Discourse, of Course

Discourse, of Course

An overview of research in discourse studies

Edited by

Jan Renkema
University of Tilburg

John Benjamins Publishing Company
Amsterdam / Philadelphia

The paper used in this publication meets the minimum requirements of American National Standard for Information Sciences — Permanence of Paper for Printed Library Materials, ANSI Z39.48-1984.

Library of Congress Cataloging-in-Publication Data

Discourse, of course : an overview of research in discourse studies / edited by Jan Renkema.
p. cm.
Includes bibliographical references and index.
1. Discourse analysis--Textbooks. I. Renkema, J.
P302.D54884 2009
401'.41--dc22 2008052214
ISBN 978 90 272 3258 8 (HB; alk. paper) / ISBN 978 90 272 3259 5 (PB; alk. paper)
ISBN 978 90 272 8981 0 (EB)

John Benjamins Publishing Co. · P.O. Box 36224 · 1020 ME Amsterdam · The Netherlands
John Benjamins North America · P.O. Box 27519 · Philadelphia PA 19118-0519 · USA

Table of contents

IV. Discourse structures

V. Stylistics and Rhetorics

VI. Discourse and Cognition

VII. Discourse and Institution

VIII. Discourse and Culture

A multiple invitation to discourse studies

Jan Renkema

1. How this book came to being

The study of discourse now has a fixed position in academic programs in communication science all over the world. In many freshman and bachelor courses introductory lectures are given, and in many master programs students spend a few months on special topics related to discourse in communication.

In 2004, the revised edition of *Introduction to Discourse Studies* appeared, a result of almost twenty-five years of academic and non-academic teaching about discourse. It was a renewal of Renkema (1992), which has been reprinted and translated several times over. The revised edition has found its place in many education programs.

This book is a kind of follow-up on that introduction, which was meant for undergraduate programs. It is a collection of twenty short papers, a *capita selecta course*, and is written for graduate programs. The selection of the twenty chapters was made on the basis of insights gained in contacts with fellow researchers whom I met while I was working as a guest professor at various universities in different parts of the world. I invited colleagues who have influenced and stimulated me in my work to write an invitation to theirs in their own area of discourse studies. This book, the result of that invitation, is a critical overview of stimulating ideas from leading persons in the field.

The aim of this book is threefold:

a. presenting material for advanced courses in discourse studies;
b. unfolding a stimulating display of research projects to future PhD students;
c. giving an overview of new developments after the 2004 introduction.

This publication is motivated by the need of teachers to have a state-of-the-art overview of the main topics in the field, and by the need of advanced students to acquire standards for developing research plans, in theses or dissertations. It gives a combination of approaches from very different schools in discourse studies, ranging from argumentation theory to genre theory, from multimodal metaphors to cognitive approaches to coherence analysis. This book not only serves as a textbook, but also as a kind of reference book for researchers who want to have an update for various main topics in the field.

The order of the chapters in this book is inspired by the arrangement of chapters of my 2004 *Introduction*, that is, starting with discourse as a mode in communication, and then going further via discourse types, structure and style to three main research areas: cognition, institution and culture. This allowed me to sort the twenty chapters in this book without relying on a non-informative, alphabetical topic order. It also avoids other problems inherent in using central topics as organizers; for example, it would be very difficult to organize around a topic such as *coherence*, which can be studied from many different points of view including discourse structure, cognition, and the relation between discourse and culture.

2. The outline of this book

I. Discourse in communication

Discourse studies is part of the much broader discipline of communication science. Discourse is, of course, always related to the world in which the interlocutors communicate. Therefore, this book starts with two chapters in which the position of discourse in communication is focused on more generally.

Rocci explores a point of view in the relation between discourse and the world: the analysis of discourse in relation to possible worlds. Words such as *wish* or *apparently* are indicators of those other worlds. The concept of *discourse worlds* is nicely clarified with an analysis of Martin Luther King's famous speech "I have a dream." Based on the so-developed discourse semantic toolbox, the student is invited to enrich the analysis by looking at other famous pieces of discourse, for example a speech by 2008 presidential candidate Barack Obama, in a search for the worlds we try to communicate in discourse.

Duszak focuses on the fact that in communication much more happens than just the exchange of discourse via patterned documents of conversations based on co-operation of the interlocutors. Many discourses are realized, so to say, "off course," such as creative language, deceitful language, etc. Inspired by this research challenge, "blended texts" (blending the visual and the verbal) are analyzed with Polish examples for which counterparts can be found easily in other languages. The analysis is based on the concept *intertextuality*, in a new, elaborated meaning, which invites the young researcher to do the same analysis in other languages and other discourse types.

II. Discourse and other communication modes

In discourse studies, the focus has been solely on the written or spoken forms for too long. An explanation for this restriction could be that discourse itself revealed more than enough interesting problems. Over the last decades, attention has increasingly turned to the direction of communication, especially to the blending of the verbal and the visual mode, as we have already seen above. The most convincing argument for exploring multimodality is that pure discourse phenomena cannot be fully understood without taking into account other modes of communication.

In **Bateman**, multimodality is not seen as "discourse plus visual" or "plus another mode." In analyzing a telephone instruction, a bird guide or a movie, we have to look for the meaning-making potential of visually, spatially and temporally-based pieces of communication. The analysis is based on the *GeM model*, in which GeM stands for Genre and Multimodality. In this model, the linguistic structure in discourse is only one of six modes. The reader is invited to analyze multimodal documents via three semiotic modes: the ("traditional") text-flow, the (spatial) page-flow and the (graphical) image-flow.

Maes and Schilperoord stimulate the researcher to look through new glasses at classical rhetoric devices — metaphor and rhyme — which have been studied for centuries solely as rhetorical figures in language. On the base of their collection of visual advertisements, Maes and Schilperoord show that *visual rhetoric* is omnipresent in advertising. In doing so, a new domain of research is opened, starting with the question: To what extent can visual rhetoric be studied in the same way as verbal rhetoric? In analyzing the interaction of visual schemes (e.g., rhyme) and tropes (e.g., metaphor), corpus research is proposed to make an inventory of all possibilities. Based on these data, experimental research is outlined to test awareness of naïve respondents and the attractiveness or estimated effect of visual rhetorical elements.

III. Discourse types

A well-known problem in discourse studies is the lack of consensus on criteria that could serve as a base for text typology or genre classification. Due to the embarrassing variety in forms and functions of discourse, the many proposals made cannot be compared easily. One of the main reasons for this is that discourse types are linked either to cognitive processes or to communicative functions, which until now have not been taken into account systematically.

Wang (Sungsoon) offers a new approach to the study of text type variation in focusing on how language users detect different text types with great ease, even when the discourse itself seems to present no explicit cues. The explanation is given within the framework of Relevance Theory, in which every utterance can be seen as an interpretive expression with degrees of interpretation constraints. The notion of *interpretation constraint* is proposed as the corner stone of an analytic tool for text type variation. With Korean examples, the reader is invited to distinguish various kinds of descriptive and interpretive utterances, degrees of interpretation and text type characteristics.

Parodi offers another new genre research from a completely different viewpoint, starting by asking which precisely are the texts that subjects are exposed to during their university careers and in daily routine professional activities in their workplace. In order to answer this question, *corpus based research* has been undertaken with a collection of about 1,000 Spanish texts containing academic and professional documents of various disciplines. This produced findings about the differences in text types between "hard science" and "soft science" that readers in other language areas should be stimulated to prove or refine. Moreover, in the finding that the number of text types in the professional area is three times as rich as in the academic area (29 versus 9), the first results also prompt an interesting didactic challenge.

IV. Discourse structures

In the study of discourse structures, the scope narrows from more external aspects — communication, multimodality and typology — to more internal aspects: the various ways in which sentences or utterances can be combined within a discourse. A commonly used distinction in structure studies is evoked by the essence of discourse itself: a structure of content units, linked by verbal ties. But this rough distinction is of little help in explaining why a discourse is perceived as coherent. The two chapters in this section deal with the puzzling phenomenon of coherence.

Le offers a model of coherence analysis in order to explore the textual *information hierarchy*. The model starts with the assumption that a reader needs three types of knowledge to establish links between discourse segments: linguistic knowledge, domain knowledge and world knowledge. The model itself is based on three main types of coherence: coordination, subordination and superordination, which makes it rather easy to delineate an insightful coherence graph of a discourse, describing the information hierarchy. This model has already been applied to academic articles and newspaper editorials in English and French, and offers the researcher a new way of exploring the question of how discourse is interpreted as coherent.

Taboada explores another intriguing phenomenon of coherence: How is it possible that we can establish relations between segments, given the fact that the *signaling of relations* is so often absent? In explicit relations there are cues like connectors, but in discourse it is said that about 50 percent of the relations remain implicit, without any cues that their status might be a cause, a sequence or any other relation. This is nicely illustrated with examples in English, Spanish and German. The chapter ends with a research proposal for a corpus study to detect the most frequent signals of coherence relations and the sources of ambiguity in implicit relations.

The results of this study would be relevant for the design of effective communication in written documents.

V. Stylistics and Rhetorics

The oldest discipline within discourse studies is *stylistics and rhetorics*: the study of the varieties in wording and composition in discourse and the effects on its audience. From the many, many approaches to style, three main views can be detected: style as a specific form for a special content, style as a choice of specific patterns and style as a deviation from average language or a kind of norm. In rhetorics, for centuries the focus has been on appropriate and effective forms of communication, mainly by analyzing what is going on in well-known documents by great masters. The three chapters in this part of the book prove that there are many new developments anchored in this traditional framework.

Kaltenbacher opens a new direction by stating that style as a choice is more than just patterns of language use dependent on the situation. With the analysis of an Austrian and an American corpus of tourist websites, it is explained clearly that *stylistic patterns and cultural identity* to a certain extent belong together. The analysis is focused on forms of obligation like *have to* and *must* or *required* and *not allowed*. The Austrian websites show a tendency to link obligation to administrative duties, whereas the American websites reveal more preference for exercising speaker's authority. Based on other results, it could be predicted that negative obligations would be more frequent in the American websites, which proved to be the case. This approach leads us closer to an answer to the old question of the extent to which culture can be tracked down in discourse.

Yang also focuses on stylistic analysis via a small subset of discourse material: modal verbs (like *may*) and modal adjuncts (like *probably*). In this approach, the notion of *register* in text types is further explored, as a style in a specific situation or profession. This means that, for example, academic writings and legal documents must differ in their use of language. An extensive corpus showed that these two text types differ in the use of modal verbs. Based on these findings, research proposals can be made about modal systems in other registers, and of course many more about characteristics of other verbal patterns in various registers.

Van Eemeren and Garssen take a very special position regarding rhetoric. They combine rhetorical insights with a critical analysis of argumentative discourse, stemming from a dialectical framework. In their so-called *pragma-dialectical approach*, they present normative quality judgments of argumentation, based on very accurate descriptions of argumentative discourse. A new focus in this approach is the analysis of strategic maneuvering, which means that in all stages of a critical discussion, from confrontation to conclusion, the parties opt for the optimal rhetorical result. The analysis of the strategic maneuvering in a tobacco advertorial for children inspires young researchers to walk their own avenue in the pragma-dialectical area of discourse studies.

The introductory book on which this publication is a follow-up (Renkema, 2004), ends with three chapters about the most important domains of discourse studies. *Discourse and cognition* deals with what is going on in our brains during the production or perception of discourse; *discourse and institution* analyzes the function of discourse in institutions — such as government, law, health and media — from a sociological perspective; and *discourse and culture* focuses on what discourse can reveal about societal characteristics, like power relations, the male–female relationship, and so on. The next chapters are sorted within these three domains, with each domain represented by three studies.

VI. Discourse and Cognition

Sadoski opens a new direction in studying cognition in discourse. The starting point is *embodied cognition*, which has as its basic assumption that all mental representations and processes are based in the body's physical interactions with the world. The most established theory is the Dual Coding Theory, which tries to explain cognition by two codes: the verbal code and the nonverbal (image) code. This theory predicts that concrete language that directly evokes sensory memories is better understood than abstract language without invoked mental imagery. An experiment showed striking results: the use of concrete language doubled the amount of gist recall in comparison with abstract language. Thus, two mental codes appear to be twice as good as one. In line with this experiment, a perspective is opened to determine which verbal discourse elements work interactively with the effects of language concreteness.

Sanders and Spooren delineate a framework for testing the cognitive status of *coherence relations* like Addition, Contrast and Cause-Consequence. They assume that all relations share four basic properties, which can serve as an underlying grid for ordering the variety of relations, for example, the basic distinctions semantic-pragmatic and causal-additive. They present an overview of empirical studies into the role of these basic properties in discourse processing. This chapter is a good starting point for research into coherence relations, because it also presents data about the use of connectives in different languages and the order of acquisition of coherence relations in child language. The practical relevance for automatic summarization is also discussed.

Louwerse and Jeuniaux apply a computational psycholinguistic algorithm to determine the degree of *cohesion* in discourse. With this technique, called Latent Semantic Analysis, the semantic relations between words, sentences and paragraphs can be determined. This technique is based on the assumption that the meaning of a word, say "father," can be determined by the words that co-occur with this word in all kinds of other discourses we have read ("job," "remote control," etc.) If we read "father" again, those latent collocations contribute to the meaning of the word. With this analysis, it proved to be possible, for example, to construct the macrostructure of a text, or to classify Shakespearean plays, or to determine whether textbooks are appropriate for their readers. The researcher is invited to expand this technique to other types of cohesion than lexical cohesion.

VII. Discourse and Institution

Wang (Jinjun) applies the "good old" turn-taking model to *institutional dialogue*. In the turn-taking model, participants are regarded as interlocutors with equal rights and obligations in changing topics or posing questions. But to what extent is this true for interaction in institutions such as media, health and education? For this study, data has been collected from news interviews, medical encounters and classroom interaction in China. It is shown convincingly that there exists a huge discrepancy in the question ratios for the participants, and hence in possibilities to control the discourse structure. With this example, researchers are invited to detect other differences between every day interactions and institutional dialogue, such as lexical choice and institutionally specific references, and to compare data from various languages.

Jacobs and Van Hout explore new ways in the study of media to analyze how *press releases*, as "preformulated opinions," find their way into the newspapers. In order to investigate the variety of discursive PR and news room practices, two methods are combined: an ethnographic approach in fieldwork for an insight into what producers and journalists really think while handling press releases, and a computer-assisted analysis with online screen registration of the writing process. With examples from a Belgium bank and an industrial institute, the researcher is stimulated to investigate the rather new form of e-releases. In doing so, more insight can be obtained into news makers and news managers on the Internet, which can help us to become more critical digital news consumers.

Kong deals with another aspect in media research. Sometimes institutions give rise to *hybrid text types*. In Chinese newspapers, an intriguing mixed type can be found: the combination of a news report and a property advertisement, the so-called "property transaction report." From a structural analysis of some examples from newspapers in Hong Kong, it appeared that the general move structure in news stories has to be specified. Moreover, it appears that this text type contains other characteristics than "advertorials." This example of analyzing a new text type may inspire students to apply a specific move analysis in order to detect new or hybrid genres in other institutions.

VIII. Discourse and Culture

Van Leeuwen uses Critical Discourse Analysis as a framework to explain how discourse is influenced by the social, economic and political world. He explores a main topic in Critical Discourse Analysis, *the presentation of social actors*, in studying how the English language allows "actors" to be presented. He also uses the discourse of the media to apply a framework of analysis by comparing two British newspapers — the more conservative *The Times* and the more sensational *Sun* — in how they represent ordinary people. The analysis shows that both newspapers can be criticized for different reasons. However, even more interesting than his findings is his systematic analytical procedure, which can serve as a toolkit for new researchers.

Lassen explores the way in which we construct our social identities in interaction. One of the important factors in this process is *gender*. The relevance of this topic is nicely illustrated with a research on demand. A Danish Bank wanted to know why women were underrepresented in management positions. In focus group interviews, the nature of stereotyping of female and male bank employees was analyzed with as overall result that each gender seems to appraise its own category more favorably. With this example, a frame is outlined to investigate whether management styles are gender specific in some industrial areas and how that can be detected in discourse. Even more important is the question of whether a masculine corporate style prevents women from acquiring high positions. This type of analysis can be based on various text types, including mission statements and job advertisements.

Wodak introduces a new branch in critical discourse analysis: the discourse-historical approach, in which the focus is not on how discourse (re)produces, for example, imbalance in power, but on how discourse mediates and has mediated this imbalance. The factor researched in this chapter is *racism*, with a focus on verbal-visual racist propaganda in election posters from an Austrian populist party. Part of the analysis considers argumentation strategies, referential strategies and strategies of negative presentation of others. In a research proposal, an outline is sketched of a comparative study of election materials in more countries and other topics, followed by a field research in which citizens are interviewed about the reception of propaganda.

3. The structure of the chapters

Because publishing a collection of papers from various academic schools faces the danger of just putting a bunch of important papers in one book without an underlying overall vision or theme, I invited my colleagues to present their ideas in a fixed format.

All contributors also accepted a strict length condition: the length (about 5,000 words each) enables MA students to prepare in a self-study of about two or three hours for a meeting with course mates, or to attend a lecture in which the topic is further discussed.

Since the book contains a great variety of approaches in the broad field of discourse studies, not all chapters may be relevant for all the students who want to explore research possibilities. Therefore, abstracts precede each chapter, just as they would in a scientific journal, presenting a glimpse of the information needed to determine whether the presented research serves a specific interest. Furthermore, all chapters are presented in the following format.

3.1 Introduction

Because discourse studies as an inter- or multidisciplinary area of research can often be very disordered and confusing, the introduction places the topic in the broad domain of discourse studies and presents information about connections with other sites on the research map.

3.2 The research challenge

Between the start and finish of a research project, anything can happen, from disappointment to the necessity to walk another road. In such a difficult endeavor as research, it could be helpful to always have one's aim as a beacon in stormy seas. This fixed point can be captured better if one is aware of the real research challenge. Therefore each chapter continues, after the introduction, with its specific research challenge. Because such a challenge is often a mix of an old problem and a new insight, all the contributors were asked to relate their challenge to "old information" in the previous book, *Introduction to Discourse Studies*, and were invited to explain that there is much more at stake than what could be told in that — or any — introductory text.

3.3 Examples

Many research questions suffer from the danger of abstractness. As soon as it comes to discourse, many research problems tend to become very diffuse or vague themselves. Therefore, each chapter contains a section with examples of discourse fragments in which the discussed phenomena can be clearly detected. These discourse fragments are real ones and not self-designed "textoides," to show what is really going on in discourse. They are given in the language under consideration, and in an English translation.

3.4 Research methods

All chapters in this book have been written by senior researchers with a thorough experience in at least some ways to answer a research challenge, from desk research to field work, from corpus linguistics to laboratory experiments. In order to guide new researchers finding their way when answering a research question, all the contributors to this book were asked to make as explicit as possible the method they saw as most appropriate to reach their research aims.

3.5 Recent research

The amount of literature on discourse studies is growing with astonishing speed. Many students have lost time-consuming energy in procuring detailed surveys or stimulating examples of research. This section in each chapter is meant to summarize important research related to the topic and to present puzzling or stimulating results. Of course, long lists of references could have been published, but the contributors have been asked to restrict themselves to key publications and recent research in their own area of research. The references have been collected at the end of the book in order to avoid duplication.

3.6 Research proposal

The main part of each chapter is a proposal, which is meant to be informative enough to discuss with a PhD student, or from which parts can be conducted by an MA student. Not surprisingly, these proposals vary in level of detail and in degree of planning. The topics are so diverse and may be, to a certain extent, incomparable. However, with this overview of twenty research proposals, this book can serve as a collection of research advertisements and as a standard of what a PhD proposal has to be, irrespective of its discourse school.

3.7 Practical relevance

Many new researchers do not — on very legitimate grounds — want to engage themselves in a research project without having an awareness of how possible results will have impact outside the ivory tower of a university. Therefore, all the contributors have been asked to conclude their chapter with some information about possible practical relevance. For some chapters this has meant more than a few remarks.

In order to make this publication extra suitable as a textbook, the contributors have also been asked to add one or more assignments that could be worked out with

Internet information. The answers or elaborations are presented in the "Key to the Assignments" at the end of the book.

At the end of this introductory chapter, I want to thank all my colleagues, who have accepted me as their Procrustes, cutting all information that could not be fitted to the bed described above. My main pleasure during this project was in knowing that we all have been inspired as we push forward new research, and in the conviction that a publication like this could make it a little bit easier for other colleagues to select from an overview of important research topics. The heavy task of collecting and editing the following chapters has been carried out by Cathy de Waele, who served as an editorial manager, and by Brigit Kolen who served as an editorial assistant. Without their assistance this book could not have been published. I hope that this publication can function as a follow-up of my introductory textbook and that it stimulates contacts between research teams of discourse studies from even more countries than are represented in this book.

Part I

Discourse in communication

Chapter 1

Doing discourse analysis with possible worlds

Andrea Rocci
University of Lugano, Switzerland

This chapter considers the relevance for discourse analysis of semantic issues pertaining to the functioning of modal operators and other "world creating predicates," which open a variety of shifted or embedded "discourse worlds" and connect these "worlds" to each other within the semantic structure of a text. A semantic toolkit is provided, drawing on possible world semantics and dynamic approaches to discourse semantics, with an emphasis on usability for discourse analysts rather than a on the formal implementation of the underlying concepts. This approach is then applied to the analysis of a fragment of Martin Luther King's *I have a Dream* speech, showing how the mapping of "discourse worlds" provides a formal scaffolding to discuss the cultural world implied in a text and relating it to its rhetorical strategy. Finally, some lines of inquiry are sketched for doing research on the relation between the worlds evoked by texts belonging to a certain genre and the pragmatic goals and activity type associated with that genre.

1. Introduction

Discourse meaning has both a *pragmatic* and a *semantic* dimension. Pragmatically, a text or speech represents a complex action — or, more precisely, an articulated proposal of a joint action to be realized with the participation of the addressee —; semantically, a text establishes a developing representation of states of affairs which hold true in some possible world.

Put in the terms of a classic model used as a foundation in Renkema's (2004) *Introduction to Discourse Studies* (henceforth *IDS*):[1] the semantic dimension is connected

1. For the presentation of Bühler's Organon model see *IDS*, Section 2.1

to Bühler's (1990) "symbol" aspect of the sign, corresponding to what he calls "representative" function; while the pragmatic one is connected to the "signal" aspect and Bühler's "appeal" function.

Studying these semantic representations is not alien to the study of discourse as social action. A large part of the perlocutionary effects of a text, that is its power to persuade, arouse emotions, entertain, in a word, its "appeal," is mediated by its ability to plausibly evoke in the mind of the addressee the representation of a world fragment. Tannen (1989) devotes a whole chapter of her fortunate book on involvement in discourse to the effects of detail that brings the addressee to imagining an experienced world (see Tannen, 1989, chapter 5).

Interestingly, the representation of human experience and human action entails the reference to a plurality of worlds, relating to desires, requirements, future possible developments, opportunities and risks, but also to counterfactual conditions and consequences, wishes and fictional states of affairs, as well as to the representations of discourses and beliefs of human agents and of the speakers themselves.

Therefore, discourses refer to the world in which the discourse participants live as well as to a host of other "worlds," which can relate in a number of ways with the participants' world. This phenomenon relies on the very basic human cognitive ability of thinking that *things might be otherwise*, that is, thinking of *alternatives*: states of affairs other than what is the case. The logico-philosophical tradition developed the theoretical notion of *possible worlds* to deal with reasoning about alternatives.[2] *Modality* is the semantic category mainly associated with the expression of thoughts about alternatives. In the logico-philosophical tradition, modality concerns, in a more restricted sense, a class of semantic notions — which include *possibility*, *necessity* and *probability* — involving the quantification of alternatives of a certain kind.[3]

Many discourse analysts have chiefly pragmatic concerns. They are interested in understanding how language is used by people to act socially and to achieve their goals in a variety of social contexts. The question might arise whether discourse scholars should care about possible worlds or they better leave the matter to philosophers and philosophically minded linguists.

---

2. David Lewis' (1973) work on counterfactuals is one of the most influential in-depth discussions of possible worlds in modern philosophical logic. The book is also noteworthy for the impact it had on the linguistic semantic analysis of modality and conditional constructions. An accessible introduction to possible worlds is Girle (2003). This work is recommended for its focus on the broader philosophical significance of possible worlds rather than on the technical details of their implementation in modal logic.

3. "At the heart of the technical and the philosophical use of possible worlds is the simple idea that something is possible if it is so in at least one possible world and something is necessary if it is so in all possible worlds" (Girle, 2003: 3).

In this chapter we would like to suggest that they should — in their own way — and that the systematic formal study of how discourses evoke worlds is currently a promising avenue of research for discourse analysis and that this kind of study is essential to provide the necessary scaffolding for research focused on the concrete cultural and experiential contents of the worlds evoked and on their appeal to the audience.

It can be useful in this connection to provide a first informal illustration of the main types of modal meanings by looking at how the capacity of envisaging these alternatives is a prerequisite of human action itself and, consequently, of our talk about action.

Human action[4] involves envisaging a state of affairs which is *desirable* (*bouletic* modality), *possible* in the future (*broad dynamic* modality), what is *needed* to bring it about the desire (the so-called *deontico-practical* modality), and what actually *can* be done by the agent (*participant internal dynamic* modality). Moreover, since our agent has to cope with her partial and fallible access to the facts, she will consider what *may* be or *must* be the case in view of the evidence at her disposal (*epistemic* modality).[5] Since people do not act in a social and cultural void, our agent's action will inevitably relate to what *may*, *should* or *must* be done according to the *law*, to culturally shared *ethical norms* or *ideals*, to the *commitments* that the agent has entered in her interactions with other people (these are different sorts of *deontic* modality). The alternatives evoked by the *basic modal notions*[6] mentioned above do not exhaust the worlds to which our discourses can refer. To them we should add at least — given their prominence in discourse — the world as represented according to other people's *reported discourses* and *ascribed thoughts*, and the worlds associated to a variety of *representations* (pictures, movies, novels, etc.), including *fictional worlds* more or less disconnected from the one inhabited by the discourse participants.

A striking variety of linguistic structures is employed to explicitly introduce new worlds in an ongoing discourse, shift from a world to another, embed a world within another, and relate one world to another by logical and other relations. These include,

---

4. We cannot enter here the discussion on the theory of action, but see Rigotti (2005) for a concise presentation of a basic model applied to discourse analysis.

5. *Epistemic* modality relates to the higher cognitive faculty of *metarepresentation*: the ability of representing one's thoughts (and other people's thoughts) *as representations* distinct from the world, and, consequently, reason about alternative representations of the world. See Rocci (2005a: 212–214) for a discussion.

6. For an in-depth analysis of the different modal notions presented in this section from the viewpoint of possible world semantics see the foundational work of Kratzer (1981), the rich summary provided by von Fintel (2006) and the discussion in Rocci (2008b), which is oriented to providing semantic tools for the analysis of argumentative discourse.

for instance, modal verbs, modal adverbs or verbal mood, lexical "world creating predicates" (McCawley, 1993: 415–430) such as *intend, want, wish, dream, fear*, reported speech indicators, conditional constructions, and certain discourse connectives like *in fact, in reality, apparently.*

2. The research challenge

Chapter 5 of *IDS* deals with the semantic, that is, representative, function of discourse, introducing discourse as having *structured* contents or meanings, whose minimal unit is the *proposition* (*IDS*: 88). *IDS* briefly introduces the analysis of the semantic contents of a discourse in terms of a structured network of propositions, which in turn gives rise to more abstract and global propositional representations of contents — *macrostructures* according to Van Dijk's model — providing a sort of summary of the contents of a text (*IDS*: 87–99).

Early studies in text linguistics — both European (Van Dijk, 1977) and American (Grimes, 1975) — devoted a considerable amount of attention to the daunting task of characterizing the referential semantics of texts, that is, how larger stretches of language in use refer to world fragments. As discourse analysis shifted towards more pragmatic and sociolinguistic concerns, very little of that early theorizing carried through to influence the actual practices of discourse analysts, with few exceptions such as Van Dijk's notion of *macrostructure* — which has been applied by the author himself to the analysis of news discourse (cf. Van Dijk, 1985).

The development of such a component remains, however, an important task for discourse studies. Media discourse is a case in point: students of the media place a lot of emphasis on how media accurately reflect (or, alternatively, distort) the world. Studies of news discourse, for instance, need a way to see how a news text comes to represent a concatenated series of events — together with their temporal and causal relations. Bell (1998) has shown that through a linguistically informed examination of the relationship between the formal organization of the news text and the world fragments and event chains it represents we can discover that "[...] news stories are regularly not saying what we think they say on first reception. They are not telling a simple, clear, tale, but are replete with ambiguity, unclarity, discrepancy and cavity" (Bell, 1998: 66). Recourse to quantitative or qualitative techniques of content analysis imported from the social sciences would hardly provide discourse analysts with the finesse and systematicity required for a semantic study of discourse.

In this chapter, a discourse semantic research program is advocated for a key dimension of meaning, complementary to the event structure focused on by Bell: the introduction of different worlds in the discourse and the connections that are established between these different worlds.

Most treatments of modality, belief and "stance" in discourse analysis do not connect it with the referential function of discourse and do not make use of any notion of *world*. An influential model for the treatment of modality in discourse analysis, for instance, is the one offered by Systemic Functional Linguistics (cf. Halliday, 1994: 356), where modality is mainly associated with the *interpersonal* dimension of meaning and treated as a *scalar* dimension. Basically, modal meanings are represented as positions in a scale between the *yes* and *no* poles encompassing *high*, *median* and *low* modalities. Consistently with the pragmatic concerns of discourse analysts, this view of modality has been mostly applied to considering the effects of modality on the speech act: for instance, its role in *mitigating* potentially face-threatening speech acts or in *hedging* assertions to avoid total commitment.

During the last decades in the field of semantics, both in formal and in cognitive research traditions, a number of conceptual tools have been developed for the treatment of reference to different worlds in discourse that could be profitably applied in the practice of discourse analysis, complementing and refining the pragmatic interpersonal view. To this date, these tools have seen limited application. Seldom, if ever, have they been put to the test of instances (let alone corpora) of actual discourse for descriptive or critical purposes. As always, it is not just a matter of mere application, but of adapting models to partially different research concerns, as well as of making them practically usable. This is the research challenge on which this chapter focuses.

3. Examples

Joseph Grimes, in a seminal book on discourse structure (Grimes, 1975), once observed that positing that the field of reference of a discourse can be removed from the spatiotemporal reality of the context of utterance is not only required to understand fictional worlds such as Middle-Earth or Narnia, but also essential to understand "motivation and inspiration":

> A leader leads by helping his followers recreate his own vision of a state of affairs that is different from the one in which they live. Martin Luther King says 'I have a dream,' and thousands of American black men and women follow him in it (Grimes, 1975: 301).

The fragment of Martin Luther King's *I have a Dream* speech to which Grimes alludes is worth quoting extensively:

(1) And so even though we face the difficulties of today and tomorrow, I still have a dream. It is a dream deeply rooted in the American dream.

I have a dream that one day this nation will rise up and live out the true meaning of its creed: "We hold these truths to be self-evident, that all men are created equal."

> I have a dream that one day on the red hills of Georgia, the sons of former slaves and the sons of former slave owners will be able to sit down together at the table of brotherhood.
>
> I have a dream that one day even the state of Mississippi, a state sweltering with the heat of injustice, sweltering with the heat of oppression, will be transformed into an oasis of freedom and justice.

Indeed, this enormously famous speech can be used[7] to provide an example of how considering the worlds introduced by discourse can provide the formal scaffolding to relate in an insightful way different aspects of the content and context of a highly valued text. In Section 6, I will provide a fragment of a micro-analysis of this text as an illustration of the kind of research proposed in this chapter.

A further illustration of the relevance of *alternatives* for understanding how people use discourse to do things within specific social contexts and activity types is offered by Gaik's (1994) paper on possible worlds in radio-talk show therapy. Looking at this hybrid forms of therapeutic discourse, where listeners call in during a radio talk show for a brief therapy session with a doctor, Gaik found that the therapeutic intervention of the doctor within the "talk-show therapy" activity type can be organized along two very different "modes,"[8] which are also found in other psychotherapeutic contexts: "classical" *therapy* and *counseling*. In the therapy mode, the doctor seeks to avoid "any prescriptive or directive role — in the interest of motivating the patient into further introspection, self analysis and eventual autonomy" (Gaik, 1994: 276). Counseling, on the contrary, is a process designed to provide *advice*, to help a person answer the question "What shall I do?"

Gaik observes that certain kinds of epistemic possibility and conditionality, which he groups under the label *irrealis*, are functional to the goals of therapy: they "present the caller with alternative hypotheses about the sources of his or her anxiety" (Gaik, 1994: 279) and motivate further introspection. As shown in the following excerpt, where the therapist answers to a woman who is anxious about her husband's way of dealing with money:

7. The speech has attracted the attention of discourse analysts for the poetic effects it achieves through a series of stylistic devices that are typical of the performed African-American sermon. See, for instance, Tannen (1989: 82–85) who focuses on the effects achieved through repetition. The semantic viewpoint offered here can easily be seen as complementary rather than alternative to these analyses.

8. These are, more precisely, two different *interaction schemes*, according to the terminology proposed in Rigotti and Rocci (2007): "The *interaction schemes* are [...] culturally shared 'recipes' for interaction congruent with more or less broad classes of joint goals and involving scheme-roles presupposing generic requirements. Deliberation, negotiation, advisory, problem-solving, adjudication, mediation, teaching are fairly broad interaction schemes; while more specific interaction schemes may correspond to proper.

(2) D: [These are irrational fears]
and not coming from your current reality at all,
but rather from something *perhaps* from your pa:st (0.5)
C: *Probably*
D: And it *may* have nothing to do with money at all.
It *may* have to do a lot with po:wer,
It *may* have to do with will you really take care
of me. Ca:n I really trust you?

If, on the one hand, the introduction of this kind of epistemic modality is functional to the goals of therapy, on the other hand, it also functions as a contextualization cue to recognize that *therapy* is the interaction scheme being proposed and to set it apart from *counseling* where such speculation would be dysfunctional with respect to the orientation towards the future actions of the patient. Gaik argues convincingly that this approach is more insightful than previous treatments that accounted for these phenomena in psychotherapeutic discourse *directly* in terms of mitigation of the speech act of the therapist: presenting a possible world to the patient's speculation is more than just "making a veiled (or mitigated) assertion" (Gaik, 1994: 287).

Expanding on these insights, in the following sections we will introduce an essential "discourse semantic toolbox" and then apply it to the analysis of a fragment of M.L.K.'s speech to show how mapping the different possible worlds introduced in discourse and their relations can lend important insights on the way in which a discourse pursues its pragmatic goals and relates to its social and cultural context.

A final — rather different — example of the relevance of the proposed line of research is provided by the genre of economic-financial news articles in the written press. Here are two rather typical fragments of business news, which evoke a fair number of different worlds:

(3) In November, Dell set up a dedicated consumer unit that includes marketing, engineering and industrial design. The company *believes* the strategy shift *can* produce more-innovative products while reducing the time needed to develop a new consumer PC to one year from about 18 months.
(*The Wall Street Journal Europe*, June 26, 2007; Page B4).

(4) Representatives of the Russian and Italian governments Saturday signed a memorandum of understanding to cooperate on a 900-kilometer, or 558-mile, pipeline. The pipeline could carry as much as 30 billion cubic meters, or 1.05 trillion cubic feet, of gas annually from Russia into Europe through the Black Sea. Construction would begin as early as next year if the project, [...], overcomes regulatory hurdles.
(*The Wall Street Journal Europe*, June 25, 2007; Page A11)

Financial news proper, as opposed to *company* news, can easily propose even more luxuriant configurations of possible worlds, as happens in this article discussing the evolution of the Dollar-Euro exchange rate:

(5) Such concerns have helped limit the dollar's losses against the euro, despite the Fed's recent moves — which once **might** have produced a dramatic fall in the dollar. The euro is "still essentially where we were at the start of December," *says* Simon Derrick, the London-based chief currency strategist for the Bank of New York Mellon. "That **I find** absolutely remarkable." Mr. Derrick ***believes*** investors **may** be focused more on the risks to growth than on those posed by inflation. They "**may well believe** that the ECB is not being reactive enough and the euro is too highly valued," he *says*.
(*Rate-policy shift could sap euro*, WSJ Europe February 1, 2008)

Also in this case, the worlds evoked by the discourse play a vital role in relating the contents of the texts to the communicative purpose of the genre. In contrast with other news genres, financial news are as much about predicting the future and evaluating possible outcomes than about reporting the past events. Future events — both in the form of forecasts and of alternative conditional scenarios — receive the same importance as the reporting of past events. This appears to be functional to the demand of readers-investors to cope with uncertainty about the future with regards to investment opportunities. Also, the use of modals and conditionals in financial news, as well as in academic economics (cf. Bloor & Bloor, 1993), has been treated as hedging of assertive speech acts motivated by face concerns. Again this approach, while justified in itself, tells us very little on the important role of these expressions in *structuring* discourse at the referential level.

4. Research method

The foundations of the method for mapping worlds in discourse proposed here lie at the crossroads of semantics, pragmatics and discourse studies. During the last few decades, a number of scholars have begun to look at discourse semantics in a *dynamic* way, which reflects how discourse participants, by exchanging utterances in a monologue or dialogue, progressively establish a shared *discourse representation*, which we could call the "world" of the text.

According to this view, the semantic representation is built gradually through successive increments, or "updates" of a *common ground* (See Stalnaker, 1973; Clark, 1996; and Renkema, 2004: 42), that is, of that fragment of the world which is already shared by the discourse participants. This is what participants take for granted at the current stage of their interaction. Following Stalnaker (1973), we can think of the common ground as a set of propositions, which *partially* define a world that the participants are sharing through communication. New utterances add new propositions to the common ground extending the world fragment shared by the participants.

Note that the common ground is underspecified with respect to the actual world, or any other single possible world.[9] In logic, possible worlds are worlds in a rather strong sense: they are complete, fully specified. That a given common ground is compatible with many possible worlds is quite natural. Consider the participants in a discussion: they will share a certain common ground, but where they disagree their views of the world will diverge. What we have just said of the common ground in general holds also for the developing "world" of the text, the discourse representation, which is a part of the common ground.[10]

Dynamic approaches to discourse semantics have provided more sophisticated models of the developing discourse representation (Kamp & Reyle, 1993). These models devote particular attention to discussing how utterances introduce new entities (*discourse referents*) into the "world of the discourse" and how these entities are anaphorically recovered by subsequent utterances which attribute new predicates to them, as in (2), where J.R.R. Tolkien paints the very first strokes of his fictional world:

(6) In **a hole in the ground** there lived a hobbit [...] **It** had a perfectly round door like a porthole, painted green.

As suggested by L. Kartunnen (1969), in a paper which is at the origins of discourse semantics, these representations are like data-bases containing records for each entity mentioned in the text — each discourse referent. The records are retrieved and updated when new predicates take the same discourse referent as their argument.

Here, we will not have much to say about discourse referents and anaphora per se, but we will focus on another kind of complication: namely the fact that the new propositions introduced in a discourse representation do not always add up to the specification of the actual world inhabited by the speaker and the hearer. What the discourse participants need to share in order to interact inevitably involves information about different possible worlds. We can say that the human universe that people share through discourse is much wider than Wittgenstein's *everything that is the case*.

Consider the following examples, taken from Kartunnen (1969):

(7) Bill **can** make *a kite*. **The kite* has a long string.

(8) John **wants** to catch *a fish*. *Do you see *the fish* from here?

---

9. In other words, we can say that the propositions in the common ground define a set of possible worlds that are consistent with them. Stalnaker calls this set of possible worlds the *context set*.

10. Clark (1996: 54) speaks of a *situational discourse record*, that part of the common ground where information about the situation talked about is accumulated.

In the above examples, anaphora fails because the antecedent and the anaphor are not in the same world. The above antecedents have been introduced in some world which is not the default world of the text: making a kite is just a *possibility of action* for Bill (dynamic modality), while catching a fish is a *desire* for John (bouletic modality).

5. Recent research

Many approaches to discourse semantics have introduced a *partitioning* of the discourse representation. Partitions go under a variety of names in the different approaches to discourse semantics: *discourse representation structures* (Kamp & Reyle, 1993), *discourse domains* (Seuren, 1985), *mental spaces* (Fauconnier, 1991), *discourse worlds* (Polanyi, 1996), *discourse universes* (Charolles, 1997), *text worlds* (Werth, 1999; Gavins, 2007),[11] *discourse contexts* (Polanyi, 2001). Here we will use the term *discourse world*, used by Livia Polanyi (1996), from which we borrow part of the graphical notation. Some of these approaches belong more or less strictly to the formal semantics tradition, others, while drawing ideas from *formal semantics* and computational linguistics, are more informal and sketchy, others still take the stance of *cognitive linguistics*. Despite their purportedly deep philosophical differences, all have much to offer to the discourse analyst who needs to forge her tools for the treatment of rich discourse samples. It is advisable, then, to become initially conversant *both* with formal and cognitive models and not letting "ease of use" dictate one's epistemological choices when they actually are at stake.

Here, a minimal starting theoretical package for using discourse worlds in empirical discourse research is offered.

Discourse worlds are a sort of cognitive work spaces set up for the specific purpose of interpreting successive utterances[12] which store the propositions that are progressively added to the common ground by the discourse. *Discourse worlds* and the

11. Sometimes the different names correspond to notational variants, while in other cases signal deeper differences between *logico-formal* (Kamp, 1981/2004; Seuren, 1985; and Polanyi, 1996) and *cognitive* (Fauconnier, 1991; Werth, 1999; Gavins, 2007) approaches in the underlying assumptions concerning the analysis of meaning.

12. Cf. Seuren (1985: 314) about his *discourse domains*: "Discourse domains are cognitive 'working spaces' set up for the specific purpose of interpreting successive utterances […] These domains are intermediate between utterances and 'the world' in those cases where the discourse is about things that are or are not the case. The (propositions in the) utterances of such discourses have truth value, but there are many discourse domains where the question of truth-values does not arise." Note the similarities and differences with what Fauconnier (1998/2004: 347) says about *mental spaces*: "Mental spaces are small conceptual packets constructed as we think and talk, for purposes of local understanding and action. They are very partial assemblies containing elements, and structured

possible worlds of logic are not the same (cf. also Polanyi, 1996: 34). From a semantic viewpoint, discourse worlds are partial, sketchy, representations — partial models — which mediate between the verbal utterances we exchange and the possible worlds we intend to talk about. While possible worlds are complete worlds, discourse worlds are just bundles of propositions partially characterizing a situation. Let us exemplify what discourse worlds are like with the business news discourse fragment presented in example (3) in the *Examples* section:

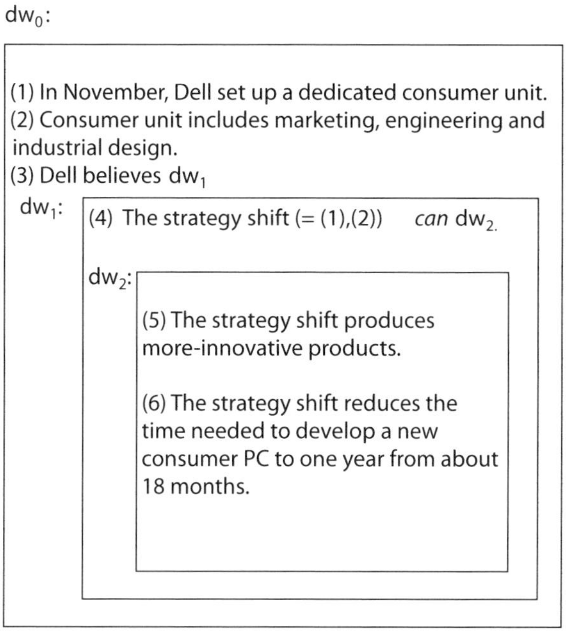

Figure 1. Discourse world partition of example (3)

The discourse world dw_0 corresponds to the basic level of the developing common ground. Propositions (1), (2) and (3) are added directly to this common ground. Proposition (3), however, contains the world-creating predicate *believe* whose second argument is not part of dw_0: the beliefs of Dell's management constitute an embedded discourse world dw_1. Proposition (4), added to dw_1, in its turn, immediately introduces — through the dynamic modal *can* — a further discourse world dw_2 relating to what the strategy will be capable to achieve. Propositions (5) and (6) are future achievements that the strategy is believed to make possible, and not just propositions that are the case according to Dell's belief. Thus their double embedding.

by frames and cognitive models. They are interconnected and can be modified as thought and discourse unfold."

The discourse worlds introduced by modals and other world-creating predicates typically do not single out one possible world. Rather they define a set of possible worlds where the propositions introduced in the dw hold. Consider the following example. The square brackets are used here as a space-saving substitute for dw-boxes:

(9) dw_0: [*John wants to* dw_1: [*hire a secretary who speaks fluent Chinese*]]

The are clearly many different possible worlds that may realize John's wants. What we know is that in all the worlds that correspond to John's wants, the proposition in dw_0 is the case.

It is worth saying a few words about the relations that may obtain between different world-creating predicates occurring in a discourse and the respective discourse worlds they introduce, as we will see that working out these relations can lend precious insights for discourse analysis.

Example (3) above presents a case of *embedding*: the dynamic possibility expressed by *can* is something that holds within the company's beliefs. Nothing is said about whether this possibility actually holds in dw_0. There are discourses, on the other hand, where successive world-creating predicates expressing the same kind of modality simply add new propositions to the same discourse world, without creating other embedded or parallel discourse worlds. In the fragment of talk-show therapy in example (2), the adverb *perhaps* and three successive occurrences of *may* all contribute to build the same epistemic dw:

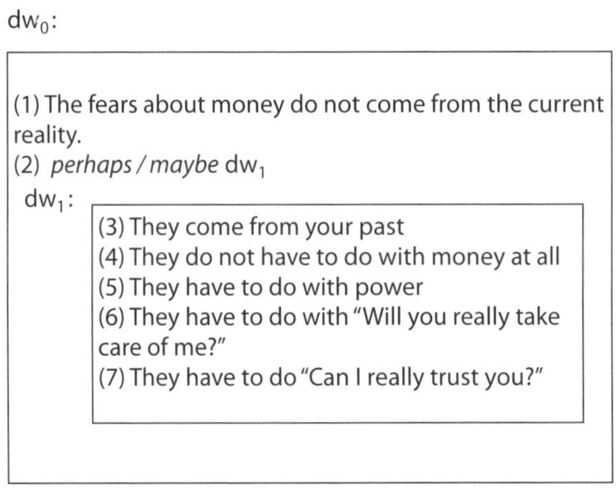

Figure 2. Discourse world partition of example (2).

A third case, about which there is a vast amount of literature in formal semantics, is represented by explicit conditional structures and implicit ones, such as those emerging from the so-called *modal subordination* (see Geurts, 1999). In these cases there is a conditional-like relation between an antecedent dw and a consequent dw. It can be a relation of *logical consequence* (let us symbolize it as dw_a: [...] ⇒ dw_c: [...]), which means that in all the worlds where dw_a is true, dw_c is also true. Or simply a relation of compatibility between the discourse worlds (symbolically: dw_a: [...] ◊ dw_c: [...]), which means that in some possible worlds where dw_a is true, dw_c is also the case. Consider the business newspaper excerpt from example (4):

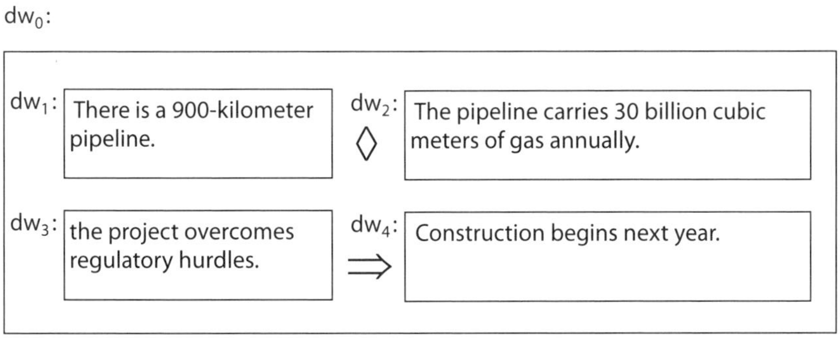

Figure 3. Discourse world partition of example (4).

In the next section, we will come closer to exemplifying a fragment of substantial research in discourse analysis. We will illustrate what could be gained, in view of our understanding of what a discourse does in pragmatic terms, from the mapping of the discourse worlds and their relations evoked by an extended discourse fragment considered in its broader communicative context.

6. Research proposal

Using a fragment from Martin Luther King's *I have a Dream* speech, we illustrate here the use of *discourse worlds* as a formal semantic scaffolding for discourse analysts interested in understanding: (a) the pragmatic and rhetorical functioning of discourse within a precise socio-historical context of communication, (b) the cultural contents of the discourse — and how they relate to (a). We hope that other researchers would follow this lead, to further develop discourse worlds as a rich tool for discourse analysis.

This enormously famous speech was delivered by Martin Luther King Jr. on August 28, 1963, at the Lincoln Memorial, Washington D.C., before a crowd of more than 200,000 civil rights demonstrators, "most of them black but many of them white" — as the New York Times wrote — as part of the March on Washington aimed to back the promulgation of the Civil Rights Act, which was stalled in Congress at the time.

We will consider here mainly the fragment quoted in (1) in the Examples section, presenting a partial discourse representation of the fragment which considers jointly two intertwined dimensions:

- The first dimension is the distinction between the information which is already part of the common ground between the speaker and the audience — the *pre-textual common ground* — and the propositions that are added to the common ground by the fragment analyzed, which we will call the *textual incrementation* of the common ground.
- The second dimension is the partitioning of both the common ground and its increment in terms of distinct discourse worlds. The discourse world dw_0 corresponds to the context of the communication event. Following Polanyi (1996), a number of features relating to the communication context[13] of dw_0 are expressed in the upper area of dw_0.

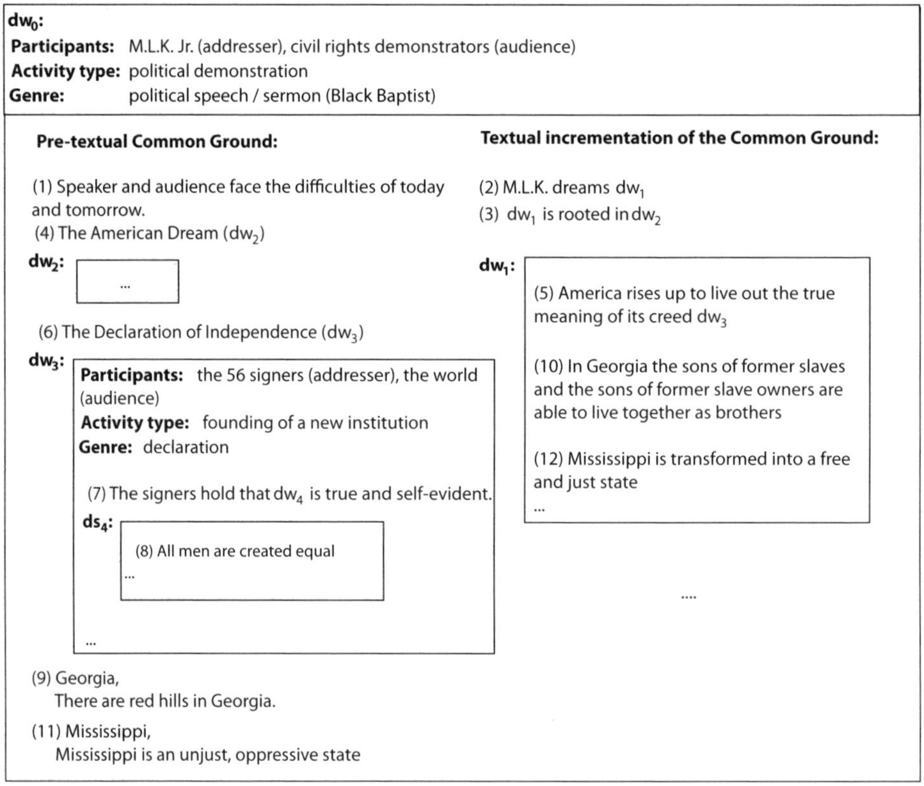

Figure 4. Partial discourse representation of example (1).

13. For a detailed discussion of the relevant dimensions of *communication context*, see Rigotti and Rocci (2006).

The left column of the representation contains common ground information. This is a partial representation as it only contains *presupposed* propositions triggered by the linguistic utterances in our fragment. Restricting ourselves to presuppositions can have a methodological value as it shows how the discourse semantic analysis of the text can serve to illuminate its communicative context.

The right column contains the propositions that update the common ground. It has to be observed that proposition (2), M.L.K.'s "having a dream," is a *fact* in the world shared by the discourse participants.[14] The content of the dream is not part of dw_0 but of a "dream world" dw_1 where the propositions (5), (10) and (12), subsequently introduced, are located. The world dw_1 is introduced as the second argument of a "world-creating" predicate — let us call it DREAM (x, dw) — whose most explicit expression is the syntactic construction "*I have a dream that... will...*" The modal *will* is an integral part of the world creating construction: it locates dw_1 in a possible future accessible from dw_0 and serves to clearly set apart dw_1 from other kinds of "dream worlds" disconnected with dw_0, such as dream experiences and fancies which are usually reported in the past tense (e.g., *I dream that I was Da Vinci and she was the Mona Lisa*). The semantics of this particular world-creating predicate, vague and rich in resonances at the same time, is difficult to pinpoint, which seems to contribute to its evocative power. Certainly, dw_1 corresponds, in part, to the argument of a *bouletic* modality: dw_1 describes a desired future state of affairs for the speaker, which motivates action. However, there is clearly more to it than the simple bouletic modality. The nature of the *dream* predicate and of dw_1 can be further illuminated if we look at the relations between dw_1 and other discourse worlds.

One such relation is established in dw_0 by proposition (3), which presents dw_1 as deeply *rooted* in the American dream. Appearing as a definite NP, the American Dream is clearly presupposed, hence its collocation in the pre-textual common ground.

Here we treat the American Dream as a discourse world dw_2. Why should the *American Dream* be treated as a discourse world?

Consider the kind of culturally shared information in the common ground that satisfies the presuppositional requirement of this definite NP: *the American Dream*, in its minimal interpretation, is the name of a set of values, a fuzzy set whose core members are to be identified with values such as freedom, equality of opportunities and (upward) social mobility. If we were to formulate these values, we would get a set of propositions. These propositions are not stored in the common ground as facts. They describe an ideal world and it would be natural to preface them with a deontic modal word such as *should* (e.g., *People should be free to pursue happiness*).

14. Interestingly, later in the speech King repeats "I have a dream now" as if to stress that his dream is a political stance that has immediate consequences in the present.

Another, perhaps more concrete, way of envisioning the American dream is as a *narrative*. Not as a concrete story but as a prototypical story, a master narrative, "cultural hypertext" (Danesi & Rocci, in press) underlying many real and fictional stories actually told in American culture (including, for instance, exemplar stories of immigrants coming to America) and drawing from a variety of "foundational texts" in American culture, one of which is the *Declaration of Independence*. Polanyi (1989) analyzed everyday American conversational narratives to show how they reflect the telling of "*the* American story," offering a striking empirical illustration of the relationship between texts and an underlying cultural hypertext.

Treating the American Dream as a discourse world allows us to interpret the relational predicate in (3) as having two homogeneous arguments (dw_1 *is [deeply] rooted in* dw_2). What does it means for a discourse world to be *rooted* in another one? This brings us to the issue of relations between discourse worlds, which we touched in the previous paragraph. Certainly this predicate entails the minimal logical relation of *compatibility*: no proposition in King's dream contradicts the American Dream, but we might be tempted to hypothesize that it also entails the stronger relation of *logical consequence*: King's dream follows logically from the American Dream. In terms of possible world semantics, it would mean that in all possible worlds where the values of the American Dream are realized, King's dream is also realized.

While it captures a basically correct insight, this translation still seems too blunt and a-historical. In fact, powerful as it is as a model for interpreting discourse worlds, possible world semantics is not well suited to capture certain aspects of discourse worlds as representations entertained by people, who may or may not be aware of their consequences. In the conclusion of her book on the telling of the American story, Polanyi (1989: 193) writes: "The Story of America is, very largely, a prolonged, complex, and sometimes tragic exegesis of those few lines from The Declaration of Independence. 'All men are created Equal.' Yes, all MEN are EQUAL. But who exactly are MEN?" (Capitals in the original). The idea of interpretive activity suggested by the word *exegesis* comes close to render the value of *being rooted* in King's text, and the dialectical, historical relationship between dw_1 and dw_2.

Polanyi's remark about the Declaration of Independence brings us to another discourse world evoked as part of the common ground of M.L.K.'s speech. Contrary to dw_2, dw_3 is an actual discourse — whose context of utterance is represented in the upper part of dw_3's box — and it is not simply evoked as a whole: proposition (7–8) of dw_3 is actually quoted. The deontic value of dw_3 is also made explicit by the use of the word *creed*. Given the institutional and foundational value of dw_3, this deontic value goes beyond the simple indication of what is good in a given culture, but assumes the nature of a commitment to which the United States are bound as an institution. On the other hand, King's reference to the *true meaning* of the Nation's creed highlights the same kind of *interpretive* relationship between dw_1 and the discourse worlds of

American culturally shared values that we hypothesized above.[15] The exact relationship between the *Declaration of Independence* (dw_3) and the American Dream (dw_2) is not made explicit in the speech, but it can be inferred that the foundational text dw_3 is one of the sources, perhaps the main source, of the values of dw_2.

By examining the relations between dw_1 and the other discourse worlds evoked by the text fragment analyzed, it was possible to elucidate aspects of Martin Luther King's "dream" that are crucial in view of the rhetorical and argumentative strategy of the whole speech. The consideration of a broader fragment would bring to light other aspects of dw_1 beyond its bouletic and deontic facets. For instance, one could see how, through the use of Biblical quotations, Biblical language, and the whole style of the speech which reminds of a sermon, King — who was a Black Baptist minister — relates dw_1 to the discourse world of the Bible. Consider, for instance, one of the final passages of the speech (italics added):

(10) "I have a dream that one day every valley shall be exalted, and every hill and mountain shall be made low, the rough places will be made plain, and the crooked places will be made straight; 'and the glory of the Lord shall be revealed and all flesh shall see it together.'
This is our *hope*, and this is the *faith* that I go back to the South with."

Through the reference to the Bible, King's dream not only reinforces its deontic modality, but acquires another one, the modality of a *prophetic dream*. The authority of the Bible not only ensures that King's dream is morally good, it also ensures that it ultimately will come to pass as part of God's promise. Interestingly in (10), dw_1 the discourse world of King's "dream" is anaphorically referred to using two nouns corresponding to world-creating predicates that have a clear *epistemic* component: *hope* and *faith*, both to be taken here in their strongest religious reading, entailing certainty rather than in their often toned down everyday use (e.g., *I hope she will get well soon*).

As we can see, studying discourse worlds is not alien to the study of discourse as social action: a large share of its power to persuade, arouse emotions, entertain, etc., is

---

15. In preparing this illustrative analysis, we wanted to focus on the power of discourse worlds as an analytical tool and we have purposefully refrained to consult the rich rhetorical and discourse analytical literature on this speech, as well as to investigate "philologically" its intertextual connections prior to the analysis. It was therefore interesting to find, afterwards, that in a 1965 sermon, titled *The American Dream* King engages in an actual *exegesis* of the same words of the *Declaration of Independence* ("It doesn't say 'some men,' it says 'all men.' It doesn't say 'all white men,' it says 'all men,' which includes black men."). In this sermon, King clearly indicates the *Declaration* as the source of the "American Dream." That these things are well-known to King's scholars (and maybe pretty obvious to many Americans) does not detract anything from the methodological value of our "naïve" discovery.

mediated by its ability to plausibly evoke in the minds of the audience the representation of world fragments: both fragments of the actual accessible world, to which react upon and fragments of other possible worlds: worlds to act towards, to comply to, to desire, to hope for.[16]

An analysis in terms of discourse worlds and the kind of possible worlds they underlie does not substitute a rich, substantial, cultural analysis of the worlds of the texts but, as we have shown above, provides its essential, and often strategic, structuring.

Insightful as it may be, discourse world analysis is better seen as a component of a more comprehensive research strategy in discourse studies.

In our own work, we have adopted a three-pronged approach, where the two other components, apart from discourse worlds are represented by

a. A speech-act theoretic treatment of the pragmatic organization of texts, subsuming also the notion of *discourse relations*, which are seen as multi utterance, complex speech acts, and addressing the notion of discourse coherence. (This component is presented in Rocci, 2005b);
b. A model of the social *context of communication* (Rigotti & Rocci, 2006) allowing for a fine grained analysis of *activity types*.

Finally, this three-fold analytical component is related, as an input, to a "normative" evaluative component, which in our own work on persuasive discourse (Rocci, 2008a) is represented by *argumentation theory* (see Van Eemeren, chapter 11 of this volume).[17]

7. Practical relevance

The practical relevance of the discourse semantic tools sketched here depends on their ability to help us understand the context and content of discourse within specific communication practices. In other words, it seems particularly promising to investigate, expanding on Gaik (1992), how discourse worlds reflect the interactional purpose of a certain discourse *genre* or *activity type*. Qualitative discourse analyses of small corpora of texts or transcripts focussing on the mapping of discourse worlds would

16. With respect to the persuasive role of experientially rich representations of the world we have already mentioned Tannen (1989), but see Cigada (2008) for an approach to the persuasiveness of narrative and description which makes explicit use of the notion of *discourse world* and considers both fictional dws and dws referring to the actual world or its possible future developments within the same overall theoretical framework adopted here (see in particular chapter 2).

17. Note that the approaches to discourse quality discussed in Renkema (2004) could take the role of the evaluative component in studies of informative discourse not aimed to persuade.

provide precious insights into the pragmatic functioning of specific genres and activity types.

An activity type where this kind of analysis appears fruitful also for its practical consequences is represented by the practice of *mediation*. Mediation is a form alternative dispute resolution (ADR), where a third party, typically a professional mediator, intervenes in a conflict "in order to facilitate a reasonable discussion between the conflicting parties, who are no longer capable of negotiating directly, but are nevertheless committed to trying to find a solution" (Greco-Morasso, 2006).

A number of discourse-analytic studies have tackled mediation as an activity type, focussing, in particular, on its argumentative aspects (cf. Aakhus, 2003; Greco-Morasso, 2006, 2008). The interest of a discourse semantic study focussed on discourse worlds emerges clearly from this literature.

Some studies have stressed the complexity of the initial common ground in mediation, and the care devoted by mediators in ascertaining the common ground[18] between the parties in order to offer a solid starting point to the mediation (Greco-Morasso, 2006: 286). This complexity can be effectively mapped in terms of discourse worlds. This mapping would have to include the (apparently) conflicting bouletic dws that define the dispute, the shared bouletic dw that prompted the parties to resort to a mediator for a settlement (e.g., we don't want to ruin our interpersonal relationship / our common business), the agreement upon "facts" of the incident but also the epistemically conflicting accounts and interpretations of what happened. This bouletically and epistemically fractured common ground has to be updated during the mediation to create a dw corresponding to a possible acceptable settlement, which the parties should arrive at with the help of the mediator.

The discourse moves performed by the mediator to facilitate agreement also involve the evocation of alternatives, most notably the evocation of the possible negative consequences of not reaching an amicable agreement. Greco (2006: 288) presents a typical example from a mediation in a dispute between business partners:

(11) **Mediator**: A:nd (.) all the time, I think, keeping in mind (.) that (.) one of the things you really want to do is — you've got a golden goose here. And it would be crazy to kill the golden goose (..).

A systematic research on the discourse worlds of mediation is yet to be done. This research could profitably start with a mapping of discourse worlds in a single mediation transcript, to later focus more in-depth on the semantics of the world-creating predicates encountered and the kind of logical relations established between worlds.

18. This operation of the mediator corresponds to the *opening stage* of the critical discussion in the pragma-dialectic model of argumentation (cf. Van Eemeren & Grootendorst, 2004 and Van Eemeren, chapter 11 of this volume).

At this point, the researcher could observe the distribution of the different kinds of dw with respect to the participant who introduced them (litigant or mediator) and the phase of the mediation process in which they occur. As a result, the researcher would be able to put forth hypotheses that relate the types of dw with the pragmatic goals of the participants, the goals of the different phases and the local aim of the speech act in which they occur.

If it is found that there are lexical or grammatical indicators (e.g., modal verbs, propositional attitude verbs, or conditional constructions) routinely associated with certain kinds of dws, the research could be further developed in a quantitative direction through the observation of the distribution of these markers in a larger corpus of transcribed mediation interactions. Here, the "manual" examination of concordances would represent a necessary intermediate step to refine hypotheses about the function of different markers before plotting their distribution in the interactions composing the corpus.

Assignment

The text reproduced below is an excerpt from the speech delivered by US presidential candidate Barack Obama on January 26, 2008, on the occasion of his victory in the South Carolina Democratic primaries.

The choice in this election is not between regions or religions or genders. It's not about rich versus poor; young versus old; and it is not about black versus white.

It's about the past versus the future.

It's about whether we settle for the same divisions and distractions and drama that passes for politics today, or whether we reach for a politics of common sense, and innovation — a shared sacrifice and shared prosperity.

There are those who will continue to tell us we cannot do this. That we cannot have what we long for. That we are peddling false hopes.

But here's what I know. I know that when people say we can't overcome all the big money and influence in Washington, I think of the elderly woman who sent me a contribution the other day — an envelope that had a money order for $3.01 along with a verse of scripture tucked inside. So don't tell us change isn't possible.

When I hear the cynical talk that blacks and whites and Latinos can't join together and work together, I'm reminded of the Latino brothers and sisters I organized with, and stood with, and fought with side by side for jobs and justice on the streets of Chicago. So don't tell us change can't happen.

When I hear that we'll never overcome the racial divide in our politics, I think about that

Republican woman who used to work for Strom Thurmond,[19] *who's now devoted to educating inner-city children and who went out onto the streets of South Carolina and knocked on doors for this campaign. Don't tell me we can't change.*

Yes we can change.

Yes we can heal this nation.

Yes we can seize our future.

And as we leave this state with a new wind at our backs, and take this journey across the country we love with the message we've carried from the plains of Iowa to the hills of New Hampshire; from the Nevada desert to the South Carolina coast; the same message we had when we were up and when we were down — that out of many, we are one; that while we breathe, we hope; and where we are met with cynicism, and doubt, and those who tell us that we can't, we will respond with that timeless creed that sums up the spirit of a people in three simple words:

Yes. We. Can.

The excerpt reproduces the final part of the speech. This rhetorically crafted electoral speech introduces a whole host of discourse worlds of different kinds, whose evocation plays a strategic role in fulfilling the interactional goals of the speech, contributing to its persuasive force.

Try to work out a discourse semantic analysis of the text in two steps.

- Firstly, mark down all the world-creating expressions that are found in the text and try to establish the kind of discourse worlds they introduce.
- Secondly, try to reconstruct a semantic representation of the speech, mapping the different discourse worlds introduced in the discourse and the propositions that populate them.

In performing the first step, one should be careful also to consider worlds that are not explicitly introduced via world-creating predicates, but are evoked through the borrowing of stylistic patterns from other speeches.

In fact, one broad kind of discourse world which is particularly prominent in the speech is the representation of the speech and thoughts of people other than the speaker. The key rhetorical role of these distinct "voices" has been pointed out by Alessandro Capone in a recent paper (Capone, 2008). This paper does not use the discourse worlds as an analytical tool and has a partly different focus. It would be particularly interesting, then, to read it after having completed the analysis and compare the results obtained.

Finally, it is worth comparing the results of the proposed analysis with the analysis of Martin Luther King's *I have a Dream* speech to find similarities and differences. Consider the context and genre of Obama's speech, and its goals and how they differ from King's speech. To what extent are these differences reflected in the semantic representation?

19. James Strom Thurmond (1902–2003) was a pro-segregation South Carolina governor and senator.

Chapter 2

Discourses "off course"?

Anna Duszak
Warsaw University

Discourse studies have traditionally focused on patterning in discourse structures, and on rationality and cooperation in discourse processing. However, a lot of communication goes "off the regular course" under the human drive for creativity, language play, prevarication, or plain desire for deceit. This chapter examines potential instances of such subversive texts. It builds its argument on the relative role of intertextuality in how coherence is established, and how it can be semantically disruptive and socially alienating. This is illustrated on the example of inter-lingual and multi-modal hybrids in Polish. It is demonstrated that such discourses thrive on global and local resources for textuality. The discussion makes points of contact with Critical Discourse Analysis, social semiotics and applied linguistics.

1. Introduction

It is not easy to locate this task in the domain of discourse studies. Discourse is a fuzzy concept and resists exclusions as much as elegant explanations. It is tempting therefore to discuss it in terms of metaphors in general, and with reference to our current undertaking in particular. I shall invoke two metaphors. First, discourse is a "JOURNEY," second, it is a "GAME." Both nominations are not new.

The first recalls the imagery that is typical of cognitive semantic views on communication and human condition in general ("life is a journey"), building up on the underlying conception of MOVEMENT (e.g., Johnson, 1987). Some authors have already stressed this nature of discourse. Cf. Krzeszowski (1997: 230), who says that discourse "is often metaphorically conceived as a journey, and this metaphor is responsible for most other phenomena making up the structure of discourse." And further on: "the concept <journey> illustrates the SOURCE-PATH-GOAL schema inasmuch as every journey has a beginning (SOURCE), proceeds along some route (PATH) and leads to some destination (GOAL)" (Krzeszowski, 1997: 245–246).

What are the advantages of this metaphor for our conceptualization of discourse? Journeys normally connote scripted actions, combining routine with readiness for adventure. We enter discourses with some expectations about the sense, relevance, or function of what is being said (written). Such disposition for critical interpretation of discourse meanings is particularly important for meta-linguistic studies. What is it then that we as discourse analysts can rely upon? Up-to-date research in text and discourse provides some useful guidance. It has anchored many cognitive aspects of discourse organization and processing: cf. especially the early strategic models of discourse comprehension (Van Dijk & Kintsch, 1983), procedural models of textuality (De Beaugrande & Dressler, 1981) or more recent accounts of "discourse pragmatics" (e.g., Verschueren, 1999). Such work has highlighted the various goals and motivations, ends and means in how people communicate through texts. It also inalienably linked language to its social embedding and ecology of use. The discourse-as-JOURNEY metaphor makes it easier to visualize discourse as a dynamic, social and interactive action in context.

This imagery accommodates other aspects of "journeying" as well: traveling needs a territory and orientation in space. Most often a flagged ground is necessary to keep us on the right track. Charting new directions needs signposting too. In discourse, this orientation function is performed by various observable features of texts or "images" (in the sense of Kress and Van Leeuwen) acting as "keys" to meaning. Generally speaking, our discourse routes and signs engage various semiotic repertories and perform various functions. As a result, we can normally allocate discourses to language systems (e.g., English, Polish, etc.) and subsystems (registers, genres, styles), as well as attribute to them particular user characteristics (e.g., attitudes and identities). This gives us the welcome sense of communicative comfort and social alignment with our partners.

The task of discourse analysis has always been to establish, describe and explain what are (relatively) stable structures, conventionalized behavior patterns or shared valuations. Like earlier text linguistics, modern discourse analysis focuses on CORE phenomena and backgrounds the peripheral. This means interest in discourses representing the highest density of co-occurring parameters of contexts, users and texts. So, for instance, on the level of discourse grammar we focus on standardized structures-in-use. On the level of connected speech we attend to what is perceptually, semantically and culturally salient. Building up on our "discourse-as-JOURNEY" metaphor, we could say that discourse analysis can provide us with a general road map only, with what might be described as a motorway system with some indications if any of side roads and country trails. Still, discourse worlds are not always easy to penetrate or understand. Next to "regular" texts, there are discourses that go "off the main track," some leading us astray and some funneling new ways to textuality. This is what happens for instance with many global intertexts (e.g., in advertising), which subvert the core and create new centers in cosmopolitan communication (cf. e.g., Duszak, 2004). That is why we should appreciate better the capacity of discourse-as-JOURNEY once we realize that discourse is also a GAME that we play, and that games are also played in alleys respecting their own rules or guarding access to outsiders. These are the various trails for rambling around, shortcutting or discovering new paths to meaning.

We are aware of course that there are no recipes for making (or unpacking) texts. Can discourse analysis guide and guard us then in a world that often thwarts the CORE and plays with resources, goals and habits? In this chapter, I focus on discourses that are heterogeneous, hybridized, and semantically ambivalent, if not vague or potentially meaningless. They are interlingual and/or multi-modal texts, a category that — variously and selectively — attracts the attention of social semiotics, multimodal discourse analysis, interactional sociolinguistics, grammar and translation theory. These are the texts that challenge mainstream logocentric approaches to communication on their regimes of linearity, cohesion, rationality and even cooperativeness. Such "off (the main) course" communications are also interesting in the light of the growing self-commodification of authors, texts and entire discourse domains. They are relevant too considering the ease or else the difficulty with their social or cross-cultural mediation. All this makes them relevant for educationally minded endeavors in discourse analysis: what tools should go into the students' traveling kit to provide them with adaptable and multifunctional instruments for opening the various doors to discourse?

2. The research challenge

In our view, discourse is a flow of repeating, re-writing, re-reading and re-interpreting "things" that stand in some relation to other "things" and that display varying degrees of semblance or idiosyncrasy in terms of text and context characteristics. A relational approach to discourses, and texts for that matter, may not disregard the general constitutive conditions on texture. Only then can we establish what is similar and what is different, or how salient (or marked) some discourses are if compared to others. The bottom question is then: "what makes discourse discourse"? (cf. Renkema, 2004: Section 3.6). This concern was first handled under standards of textuality (De Beaugrande & Dressler, 1981). Out of the seven constitutive criteria nominated, we select intertextuality as a major controller of the relative proximity and distance between texts. The concept of intertextuality, and its later cognates, can inform our understanding of the specific nature of many discursive hybrids in the sense intuited here.

This chapter departs from Renkema's discussion on "What makes discourse discourse?," and specifically from his treatment of intertextuality. Renkema defines intertextuality as follows:

> *Intertextuality* means that a sequence of sentences is related by form or meaning to other sequences of sentences. This chapter is a discourse because it is related to the

> other chapters of this book. And this book is a discourse because it is a member of the group of textbooks. An example of intertextuality where the two sequences are related by meaning is a news bulletin on a topic that has previously been dealt with in a news program (Renkema, 2004: 50–51, emphasis in the original; cf. also page 54).

This description is an example of an elegant definition trying to pin down the essence of what intertextuality is (does) in discourse rather than hedging at what it may be (doing). It is a simplification for instance to define intertextuality as some "relation" existing between "sequences of sentences," especially as a giant leap is done right away, when intertextuality is redefined as a link between the "chapters of this book." A still more demanding task confronts the reader when he/she is asked to see intertextuality between "this" and other "textbooks." To a careful student it may not be clear to what extent intertextuality is a matter of language and to what extent it resides in the knowledge of the world. Last but not least, the formulation that an intertextual relation can be established "by form **or** meaning" (emphasis added), may suggest that the two can be kept separate in analyzing how discourses inter-communicate. We have to remember though that intertextuality is a particularly troublesome parameter for text studies.

I believe that intertextuality serves a primary function in regulating our understanding, acceptance and valuation of discourses in general and in the case of discursive hybrids in particular. Perhaps better than other standards of textuality, it demonstrates the fuzz underlying human decisions on how discourses mean, what associations they entail, and what connections they immobilize. On this view, intertextuality easily fits into our metaphor of discourse-as-JOURNEY, making it possible to label texts for their capacity of movement, whether traveling back and forth in time, heading straight on or sideways, or perhaps making detours. It illustrates the complexity of the relation between form *and* meaning, suggesting where it should be more transparent and where it could remain obscure. By and large therefore, intertextuality also determines the rules of the discursive GAME, making it clear that our decisions in discourse depend on our access to the semiotic resources and cultural values that underlie it.

Finally, is the intertextual potential of discourse an asset or an impediment in communication? Is it helpful for our orientation on the map, or is it more of a peril lurking on the side of the road? Some see it indeed as a source of ambiguity and uncertainty in discourse (e.g., De Beaugrande, 1996: 65, or Fairclough, 1992: 135–136, who talks about "resistant interpretations" for texts intertwined in unclear intertextual connections). It leaves no doubt that intertextuality opens the door wide to various forms of subversive, non-serious, creative, or prevaricate uses of language, a style that is increasingly valued in the world of self-promotional and commodified discourses. It lies at the bottom of parody, irony, provocation, taboo breaking or de-sacrilization. At the same time, it essentially redefines our initial question, "What makes discourse discourse?" into: "What makes discourse discourse *to you*?"

3. Examples

This section provides some illustrations of hybridized texts circulating in Polish, mainly in public discourse spaces. The semiotic blending involves various resources and codes, the visual and the verbal, English and Polish. The choice of the examples and their explication reflect a localized perspective, yet many of such texts (images) display global patterning that makes them interpretable outside of their immediate context of operation. As argued by Duszak (2004: 119ff.), the peripheral nature of such communications may actually ease their spreading, intersemiotic breeding and re-contextualization across various discursive spaces, slowly destabilizing our sense for what is CORE in communication. Above all, the "physicality" (after Duszak, 2007) of many inter-semiotic hybrids powers the current trend for visual, prevaricate or "non-serious" communication (cf. Clark 1996: 363ff.), enhancing the self-promotional character of many modern language GAMES. The examples that follow illustrate such capacities of discourses to exploit the tug-of-war between perceptual and semantic salience, between seriousness and play, compliance and subversion. These are the texts that leak their meaning and contextual function rather than build them on particular intertextual chains in our discourse experience (cf. the "textbook" domain above). Some patterning is discussed in how such semiotic games can be played.

Examples 1 and 2 are instances of a single macrostrategy. Here two traffic code signs are vulgarized in inter-semiotic hybrids.

Example 1:

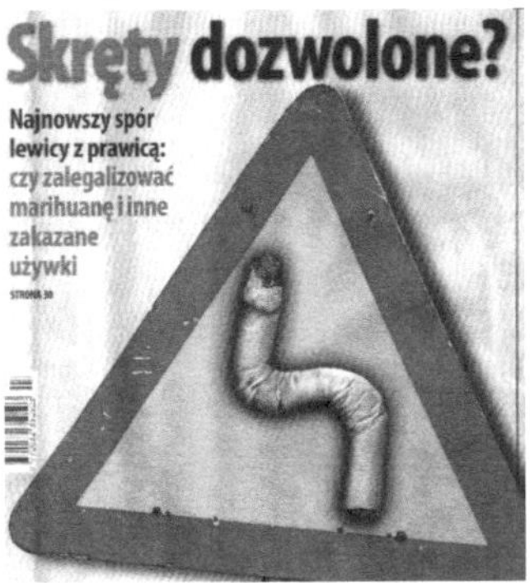

Example 2:

Example 1 is a good candidate for a global intertext, considering its perceptual and semantic salience, if not its ideology of a "warning," which is likely to be inferred internationally. We could assume that the message is vision dominated, highlighting two focal elements (the generic traffic code triangle and a twisted cigarette joint). The first clue pulls towards the traffic code and its ecology of use. Images parasitic on the traffic code are extremely productive in all sorts of inter-semiotic promiscuity, at least in Polish, mainly as semiotic vulgarizations in business, education, entertainment and advertising. In turn, the second clue, the burning cigarette, vectors towards a topical domain, that of discourses on consumption and behavior patterns, especially addiction, health education, or restrictions on conduct in public spaces. We may therefore assume that this sign could be perceptually salient and semantically (and pragmatically) analyzable in various linguistic environments. It is more of an open question what falls out and how relevant this might be for our interaction with such texts in particular environments. Here the knowledge of the language is important and conditional for more subtle readings of the message. In Polish the word *skręty* can be ambiguous, meaning *turns* (on the road) and (cigarette) *joints* for smoking. Hence the combination of the verbal and the graphical elements has perceptual and cognitive proximity. As a result the headline *Skręty dozwolone?* [*Joints allowed?*] prompts an intertextual dialogue across the two social domains, driving and addiction, sending a coherent message of a "danger" you are being cautioned about.

The *wSTOP do baru* example, on the other hand, is more complex even though equally potent as a global intertext. It is likely to send similar hints to people, no matter whether they speak Polish or not: "discontinue moving" (and look around). Or even: "you must stop here" (there is a bar right here that you must not miss). Yet, the form of the sign means more to those who speak Polish, and still more for those who know its orthography well. The text "sells" for a spelling (and pronunciation) error in the Polish word *wstąp* (*step into / inside* [*second person singular imperative*]). The nasal vowel *ą* in *wstąp* [fstomp] is replaced by *o* [o] as in STOP. The sign is then an instance of language play, or — which is not to be excluded — an accidental result of the maker's poor knowledge of Polish spelling rules. This means that the recognition of the error, and the ensuing endorsement of some creativity (or prevarication) on the part of the sign's producer demands the ability to make more subtle distinctions for Polish.

Examples 3 and 4 are perhaps less perceptually salient, yet they too bifurcate intertextuality across two semiotic systems: the verbal and the digital.

Example 3:

Example 4:

> 3maj się [Keep well]
> (in Dąbrowska, 2004: 269)

At first glance the discourse function of the digital is superficial and limited to the formal (physical) recognition of what is written, or rather what is said while reading. In this way the digitals fill in the missing links in each wording, and thus make it interpretable. Like with the above images, they invoke topical intertextuality, pulling towards various discursive domains. The first sign activates such discourses as *car repair, car dealers* or *second hand cars*. The second is likely to activate other formulaic expressions, such as greetings or farewells. Both images can be located within central social domains: (car) advertising and purchase, on the one hand, and electronic communications (*sms, e-mail*), on the other. Both domains, however topically distant, borrow eagerly from the digital code.

If context remains a viable indicator for the meaning of both signs, the power of the digital is not quite the same in each case. In Poland today the *CAR4you* is generally meaningful independently of one's command of English. It is a commercial buzz word, a sign that connotes rather than denotes meaning, yet hardly requires any translation. In contrast, the *3* in *3maj się* cannot be understood without some knowledge of the Polish language. The sign is a local product of a global pattern. There is a difference too in how each digital "enters" the verbal code. In Polish *3* (*trzy*) simply replaces the first four letters of the verb "*trzy*maj się" (*keep well*). It is a prosodic (visual) "substitute" of a part of a word. In English, on the other hand, we need to infer that *4* reads "for" and not "four," which can be done only once we venture an assumption about the meaning of the whole sign.

In the last two examples the hybridization is less perceptually salient.

Example 5:

> *A ja? […] nołproblem, facet. Nie bądź spięty. Nikt ci niczego nie broni. Kochamy cię, stary. Łilawju, ewrysingforju*
> And what about me? […] no problem, man. Relax. You are forbidden nothing. We love you, old man. Weloveyou, everythingforyou.
> (Varga Krzysztof, *Tequila*, 2001: 21 in Kozak, 2004: 147, transl. J.Kozak)

Example 6:

> *Był luzerem od chwili narodzin. „Borntubiluzer," to jest tytuł na numer, na wielki hicior.*
> He was a loser from birth. "Born to Be a Loser," this is a title for a piece, a grand fat hit
> (Varga, page 53 – transl. J. Kozak).

The (italicized) examples need to be located in a particular linguistic system before deterioration of some wordings is detected or some assumptions about the texts' coherence can nonetheless be made. Reluctantly perhaps, speakers of Polish will identify these texts as Polish even though they incorporate non-Polish words — most probably importations from English. In fact however, both language systems, Polish and English, are pidginized here. *Luzer* is not a Polish word, nor is English as it comes. As Kozak shows in the translations, it is far from easy to translate into the source language. The translatability or untranslatability of such inter-lingual hybrids is of some concern to translation theorists and practitioners (the cross-cultural mediation of *Clockwork orange* is sometimes discussed as a first illustration of such problems, cf. Hejwowski, 2004).

4. Research method

There is no space here to redefine intertextuality in a way that could reach a reasonable level of explanatory completion (for some overview or references see Duszak, 1998: 219ff.). In this sense, my coverage of the topic here remains modest and selective only. Some guidelines for further elaboration are however in order. Relevant are such cognate concepts as *heteroglossia*, *polyphony*, *dialogicality* (after Bakhtin, 1986) and above all *interdiscursivity*, or *interdiscursive dialogicality* (Scollon & Wong Scollon: 2003) (cf. however Fairclough, 1992, for a distinction between intertextuality and interdiscursivity). The origins of the term *intertextuality* are non-linguistic (Kristeva, 1968) and have semiotic, literary and philosophical foundations. In some sense, intertextuality replaced reference to phenomena that were also (or earlier) analyzed under such labels as text transformations, stylization, parody, citations, travesties, etc. In contrast to earlier formulations, it afforded a new perspective on texture, evolutional and relational simultaneously, described sometimes (after Kristeva) as *vertical* and *horizontal*. So, any text enters into relations with other texts that make its context, networking as a result within entire discourse worlds. Yet, there is also an osmotic relation between the textual and the societal, the past, the present and the future, with history "entering" texts and texts "entering" history. This position communicates well with the basic tenet of contemporary Critical Discourse Analysis that discourse is socially *shaped* as well as socially *constitutive*:

> Viewing language use as social practice implies, first, that it is a mode of action (...) and, secondly, that it is always a socially and historically situated mode of action, in a dialectical relationship with other facets of "the social" (its 'social context') — it is socially shaped, but it is also socially shaping, or *constitutive*. (Fairclough, 1995: 131, emphasis in the original).

It was an important contribution of text linguistics to show that intertextuality does not reside in form repetition, or presence of the linguistic form for that matter. On the contrary, intertextual linking often depends first of all on the availability of non-linguistic knowledge, especially cultural knowledge, for making bridging connections between texts, topics or strategies (e.g., Hatim & Mason, 1990: 124). Essential is also our general ability to reason, conceptualize abstractions or establish analogies, all of which underlies decisions on *structural* intertextuality, as when kinship between texts is conceived of in terms of style, textual format, ideologies or writing conventions.

This does not mean though that we should dismiss of the (observable) form in analyzing how intertextual meanings emerge in communication. This would be counter-intuitive in particular in the context of our immediate interest. Some relevance of form was acknowledged too in text linguistic research on intertextuality. Malmkjæker and Anderson (1991: 469), for instance, argue that in many cases the establishment of an intertextual relation is dependent on the existence of concrete texts (as with parodies or reviews). Plett (1991: 7) stresses that *material intertextuality* is particularly easy to detect as the type of intertextual relation that consists in the repetition of signs (see also Helbig, 1996). The role of the perceptual was presupposed in a first categorization of complex discourses. Namely, Hausenblas (1966) argued that complex discourses incorporate "foreign" ("strange") texts (e.g., citations or graphically highlighted parts of bigger wholes).

Today, with the rising use of inter-semiotic texts, we can observe even more attention being paid to the perceptible in complex signs, or to the material context of their placement. Van Leeuwen (2005: 237), for instance, points to the role of "spatial co-presence" in itemization of televised news. Within their model of "place semiotics" (*geosemiotics*), Scollon and Wong Scollon (2003: 167) speak of "*interdiscursive dialogicality*," which they define relative to semiotic aggregates, or "intersections of multiple discourses" and "interaction orders" with them, that happen "in such places as restaurants or neighborhoods, street corners in cities or shopping malls." Here, the physical location of the text serves as an additional prompt for its intertextual meaning potential.

Quite importantly for the current discussion, intertextuality connotes another important concept, and namely that of (re)-contextualization. On the one hand, no text is "the same" on its subsequent actualizations: every reading of the same excerpt from a book is a "different reading," or reading of a "different text," activating diverse intertextual links. The extent of that difference varies, depending on, say, the type of audience, the occasion, the purpose, the concentration of the reader, the state of his (her) mind, or the modulation of the reader's voice, if the reading is done for an audience. On the other hand, texts may be, more or less purposefully, adjusted to suit various situations, users, genres or ideologies. This is a well-known issue in Critical

Discourse Analysis, as when strategic choice has to be made whether to call actors *freedom fighters* or *terrorists.*

Intertextuality and re-contextualization are two sides of the same coin. Both are a matter of degree, especially given the steady blending of textual and contextual features in how many communications are structured and enacted (e.g., the leveling of the distinction between the private and public, between the informal and the formal, or the concept of intertextual genre). Many hybridized discourses are propelled by interdiscursive dialogicality that stems from the perceptual salience of their form and the ideological stigmatization of their meaning. As I shall argue below, such texts send multiple, and possibly confusing signals where to go or how to make the best shortcuts in order to arrive at the intended meaning, if such meaning can be established without "any reasonable doubt" at all.

5. Recent research

The images in Section 3 illustrate the type of inter-semiotic — inter-lingual and multimodal — hybrids that are of interest here as examples of language play in a globalizing world. Linguistic dispersion is important: among them are visuals which at the same time are **bilingual** texts or intra-lingual variants of texts, showing as a result varying potential for intercultural mediation. In approaching such hybrids, I assume that there is a bifurcation in how their intertextual potential is constructed in interaction. This bifurcation stems from the intertextual disposition of every code involved. In our case, this means intertextual linking between and through the resources of the visual codes (traffic and digital) and the verbal (English and Polish), each of them opening up spaces for meaning enrichment. The component parts of each image have a perceptual salience that "forks" our attention as well as our search for associations, taking us astray as it were from the text into densely populated discourse worlds that surround it. On the other hand, an integrated holistic interpretation seems a natural, default, striving in communication. That is, we tend to conceptualize a hybrid as an integral sign that has its own potential for usage and intertextual linking. As a result, we make detours, trying to return to our point of departure, and view it through the prism of what we saw on both tours, guided by the visual and the verbal cues respectively.

This rough itinerary begs for some untangling of its metaphorical tips. Speaking of bifurcation, I imply that each semiotic code pulls towards its own CORE discourse worlds. Admittedly however, the case is complex. In fact, we are dealing not with a simple bifurcation of intertextual resources, but with a dispersion of intertextuality cues, easily sliding off the main track and into an open periphery of textuality. This is a likely supposition considering that, for instance, even an apparently central traffic sign may be multi-modal, as when the visual and the verbal are merged into one complex form (cf. the "give way" or "stop" sign, which speak through the visual and the verbal at the same time). There may be intertextual "offshoots" too, once we remember that traffic regulations may include signs that are already visual hybrids (e.g., the geometric size of the "warning" sign and the drawing of an animal, cautioning drivers of crossing animals).

If the intertextual potential of hybrids normally disperses our search for meaning, then context may ease taking the right course. The fact that a hybrid is placed in an advertisement column can funnel our interpretation along some cues (e.g., verbal and topical) rather than others (e.g., the visual of graphic design). The appearance of a sign at a particular place may encourage us to maximally reduce our efforts for processing and elaboration, as could be the case with the *stop-bar* example above (example 2). This does not change the fact that all signs have a potential to re-contextualize, that is, to locate in various contexts. It stands to reason that in the case of hybrids the intertextual potential is high, due to the very nature of such formations. This capacity for re-contextualization applies to the sign in its physical integrity as well as to its component parts. In this way hybrids bifurcate our search for contexts, opening a pool of possible contextualizations and showing a varying potential for re-use for similar or countering purposes (e.g., the warning function connoted by a triangle in the context of driving regulations may be replanted to signal other "threats" or parodied for commercial purposes of attracting attention to some commodities).

With reference to what was said above, our road map may not disregard individual (or group) capacities of users to find orientation in discourse worlds. This shifts our original attention from the composition of the sign on to the characteristics of its users. This is of course more of a change in perspective than a real redefinition of the object of our analysis: things communicate only when they are interpretable, that is, they must be meaningful to people. The point is that the same sign never means "the same" to all of its potential users. Therefore, we need to inquire into the variation with which people recognize, interpret and evaluate inter-semiotic hybrids, and ultimately how they locate them in the contexts familiar to them. This is an important aspect of any approach to multi-modal communications, especially if one remembers about the unifying, or else the alienating role of texts (images) in social life. Still, for this variation to be spelt out, we need to return to the characteristics of the code and the environment of its operation. Namely, we are talking here about access to relevant codes and contexts, and a general experience with similar texts. The availability of the knowledge of English and Polish becomes an issue.

6. Research proposal

Intertextuality is a pervasive feature of communication, integrating yet also diffusing, what discourses say and do in social contexts. Hybridized images enhance this associative potential of any texture. This they do through vulgarization of form and meaning (cf. the twisted cigarette in the triangle of the traffic code sign, or distorted English in Polish texts). Important is their ability to "cross" contexts, as when a traffic sign is made to function outside of its central ecology of use (roads, manuals for learner drivers), in a peripheral setting of commercial or social advertising. From the perspective of their intertextual potential, hybridized discourses are poly-vocal in that they resound in many voices, and poly-spatial in that they can spread across various contexts. Many of them can function as intertexts, bridging global and local communication strategies and values. So, on the global side they capitalize on visualization and promotional strategies, or the reference to English as the global *lingua franca*. On the other hand, however, much of what (and how) they communicate is regional, specialist, idiosyncratic or simply vague.

Today the meta-theoretical potential of such hybrids remains largely unexplored. A part of the problem may be that such hybrids are not "prestigious" enough to make them eligible for more systematic analyses. Users too often disregard such texts as fleeting, vague and undeserving of serious attention. Such dismissive attitudes are not necessarily legitimated in the face of growing hybridization of discourses and social knowledge in general, with the mixing of semiotic resources — languages, words and images — becoming a strong undercurrent in modern communication.

There are many ways in which such hybrids could be studied and handled for research and educational purposes. Apart from the mainstream area of social semiotics and multi-modal discourse analysis, we could envision their relevance for translation theory, foreign language pedagogy or language policy. These are diverse frameworks, making it necessary to adjust our discourse tools for specific priorities of research. For instance, we might interpret such formations against such concepts as *pidginization* of languages (and texts) and *interlingual borrowing*. For Polish this would mean revisiting the regime of purist thinking in linguistics, the so-called "language culture," especially among more traditionally minded linguists, (cf. Buttler et al., 1971; Miodek, 1996; Pisarek, 1999; Pisarek & Zgółkowa, 1995; cf. cognate terms in other languages, esp. *Sprachkultur* in German). Other areas of research could invoke studies in *social accommodation* and *convergence* (*divergence*) as well as code-*switching* and code-*crossing*, putting focus on attitudes to language users and resorting to frameworks informed by social psychology and discursive construction of social identities; cf. e.g., Benwell & Stokoe, 2006). Last but not least, we might want to consider the role of *domestication and foreignization* (taken from translation studies mainly after Venuti, 2000) in how language contact is mediated.

7. Practical relevance

Multimodal texts receive increasing attention among linguists and communication scientists in general. Considerable work has been done first of all within social semiotics (cf. Kress & Van Leeuwen, 1996; Van Leeuwen, 2005; Scollon & Wong Scollon, 2003), but multi-modal discourse analysis is also coming forward (cf. O'Halloran, 2004 for some overview; cf. also other contributions in this volume). Much of this research has focused on compositional structure of images, often as a follow-up to text organization models (especially Kress & Van Leeuwen). Some believe however, that human interaction with multi-modal texts is likely to be multidimensional and holistic rather than linear (cf. Crystal, 2001). It was also argued that semiotic resources specialize in their meaning potential. So, for instance, Lemke (2004) speaks of semiotic *incommensurability*. He argues that no two semiotic resource systems "are capable of producing exactly the same meaning potential in a text or artifact," that is, to put it crudely, there is "no image that corresponds exactly in meaning to a word, phrase, or sentence." Such varying affordances of semiotic resources are important from the perspective of any "inner" dialogue within semiotic aggregates. They are also relevant for assessing the intertextual potential of such hybrids, and their ability to cross contexts of use, especially if such contexts should select, preferably or exclusively, for some codes only (e.g., the traffic code in its central and vulgarized uses). This complexity of inter-semiotic formations begs for more attention especially against the rapid proliferation of interaction patterns exploiting perceptual, cognitive and social hybridization.

By and large, it is only natural that discursive hybrids should constitute a viable yet also a demanding task on the agenda of multi-modal discourse analysis. This applies as well to the discourses that I have somewhat arbitrarily labeled here as going "off (the main) course" of any textual canon. I admit that the category is fuzzy and deliberately open, as our ultimate judgment on texts is largely a matter of subjective evaluation as much as it is the result of socialization in particular orders of discourse. That is, to revive the earlier metaphor of discourse as a JOURNEY, it depends on our point of departure (ethnic, educational, professional, ideological) and the field of vision that it affords to us. Even though my interpretation of the phenomena owes a lot to what goes under prevarication (cf. Hockett, 1966), or non-serious communication (Clark, 1996), it is not to be limited to such uses of language. Prevarication may be neutralized under the consensus that playfulness and innovativeness are the rules of the discourse-as-GAME. This becomes particularly valid once we agree that such a style of communication is turning into a central mode of social action especially in the public domain (cf. Duszak, 2004, 2007). This, in turn, can only upgrade the relative social weight that should be attached to how people cope with visual texts, and how the "physicality" of such texts can enhance their communicative and social values. As already pointed out (see Section 6), such "new pidgins" also carry an educational potential for applied linguistics, especially for translation and foreign language teaching involving English and a "minor" language.

Assignment

See what sense you can make of the hybrids below.

Task 1. *eLIEtes*
Can you, without a context, guess what word is being played with? What sense can you make of this play? What could be the function of the capitalized section of the word?

Task 2. *Zechciałbyś sforwardować to do niej?*
Provided you do not speak Polish, is there anything that you can figure out from this text?

Task 3. *„Idź na bekjard, wyrzuć garnek. Wymapuj podłogę, a potem wywaksuj. Weź insiurę na karę i jedź do Stanleya na korner, kup, com ci mówił. I łaciuj jak jedziesz, bo zrobisz akcydent."*
Provided you do not speak Polish, is there any meaning that you can figure out from this text? If so, then how is this possible? Can you locate the text in a discourse domain? Can you hypothesize on similarities and difference between this text and the example in Task 2?

Task 4.

What elements are perceptually salient in this image? How does their salience affect your interpretation of the entire image? What, do you think, is this text about, and in what context could it appear? Does it have any global potential for meaning? Could it be made to fit language contexts other than Polish?

Find "within" your own language, or languages of your choice, examples of textual hybrids that replicate or exploit such patterns as the ones discussed in this chapter. Try to establish other patterns in hybridizing the visual and the verbal for purposes of prevarication, language play or creative advertising in the social context that you are familiar with. See if such patterns change over time and, if so, to what effect and why. Probe people's attitudes to interaction with such texts: when (and why) do people show interest in interpreting such texts, and when (and why) do they reject cooperation? Check the recognition, interpretation and appraisal of a single textual hybrid with various populations of users (e.g., varying in age, level of knowledge of a language [jargon, style], education and profession, hobbies, etc.) and discuss the results. Can an analysis of hybridized texts inform our general understanding of how people use perceptual and semantic salience in communication?

Part II

Discourse and other communication modes

Chapter 3

Discourse across semiotic modes

John A. Bateman
Bremen University

The analysis of distinct semiotic artefacts such as page-based documents in both print and electronic form as well as time-based media, such as film, reveals a range of semiotic modes at work. Although sharing common substrates, such as the visually perceived two-dimensional page or screen, these semiotic modes need to be carefully distinguished. In this chapter, I define three distinct semiotic modes — text-flow, page-flow and image-flow — and show something of the distinct kinds of discourse that are possible within them. In essence, text-flow supports a linear unfolding of logical text organization and includes motivation for basic text-formatting options; page-flow draws in the two-dimensional possibilities of the page for expressing rhetorical relationships via spatial proximity and grouping; and image-flow uses the space of the page or a presentation in time for carrying an unfolding conjunctively-related discourse.

1. Introduction

It is increasingly common to find analyses of communicative artefacts that, on the one hand, draw on results and methods from linguistics and, on the other, address "texts" combining a variety of presentational modes. When analyzing an advertisement, for example, we rarely feel it sufficient nowadays to extract the verbal from its usually highly graphically loaded context and consider it in isolation as an example of "advertising" language. This stronger orientation to the "visual" can be observed in many disciplines involved with communication; some even talk of a "pictorial" or "visual" turn in which the previous monopoly of the written text has been overthrown, for better or for worse.

The areas of linguistics that have been most closely involved with this extension are naturally those that already deal with discourse. Discourse analysis, text linguistics, pragmatics and related areas within several theoretical orientations are all now facing issues that arise when the artefact under investigation mobilizes a variety of modes of presentation in order to communicate. But, although increasingly widespread, this extension of linguistics and discourse analysis to a kind of "multimodal linguistics" is fraught with analytic dangers. Precisely because there are many schools of linguistics with well developed styles of discourse for constructing analyses, the issue of "linguistic imperialism" — where all semiotic modes are made to resemble language, regardless of whether this is justified or not — must be seriously addressed.

Armed with sophisticated tools of linguistic analysis, the would-be multimodal analyst sets off, confident that multimodal communicative artefacts will quickly give up their secrets. It is hoped that this will produce research results that are rather more colorful and exciting than those generally managed within discourse studies, and which will then also awaken a broader interest than discourse studies traditionally enjoy. In addition, particularly for research students, this kind of analysis simply looks like a lot more fun than painstaking linguistic analyses; the lure for young researchers is therefore considerable.

The main problem with this is that multimodal communicative artefacts are not simple at all — in fact they are more complex than the traditional quasimonomodal texts on which much of linguistic text analysis is based: necessarily so, because such verbal texts are just one (optional) component of a semiotic complex of presentational resources. Approaching multimodal artefacts with the tools of linguistic analysis needs then to be undertaken with care. It is seductively straightforward to obscure relatively superficial interpretations behind apparently technical discourse where the analysis does not go substantially beyond what is readily available to inspection. In such cases, the main problem is that the rich interpretative schemes provided from other areas of study, here most relevantly linguistics and discourse studies, all too easily swamp the rather weak signal that we are currently capable of receiving from the multimodal artefacts themselves.

2. The research challenge

The principle challenge for discourse studies and their application to multimodal artefacts at this time is that our understanding of the meaning-making potential of visually-, spatially- and temporally-based artefacts is still surprisingly weak. Our sophisticated theories easily overrun the information that we are actually capable of extracting from the artefacts themselves. We can usefully cite here a rather strong claim made by Halliday with respect to grammar and discourse: "a discourse analysis that is not based on grammar is not an analysis at all, but simply a running commentary on a text" (Halliday, 1985: xvii). While opinions differ, especially among discourse analysts, of the extent to which grammar needs to be consulted, the warning remains particularly apposite for multimodal discourse analysts — for this is precisely what we most usually find in "analyses" of multimodal artefacts: not analyses, but "running commentaries"; for an accurate critique of this tendency, see Forceville (2007), as well as a general call for more empirical responsibility by Kaltenbacher (2004).

Getting further with the analysis of the discursive aspects of multimodal artefacts demands that we get beneath the surface. To do this, we need to develop frameworks for analysis within which empirical research can be conducted — and this involves concerning ourselves with the issue of just how we can analyze multimodal artefacts in a way that places the analysis on sound empirical and scientific foundations. Analysis of this kind is still largely beyond the possibilities of informal discourses of multimodal "analysis," even those that consider themselves "linguistic" in orientation: it remains difficult to say that an explanation is "wrong," that it does not match what an artefact itself brings to the interpretation. But unless we can do this, we are unlikely to proceed beyond statements reaffirming our starting points.

This raises intriguing scientific questions. Whereas few probably would seriously claim that there is anything in multimodal artefacts analogous to natural language syntax — i.e., there will be no "ungrammatical" multimodal artefacts — it is unlikely that all multimodal artefacts that can be created are necessarily interpretable. If the demands placed on visual and spatial perception are too high, then the artefact will not even be "perceivable." What are the limits here? Many suggest that multimodal artefacts are analogous to texts or discourses, i.e., that we interpret the elements in a multimodal artefact and put these together in order to create a coherent "story" about what is meant. But we have no models of discourse structure that are based on a spatial/visual material base instead of a verbal/acoustic one. The move to two (and three/four) dimensions is a fundamental distinction: what consequences does it have? Clearly, simply assuming that the same kinds of meaning are to be found provides interesting hypotheses but unless we can test such hypotheses and possibly show them wanting, there will be no progress beyond the null hypothesis of similarity.

3. Examples

Consider the page shown to the right below. Despite the fact that this is a relatively simple multimodal document page, it still presents problems that most multimodal analysis frameworks are ill equipped to address. In particular, although the page is professionally designed, its communication of rhetorical organization has become distorted; that is, the spatial layout of the page communicates relationships between elements that were not intended and which, even worse, are actually false (cf. Bateman,

2008, chapter 4). To show this analytically, we need to be able to distinguish several layers of description. In particular, we must be able to characterize both the visual structure of multimodal artefacts and the likely discourse interpretations of that structure independently of one another so as to be able to contrast and compare their interrelationships.

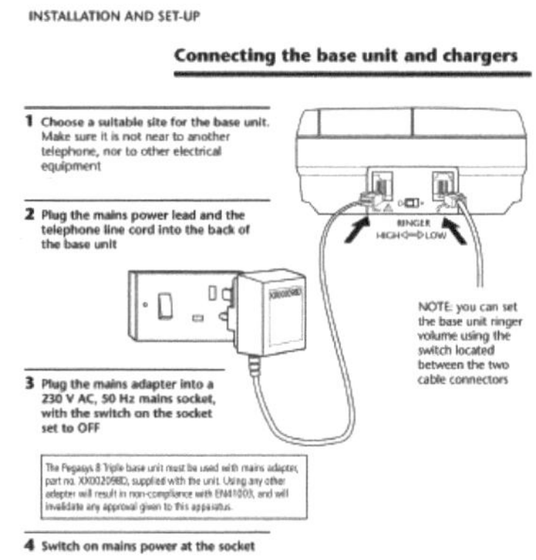

Figure 1. Telephone instructions.

Even well established characterizations are often less helpful here than might have been hoped. Often little more is provided than suggestive proposals. One characterization by Kress and Van Leeuwen (1996), for example, describes page layouts in terms of a left-right dimension of "given"-"new" and a top-bottom dimension of "ideal"-"real." This characterization is still empirically under-evaluated: it is unclear both what it means, i.e., what implications follow from an analysis in its terms, and to what units it can apply. In the page on the left below, for example, we can ask just where on the vertical axis any division into ideal and real can be found. Is the ideal the heading above the horizontal line, including the icon top-right, or does the ideal include the picture, or does the real include the main body text? And what would it concretely mean for our interpretation to decide on one of these rather than another? When texts are already "charged" ideologically, as is often the case with artefacts analyzed with Kress and Van Leeuwen's account, one can use the ideal/real distinction as a starting point for discussion; but, as both examples here show, it is actually rather unclear just on what foundation such discussion rests. Similar problems can be mentioned for the vast majority of constructs proposed in the area. And when we move from static to dynamic artefacts, the problems multiply.

Figure 2. Bird guide 1.

4. Research method

A research method to take us further can be built drawing more closely on the methods of empirical investigation pursued in linguistics. Here, fine-scaled descriptions of linguistic phenomena, the data, are examined in order to build theories that explain those data. We need to adapt this approach to multimodal artefacts, also. In particular, we need to incorporate methods of empirical study developed within corpus-based linguistics (Sinclair, 1991; Biber et al., 1998; McEnery & Wilson, 2001).

Checking hypotheses against a corpus, i.e., a "large and principled collection of natural text" (Biber et al., 1998: 4), has already brought substantial advantages for the analysis of language when compared with earlier "armchair"-theorizing. The analyst is constantly confronted with how language is actually used, rather than relying on intuitions or artificial examples, and has access to a richer basis for constructing theoretical models. Modern corpora support these activities directly by annotating their contained data. Annotation adds specially selected information to a corpus that allows queries to be formulated at levels of abstraction nearer to those of the analyst (and to the theories applied) than to the raw data. The more the format of stored data can be made to support the activity of searching for patterns, then the more valuable that corpus becomes as a tool for empirical investigation. Sophisticated treatments now commonly invoke multiple layers of annotation in order to describe data from various perspectives simultaneously. Significant progress has been made in this area and international standards for linguistic annotation are beginning to emerge (cf. Ide et al., 2003).

With an empirical anchoring of this kind, we can also target similar progress in the understanding of multimodal artefacts. But to carry out such investigations, we also need multimodal corpora. For some classes of multimodal data, particularly time-based data, corpora are already becoming reasonably established — for example, spoken language corpora that also include video recordings of the interaction are well accepted. Such corpora need to make particularly intensive use of annotation layering: layers commonly employed capture aspects of intonation, syntactic structure, distance (proxemics), gesture (Kranstedt et al., 2002), and other details of the context of interaction (cf. Norris, 2002, 2004).

The situation for multimodal documents, i.e., multimodal artefacts that rely on visual perception and spatial organization rather than time, is unfortunately quite different. There we are still very much at the beginning and design criteria are few and far between. A central question is still just what kind of annotation layers are going to be necessary and useful for furthering analysis. Typically we will want to have layers both that capture aspects of the documents' form, i.e., which represent the expressive resources (in whatever presentational modalities) deployed in a document, and that cover selected aspects of their functional organization. When we have layers of this kind, we can explore how they relate and under which conditions they relate.

One multimodal analysis scheme of this kind has been developed within the GeM (Genre and Multimodality) project (cf. Delin et al., 2002; Bateman, 2008). The GeM model defines the layers of description for multimodal documents shown in Table 1. The model claims that these layers are the fewest required for doing justice to page-based documents — there are certainly more, but without these we will be leaving crucial components of almost any multimodal document out of the picture. The formal specification of the layers defined by the GeM model then provides the basis for the construction of multimodal document corpora conforming to the most recent recommendations and standards for linguistic corpus design.

Placing multimodal document analysis on a firmer empirical basis then proceeds by selecting documents for inclusion within multimodal corpora and by "marking up" these descriptions with descriptions at each of the layers proposed by the model. This enables us to draw extensively on our experiences from linguistics concerning just how to investigate complex meaningful artefacts, while still assessing critically (and empirically) the suggestions arising from linguistics concerning how multimodal artefacts work. This is particularly important at this time because, despite the youth of the linguistic approach to multimodal documents, there are already many signs of suggestive claims turning into a regular folklore of multimodal meaning; that is: theoretical "artefacts" are being "turned into facts" (cf. Bordwell, 1989: 241).

Research of this kind is also a prerequisite for building accounts that are couched less narrowly within the terms of particular linguistic orientations. There are several distinct communities studying multimodal artefacts from different perspectives and the accounts being developed do not draw on each other to anywhere near the extent they should (cf. Bateman, 2008, chapter 2). Empirical investigation will encourage verification and dialogue across distinct approaches.

5. Recent research

Analysis according to the GeM scheme provides several independent descriptions, one for each layer. Given these, we can search for generalizations by examining whether patterns of co-selection across the layers can be reliably established (cf. Bateman et al.; 2002; Thomas, 2007). If such patterns of co-selection are revealed, it can be assumed that theoretically independent choices are in fact being constrained so as to preclude or restrict choice. Our recent research has now begun to uncover several generic sources of such constraints. One is an extended notion of **multimodal genre** that incorporates aspects of the historically situated production and consumption of artefacts (Kress & Van Leeuwen 2001; Bateman, 2008: chapter 5). Another source is the existence of distinct **semiotic modes** that combine particular expressive resources with particular kinds of communicative goals. There is no doubt an entire range of semiotic modes

Table 1. The primary layers of the Genre and Multimodality framework for page-based artefacts

Layout structure	the nature, appearance and position of communicative elements on the page, and their hierarchical inter-relationships
Navigation structure	the ways in which the intended mode(s) of consumption of the document is/are supported: this includes all elements on a page that serve to direct or assist the reader's use of the document
Linguistic structure	the linguistic details of any verbal elements that are used to realize the layout elements of the page/document
Content structure	the content-related structure of the information to be communicated — i.e., the propositional content or, appealing to the terms of linguistic register theory, the "field" of discourse (cf. Martin, 2001)
Rhetorical structure	the rhetorical relationships between content elements: i.e., how the content is "argued," divided into main material and supporting material, and structured rhetorically
Genre structure	the individual stages or phases defined for a given genre: i.e., how the delivery of content proceeds through particular stages of activity

waiting to be discovered, each of them supporting particular kinds of meaning-making potential — their own "logic" (cf. Kress, 2003). Three distinct semiotic modes will be introduced here. Traditionally these distinctions have not been made, thereby confusing issues of document layout, picture analysis and text formatting.

The first mode, called *text-flow*, is found within page-based artefacts whenever there is verbal text. Here the visual line of the developing text provides a basic one-dimensional organizational scheme. Although this may incorporate contributions involving other presentational modes, such as diagrams, tables, and related texts (e.g., footnotes, side notes, etc.), the important distinguishing feature of this mode is that the spatial nature of the page is not made to carry significant meanings in its own right. It is closely related to Twyman's (1979) "linear interrupted" category and is the semiotic mode underlying those kinds of basic text-formatting formerly labeled "paralinguistic" (cf. Crystal, 1979).

The second, termed *page-flow*, is found whenever a page-based artefact starts to utilize its full two-dimensional spatial extent for expressing communicative purposes. This mode can combine elements in any of the semiotic modes appearing on a page, including text-flow, diagrams, graphs and so on, but adds to the individual contributions the possibility of spatially-signaled rhetorical relations supporting the communicative intentions of the artefact. This mode is quite distinct from images or diagrams and has often been overlooked — for exceptions, see Rutledge et al. (2000) & Bateman et al. (2001).

Finally, the third mode, termed *image-flow*, is used to organize sequences of graphical elements rather than the text organized by text-flow. This must be distinguished as a distinct semiotic mode because the sequence relationship carries here a very specific range of additional meanings over and above those in the contributing images. These relations have been analyzed from several perspectives but are most clearly relatable to conjunctive relations proposed for discourse semantics (for example: temporal sequence, temporal simultaneity, contrast, etc.: Martin, 1992). In its spatial instantiation, this mode resembles the panel-to-panel relations set out for comics by McCloud (1994); in its temporal instantiation, it captures notions of filmic montage (cf. Bateman, 2007).

6. Research proposal

The semiotic modes introduced in the previous section augment previously suggested modes such as "diagrams," "graphs," or "verbal text" itself. These previous divisions are also in need of refinement however. Research here is complicated in two ways. First, semiotic modes are often simultaneously active in multimodal artefacts; their particular patterns of mobilization depend on the individual multimodal genres involved. Second, semiotic modes are also commonly "composite" in nature. Composite modes have not received sufficient attention to date, although even some of the traditional "modes" are inherent composite. A classic example of a composite mode is spoken discourse, where the grammatical and semantic patterning is co-articulated with control of the speech signal (loudness, speed, rhythm), bodily gesture and facial expression.

It is actually an open question the extent to which such composite modes may be decomposed: spoken discourse appears to have developed over time as first and foremost an integrated semiotic mode. It is not the case that we have developed modes of gesture and of intonation and then somehow combine them; they were, arguably, always co-present and have influenced each other during their development. Page-flow is also an essentially composite semiotic mode, in that the elements it combines are not of its own making: page layout relies on individual elements, blocks of text, diagrams, framing lines, etc., but adds something more to the page than the elements in isolation. Film may also demand a treatment as essentially composite. It remains for future research to explore the full potential of these modes as well as to address the question of which further modes will need to be recognized.

The ability of multimodal artefacts to combine differing semiotic modes — either explicitly by framing (such as a newspaper or computer screen shown in a film; or a video embedded within a web-page) or "implicitly" by virtue of their inherent design — is no doubt one of such artefacts' major strengths. But it is also one of the main sources of complexity in their analysis. Despite the current explosion in semiotically-based "multimodal" studies, the methods employed are often not up to the complexity of the artefacts analyzed and, as a consequence, the results obtained are still too often presented in idiosyncratic ways, with little constraint on the style of analysis carried out and the kinds of conclusions drawn.

The main task for the immediate future must therefore be to undertake detailed empirical analyses with respect to more representative samples of multimodal documents. And, in order to obtain sufficiently precise analyses, we need to do this by drawing on linguistic methodology rather than, for example, media studies, visual semiotics or other areas where design and text-graphics combinations have been addressed hitherto. Analyses couched in terms of the annotation layers of the GeM model, for example, give us a concrete place to start when comparing diverse artefactual solutions to multimodal communication tasks.

The first move in such investigations is therefore to consider larger and more representative selections of documents. Instead of comparing or describing isolated artefacts as currently often the case, projects can be defined ranging in size from small, possibly group-based pieces of work up to substantial corpus collection efforts. In all cases, the documents collected need to be explicitly situated with respect to some selected set of dimensions drawn from multimodal genre — these may include combinations of target audience, particular type of document (glossy magazine, webpage, newspaper), historical period of production, area of content, communicative function (inform, persuade, etc.), and so on. Here, research concerns the extent to which differing communicative genres rely on differing layout choices. Detailed work of this kind is sorely needed in the area of multimodality at large, since all too often analysis remains "instantial," i.e., concerned with the individual case with little chance of reaching motivated generalizations.

With multimodal corpora (large or small) in particular genres available, we can subject proposals concerning the working of multimodal artefacts to more rigorous investigation than has been the case so far. For example, we mentioned Kress and Van Leeuwen's claim that a page can be divided up into regions of distinct information status above: is it correct? At present, we simply do not know — but addressing this question to a selected corpus of examples would tell us more. Alternatively, several proposals have been made concerning the relations presumed to hold between text and graphics in documents (cf. Marsh & White, 2003; Stöckl, 2004; Martinec & Salway, 2005; Kong, 2006) — but the empirical accuracy, completeness and applicability of these accounts is in urgent need of corpus-based investigation. In any given corpus, we could ask to what extent the proposed classifications cover the data. Reporting on such efforts would again take us considerably further than where we are now.

The study of multimodal artefacts has therefore reached an interesting stage. Although there is a tendency to see everything from book pages to films to art installations to museums to entire cities as "multimodal texts" to be analyzed, without first getting down to the basic work of detailed analysis of selected collections of data, accounts will remain promissory and progress fragmented. This will not convince the broader research community that useful work is being undertaken; in fact, as Müller (2007) sets out, the traditional strong "anti-visual bias" is still alive and well. Also problematic is fragmentation within the field. In a recent survey of the more established areas of visual communication, Barnhurst et al. (2004) distinguish three broad orientations: *visual rhetoric*, looking at visual persuasion, *visual pragmatics*, concerned with the practices of production and the reception of visual artefacts, and *visual semantics*, which focuses more on the intrinsic form and structure of communicative visual artefacts. The analyses and methods proposed rarely go beyond the individual communities concerned.

One way to move forward would be by achieving clear, empirically sound and effective analysis results. By *combining* distinct layers of analysis within a single, coherent and evaluable model such as that proposed in the GeM framework, we should be in a better position for this and for achieving an understanding of how multimodal artefacts function.

7. Practical relevance

The practical relevance of more detailed, empirically founded, and critical analyses of multimodal artefacts is considerable and growing. Supported by the technological advances that make it as easy to include pictures in an artefact as was formerly the case for text, artefact designers of all persuasions, ranging from the amateur to the professional, increasingly employ multimodal resources. But this has led to an accompanying increase in the "communicative load" that the visual modes are being made to carry and deploying a multiplicity of modes is not automatically and easily correct. This has raised awareness of the need to get presentation design "right" in some sense, to make artefacts intelligible for their recipients and effective with respect to their design goals — leading to new organizations, such as the *Information Design Association* (Waller, 1996), new journals, such as the recently merged *Information Design* and *Document Design* journals, *Visible Language*, *Visual Culture*, *Visual Communication* and others, and even new professions, such as that of the "Information Designer."

Bad design has a range of significant negative consequences. For example, users of documents such as instruction manuals have been shown to overwhelmingly blame themselves when they fail to understand a document, even if the blame would more appropriately be assigned to poor design (Schriver, 1997: 216–219). This can lead to debilitating loss of self-esteem. Undesirable effects have also been demonstrated in financial terms, where poorly designed documents such as forms lead to incorrect or incomplete responses (Schriver, 1997: 332). Customers are also increasingly making decisions on the basis of their impression of the companies that they deal with: and unfriendly documents are part and parcel of the entire image that a company creates for itself (cf. Waller & Delin, 2003). We can also therefore apply our finer account of visual and rhetorical organization, and possible mismatches between these, to practical concerns of document re-design and critique (Delin & Bateman, 2002).

Even when a document designer has done their job well and set reasonable demands on a reader, used the visual resources consistently, etc., it is still by no means clear that a reader will be in a position to recognize and interpret the visual modalities deployed without appropriate training. Recognition of this problem has led to increasing attention to multimodal literacy (cf. Kalantzis & Cope, 2000; Kress, 2003). Ever more educationalists are proposing the inclusion of multimodal literacy as an explicit part of the teaching curriculum, just as verbal literacy has always been. Explicitly learning how to deal with multimodality is expected to make the mechanisms of multimodal meaning-making more visible, thereby allowing them to be discussed and, subsequently, to be deployed more effectively in students' own work (cf. Goodman & Graddol, 1996; Unsworth, 2001, 2007).

In all of these areas, achieving more explicit representations and methods for approaching the diverse contributions of semiotic modes to a multimodal ensemble is a critical enabling step.

Assignment

A range of assignments developing the kind of awareness necessary for theoretically sound and practically useful multimodal analysis can be designed using just two of the GeM annotation layers described in Table 1 above: the layout layer and the rhetorical layer; several analyses of this kind have already been published (cf. Delin et al., 2002; Delin & Bateman, 2002; Bateman, 2008).

Examine carefully the relationship between structural layout relations, expressed predominantly visually by spatial configurations of more or less similar page elements, and rhetorical structures analyzing the functional organization of the communicative message. Pay attention to the expressive resources being used. Consider these against the intended rhetorical organization and notice just how flexibly those meanings can be brought across when multiple semiotic modes are available.

Compare the figures below. The left figure is the same as was shown above and is from 1994, whereas the right figure is from 1996. Keep this in mind while comparing these figures.

Answer the following questions:

- What layout structures are employed?
- Do you think the year they were published is of influence?
- What semiotic modes can be found in the artefacts?

Figure 3. Bird guide 1.

Figure 4. Bird guide 2.

- And to what extent are rhetorical purposes expressed through these artefacts?

For further excercise, take a collection of pages from artefacts of a particular kind — text-books, tourist guides, instruction leaflets, popular magazines, and so on — and from different time periods — e.g., pages from now, from the 1990s, the 1970s, the 1950s, and so on — in order to compare these broadly in terms of the multimodal resources they mobilize. Answer your questions in the same manner as you did for the first task.

Chapter 4

Schemes and tropes in visual communication

The case of object grouping in advertisements

Alfons Maes and Joost Schilperoord
Tilburg University

This chapter deals with the scheme-trope distinction in the visual medium. It discusses the question whether and how the visual medium is equipped to express tropes (like metaphors) and schemes (like rhyme), and how content and form based figuration interact in visual rhetoric.

Examples are taken from the well-defined genre of (print) advertisements which is a rich source of rhetorical figuration. The article shows how one particular form based scheme, i.e., object grouping, can be used to highlight the relationship between different conceptual domains.

1. Introduction

Ever since the ancient Greeks turned rhetoric into an honorable field of scientific investigation, its testators, for example, colleagues working in the field of *discourse and communication studies* concentrated almost exclusively on the study of language as the privileged expression modality for rhetorical figuration. Rhetorical figures, which can broadly be divided in formal devices (often called *schemes*) and meaning devices (*tropes*) have typically been described in relation to language as primary input modality (think of the term "figures of speech" as a synonym of rhetorical figures). Thus, rhyme (a prototypical rhetorical scheme) is defined as a repetition of identical or similar sounds in two or more different words, metaphors (a prototypical trope) as language that directly compares seemingly unrelated subjects. Most of the research on metaphors has been devoted to *linguistic* expressions of metaphors (e.g., Bowdle & Gentner, 2005; e.g., Deutscher, 2005; Fauconnier & Turner, 2002; Gentner, Bowdle, Wolff & Boronat, 2001; Gibbs, 2005). Since the seminal work of Lakoff and Johnson

(1980), we know, however, that metaphors are a conceptual rather than a linguistic phenomenon, which implies that not only language can be used as a stepping stone for metaphoric conceptualization. Recent work shows that other modalities — visuals, gestures and music — are capable of expressing metaphoric conceptualizations as well (Cienki & Müller, 2008; Forceville, 2006; Zbikowski, 2002).

The visual medium is particularly suited to express rhetorical figuration. Visual rhetoric has attracted a great deal of attention from researchers working in the field of consumer research, communication, and cognitive linguistics (McQuarrie & Mick, 1999; McQuarrie & Phillips, 2008; Scott & Batra, 2003; Teng & Sun, 2002; Van Mulken, Van Enschot-Van Dijk & Hoeken, 2005). Both meaning-based rhetoric like metaphor (e.g., Forceville, 1996) and formal rhetorical devices like perspective or orientation (e.g., Peracchio & Meyers-Levy, 2005) have been studied, often in relation to persuasion or consumers' responses. The explosion of visual communication in about all aspects of daily life and society, together with the strong tendency of human communicators to exploit the communicative potential of non-literal expressions makes it important for scholars in the field of discourse studies and communication sciences to focus their attention on the communicative potential of visual rhetoric.

In this chapter, we will deal with a small portion of this ambitious research agenda. We will discuss the validity of the scheme-trope distinction in the visual medium.

2. Research challenge

The rich and sound research tradition in the field of language based rhetorical figuration is an attractive starting point for the study of visual rhetoric. The question is whether and to what extent concepts and characteristics developed in the study of language based rhetoric are valid and fruitful in studying visual rhetoric. In taking this perspective, many interesting research questions present themselves:

- Do arbitrary sign systems (like language) and analogical sign systems (like vision) have equal potential to create rhetorical figuration?
- Do they have similar atomic units and structural relations to express rhetoric figures?
- Is it possible to distinguish *structural* and *semantic* classes for visual rhetoric which are similar to verbal rhetoric?
- In comprehending visual rhetoric, do people engage in *processes* which are similar to processing of verbal rhetoric?
- Does visual rhetorical figuration have *rhetorical effects* which are similar to those of verbal rhetoric?

Enough for a lifetime research agenda, too much for a short chapter like this one. Therefore, we restrict ourselves to a small but tasty portion, i.e., the validity of the basic distinction between form based and content based rhetoric for the visual medium. These are the questions:

- Does the visual medium have the potential (atomic units, structural relations) to express tropes (like metaphors)?
- Does the visual medium have the potential to express schemes (e.g., rhyme)?
- How does content and form based figuration interact in visual rhetoric?

In discussing these questions, we will restrict ourselves to the well defined genre of (print) advertisements, which is a rich source of rhetorical figuration. Moreover, we shall focus on the ways in which the specific depiction of objects is employed to get a certain message through. We will show how tropes are expressed in printed ads and how the form based scheme of *object grouping* can be used to highlight the relationship between different conceptual domains.

3. Examples

The crucial difference between *schemes* and *tropes* can be characterized as follows. Tropes *establish* a conceptual link between constructs, whereas schemes *emphasize* this conceptual link by exploiting formal characteristics of signs. Take (1) and (2) as examples of both types of figures:

(1) My *car* is (like) a *hippo.*

(2) More *madness* than *sadness.*

For an interpreter to be able to tag (1) metaphorical, s/he has to know what this sentence is about (my car) and what is said about it (is a hippo), and how the predicate can be meaningfully exploited to assert something about the subject construct (e.g., my car is as robust as a hippo). Conversely, an interpreter can easily detect that two words in (2) sound alike, even without knowing what these words mean. Hence, tropes are conceptual, and schemes are formal.

There is ample evidence for tropes being at work in the visual medium. Printed advertisements frequently use metaphoric comparisons in which products or services are meaningfully related to some relevant conceptual domain. Mainly, three structural types of visual metaphor are distinguished (e.g., Maes & Schilperoord, 2008; Phillips & McQuarrie, 2004). In Figure 1, one object (the car) is *juxtaposed* to the other (the hippos); in Figure 2, one object (wine) is *replaced* by another object (custard), and in Figure 3, the two objects (scourer, tooth brush) are *fused* into one object. The three

Figure 1. LANDROVER IS (LIKE) HIPPOPOTAMUS

Figure 2. AH CUSTARD IS (LIKE) GOOD WINE

Figure 3. SCOTCH BRIDE IS (LIKE) TOOTH-BRUSH

structural types enable interpreters to map relevant relations and attributes from one object to the other.

Less clear is whether the counterpart of a verbal scheme (like rhyme or alliteration) exists in the visual domain. Words do sound in a certain way, and the way they sound is by default not related to what they mean (with a few exceptions like "cuckoo"). This is actually what makes language arbitrary or symbolic: the convention based relation between what words "look or sound like" and what they mean. Visual signs, on the other hand, may be claimed to lack this arbitrary relationship as they refer to objects by mere *analogy*. This difference between the two sign systems has led some scholars of visual rhetoric to the conclusion that there can be no such thing as a visual rhetorical scheme, because visual signs lack the so called double articulation of linguistic signs (see, for example, Phillips & McQuarrie, 2004: 137).

This conclusion is off the mark, however. First, many visual signs (from speech balloons in cartoons to road traffic signs) are the result of rules or conventions, just like linguistic signs. Furthermore, both in the arts and in advertising, artists and designers exploit formal characteristics of visuals in an attempt to highlight or emphasize particular conceptual content. A case in point is the way in which the meaningful visual resemblance between two objects is suggested by particular visual manipulations, such as perspective, spatial orientation, size, color or shape. Such resemblances are obviously coincidental, as are two words that sound alike. But just like poets may exploit *rhyme* purposefully, visual designers exploit formal aspects of the visual modality that do not concern the objects themselves, but the way they are depicted.

Let us return to Figure 1. The metaphor LANDROVER IS HIPPOPOTAMUS is not expressed just by showing the two objects, but also by making them look similar (notice the resemblance between the ears and the driving mirrors, the nostrils and the headlamps and so on). The link between the two constructs is furthermore suggested by displaying them from an identical frontal perspective and by projecting them on an imaginary diagonal line. Such formal visual devices, i.e., structural means that do not concern what we see, but the way we see what we see, result in what Gestalt psychologists have termed *grouping* (Schilperoord, Ferdinandusse & Maes, 2008; Schilperoord, 2007; Teng & Sun, 2002). Object grouping, we believe, and the visual means by which it is established, can be regarded as the visual counterpart of verbal schemes. The next section describes the contours of a research method that we have developed for the analysis of visual schemes.

4. Research method

To study how visual trope-scheme combinations are used to mark conceptual relationships between objects, we present a research method that enables us to distinguish clearly *what* we see in advertisements, and *how* we see what we see. The method consists of a three step procedure aimed at analyzing systematically trope-scheme combinations, in this case applied to advertisements. The method reveals the formal visual devices that ad designers employ to suggest a certain relation between objects. Two types of devices can be distinguished: devices involving the *outer appearance* of objects, like their size, colour and shape, and *pictorial techniques* like spatial orientation, repetition of objects and perspective. However, a clear picture of how such devices contribute to the overall message of an advertisement can only be achieved if we unravel what that message entails. Therefore the first analytical step is:

STEP 1: WHAT?

(i) Explicate the main claim of the advertisement in terms of the depicted objects.

This step pertains to *what* we see in an ad. An ad's claim can be phrased in terms of (at least) two objects together with a certain *relation* holding between them. One of these objects is always the *topic*, e.g., the thing being advertised, while the other one is called the *attribute*. The relation between the objects may be causal ("topic *leads to* attribute"), predicative ("topic *has/is* attribute") or merely associative ("topic *is associated to* attribute"). Hence, the general format of an ad's main claim can be given as [X ~ Y], where X is the topic of the message, Y is the attribute and ~ the relation between them. Depending on the nature of the relation the main claim can be refined to [X CAUSES Y], or [X HAS PROPERTY Y], and so on. If we apply this first analytical step to Figure 1, we get LANDROVER IS HIPPOPOTAMUS, where "Landrover" is the topic and hippopotamus is the attribute, and the relation is one of predication. The ad claims that its product shares certain properties with hippos, like their strength, robustness and so on, so the relation is one of predication. Clearly, if an ad is metaphorical, its claim is always done indirectly; after all, a Landrover (or any jeep for that matter) is *not literally* a hippopotamus. As a rule of thumb, in rendering the ad's main claim explicit, the analyst should always ask whether a certain object is shown in order to actually *refer* to it, or whether it's used to make some claim about another object in the same ad. In grasping the message expressed by the Landrover ad, the viewer is not supposed to interpret the image of the hippo as one that should call to mind that particular animal. Rather, it is shown to predicate something about the topic object.

Next, we turn to "the how" of what we see, e.g., the formal visual devices that may be involved in an ad's design. This analytical step involves answering the next two questions:

STEP 2: HOW?

(ii) Does the ad ostensively employ similarities or dissimilarities in the *outer appearance* of the depicted objects?
(iii) Does the ad employ *pictorial techniques* like object perspective or spatial orientation?

In essence, this step boils down to a careful scrutiny of a myriad of perceptual features of an image, as listed (non-exhaustively) in Table 1, which we refer to by using the umbrella term *object grouping.* Many of these devices can actually be witnessed in the Landrover ad, as indicated in Table 1. For more details about these devices, see Ferdinandusse et al. (ms).

Table 1. Object grouping devices and how they apply to Figure 1 (yes or no)

Object grouping devices	Applied to Figure 1
objects have similar shape	No
parts of objects have similar shape	Yes
objects have similar size	No
objects are made to have similar size	Yes
objects are spatially aligned	Yes
objects are placed at equal distances from each other	Yes
objects have similar spatial orientation	Yes
more than one attribute object depicted	Yes

The analyst should be aware of the fact that object grouping may not always be used functionally, but can also be used for mere ornamental reasons, just to decorate the overall image. Therefore, there is one more step needed in the analytical procedure.

STEP 3: WHY?

(iv) Explicate, if possible, the function of formal visual devices in terms of (i), the main claim of the ad.

This final step once again stresses the vital importance of step (i). The function of object grouping can only be established if one knows exactly what message it is supposed to interact with. Hence, its function in Figure 1 can only be grasped as long as we are aware of the fact that this message aims at claiming a conceptual *relation* between Landrovers and hippos. Object grouping can be said to stress this conceptual relation, just like verbal rhyme may be used by the poet to stress the conceptual relation between two lines in a poem. This, we think, is the proper way of stating how rhetorical schemes and tropes hang together. The next section attempts to probe deeper into the relation between visual schemes and tropes.

5. Recent research

Advertisements often show complex interactions between conceptual meaning and the perceptual template of object grouping. To get a feel of the possibilities, we discuss the ads in Figures 4, 5 and 6, together with the already discussed Landrover ad (Figure 1). In all these cases, objects are grouped by exploiting perceptual variables, either based on outer appearance or pictorial techniques. The grouped objects express a non-literal similarity or a conceptual link between a topic object (the product) and a particular category of objects (the attribute). The Landrover ad (Figure 1) represents the simple case: the perceptual characteristics discussed above establish a membership relationship between the topic object (the car) and the attribute object (the hippopotamus), and, by generalization: the category of strong, robust objects.

Figure 4. Barclays.

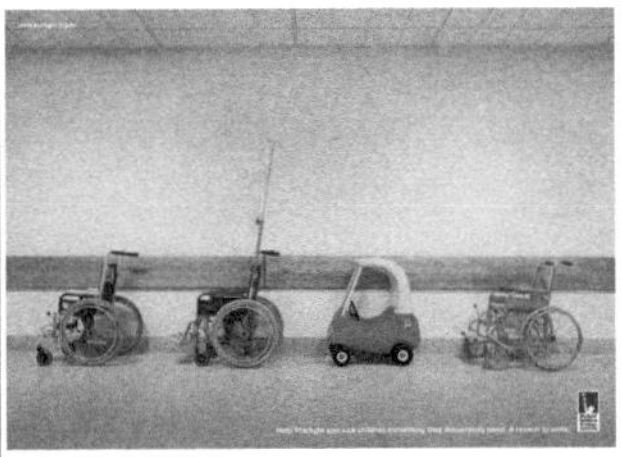
Figure 5. Starlight.

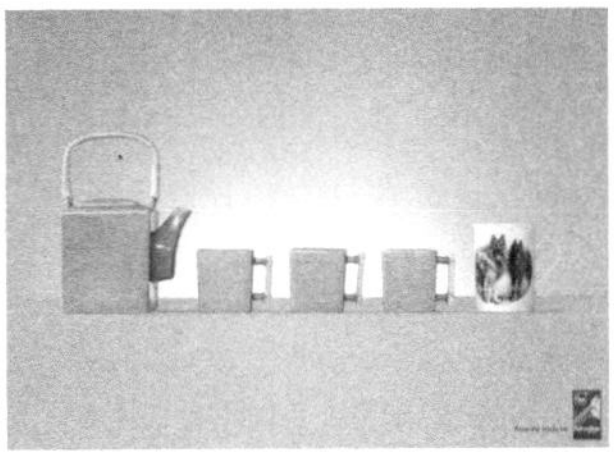
Figure 6. Chux dish brush.

The Barclay ad in Figure 4 is more complex: it shows a series of beau ties with a snake hanging among them. Here, perceptual grouping (proximity, lining up, shape of ties) is not used to suggest conceptual similarity, but to emphasize conceptual *differences* between Barclays bank and its competitors in the market. Either, the ties refer to the reliable investments of Barclays, which are contrasted to the unreliable investments of other banks, represented by the snake. Or, Barclays is seen as the sly snake under the bankers, and hence attractive for smart and daring investors.

Precisely the opposite relation between perceptual grouping and conceptual categorization can be found in Figure 5, an ad from Starlight, an organization that tries to raise funds for buying toys for hospitalized children. Perceptually, the toy in the row of wheel chairs conveys a double message: on the one hand, it is lined up the same way as the wheel chairs, on the other hand it quite ostensively differs both in shape and color from the other objects in the row. That way, it supports the conceptual message of the ad: despite the fact that they do not belong to the category of medical equipment, children's toys belong in hospitals just like wheelchairs do.

Things may be further complicated by looking how perceptual grouping relates to the conceptual category in the Chux-ad in Figure 6. The message this ad conveys is that if you don't use this kind of dish brush, your set of nice cups will soon be incomplete, because you will damage your cups with the wrong equipment. As in Figure 5, one of the objects lined up is visually very different from the other objects (one "ugly" cup in a set of design cups). But unlike Figure 5, the conceptual conclusion is not that the ugly cup should be included in the suggested category, rather, it shows the unwanted result of *not* using the product. Further research should reveal how precisely this grouping pattern is employed and how it is involved in communicating the conceptual message.

Summarizing things so far, perceptual grouping based on object internal or pictorial variables can be seen as a powerful rhetorical device used to suggest a relevant conceptual (categorical) link between concepts in an advertisement. Perceptual compatibility can either suggest category inclusion (as in Figure 1) or exclusion (as in 4). Likewise, perceptual incompatibility can either suggest category inclusion (as in 5) or category exclusion (as in 6).

6. Research proposal

The previous section has shown that visual schemes, in particular object grouping, can be used to emphasize different types of associations between elements coming from different conceptual domains. Different methods and research perspectives can be used to further develop and validate the analytical ideas presented above, so as to come to grips with the analytical characteristics, the processing, and the rhetorical effects of visual scheme-trope combinations in advertisements and other visual communicative messages.

First, corpus research is needed to make an inventory of meaningful schematic elements in advertisements. Ferdinandusse (2007) has shown that a number of traditional laws of Gestalt are a suitable starting point to fruitfully classify systematic schemes in advertisements: closure, symmetry, similarity, regularity and orientation, good continuation. In follow up analytical research, the coding of these principles needs further corroboration, for example on the basis of interrater agreement tests.

Second, experimental research is needed to find out whether naïve respondents are aware of these regularities. One method of doing this is by asking respondents to draw visual reminders for ads they are exposed to (without allowing them to use verbal elements), and to see to what extent the schematic architecture and perceptual regularities of an ad is reflected in the drawings. These drawing results can shed light on the awareness of respondents for these schematic elements. For example, Figure 7a, b and c show examples of drawings that were produced by subjects after they were shown the ad in Figure 1. They illustrate the three main strategies in such a drawing task: using the topic domain as a reminder (version c), the attribute domain (version a) or the schematic architecture (version b) of the ad. Proportional distributions between these strategies can give a first indication of the natural relevance of these schematic elements. These distributions can be compared with the strategies used to draw advertisements with similar schematic elements which however do not support any conceptual link between an attribute and a topic domain, for example a number of bottles of wine lined up "schematically" in an ad merely to form a set.

Figure 7a. Attribute domain.

Figure 7b. Schematic architecture.

Figure 7c. Topic domain.

A further stage in the experimental control of this issue is to construct two versions of the same advertisement, which differ only in the semantic meaning of the visual schemes used. Take, for example, a car ad, showing five cars lined up from left to right in the ad, with the caption: "Escape the regularity, as regularly as possible." The caption enables respondents to understand the line-up regularity of the five cars. Adding or deleting the caption enables us to manipulate the meaningfulness of the visual scheme. This material can be used in drawing experiments, in experiments in which respondents have to paraphrase or evaluate ads, as well as in more controlled experiments, in which online processes are measured, e.g., by using eye tracking.

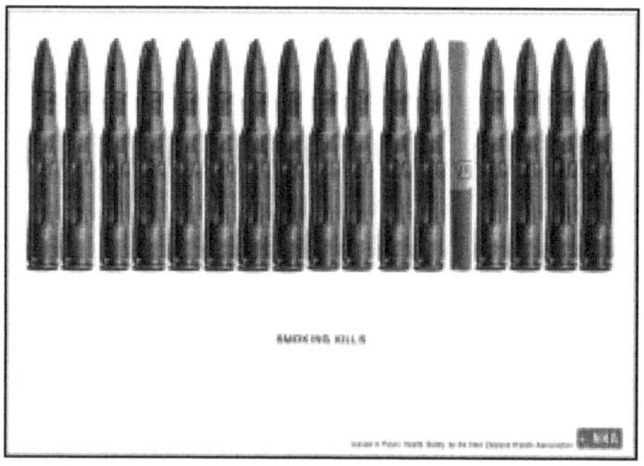

Figure 8a. Good continuation.

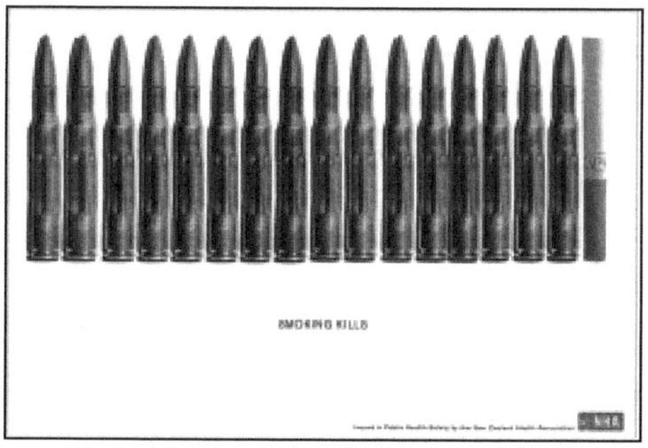

Figure 8b. Closure.

Manipulating versions of the same ad can be used to test other characteristics of perceptual grouping as well. Take Figure 8, expressing the metaphor CIGARETTE IS BULLET. The two versions make clear that the topic object (cigarette) can be ordered either in between the other objects (8a) or as closing off the set of objects (8b). In Gestalt psychological terms, these patterns are called *good continuation* and *closure* respectively.

Ferdinandusse (2007) has argued that the conceptual import of the *good continuation* variant (8a) may be that the viewer psychologically organizes the objects as "more closely" related to the other objects, whereas the *closure* variant (8b) may result in a mental separation between the topic object and the other members of the set, more or less similar to the effect suggested in the analysis of rhyme schemes in poetry (Tsur, 1992). This hypothesis can be put to a test by systematically presenting respondents with one of these versions and ask them to rate the perceptual resemblance between topic (cigarette) and attribute (bullet) object, followed by a free production task in which they verbalize the conceptual content of the ads. These methods enable us to see whether respondents spontaneously or explicitly process these Gestalt inferences. Preliminary results of a pilot experiment using these methods show that respondents judged the level of similarity of bullet and cigarette in the (8a) version higher than in the (8b) version. Such an outcome suggests that we are on the right track.

Third, various offline techniques present themselves to evaluate the attractiveness or estimated effect of ads with and without schematic elements. Respondents can be asked to rate the attractiveness of different versions of the same ad (with and without visual schemes), as well as their behavioral intentions with regard to the products presented in the ad.

7. Practical relevance

Our research on visual rhetoric and visual metaphors first and foremost serves theoretical aims and ambitions. We investigate visual communication from a cognitive information processing perspective; that is: we ask questions about the way people process visual information, the conceptual structures that can be expressed visually, the various structural and syntagmatic variants for constructing visual rhetorical figures, and their rhetorical effect on target audiences.

The practical relevance of the research described above can be seen in both a narrow and in a broad perspective. The first perspective has to do with a better understanding of a prototypical case of persuasive communication, the genre of advertisements, which serves to sway an audience into forming beliefs about consumer products, and into contemplating actions (i.e., to buy and to use the product). Viewed from a more encompassing perspective, however, this research contributes to the understanding of how people process visual information in everyday information processing tasks and how visual cues can manipulate these processes. In his latest book, *An Assault on Reason*, Al Gore speculates about verbal and visual information processing as follows: "I believe that the vividness experienced in the reading of words is automatically modulated by the constant activation of the reasoning centers of the brain that are used in the process of co-creating the representation of reality the author has intended. By contrast, the visceral vividness portrayed on television has the capacity to trigger instinctual responses similar to those triggered by reality itself — and without being modulated by logic, reason and reflective thought." (Gore, 2007: 19) However much we appreciate his passionate attempt to make us realize the seriousness of global warming, Gore certainly is not a cognitive scientist. At the very least, the views he expresses are not warranted by recent developments in the fields of visual and verbal cognition. Verbal and visual information may employ different regions and tracts in our brain, and the processing of these types of information may use their own set of cognitive processes and structures, but in the end, both types of information result in sets of unified conceptual structures, enabling people "to talk about what they see" (Jackendoff, 1987) or to visualize what they have read or heard. Whether or not such processes are modulated by logic, reason and reflective thought is *not a matter of the format by which information comes to us, but by its contents*. Pictures may seduce people, but so may words and language. Conversely, visual information may just as well lead to a better and more thorough understanding of the world surrounding us, as is testified by Gore's own movie *An Inconvenient Truth*. So what matters are *not our prejudices* regarding the visualization of contents, but what *scientific research* may enable us to find out about the structure, process and meaning of visual information.

Assignment

Figure 9 shows three ads (Guitar, Champagne, and Beer) that all contain the image of an exploding atomic bomb. Use the analytical method laid out in Section 4 to answer the following questions:

Figure 9a. Guitar.

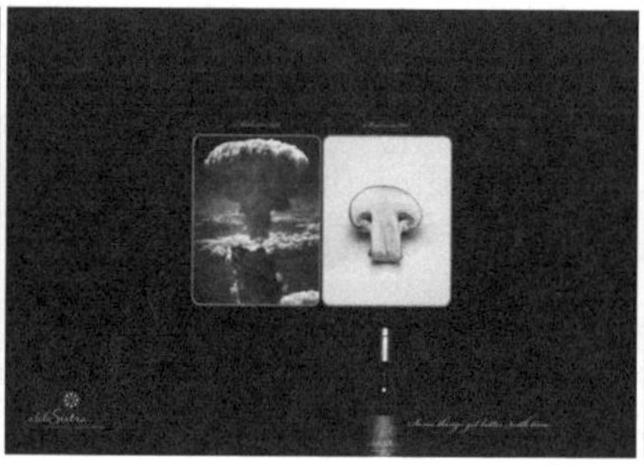

Figure 9b. Champagne.

Figure 9c. Beer.

WHAT?

1. What are the central claims expressed by these ads?

HOW?

2. Which of these ads shows object grouping?
3. What perceptual features are used (compare the list of features in Section 4)?

WHY?

4. Which of the ads uses the image of the bomb metaphorically?
5. Explain how the metaphorical relation between topic and attribute is expressed?
6. Explain the use of object grouping in the non-metaphorical ad(s).

IN SUM

7. Summarize the differences and commonalities of the three ads.

Part III

Discourse types

Chapter 5

Text types and dynamism of genres

Sungsoon Wang
Sogang University

Past studies of text or discourse type classification were static and did not account for the dynamic phenomenon of constantly changing or newly created genres, because they were based on surface linguistic forms or functions of particular genres under investigation. In this chapter, I introduce a different approach to text type variation, which attempts to identify the underlying mechanism of text type variation from a cognitive pragmatic perspective, by using relevant theoretic notions of utterance types for text analyses. Recently applied studies are also introduced, regarding the broad-genre approach for the language learning classroom and the notion of persuasion with a focus on gradient persuasion strategies across genres. Future research proposals are presented, based on the idea that this model of text type variation can be exploited for a systematic genre analysis in connection with the dynamic nature of genres and can also provide prototypical text types for practical application.

1. Introduction

Classifying discourse/text types is an important area in discourse studies and is a prerequisite to any comparative text analysis, because it situates particular texts relative to a range of texts with many different functions and different forms as well. It has also received much attention from the scholars in applied linguistics, because analyses of particular discourse types, often called genre analysis, are applicable to document design or pedagogy.

The definitions of the terms used in this chapter need to be clarified, because, with the increasing popularity of discourse studies and especially genre analysis in recent years, the three notions of discourse type, text type, and genre are often used interchangeably in literature. The notion of text involves text-internal linguistic elements while the notion of discourse is used as an umbrella term, which involves both text-internal and text-external elements. Like discourse types, genres (e.g., news reports, academic papers, poetry) involve both text-internal and text-external contextual elements. Genre is defined as a particular type of communicative event that has a particular communicative purpose recognized by its users, or discourse community (Swales, 1990). Text types (e.g., expository, narrative, poetic) involve text-internal elements (Pilegaard & Frandsen, 1996) such as surface linguistic features and textual functions. Although there is no strong consensus on the distinction between genre and text type (Paltridge, 2002), the distinction has generally been recognized as useful and is employed by a number of scholars, especially in the field of language teaching or learning. Coe (2002) defines genre as a functional relationship between a type of text and a type of situation.

The research into discourse or text typology starts from the idea that people have certain intuitions regarding discourse types, so it is necessary to have a system of discourse classification regarding these intuitions, within which discourse characteristics can be related to the kinds of discourse. To characterize the different discourse or text types, a number of scholars have presented models of discourse classification, based on discourse form and function or on a combination of form and functional differences, for example, description, narration, exposition, argumentation and instruction based on human cognition, and notional types realized by surface structure types in monological discourse such as narrative, procedural, behavioral, and expository discourse (see Renkema, 2004). Biber (1989) categorizes eight different text types from the "multi-feature/multi-dimensional analysis" of large corpus data where five dimensions are labeled, based on a particular set of lexical and syntactic features that frequently co-occur in texts and reflect common communicative functions. The criteria for distinguishing between two texts are the presence or absence of elements of structure or types of sentences, clauses, or words. However, the categories vary with different authors and the characterization of surface linguistic features has often led to an overlap in different categories.

2. The research challenge

The discrepancy in the number of text types suggested by the scholars is due primarily to the fact that discourse types are linked either to cognitive processes or communicative functions that have not been taken into account systematically in typologization (Pilegaard & Frandsen, 1996). What is also needed in addition to the surface phenomenon of text types, is a consideration of the underlying textual processes that contribute to the meaning of a text and alters their text type categories. Moreover, the typologies have not been fully developed into a typology of all possible discourse types; in contemporary discourse studies; few attempts at an all-encompassing classification can be found (Renkema, 2004).

In the field of applied linguistics, researchers such as Swales (1990) and Bhatia (1993) developed a more focused methodology, which they referred to as genre analysis. Genre analysis deals with the description of functional variation, based on statistically significant features of lexicogrammatical features and discourse structure of specific genres and how they are used in sociocultural contexts. These studies are descriptions of specific genres rather than comparisons of different text varieties, because the focus of these works was on ESP for learners from a specific discipline (Bhatia, 2004). There were also attempts to concentrate on the use of particular linguistic items in specific text types, using large corpora of text.

In a more recent view of genre studies, however, previous studies of text type are seen as static, idealized characterizations of functional varieties rather than a reflection of the real world of constantly changing or newly created (e.g., email) dynamic genres. Due to this complexity, genre identification is an issue for both genre theorists and practitioners: For example, an instruction text for medical products may give background information and explain how to use the product, while simultaneously satisfying government regulations (Askeheve & Swales, 2000); a text may be a typical example of one genre, or a less typical one, but still be considered to be an example of the particular genre (Paltridge, 2006). The issue of genre identification is, thus, a complex one and requires a flexible, rather than static, view of what makes users of a language recognize a communicative event as an instance of a particular genre (Paltridge, 2006: 89). Swales (2002) has recently viewed genres as "resources for meaning," rather than "systems of rules."

With the increasing awareness of the dynamic nature of genres, recent studies emphasize the explanatory account of the form-function relationship to answer the question why there are particular linguistic forms in a particular genre (Bhatia, 2004). Members of the discourse community now become the primary focus of the analysis, equal to, if not more important than, the actual text. Analysis thus becomes more ethnographic (Berkenkotter & Huckin, 1995) and genre is conceived as a dynamic phenomenon, subject to change and adaptation by the participants, in contrast to the somewhat static original text-bound conceptualization.

Though there will no doubt be much more at stake than what could be told about text types in an introductory text, an interesting question is how language users can detect different text types with great ease. Another question is how we can approach an all-encompassing classification of text or discourse types: Although the "all-encompassing" classification is useful for its practical application, there may be an endless continuum of genres mixing with one another to form generic blends subject to change and adaptation by the participants.

3. Examples

Consider the following Korean examples of two different texts from two different genres, followed by their English translations: a paragraph from an academic research paper and a news article.

Text 1: Research Article

> 말뭉치는 유용하고도 쉽게 접근 가능한 언어자료들을 기술언어학자 혹은 이론 언어학자들에게 제공한다. (Johnson & Johnson, 1998) 뭉치 언어학" (corpus linguistics)은 "말뭉치"를 기반으로 한 언어학의 한 분야이다. 그러나 "뭉치 언어학"은 다른 언어학 분야들과 쉽게 비교하기가 어렵다. 그것은 "뭉치 언어학"이라는 분야는 연구의 영역에 의해 구분된 것이 아니라 연구 방법론에 의해 구분된 것이기 때문이다. 그러므로 원칙적으로 "뭉치 언어학"은 음운론, 통사론, 사회 언어학 등의 다른 언어학 분야와 "말뭉치"를 매개로 하여 비교적 쉽게 결합될 수 있다. 다시 말해서 "뭉치 언어학"의 연구 기법과 음운론, 통사론, 사회 언어학 등의 연구 내용을 결합하는 것이다. (영어교육 Dec 23. 2007)

Translation:

> Corpora provide descriptive linguists or theoretical linguists with useful and easily accessible language resources (Johnson & Johnson, 1998). Corpus linguistics is one field of linguistics based on corpora. But corpus linguistics is not really comparable to other fields of linguistics because the field of corpus linguistics is not divided by research areas but rather by research methodologies. Therefore, corpus linguistics in principle can combine relatively easily with other fields of linguistics such as phonology, syntax, and social linguistics. In other words, it is relatively easy to combine corpus linguistic methodology with the research content of phonology, syntax and sociolinguistics. (English Education, Dec. 23, 2007)

Text 2: News Report

> *박근혜 전 한나라당 대표, "공천 지연 다른 의도 있지 않나?"*
> 박근혜 전 한나라당 대표가 2일 최근 논란이 되고 있는 총선 공천 시기 문제와 관련해 "석연찮은 이유로 공천을 미룬다는 것은 다른 의도가 있는 것 아니냐"며 직접 이명박 대통령 당선인을 겨냥했다. 이에 대해 이 당선인 측은 "할 일이 태산 같은데 밥그릇부터 챙기겠다는 것이냐"며 강하게 반발하고 있어 공천 시기를 둘러싼 내홍이 폭발 직전이다. 여기에 강재섭 대표도 "공천권 없는 사람은 말하지 말라"며 싸움에 끼어들어 공천 문제를 둘러싸고 한나라당이 어수선한 상황이다.

Translation:

> *Former representative Park Keunhye asks, "Isn't there another intention in delaying the nomination?"*
> In the Grand National Party, the conflict is being aggravated by the delay of the

nomination of parliamentary candidates. Park Keunhye, the former representative of the Grand National Party, directly *targeted president-elect* Lee Myungbak regarding the controversy over the nomination period of the parliamentary candidates: "Isn't there some other intention with some dubious reason?" The president-elect's side is dead against her: "Does she only take care of *her bowl of rice* even though we have mountains of work to do?" The inner party disturbance immediately *precedes an explosion*. The current representative Kang Jaesup intruded upon this matter, "Don't talk if none of you is in charge of the nomination." The Grand National Party is in chaos *being surrounded with this matter*.
(Jan. 3. 2008 Dong-a Daily Newspaper)

Readers of these two texts would recognize (text 1) as an academic text and (text 2) as a news report. One of the questions in text type research is how language users can detect different text types with great ease when the discourse itself seems to present no explicit cues. Wang (2001) attempts to identify the underlying mechanism of linguistic variation of different text types within the framework of Relevance Theory (Sperber & Wilson, 1986/1995), rather than to classify different text types. To illustrate this, she presents prototypical examples for different text types within the proposed framework.

4. Research method

The text type differences are explained through analyses of dominantly used utterance types in a cognitive pragmatic perspective, based on Relevance Theory in Wang (2001). In the Relevance Theory, inference making is viewed as a constant feature of communication geared towards perceiving one's intention. The Relevance Theory's concept of utterance types is that every utterance is an interpretive expression of a speaker's thought; the speaker's thought can be used to represent things in two ways: descriptively or interpretively. When an utterance is used interpretively, it imposes more layers of implicature on interpretation than when it is used descriptively.

To illustrate, utterance (3), (B1) is used descriptively to represent a deterministic state of affairs of the speaker's intention.

(3) A1: 내일 피크닉에 오니?
Are you coming to the picnic tomorrow?
B1: 응 갈께.
Yes I'm going.
A2: 민수는 뭐래? 온대?
What did Minsoo say? Is he coming?
B2: 내일 비가 안오면.
If it doesn't rain tomorrow.

On the other hand, utterance (B2) simultaneously informs A of what Minsoo said, implying that Minsoo will not come if it rains tomorrow, and expresses B's attitude to what has been said in a skeptical or doubtful tone. (B2) is interpretive here in the sense that A has to interpret how B interpreted Minsoo's thought. In this case, the interpretive utterance (B2) imposes upon the hearer more layers of implicature and, thus, there is less interpretative constraint (I-constraint).

The utterance types broadly range from tightly constrained and descriptive uses (e.g., assertion, imperative) to loosely constrained and interpretive uses (e.g., report/quote, interrogative, echo, irony). Metaphors are categorized into two types: ordinary metaphors and creative metaphors. The dominantly used types of referring expressions in texts are additionally analyzed for a more micro-level analysis. These linguistic features are analyzed along with interpretation processes from three different text types from three different genres which have different salient communicative purposes (academic text, news text and poetic text) and show that text types vary according to the extent to which the texts provide information for interpretation; text types are thus the result of interpretation based on human cognitive capacity. The types of utterances and referring expressions are presented in Table 1.

Table 1. Examples of types of utterance and referring expressions

Types of utterance	Examples
1. Descriptive	
Des + Ø	(1) Variables of state are divided into two classes.
Des + Or-meta	(2) The arrival in Beijing of a Taiwanese business delegation seemed to have broken the ice. (in news)
Des + Cr-meta	(3) Bud knocks on winter's wall on death's door. (in poem)
2. Interpretive	
Int + Echo + Ø	(1) "We are going to restrict foreign business." (quote)
Int + Echo + Or-meta	(2) "It's a lot better than living under missile threats."
Int – Echo + Cr-meta	(3) "Who cares/who cares?" (personification of wind)
Int – Irony + Ø	(4) It's a lovely day for a picnic. (when it rains)
	(5) Once below a time, I lordly had the trees and leaves. (in poem)
Int – irony + Cr-meta	(6) Progress is a comfortable disease. (in poem)
Types of referring expressions	**Examples**
Same NP	corpus – corpus
The + NP	variables of state – the variable
Pronoun	corpus linguistics – it
Synonym	the government – the country
Or-metaphor	the war of words – the conflict
Cr-metaphor	the busy monster – man unkind (in poem)

The utterances for text type analysis are categorized into nine types on a numerical scale of I-constraint according to the degrees of I-constraint as in the table where the analytical unit is a proposition. The number is added starting from 1 (Descriptive + Ø) to 5 (Interpretive-Irony + Creative metaphor) as a layer of implication is added to the utterance. The numbers are assigned to each utterance in a text and the degrees of I-constraint are compared.

To return to the text samples, the utterances in text (1) are descriptively used throughout the text in an assertive way, which indicates a tight I-constraint. Academic text is usually written to inform the reader about new topics; the writer starts from the assumption that the writer's knowledge on the topic is not shared with the reader. In this text-external context, text (1) focuses on the explanation of what *corpus linguistics* is and the same NP is used for its referring expressions, for example in the chain *corpus linguistics – corpus linguistics – corpus linguistics* as underlined. Text (1) can be called "expository text type with an informing function."

In text (2), interpretive utterances are dominantly used by quoting what the politicians said in the conflict around the delayed nomination. One example chain of referring expressions is *the conflict – the controversy – disturbance – this matter*. Metaphors are often used, as in *targeted president-elect*, *her bowl of rice*, *precedes an explosion* and *surrounded with this matter*. Text (2) is less tightly constrained than text (1) by inviting more of the reader's knowledge in the interpretation. Text (2) can be called "narrative text type with an evaluative effect," in the sense that readers evaluate the topic based on the quoted speech despite the fact that the writer does not directly state what the reader should think about the topic.

This approach focuses on identifying the underlying mechanism of linguistic variation, based on the investigation that a particular text types keeps some constant degree of I-constraint throughout the text; different text types form a continuum in varying degrees of interpretative constraint. There are, theoretically, numerous text types in the continuum, since the boundaries are not numerically clear-cut in actual texts, but we conventionally label generally recognized text types such as the expository, instructive, narrative, or argumentative according to intuitively recognized functions of the text. The non-discreteness of linguistic phenomena in the continuum will be accounted for in terms of the fuzzy borderline areas between different text types, treating them as prototypes.

This approach to text types reflects the dynamic aspect of genres in relation to contextual variations by showing in a predictable way that the degrees of I-constraint vary for different textual functions.

5. Recent research

The I-constraint approach to text type variation provides a new text analytical tool in the area of genre analysis. This approach to text type variation has been applied to learning genres in the classroom (Wang, 2005a). The basic claim is that if teachers are equipped with a linguistically principled knowledge of text type variation as proposed above, they can deal with text types more systematically for classroom practice. I, Wang, show a way of comparing different or similar text types based on the distinction between the text type and the genre as two separate entities because, once students raise their awareness of linguistic and functional variation from a variety of text types, they can use the text types according to the changing purposes of genres. This implies that such an approach prepares students for the unpredictable genres they may face in the future. Coe (2002) notes that text types survive because they respond effectively to recurring situations. The distinction between the two notions of genre and text type is also discussed in Biber (1989) and Paltridge (2002) in the sense that a genre can vary in its linguistic characteristics and that different genres can be similar in linguistic characteristics.

Another applied study is on the notion of persuasion in the field of genre-based teaching of writing. (Wang, 2005b). It is argued that composition teachers need to know a broad concept of persuasion as recognized in different linguistic forms according to different communicative purposes; teachers have dealt with persuasion by teaching some variant of classical argument, but argument is one form of persuasion — not the only one and often not the most effective (Coe, 2002; Andrews, 2005). Persuasion is defined as all linguistic behavior that attempts to either change the thinking or behavior of an audience, or to strengthen its beliefs (Virtanen & Halmari, 2005). Through text analysis from a pragmatic perspective, with the idea that genres are fundamentally persuasive, she shows how persuasion is achieved differently according to different communicative purposes including the situational context, and how different persuasion strategies vary across different genres and even within one genre. Ostman (2005) argues that persuasiveness is a gradient phenomenon which takes place on several levels, from explicit choices of meaning to implicit choices expressing ourselves in relation to the demands of the cultural context at hand, in relation to our reader or co-interactant.

This study points out the classroom problem of current English writing instruction in Korea, which focuses on five-paragraph essays with a narrow concept of persuasion aimed at general educated readers. The claim in this study is that writing teachers should help students become versatile writers, able to adapt to the wide variety of types of writing tasks they are likely to encounter in their lives, because different writing situations require different types of writing (Coe, 2002); students' genre theories are fully limited and constricting in relation to the pedagogical genres known as the research paper, the essay, and the paragraph, and students are often shocked by the degree of disparity they find between what they have learned in school and the workplace expectations they find (Bhatia, 2004).

6. Research proposal

Although the analytical results in this work are based on a small set of data, its extended study of larger corpus data analysis will be a necessary step toward a further validation of the theory to make it more firmly grounded. It also awaits further empirical study of the processing perspective, e.g., whether coherence for non-problematic comprehension of text can be attributed to the constant degree of I-constraint throughout the text. The above study suggests that some constant degree of I-constraint forms text coherence; if this is the case, the matter of constancy can be exploited for text production and text evaluation. Another question in the processing perspective is whether loosely constrained utterances cost more processing effort than tightly constrained utterances.

The utterance types and referring expressions in the I-constraint approach to text type variation as introduced in the previous section provides a new text analytical tool for genre analysis. In genre analysis, we may start from typical generic patterns in the texts we are interested in (a text-first approach) or from a particular context of the texts (a context-first approach) we want to investigate. One can either pursue an analysis of prototypical text types starting from a text, or a flexible analysis of a variety of text types involving subtle linguistic variations in relation to the contextual variation.

Although recent research in genre studies is concerned with investigation of the correlation between text-internal and text-external elements in the real world of discourse (Bhatia, 2004), it does not mean devaluing surface linguistic features. It rather implies that investigation of text surface features should continue in connection with contextual factors that influence language users' choice of language to explore generic resources and to explain why language users use the language the way they do.

Recently, the phenomenon of genre mixing or hybrid has received much attention from the scholars in the field of genre analysis. For example, Kong (2006, this volume) shows that property transaction reports are a hybrid genre that combine the voices of property agencies (promotional character) and journalists (news report character) in a very subtle and sophisticated manner to accomplish the practices of the two communities in practice. He argues that prototypical categories are little more than tools. Prototypical categories are useful in the sense that some notions of the genre in question are needed for us to understand how resources are drawn on and then mobilized. He points out that discourse analysts have to be flexible with any tools that they are employing. Lauerbach (2004) analyses political interviews of two different companies using the notion of hybrid genre.

It will be also interesting to investigate how the subservient functions of different text type units are combined for a generic communicative purpose in a mixed genre (see also Askehave & Swales, 2000) or how utterance types change in terms of I-constraint in a hybrid genre. Text types construct a variety of genres in various permutations and combinations in actual discourse.

When we examine the context of the texts, the categories of context are not fixed and vary with authors. One generally accepted category of context in literature is Register Theory, which defines field, tenor, and mode as three contextual configurations (Halliday, 1994, second edition). But, even within one category of context there are variations, for example, in news text (Vestergaard, 2000): a field can be either business or sports. By expanding the categories of context in this way, we may move toward a more resourceful and systematic genre theory. Such research will be useful because prototypical generic convention is, though necessary, "not sufficient for any subsequent exploitation or manipulation of generic conventions in real life professional contexts" (Bhatia, 2004).

Additional linguistic features other than utterance types and referring expressions could also be included in future analyses with the question of whether or not the inclusion of such features would reveal the same phenomenon of text type variation as presented in Wang (2001); for example, the degree of I-constraint can be examined from the use of adjectives, verbs, verb tense, and discourse connectives. Such an analysis can also be carried out within a particular text type for a focused investigation of subtle linguistic variations as well as more than one text type. The outcome of such research will provide additional resources of cohesive devices in addition to the descriptive and interpretive utterances for learning writing or document design.

A recent development is to define appropriate levels of discourse description and develop ways of genre categorization which reasonably reflects a complexity of genre and a flexible view of genre identification. Bhatia (2002) presents three levels of conceptualization with generic value at the top, genre colony second, and individually identifiable genre constructs third. Grabe (2002) proposes narrative and expository macro genres as two ways of constructing and interpreting texts because the two macro genres provide a productive means for understanding the different purposes of texts. Paltridge (2002) presents an overview of the use of the two terms, text type and genre, commonly used by scholars in language teaching. Terms such as genre set, genre chain, or genre network are also used (Swales, 2002; Paltridge, 2006) instead of just labeling a text as a single genre. For example, an understanding of a group of (academic) genres is required by many US graduate students. Though the scholars have used the terms for their individual studies, little attempt has been made to reach a general consensus for defining the levels of discourse description.

Also relevant here is the future study of stylistics, because the text type continuum includes both nonliterary and literary texts. Recently, stylistics have become increasingly aware of the need to cross the boundary between literature and non-literature in developing a view of literature as a historically and culturally defined type of discourse rather than as a linguistic category independent of other discourse types (Semino & Culpeper, 1995).

7. Practical relevance

Genre analysis is closely related to research into document design, developing language learning instruction, and professional writing. In this connection, further research on developing linguistic strategies which vary the degree of I-constraint will be useful for the practitioners in the field in the sense that choosing a particular text type is a matter of controlling the degree of I-constraint given a particular communicative goal.

Organizational communication is a much more complex affair than academic communication and the research generated by this practical teaching need has been far greater than we could ever have imagined. Effective public documents affect how well the government can perform its tasks (Janseen & Neutelings, 2001). Relevant questions are how public documents could be optimized and how the writers of public documents be trained to become better writers.

In the language learning classroom, the comparison and contrast of text types is considered an important component in raising awareness of what language does in the relationship to language and contexts of use (Wennerstrom, 2003), and in developing a sense of generic variation in one genre as well as across the different genres. The "contrastive principle" states that awareness of the operation of language in all texts is usually best stimulated when texts are compared and contrasted. If teachers are equipped with a linguistically principled knowledge of text type variation as proposed above, they can deal with text types more systematically for classroom practice.

Similarly, persuasion strategies can be compared across genres in a gradient scale (Ostman, 2005) for classroom practice. Focused investigations of persuasion strategies in a variety of specific discourses can be explored in future research.

Finally, a number of recent studies emphasize the genre approach to writing rather than using only a process approach (Hyland, 2004). Badger & White (2000) propose a process-genre approach based on the idea that writing involves knowledge about language and the context in which writing happens, especially the purpose of the writing (as in a genre approach) and skills in using language (as in a process approach).

Assignment

The two texts below are often termed as persuasive text type for an advertisement and as narrative text type in a novel, respectively. Through an analysis of utterance types and referring expressions, explain how these two text types are different. Explain also how the different textual functions arise. Text (4) is accompanied by a picture of a man standing beside a person who is lying flat on a seat folded flat and another picture of an ordinary airline seat.

(4) ***Air France is about to prove that***
lying flat on your back in the air
is not just an illusion.
Your eyes are heavy, very heavy.
Now all you can hear is my voice
You're on the L'ESPACE 180 seat.
It reclines through 180.
You feel relaxed. Very relaxed.
Its surface is so smooth that you can even sleep on your stomach.
You're feeling just fine.
You are sleepy.
Now you're going to sleep. Sleep.
One, two, three…you are asleep.
YOU WILL ALWAYS HAVE A REASON TO FLY AIR FRANCE.

(5) ***The House of the Seven Gables***
Halfway down a bystreet of one of our New England towns stands a rusty wooden house with seven acutely peaked gables, facing towards various points of the compass and a huge, clustered chimney in the midst. The street is Pyncheon Street, the house is the old Pyncheon House; and an elm tree of wide circumference, rooted before the door, is familiar to every town-born child by the title of the Pyncheon Elm. On my occasional visits to the town aforesaid, I seldom failed to turn down Pyncheon Street for the sake of passing through the shadow of these two antiquities — the great elm tree and the weather-beaten edifice.

Chapter 6

Academic and professional written genres in disciplinary communication

Theoretical and empirical challenges

Giovanni Parodi
Pontificia Universidad Católica de Valparaíso

Corpora of natural, annotated texts have had a significant impact on linguistic analyses over the previous two or three decades. The relevance of a corpus based approach is that it helps construct empirically founded descriptions to study genre and register variations. Supported by the computational advances that make it possible to work with incrementing corpora, researchers capitalize from corpus linguistics principles and may explore all dimensions of language, including semantics and multimodal discourse. In this chapter, I will report a research study based upon the largest available on line corpus (57 million words) of written specialized discourse of Spanish on four disciplines: Psychology, Social Work, Industrial Chemistry, and Construction Engineering. In essence, a description and analysis of a corpus of 940 texts is presented. Some of the genres detected are shared by some disciplines and also employed in academic and professional settings, but important distinctions are detected. Thus, it is clear that access to disciplinary knowledge is constructed through a varying repertoire of written genres depending on disciplinary domain and on academic or professional field.

1. Introduction

In this chapter, I focus on a leading question from a corpus-based empirical approach: What are the prototypical written genres that circulate in academic and professional similar disciplinary domains of knowledge? I believe that specialized written discourse literacy at academic university and professional fields has just begun to be explored in most countries of the world. Thus, one way to access the disciplinary written genres employed by academia and professional workplaces is to start from the assumption that all materials read in these contexts reveal relevant data about written communication means and knowledge organizations.

At first glance, it is increasingly common nowadays to find research studies based on large corpora of natural complete texts, employing computational support and statistical techniques. New frontiers are being explored from these perspectives, and refreshing and robust empirical results facilitate interesting new areas of study. Following this approach, research into the English language, as well as certain European and Asian languages, has revealed that linguistic studies based on large corpora of digital texts do not always corroborate the researchers' initial intuitions. Genre descriptions must be based on sufficient texts of naturally occurring language use to ensure that the regularities and patterns observed reveal actual characteristics of the genres under study. The use of computer-readable corpora as well as the availability of computer programs has boosted linguistic research in a way that was previously unpredictable.

Research describing specialized genres based on Spanish corpora and used in academic and professional settings is relatively scant. Most of the research produced in the Spanish language on specialized discourse addresses the so-called specialized-disseminating discourse of magazines, journals, and newspapers (Cademártori, 2003; Calsamiglia, 2000; Ciapuscio, 2003; López, 2002), or it focuses on discourse markers in a variety of genres (Martín Zorraquino & Portolés, 1999; Montolío, 2001; Portolés, 1998). Other studies concentrate on few linguistic features in small and exemplary texts (Harvey, 2002) or on specialized terminology (Cabré, 1999, 2002; Lorente, 2002). It is difficult to find research into Spanish genre classifications and descriptions, based upon large corpora of texts which are fundamental reading material in university programs and in professional organizations on the same disciplinary domains.

The idea behind a corpus is that it represents a language variety in some domain. This makes the approach ideal for researching prototypical and identifying features, for example, of academic and professional genres. In other words, priority is given to what frequently and typically occurs based on descriptions of the regular uses and also based on the comparison of one genre type to others, or of genres on varying degrees of specialization, or of genres on different language modes (e.g., written or spoken).

Thus, in what follows, some challenges on this research area are introduced, some techniques for gathering and manipulating corpora are revised, new frontiers of "language-in-use" research are envisioned. All of this will be accomplished on the framework of the analysis and description of genres detected in the PUCV-2006 Academic and Professional Corpus. Connections and differences are explored and also compared between the nine genres identified in academic settings and the twenty-eight genres collected in professional workplaces.

2. The research challenge

One of the main challenges for discourse studies and their future projections to empirically founded genre research is to find ways to reach robust results, based on large corpora as a way of describing linguistic and discourse variations in greater detail; also, constructing a wide overview of similarities across languages, across disciplines, and across different institutions and workplaces. It is highly important to overcome the study of fragmented texts or exemplary documents, just focused on one single variable. The number of annotated corpora of diverse nature, available in digital format and uploaded onto websites, is still surprisingly small and of restricted nature.

If we want to move forward in the study of genre and genre variation, an approach following corpus-based principles and corpus linguistic methodologies should be followed. In particular, we also need to widen the frontiers of some restricted conceptions of corpus studies, in which a cognitive dimension is rejected or denied. A multidisciplinary perspective is highly required.

A corpus approach provides a large-scale evidence-based research tool into language use and helps discover with reliable methods discourse variability across disciplines, registers and, of course, genres (Biber, 1988, 1994, 2006; Biber, Connor & Upton, 2007; Parodi, 2005a, 2007a 2007b). Also, genre research has capitalized enormously from data gathered based on corpora analysis, and new areas and procedures are being explored from these principles, sometimes combining qualitative and quantitative methods. However, research describing linguistic features of specialized academic and professional genres — based on Spanish data and employed in academic and professional settings — is relatively scant or non-existent.

The increasing importance of genre variation across disciplines as an explanatory factor for diverse knowledge construction within discourse communities has been recognized over the past years. The perception that there is no core disciplinary discourse per se and that it is better to talk about disciplinary discourses in plural (Hyland, 2000) is becoming more accepted among researchers. Essentially, genres are social, cognitive, and linguistic constructions that help group texts together and represent how writers/speakers and readers/listeners communicate and use language to interact in recurring situations (Parodi, 2008a). One way of characterizing genres is in terms of the communicative purposes that the writer/speaker conveys through language: e.g., to report, to describe, or to argue. Also, the participants may be specified or described in terms of the degree of specialization, the number of people included, the relation between them: e.g., specialist to specialist, a group of scientists to a large audience, or from a teacher to his or her students. Discourse organization in terms of rhetorical and linguistic recurring features also applies (e.g., narration, exposition, or argumentation). This classic three-pronged variable construction has its origin in Bajtin's ideas: topic, style, and textual composition.

However, the degree to which social, contextual, rhetorical or linguistic features are included and emphasized are highly relevant to approach an understanding of the different ways genres may be conceived of. Alternative schools offer possibilities that are not always compatible among them. Some are based on abstract guiding frameworks or forms of social actions, or recurring linguistic structures, or rhetorical options from which to choose. Some of them are more linguistically oriented and accept that genres can be taught in schools, exposing students gradually to more complex ways depending on lexicogrammatical organizations; while others defend the communicative value of genres and are against the idea of transforming genres in materially objective artefacts of linguistic organizations that may reduce texts to fixed templates. Another more complex way of approaching genres is a multidimensional orientation that emerges from interdisciplinary studies where language, cognition and society constitute three nuclear issues that are linked together.

This general but also complex overview of the different alternative conceptions of genre may confuse the novice, but also the expert. Systemic Functional Linguistics (SFL), New Rhetoric (NR), Semiolinguistics (SL), Communicative Procedural Text Linguistics (CPL), Interdisciplinary Text Linguistics (ITL), Genre Analysis (GA), among others, are all labels that represent options to be explored. Highly relevant differences are detected among them; differences that must be analyzed by those interested in the study of language from these perspectives. It is interesting to see how cognitivism and contextualism in linguistic studies have evolved and influenced genre theory. The cognitive approach to language emerged slowly into linguistic research, so the progressive process of constructing complex scientific and multidimensional objects became more accepted, revealing almost all its features and different dimensions and planes. Genre, therefore, remains an elusive term for those who do not have clear tenants or adhere to existing theories. As we shall see below, however, combining interdisciplinary approaches which focus on several aspects could offer a harmonizing proposal.

Our approach towards the study of genres is decidedly interdisciplinary and of a psycho-sociolinguistic nature (Parodi, 2005b, 2007a, 2008a, in press-a). The texts collected are considered as linguistic units produced in cognitive and social contexts, that is, whose function is constructed through complex semiotic and cognitive processing. From this perspective, genres are linguistic organizations with meanings in virtue of producers/speakers and readers/hearers with specific purposes, based upon prior knowledge constructed from cognition in specific social contexts. In other words, discourse genres are conceived of as meaning processes and products of discourse, cognition and context, and, at the same time, as forming tools that, in part, help people construct their world and their environment.

3. Examples

In order to show genre identification and distinctions, we will provide a few examples from some of the genres identified in the PUCV-2003 Corpus (Parodi, 2005a), accompanied by the corresponding translation into English. The principles of genre classification are described, explained and exemplified in Parodi and Gramajo (2007), and more recently in the analysis of a larger and wider corpus, in Parodi, Venegas, Ibañez and Gutierez (2008).

The identification of different genres, based on a group of categories, still presents problems for researchers. No definitive consensus has been reached. In particular, some of the problems emerged from the different existing conceptions of genre, and the undetermined variables accepted as minimum requirements to be considered. In order to show part of the emerging classification that follows our principles, some passages were extracted from one of our corpora representing five different genres: Glossary, Instructive, Textbook, Regulation, and Technical Description. The examples belong to two disciplinary domains: Commerce and Maritime Engineering. We will also give the codification number in each case, so it is possible to check the whole annotated texts online in our website and get more information about them: www.elgrial.cl.

One of the most striking aspects of the possibility to observe and compare these examples is that the distinctive features emerge clearly and, even though some characteristics may overlap, subtle differences prevail. The Textbook and the Instructive show their didactic rhetorical tools (lots of pedagogical clues can be detected). Thus, they act as disseminating discipline knowledge material, facilitating through different means the learners' experience and understanding of the new subject matter. On the other extreme, we analyze the Regulation and the Technical Description, both very concrete with a strong reference focus and paying less or rather no attention to helping the reader grasp the contents.

Now let's look at the examples:

a) TEXTBOOK (CTC-COM-ma1)

Poner Atención:

I. LA CUENTA

"Es una agrupación sistemática de los cargos y abonos relacionados a una persona o situación de la misma naturaleza, que se registran bajo un encabezamiento o título que los identifica."

II. CONCEPTOS

a) Las anotaciones registradas al Debe de la cuenta se llaman: Cargo.
b) Las anotaciones registradas al Haber de la cuenta se llaman: Abono.
c) La suma de los Cargos se llama: Débito.
d) La suma de los Abonos se llama: Crédito.
e) La diferencia entre Débitos y Créditos se llama: Saldo.

RECORDAR:

GANANCIAS > PÉRDIDAS = UTILIDAD DEL EJERCICIO
GANANCIAS < PÉRDIDAS = PÉRDIDAS DEL EJERCICIO

Translation

Important:

I. THE ACCOUNT

"It is a systematic grouping of the charges and payments related to a person or situation of the same nature, registered under a heading or title that identifies them."

II. CONCEPTS

a) Entries registered as credit in the account are called payments.
b) The total sum of all the Charges is called: Debit
c) The total sum of the Payments is called: Credit
d) The difference between Debits and Credits is called: Balance

REMEMBER:

PROFITS > LOSSES = PROFITS OF THE EXERCISE
PROFTIS < LOSSES = LOSSES OF THE EXCERCISE

b) INSTRUCTIVE (CTC-MAR-in42)

INSTRUCCIONES DE LLENADO DE LA CONTINUACIÓN DEL INFORME DE IMPORTACIÓN

Cuando proceda el uso de este formulario, deberá ser emitido conjuntamente con el informe de Importación y este último no tendrá validez si a él no se encuentra(n) adjunto(s) el(los) formulario(s) "Continuación del Informe de Importación" que corresponda(n).

1. Presentación (Número y fecha).

Deberá indicarse el mismo número y fecha de presentación del Informe de Importación.

2. Entidad que presenta el Informe de Importación y Código.

Deberá indicarse las mismas del Informe de Importación.

3. Número, fecha y firma autorizada entidad emisora.

Número, con su correspondiente fecha y firma autorizada con el cual el Servicio Nacional de Aduana cursa el Informe de Importación.

Translation

INSTRUCTIONS TO FILL IN THE CONTINUATION OF THE IMPORTING REPORT
Whenever the use of this form is required, it should be issued with import's report. The latter will have no validity unless attached to the corresponding "Continuation of import Report".
1. Presentation (Number and date)
The same number and date of presentation of the Import Report should be stated.
2. Company presenting the Import Report and the Code Import.
Same should be stated for Import Report.
3. Number, date and authorized signature of issuing entity.
Number, corresponding date and authorized signature with which the National Customs Service issues the Import Report.

c) REGULATION (CTC-MAR-rg45)

III TRASLADO DE MERCANCÍAS DESDE EL PUERTO O AEROPUERTO AL RECINTO DE DEPOSITO.

Las normas contenidas en esta apartado solamente se aplicarán cuando el recinto de depósitos esté ubicado fuera de la zona primaria del puerto o aeropuerto de arribo de la nave.

1. La compañía de transporte debe entregar las mercancías al almacenista dentro de las 2 horas siguientes a la hora de salida de la Zona Primaria del puerto o aeropuerto de arribo de vehículo
2. La responsabilidad ante el Servicio de Aduanas de la entrega de las mercancías al almacenista es de la compañía de transportes que realizó el flete internacional, independiente de la empresa que efectuó el traslado desde la zona primaria al almacén.

Translation

III. TRANSFER OF MERCHANDISE FROM THE PORT OR AIRPORT TO THE PLACE OF DEPOSIT.

The norms contained in the section will only apply when storage is located out side the primary zone of the port or airport of arrival of the vessel.

1. The shipping company must deliver the merchandize to the head of the warehouse within the 2 hours following departure time from the port or airport primary zone of arrival of the vehicle
2. Responsibility before customs services for delivery of the merchandize to the head of the warehouse lies on the shipping company, which transferred the goods from the primary zone to the warehouse.

d) TECHNICAL DESCRIPTION (TC-COM-dt 16)

I. EVOLUCIÓN HISTÓRICA DEL CONTENEDOR

El Contenedor como nuevo elemento de transpone ha revolucionado el transporte marítimo, las naves comenzaron a adecuarse para una operación expedita hasta llegar a las naves especialmente construidas para contenedores y los puertos se han visto obligado a adquirir elementos que faciliten el mejor manipuleo.

II. DEFINICIONES DE CONTENEDORES

1. Contenedores para uso general son aquellos totalmente cerrados, teniendo todas su paredes rígidas, como así también el techo, el piso y además una de sus paredes extremas está provista de puerta.
2. Contenedores para uso especifico son aquellos destinados al transporte de mercancías generales construidos con características especiales, de tal forma de facilitar el embarque o descarga ya sea por la puerta extrema o teniendo funciones específicas, tales como la ventilación de la carga.

Translation

I. HISTORICAL EVOLUTION OF CONTAINERS

The Container, as a new transportation device, has revolutionized maritime transportation; Vessels began to adapt for more efficient operation, until the stage when vessels were built specially for container handling and ports have been forced to purchase elements that help handle the process.

II. DEFINITIONS OF CONTAINERS

1. Containers for general use are completely closed units, surrounded by rigid walls, a rigid floor and ceiling, with a door in one of the extreme walls, as thus also the ceiling, the floor and in addition one of its extreme walls is provided with a door.
2. Containers for specific use are those units destined to the transportation of general merchandize, which have been built with special characteristics so as to facilitate loading or unloading, whether through the extreme door or having specific functions, such as ventilation of the load.

4. Research method

There is a number of interesting research methods available nowadays to study genres that may help us fill the gap of non-existing corpus-based information. One key point is to produce empirical investigations based on large corpora, with annotated texts, and supported by statistical techniques. In what follows, one research method will be described within the corpus-based corpus linguistics perspective (Biber, 1988; Biber & Tracy-Ventura, 2007; Parodi, 2005a, 2007b). The description of the methodological steps was part of a research project conducted in technical professional secondary schools in the city of Valparaíso, Chile (Parodi, 2005a)

Multi-feature and multi-dimensional analysis: Methodological steps

To perform a complete multi-functional analysis, a series of decisions and rigorous steps must be followed (see for more details Parodi, 2007b). They can be summed up in the following twelve key points:

1. Design, collection, organization, and digitalization of a corpus.
2. Selection of a set of linguistic features based on a specialized bibliography and according to the registers considered in the analysis.
3. Functional characterization of the linguistic features selected.
4. Availability of computer programs that can automatically tag the texts in plain format (ASCII or txt).
5. Automatic tagging and parsing of the texts in the corpus.
6. Manual or (semi)automatic database queries to each text to determine the occurrence of the features under study.
7. Elaboration of normalized data tables, given the different number of words between texts.
8. Application, with the aid of computer programs, of factor analysis to the frequency of feature occurrences. The reason for this is the need for a reduction of the variables involved and for the determination of co-occurrence patterns in the linguistic features.
9. Establishment of a set of factors (each factor is made up of a set of linguistic features) through factor analysis with some kind of rotation (Varimax, Cuantrimax, Oblimin, etc.).
10. Functional interpretation of the factors, resulting from the factor analysis, from the co-occurrence of features, thus constituting an underlying dimension of variation.
11. Confirmation or refutation of the interpretation of the factors through the estimation of the factor loadings.
12. Estimation of the dimension scores. In this step, the scores for each register in each dimension are compared, and the linguistic and functional similarities and/or differences are studied.

Linguistic features

In order to select features for analysis, a bibliographical search must be initially carried out with the purpose of identifying representative categories that show functional relevance in a language (e.g., Spanish). Then, the researcher should be able to elaborate a matrix with a number of selected features (in our example, a total of sixty-five linguistic features we identified). Table 1 provides the features, grouped into sixteen more general categories (identified by means of capital letters).

Table 1. Sixty-five linguistic features in Corpus PUCV-2003

El Grial PUCV-2003 Corpus Project: Linguistic Features

A. Verb tense markers
1. Indefinite Past (indicative)
2. Imperfect Past (indicative)
3. Perfect Past (indicative and subjunctive)
4. Present (indicative and subjunctive)
5. Future (indicative and subjunctive)
6. Periphrastic Future

B. Verb Markers
7. Indicative/imperative
8. Subjunctive/imperative
9. Indicative mood
10. Subjunctive mood
11. Imperative mood

C. Verb Inflections
12. First singular
13. Second singular
14. Third singular
15. First plural
16. Second plural
17. Third plural

D. Personal pronouns
18. First person singular
19. First person plural
20. Second person singular
21. Second person plural
22. Third person singular
23. Third person plural
24. Demonstratives

E. Nominal Forms
25. Nominalizations
26. Nouns (common and proper)

F. Passive Forms
27. Passive with «se»
28. Passive with "ser" without agent
29. Passive with "ser" with agent
30. Passive with "estar"

G. Lexical Specificity
31. *Type/token per form* relation
32. *Type/token per lemma* relation

H. Stative Active Forms
33. Ser
34. Estar

I. Verb Types
35. Public
36. Private
37. Persuasive
38. Perceptive

J. Modal Verbs
39. Possibility
40. Necessity
41. Obligation
42. Volition

K. Modality Markers
43. Hedges
44. Boosters

L. Adverbs
45. Place
46. Time
47. Manner
48. Quantity

M. Subordination Markers
49. Noun clauses with «que»
50. Relative adjective clauses
51. Adverbial clauses of reason or cause/effect
52. Adverbial clauses of concession
53. Adverbial clauses of condition
54. Adverbial clauses of time
55. Infinitive phrases in nominal function

N. Prepositional phrases and adjectives
56. Prep. Phrases (noun complement)
57. Attributive adjectives (descriptive)
58. Predicative adjectives
59. Demonstrative adjectives
60. Participles with adjectival function

Ñ. Coordination Markers
61. Adversative, additive and disjunctive conjunctions

O. Negation Markers
62. Negation adverb
63. Adverbs of temporal negation
64. Negation conjunction
65. Negation pronouns

Table 2. Academic Corpus of PUCV-2006: Number of words and percentages

	Number of Texts	%	Number of Words	%
Psychology	227	**46**	22,163,379	**39**
Social Work	142	**29**	16,343,175	**30**
Construction Engineering	69	**14**	8,813,663	**15**
Industrial Chemistry	53	**11**	9,304,407	**16**
Total	**491**	**100%**	**56,624,624**	**100%**

A functional description of each of these features plus their relation to certain registers and a detailed bibliographical reference can be found in Parodi (2007b).

5. Recent research

Our most recent research aims to describe and understand the written genres that circulate at four university undergraduate programs and their corresponding professional workplaces, by collecting and studying the written texts that are read in these contexts and through which particular knowledge provides access to disciplinary interactions. We examine assigned student readings in four academic degree programs and the written texts that form the core of daily written communication in professional settings that correspond to these disciplines. The areas involved are: Basic Sciences and Engineering (Industrial Chemistry and Construction Engineering) and Social Sciences and Humanities (Social Work and Psychology) Table 2 provides figures that give a first overview of the academic corpus.

Taking into account the number of words collected, Table 2 reveals that texts belonging to Psychology and Social Work represent (respectively 39% and 30%) more than two times the reading material students in Industrial Chemistry and Construction Engineering (15% and 16% respectively) face as part of their study programs. This same comparison in terms of books is doubled, that is, it is almost four times. There is no other report of a written academic corpus available in the Spanish language of such dimension that is so representative and so thematically focused. A corpus of such size, close to 60 million words, in digital format (and available on line), morphosyntactically tagged and parsed, organized by subject matter and genres, becomes a fundamental tool for cutting edge research.

A first attempt at a more in-depth analysis of the written material collected and a classification as to the genre types follows, using the communicative-functional and textual-discursive linguistic taxonomy, as proposed by Parodi, Venegas, Ibáñez and Gutiérrez (2008). Below, in Figure 1, nine genres are identified along with figures of the number of texts collected.

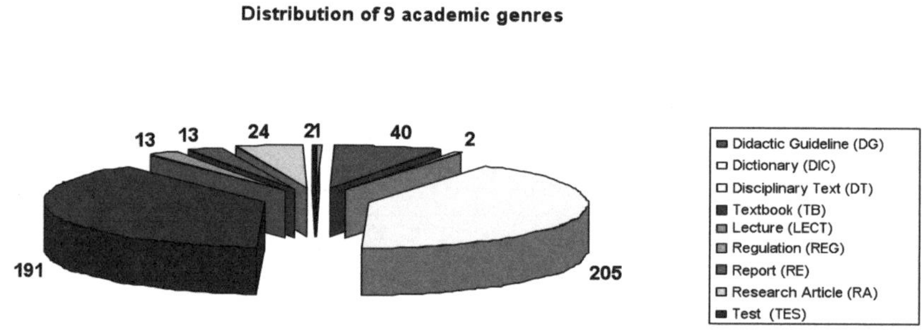

Figure 1. Distribution of academic genres.

As we can see from Figure 1, a quite heterogeneous panorama with clear concentrations emerges from the data presented. Two genres are by far the most frequent: Disciplinary Text (DT), with 205, and Textbook (TB), with 191. This provides and overall initial situation that combines, on the one hand, disciplinary knowledge as presented in subject matter books concentrating specialized knowledge in each domain (DT), sometimes with a high degree of discourse complexity; and TB, on the other hand, which, although oriented towards disciplinary knowledge, has a didactic and more disseminating character. TB generally uses more educational resources, such as graphs, tables, diagrams, etc., in a more systematic manner and incorporates exercises and other practical applications in order for readers to access, develop and test their knowledge (Parodi, 2008c).

Let's move now to the analysis of the professional corpus. It is worth noticing that the collection and description of the professional corpus is of a different nature compared to the academic one. Thus, our aim was to gather a representative corpus of the genres that circulate in daily written communication in institutional environments. A collection of 449 texts was gathered. They were classified according to the Parodi, Venegas, Ibáñez, and Gutiérrez (2008) criteria, and twenty-eight genres emerged. Table 3 summarizes the genres, identified in alphabetical order:

As observed in this table, a large number of genres was detected. Some of them are very specialized and are used in very restricted situations (e.g., CB, QUOT, and BS). Some others are genres that circulate in every day life, such as NEW, DIC, and PLA. Just a few genres show commonalities with academic domains (e.g., TB, DIC, DT, and LECT). It is highly interesting to note that most genres collected in written professional communication reveal a repertoire that does not occur in academic life. It is clear this repertoire of genres is richer and more diverse. This was unanticipated. The diversity of genres these professionals must face, read, and comprehend in daily activities is an issue in which universities do not seem to help by developing the necessary literacy skills, based on the genres employed in the academia.

Table 3. Professional genres

Professional Genres in PUCV-2006 Corpus			
Bidding Specification	BS	News	NEW
Brochure	BRO	Observation Guideline	OG
Calculation Log	CM	Operating Manual	OM
Call for bids	CB	Plan	PLA
Certificate	CERT	Quotation	QUOT
Commercial Catalogue	CC	Record	REC
Development Plan	DP	Regulation	REG
Dictionary	DIC	Report	REP
Disciplinary Text	DT	Research Article	RA
Law	LAW	Research Project	RP
Lectura	LECT	Statement	STA
Medical Order	MO	Test	TES
Medical Report	MR	Textbook	TB
Memorando	ME	Thesis	THE

Figure 2 shows the professional genres' distribution which occurs across the four disciplines (Social Work, Psychology, Construction Engineering, and Industrial Chemistry).

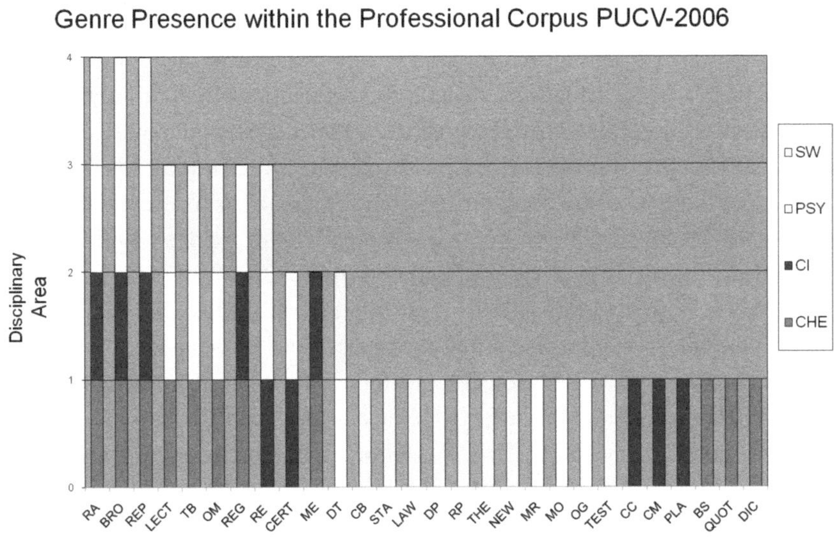

Figure 2. Professional genres' distribution in the four disciplines.

This disposition of the 28 genres follows a progressive organization from occurrence in all four disciplines to only one. As the most significant finding, three genres are shared by the four fields of professional activities: Research Article (RA), Brochure (BRO), and Report (REP). All of them reveal an important degree of specialization and are typical of discourse interactions in specific communication environments. Five genres (TB, LECT, OM, REC, and REG) occur in three of the areas, and three (DT, CERT, and ME) occur in only two disciplines. Therefore, eleven genres are shared in some degree among the areas of specialization.

These findings reveal the significance of studying language use in academic and professional settings and confirm the need to create specialized instructional materials on the basis of empirical descriptions. The evidence also suggests that there are relevant arguments to differentially pay attention to the written linguistic specialized material that circulates in both educational and professional settings. All students should practice with a wide variety of written genres, since in their professional lives they will come across a richer repertoire than in university contexts.

6. Research proposal

A group of motivating questions to research on this area of discourse studies remains. Theoretical, methodological, as well as empirical issues must be faced and approached with new and integrating approaches. Spoken or oral genres in Spanish have not been fully investigated until now. Just some small corpora are available. A rather similar situation takes places in other languages. It is true that researching with spontaneous spoken interaction involves new and not-yet-overcome great variety of problems, but the next move in such orientation is therefore to consider gathering representative empirical data from varying situations, origins and interactions in different languages.

It certainly remains for future research to explore all the potentiality that the corpus-based approaches and connecting techniques to genre description and analysis may bring in (whereas of spoken or written nature), as well as to address the still not-fully answered questions such as the status of generic conceptions and the categories and dimensions involved in an operational definition. One of the main tasks for the near future must be to integrate divergent positions in search for a multilevel, multidimensional, and inter- or transdisciplinary perspective of genre and genre variation.

One way to move forward would be to follow some regular research protocols in order to produce comparable effective analysis and robust results. By employing some similar empirical principles, we should be in a better position for achieving a wider understanding of genre variation across academic and professional domains, and across disciplines.

With this purposes in mind, I will briefly sketch some of the methodological principles followed to collect and process the academic and professional PUCV-2006 Corpus.

Constitution of Corpus PUCV-2006

Since we wanted to collect the reading material employed in four university undergraduate programs, and also gather a sample of the texts employed in the workplaces as prototypical reading material employed by professionals graduated from these four disciplines, specific methodological steps were followed into different stages according to each corpus requirements and characteristics.

Academic corpus: Main steps

- Construction of a database with the complete curricula of the four degree programs (including the syllabi of all required courses).
- Construction of a database with obligatory bibliographic references of all required courses.
- Collecting the texts from the corresponding libraries and professors' offices.
- Photocopying of each text in order to maintain a database in paper format.
- Scanning and digitizing all texts.
- Processing all plain texts (txt*) through tagger and parser El Grial and uploading of all texts to the website www.elgrial.cl.

Professional corpus: Main steps

- Construction of a database with the names and addresses of all professionals graduated from the four degree programs during the last five years.
- Telephone and email contact with professionals in order to organize interviews in their workplaces.
- Personal interviews with a similar number of professionals in each discipline to obtain samples of written material they use in daily written communication.
- Photocopying of each text in order to maintain a database in paper format.
- Scanning and digitizing all texts.
- Processing all plain texts (txt*) through tagger and parser El Grial and uploading of all texts in the online website www.elgrial.cl.

By following these steps we were ensured the creation of databases that accurately reflect the written texts subjects were exposed to during their university careers and in daily routine professional written communication activities in their workplaces.

7. Practical relevance

The practical relevance of collecting corpora of natural, machine-readable texts from a variety of written and oral interactions is, on the one hand, that it helps construct empirically founded descriptions to study genre and register variations. Such an approach to language use, based on large amounts of real data, also allows contrastive research which helps discover emerging text and discourse features that would be impossible to identify with isolated and exemplary text samples. On the other hand, supported by the computational advances that make possible to work with *annotated* texts, researchers capitalize from corpus linguistics principles and may explore all dimensions of language, including semantics and multimodal discourse.

Although corpus linguistics may be conceived of as a methodology in the first place (an approach followed by Parodi, in press [a], and described by Tognini-Bonelli, 2001, as "corpus-based"), it is also possible to argue in favor of a more theoretical position. Such a theoretical approach to corpus linguistics is what Tognini-Bonelli proposes as "corpus-driven." Exploring theoretical perspectives provide access to researching links between language, cognition, and society and the nature of the units under study, both areas which still need closer investigation.

Considering the empirical results of the research reported here, the analysis provided by the genre descriptions helps discover fundamental discursive distinctions between, on the one hand, Social Sciences and Humanities and Basic Sciences and Engineering; on the other, interesting differences that have emerged from the comparison of academic and professional corpus in similar disciplinary domains. Thus, we are beginning to realize and understand that the texts employed as reading material in some academic fields ("*hard sciences*": Basic Sciences and Engineering) are not the same as in other scientific areas ("*soft sciences*": Social Sciences and Humanities). The relevance of these findings shows that the discourse of social sciences is constructed and re-constructed through different linguistic and functional dimensions and also text features which give form to prototypical written genres that circulate in disciplines such as psychology and social work.

The written text analysis showed a distribution of nine academic genres and twenty eight professional genres. The general results show some cross-discipline differences where, for example, Industrial Chemistry (two genres) and Psychology (nine genres) are at the extreme poles of the continuum. Also interesting are the intra-disciplinary variations in the academic corpus. In general, more disseminating-reader-oriented genres were found in the fields of Basic Sciences and Engineering, with a particular high frequency of Textbook and Didactic Guideline (especially in Industrial Chemistry). Social Sciences and Humanities showed a richer variety of genres, but with a major concentration on disciplinary-specific focus with minor emphasis on didactic resources (important occurrence of Disciplinary Text).

This variety of reading materials depicts the most common academic genres students encounter in daily university discourse activities. The primary genre identified in this research is one oriented to specialized knowledge (Disciplinary Text). Textbooks are also used and they combine instructional devices such as examples, diagrams, and problem solving exercises. These two genres represent important academic tools that open pathways to knowledge to novice students.

The professional corpus collected in the study reported here showed a richer repertoire of written genres (twenty eight genres) with almost four times the variety detected in academic corpus (nine genres). As expected, the professional corpus reveals a tendency towards more specialized genres that clearly identify communicative interactions in highly specific social routines, such as those implied by Quotations, Bidding Specification, Report, Statement, and Calculation Log.

Full participation in disciplinary and professional cultures demands informed knowledge of vital written genres. Genres are intimately linked to the discipline's norms, values and ideologies. They pack information through which these professionals communicate with their peers. Understanding the genres of written communication in a field is, therefore, essential to professional success. The discourse and cognitive demand these genres impose upon professionals cannot be determined in the framework of the preset study, but it is a challenging open area of research. Also, these findings help infer information about the activities or practices in which genres are embedded.

Research studies like the one described here also have pedagogical implications concerning: (a) the selection of written genres, (b) the elaboration of teaching materials, and (c) the preparation of language tests of a different nature, such as the assessment of disciplinary contents and of specialized discourse comprehension. This is because the genres detected in each discipline help describe the characteristics of the type of language use employed in written communication students and professionals are exposed to. According to the results analyzed before, students from the four disciplinary domains being studied need to develop their discourse and cognitive skills at mastering a very particular, specialized variety of written Spanish — academically dense prose in lexical, morphological, and syntactical terms — typical of the disciplinary texts and technical textbooks.

Assignment

A variety of questions and assignments focusing on genre conceptualizations, genre descriptions and classifications can be proposed. Also, assignments on genre analysis and identification of prototypical features of different level, dimensions, and nature are of interest.

1. Explore the references in this chapter and identify similarities and differences in which the degree of social, contextual, rhetorical and linguistic features are included and emphasized in defining genres. Try to identify approaches and schools; also try to find divergent and complementary emphasis. Which school or approach would best fit your research interests?
2. Why is it important to identify discourse genres in academic and professional domains? Is just because of a linguistic interest in text structures? Is it because there is a connection between discourse, cognition and society?
3. Based on the data presented in this chapter, which are the genres that are detected in both academic and professional corpora? What teaching implications, apart from the ones mentioned here, could be proposed from the data for university programs?

Part IV

Discourse structures

Chapter 7

Why investigate textual information hierarchy?

Elisabeth Le
University of Alberta

This chapter aims to underline the benefits of working with textual information hierarchy in discourse studies. This hierarchy is revealed by the application of a model of coherence analysis that is based on cognitive psychology. It is claimed that the model allows to link micro- and macro- uses of language at the text and society levels. The model has been used to investigate formal textual characteristics. Used in connection with contextual analyses, it has also been instrumental in explaining how texts function in society. Furthermore, the model allows the combination of the benefits of qualitative and quantitative studies. On the one hand, the revealed textual information hierarchy functions as a grid on which a broad, detailed qualitative study can be grounded; on the other, it exposes the most salient elements that can be investigated further with a quantitative study.

1. Introduction

A coherent text is recognized by the global meaning that readers can make of it (Givòn, 1995; Hobbs, 1979; Sanders et al., 1992). To help their readers make sense of a text, authors link new and old information within sentences and paragraphs, i.e., they build the textual coherence at micro- and macrolevels as they go through the writing process (Kintsch & Van Dijk, 1978). This chapter presents a model of coherence analysis, and shows how it can help link micro- and macro- uses of language at the text and society levels by revealing textual information hierarchy.

In this work, coherence is reconstructed with a formal model of analysis (Le, 1996) that integrates work done on processes of text production and interpretation by Van Dijk (1980), Kintsch (1988, 1998), Hobbs (1985), and Daneš (1974, 1989). In this integrated model based on cognitive psychology, coherence links between syntactic sentences are established on the basis of logico-semantic relations existing between pairs of sentences. The three basic relations of coordination (elaboration and parallelism), subordination and superordination are Hobbs' relations of expansion that have been completed. Once relations of coherence have been defined between the text sentences, the themes and macrostructures on which the text argumentation is based are determined with the application of formal rules. While readers may not reconstruct the text coherence in exactly the same manner as authors established it, there is a limit to the number of possible readings for each text. It follows that the number of coherence reconstructions that can be done for each text is also limited and thus, the model presented also provides a process of verification for the analysis.

This model of coherence analysis has been used to investigate formal textual characteristics. Used in connection with contextual analyses, it has also been instrumental in explaining how texts function in society. The model itself relates more particularly to chapters 5 ("Structured content"), 6 ("Discourse connections"), and 13 ("Discourse and cognition") in Renkema (2004), but it has been applied in relation to issues treated in chapters 14 ("Discourse and institution") and 15 ("Discourse and culture").

2. Research challenge

> Discourse studies is the discipline devoted to the investigation of the relationship between form and function in verbal communication… The investigation of the relation between form and function requires contributions from different disciplines such as linguistics, literature, rhetoric, stylistics and pragmatics as well as other fields concerned with verbal communication such as communication science, psychology, sociology and philosophy. Discourse phenomena cannot be studied adequately from just one of these perspectives (Renkema, 2004: 1–2).

Faced with such an encompassing approach that is necessarily labor-intensive and therefore time-consuming, discourse analysts could contend themselves with focusing on a small part of a larger project and accept to run the risk of not being able to link form and function. What if their intention is to start their analysis with micro-linguistic elements (i.e., form) and finish it with the text function in society? If their aim is to "detect societal problems" in order to empower "powerless groups or minorities" (Renkema, 2004: 282) as in Critical Discourse Analysis, how are they supposed to proceed? How could they reconcile the length of time needed for the breadth and rigor of their scientific analyses with the time constraint inherent to social action?

A first answer to come to mind would certainly be to encourage work in multidisciplinary teams. This would indeed greatly facilitate a multi-perspective approach on a sizeable corpus. Unfortunately, practical considerations often get in the way of such an optimal situation. So what can be done? Many discourse analysts succeed in working independently by focusing on a few selected features and / or analyzing a very small number of texts. In some cases, this has raised concerns about the relevance of the analyzed features and most often, about the analyzed texts' representativity; in other words, discourse studies (as qualitative studies in general) have often been criticized for the small size of analyzed corpora. While the validity of qualitative analysis is not questioned in this chapter, it is still relevant to look at practical means for combining qualitative and quantitative approaches to discourse studies.

Though certainly not sufficient in itself, it is claimed that the model of coherence analysis presented in this chapter presents two major advantages: it allows to a certain extent for the combination of depth and breadth that is provided respectively by qualitative and quantitative approaches, and it enables to link cognitive processes with social matters. Indeed, the coherence analysis brings to the fore macrostructures, i.e., the information most likely to remain in long-term memory (Van Dijk, 1980). On the one hand, the revealed textual information hierarchy functions as a grid on which a detailed qualitative study can be grounded; on the other, it exposes the most salient elements that can be investigated further with a quantitative study.

3. Examples

For an illustration of how this model of coherence analysis functions, let us use the following paragraph from Hobbs (1983: 245) on discourse models:

1. In many formal methods for analyzing discourse, there is the requirement that the theories or account of a text must be generated automatically, or at least that there is "inter-coder reliability."
2. There is no room for the analyst's unique insights.
3. But these requirements place an undue burden on a science of discourse.
4. In no science are constraints placed on the process of arriving at a theory.
5. The constraints are applied in its validation.
6. We have been trying to develop a mode of analyzing discourse in which the discourse analyst can appeal to the full range of his knowledge of the speaker's culture and can use unconstrained ingenuity in constructing theories of a text.
7. However, when it comes to validating a theory of a text or deciding among competing theories, he [the analyst] must encode the theories in a formal representation and subject them to precise criteria, including at least the criteria of coherence.

Three different types of knowledge allow us to establish links between these syntactical sentences (or "T-units"; see Renkema, 2004: 226). The sentences have been numbered for easier reference.

First, linguistic knowledge (syntax, lexico-semantics, and morphology) allows for the construction of a text-based model of the text (Renkema, 2004: 234). For example, "these requirements" in sentence 3 are the fact that "theories or account of a text must be generated automatically, or at least that there is 'inter-coder reliability'" (sentence 1). The word "constraints" is presented with the same referent in sentences 4 and 5. The "theories of a text" in sentence 6 are examples of the general "theory" of sentence 4, referred to by "its" in sentence 5. "Constraints" in sentence 5 and "unconstrained" in sentence 6 are morphological variations of the same concept, which is also found in "requirements" in sentence 3. The "theories" in sentence 6 are the same "theories" in sentence 7.

Then, cotext (i.e., verbal context) completes this text-based model. When the author says that "there is no room for the analyst's unique insights" (sentence 2) and when he talks about "these requirements" (sentence 3), he means this "in [the] many formal methods for analyzing discourse" of sentence 1.

However, this text-based model is not sufficient to build the text coherence. Domain (i.e., expert's) and world knowledge (general knowledge that is not linguistic and that cannot be derived from the text) are used, and this results in the construction of the text situational model (Renkema, 2004: 234). For example, we know that the automatic generation of the account of a text and "inter-coder reliability" (sentence 1; also referred to as "these requirements" in sentence 3) do not take account for the "analyst's unique insights" (sentence 2); these expressions oppose each other. The "science" in sentence 4 refers to all types of science, while the "science of discourse" in sentence 3 is only one type of science, which is constituted by the "theories of a text" of sentence 6. "Constructing" (sentence 6), "validating", and "deciding among competing theories" (sentence 7) represent different steps in working with theories. These links that we have just established between the different sentences of the text by using linguistic knowledge, cotext, domain and world knowledge are used to determine the types of coherence relations between sentences.

The model is based on three main types of coherence relation: coordination (elaboration/opposition and parallelism/contrast), subordination and superordination. They are all grounded on the logico-semantic relation of inclusion and correspond to Hobbs' relations of expansion (1985) that were later elaborated by Le (1996).

4. Research method

To establish the type of coherence relation between two syntactical sentences (or T-units; see Renkema, 2004: 226), S1 and S2, the analyst looks for two elements (p1 and a1) in S1 and two elements (p2 and a2) in S2 such that a1 and a2 on the one hand, and p1 and p2 on the other hand are linked by a logico-semantic relation of inclusion.

For example, S4 in the example above, contains p4 ("constraints") and a4 ("theory"). S5 contains p5 ("constraints") and a5 ("its"). We have p4=p5; we also have a4=a5 inasmuch as "its" refers to "theory." This configuration of links (i.e., a1=a2 and p1=p2) corresponds to the relation of coordination, more specifically of elaboration.

The analysis below indicates which pairs of elements were selected from each sentence, and the type of coherence relation that is established between these sentences. When an element is given between square brackets, it means that this element is implied (usually from the cotext). Linguistic knowledge (including information provided by the cotext), domain knowledge and world knowledge are used to determine how one element from a sentence is linked by inclusion to an element of the other sentence. (The explanation of this analysis is given as an assignment at the end of this chapter.)

1 many formal methods (generated automatically, inter-coder reliability)
2 [many formal methods] (analyst's unique insights)
→ coordination (opposition)

2 [many formal methods] (analyst's unique insights)
3 [many formal methods] (these requirements)
→ coordination (opposition)

1 many formal methods (generated automatically, inter-coder reliability)
3 [many formal methods] (these requirements)
→ coordination (elaboration)

3 requirements (science of discourse)
4 constraints (in no science [= in science, in general])
→ superordination

4 constraints (theory)
5 constraints (its)
→ coordination (elaboration)

5 constraints (its [= science, in general])
6 unconstrained (theories of a text)
→ subordination (opposition)

3 requirements (science of discourse)
6 unconstrained (theories of a text)
→ coordination (opposition)

6 theories of a text (constructing)
7 theories (validating, deciding among)
→ coordination (parallelism)

3 science of discourse (these requirements [= generated automatically, inter-coder reliability])
7 theory of a text (must encode the theories … and subject them…)
→ coordination (parallelism)

The above configuration of coherence relations is represented in the following coherence graph (coordination-elaboration: →; coordination-opposition: ↔; coordination-parallelism: ⥣ ; subordination: ↓ ; superordination: ↑; subordination / superordination-contrast: ↨).

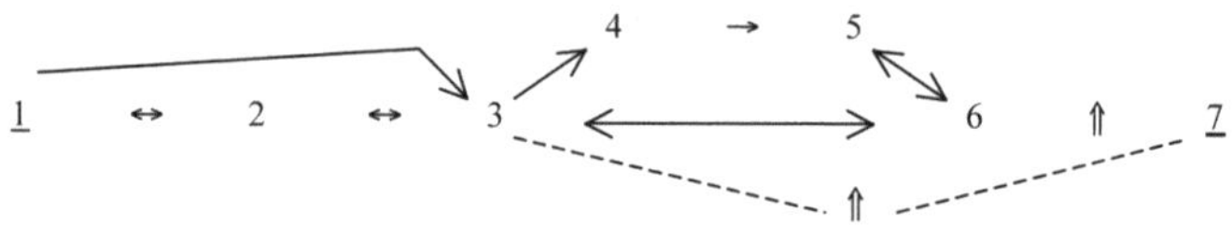

Figure 1. Coherence graph.

A typographical paragraph is supposed to present one main idea; it contains a theme (i.e., the "aboutness" of the paragraph — underlined on the coherence graph) and a macrostructure (i.e., the gist of the paragraph — in bold on the coherence graph) that are both defined with the application of formal rules. In general (i.e., there are exceptions), the first unit at the highest level of hierarchy is the theme, and the last unit at the highest level of hierarchy is the macrostructure. This does not necessarily coincide with the first and last sentences. Sometimes, one sentence is both theme and macrostructure. Although they are defined with different (formal) rules, the "macrostructures" defined by this model of coherence analysis correspond to Van Dijk's concept of macrostructures (1980). One of the advantages of defining themes in this manner is that it makes a functional perspective analysis of the text (Daneš, 1974) possible at different levels. The different hierarchical levels correspond to levels of generality or abstraction of the semantic content in the sentence.

A typographical paragraph may occasionally contain more than one main idea, especially when two or more main ideas are put into parallel. In such cases, the typographical paragraph does not represent one discursive unit but several, one for each main idea it contains. These discursive units are called "macrostructural bases." Most of the time, a typographical unit contains only one macrostructural basis. When it contains more than one, the division between two macrostructural bases appears on the coherence graph: it occurs where a sentence is linked to preceding sentences in the same paragraph by relations of coordination-parallelism (or coordination-contrast) only.

In the above example, sentences 4 and 5, although apparently at the highest level of the hierarchy (i.e., they are superordinate to all other sentences), are neither theme nor macrostructure: they express principles that link sentences 3 and 6 as shown by the relation of coordination-elaboration between these two sentences, and thus, as an exception to the general rule, they are not taken into account in the definition of the theme and macrostructure. In these conditions, sentence 1 is the theme. Sentence 7 is the last sentence of the typographical paragraph; being linked to preceding sentences of the paragraph (sentences 3 and 6) only by relations of coordination-parallelism, it constitutes a macrostructural basis by itself and is the theme and macrostructure of this unit. Sentences 1 to 6 form the first macrostructural basis; sentence 6 is the last one at the highest level of hierarchy (since neither sentence 4 nor 5 are taken into account), and thus sentence 6 is the macrostructure of the first macrostructural basis.

Once macrostructural bases, their themes and macrostructures are defined for each paragraph in a text, a first-level-of-analysis verification can take place. The theme(s) and macrostructure(s) placed one after the other in their order of appearance in the original text must present a faithful summary of the text. The only adjustments that might need to be done are to replace referential words (e.g., personal pronouns) by their referents.

The automatically generated summary of the paragraph analyzed above comprises sentence 1 (theme of the first macrostructural basis), sentence 6 (macrostructure of the first macrostructural basis) and sentence 7 (theme and macrostructure of the second macrostructural basis):

> In many formal methods for analyzing discourse, there is the requirement that the theories or account of a text must be generated automatically, or at least that there is "inter-coder reliability." We have been trying to develop a mode of analyzing discourse in which the discourse analyst can appeal to the full range of his knowledge of the speaker's culture and can use unconstrained ingenuity in constructing theories of a text. However, when it comes to validating a theory of a text or deciding among competing theories, he must encode the theories in a formal representation and subject them to precise criteria, including at least the criteria of coherence.

At the paragraph level, the automatically generated summary might not be considerably shorter than the paragraph itself. The difference in length between the original text and its automatically generated summary increases the higher the level of analysis. Indeed, this type of coherence analysis is recursive.

Any text composed of more than one typographical paragraph can be analyzed further using the same method. Each successive level of text organization corresponds to a new level of analysis, and each level of analysis is verifiable. Once the macrostructures have been identified, the links between them are analyzed in terms of coherence using the same coherence rules as at the typographical paragraph level. Similarly, higher level themes, macrostructures, and discursive units are defined, and the same type of analysis verification with the automatic generation of a summary takes place.

This goes on until the highest level is achieved (for a complete presentation of the model of coherence analysis and the definition of all rules, see Le, 2006b: 197–209).

Thus, this model of coherence analysis takes into account the "analysts' unique insights" through their use of linguistic, domain, and world knowledge, and it allows for verification of the analysis with the automatic generation of summaries at each level. Furthermore, the model takes into account the fact that different coherent readings of a same text are possible, but also that this number of coherent readings is limited. More than one automatically generated summary might be acceptable at each level, but each automatically generated summary must be deemed to represent the original text faithfully. This model of coherence analysis was first elaborated and verified through its application to academic articles; it has since been applied to newspaper editorials.

5. Recent research

The model was first applied to French and English academic articles. The most interesting findings concerned the establishment of a typology of paragraphs according to the configuration of coherence relations between their sentences (Le, 1999). It was shown how native speakers use and combine different types of paragraphs in the construction of their argumentation. It appeared that in the field of Public International Law, English authors would tend to build their argumentation within their paragraphs (i.e., by using complex paragraphs that contain different argumentative stages), while French authors would use paragraphs to build their argumentation (i.e., in presenting different argumentative stages in separate paragraphs). In defining first steps towards a grammar of paragraphs, this work showed how the model of coherence analysis provided tools to compare textual organization across cultures. Another tool was produced by the definitions of indexes of linearity (Le, 2002c), based on the number of successive units in linear progression according to the functional perspective (Daneš, 1974, 1989) and linked by the coherence relation of coordination.

A second strand in the application of the coherence analysis relates to its relevance for pedagogical purposes. While the model could be used in any matter involving text structure, it was applied to underline the importance of paragraph division for the global meaning of a text. This is particularly pertinent for translators who do not always keep the paragraph boundaries of the source texts (Le, 2004b).

Finally, the most recent and larger part of the model's application has been done in relation to newspaper editorials and their function in society. On the one hand, the definition of themes (i.e., the starting point of the argumentation) and macro-structures (i.e., the ending point of the argumentation) at different levels establish the text's hierarchical argumentative structure that functions as a reference grid for the study of specific structures. In particular, it was used to explain: (1) how explicit mentions of external sources of information achieve a specific persuasive effect (Le, 2003); (2) how editorialists use metadiscursive markers to establish their authority (Le, 2004a) and an indefinite pronoun to strengthen their argumentation (Le, 2007); and (3) what types of complex speech act editorials represent (Le, in press). On the other hand, macrostructures, as the most salient sentences, are especially useful in that they draw our attention to the information most likely to remain in long-term memory. They have been used: (1) to study the concept of Europe as constructed by *Le Monde* (Le, 2002a); (2) to show how *Le Monde*'s discourse on human rights belongs to a discourse of French national identity and thus how the newspaper's comments on the humanitarian situation in Chechnya could have resulted in an intercultural impasse (Le, 2002b); (3) to examine the extent to which the representation of a national identity is a "prisoner of its past" and thus represents an obstacle to the improvement of intercultural communication (Le, 2006a); and (4) to examine the phenomenon of the "international media echo" in which journalists of different cultures report on each others' societies and become active participants in international relations (Le, 2006b).

To recapitulate, the textual information hierarchy that is revealed by the application of the model of coherence analysis has until now facilitated the study of specific structures in their cotext, the function of texts in their culture, the comparison of texts across cultures, and the effects of texts across cultures. In revealing macrostructures, the application of the model has narrowed the focus of analysis to the most salient information and thus rendered the combination of qualitative and quantitative approaches less onerous.

Alongside these avenues of research, a few others would also merit exploration. For example, the application of the model could be fruitful in the comparison of texts across genres; it would also be interesting to see how the model could be used or adopted for the study of oral texts. Furthermore, other studies could investigate links between the types of knowledge used to build coherence of a text (i.e., the micro-elements in the text construction) and the function of this text in society (i.e., the macro-perspective of the text) as it might be very revealing of persuasive strategies. It is this last idea that is briefly developed below.

6. Research proposal

This section presents the first stages in the elaboration of a research proposal. It starts with general considerations raised by the model, and ends with a more specific direction for research. A few questions are given in italics to guide further reflection. Indeed, the ideas proposed in this section would need to be developed according to the analyst's particular interests; then, on the basis of a solid and relevant review of literature, the research question would have to be better circumscribed for this to constitute a genuine research proposal.

In writing a text, authors choose and link specific words intra- and inter-sententially in order to perform a specific function in society with their text (texts written for the author's personal purposes only are not considered here). A basic condition for the text to perform the function for which it was intended is to be understood the way the author meant it, i.e., for its coherence to be reconstructed in a manner similar to the one the author originally built. The reading of a text, i.e., the reconstruction of its coherence, amounts to building knowledge upon knowledge. In writing their text and building its coherence, authors presume that the audience possesses a certain type of linguistic, domain and world knowledge that will enable them to reconstruct the text coherence. Thus, the question arises as to what type of linguistic, domain and world knowledge authors presume their audience to have for their texts to function as they intend them to. Some of the more specific questions that arise are:

As regards linguistic knowledge,

- What is the proportion of implicit vs. explicit elements used in the reconstruction of coherence? Can the implicit elements be categorized? In which types of category? Could this information be related to the level of language proficiency necessary to receive the text?
- How far from each other (in terms of number of sentences, words) are the elements that are being linked in the construction of coherence? Does this relate to various levels of readability, and how?
- Is there a relation between the type of cohesive links on which the reconstruction of coherence rests and readability levels?

As regards domain knowledge,

- What type of domain knowledge is necessary to reconstruct the text coherence? How accessible is the text to readers with a variety of expertise levels?

As regards world knowledge,

- In the reconstruction of coherence, elements from different sentences are being compared. For example, in a *Washington Post*'s editorial, "A City in Ruins" (8 February 2000), the expressions "Hitler's troops" and "Russian generals" needed to be put into parallel for the complete text coherence. In the editorial's cotext, this meant that the actions of the Russian army in Chechnya were compared with those of Hitler's troops during the Second World War (Le, 2000). In a specific text, which elements of world knowledge that are appealed to by the author need to be associated in order to build coherence? What (new) ideas do these associations bring to mind, i.e., what ideas are reinforced by the reconstruction of coherence in the text?

- Which information is presupposed at the different levels of coherence? Is there a connection between the type and content of presupposed information at each of these levels? Which one(s)?

In general,

- What is the proportion of linguistic vs. domain vs. world knowledge needed to reconstruct the text coherence?
- Can this information be used to define indexes of linguistic readability (i.e., referring to linguistic knowledge), expertise readability (i.e., referring to domain knowledge), and cultural readability (i.e., referring to world knowledge)?

The questions above can be grouped into two large connected categories. One refers to the issue of different types and levels of readability (see Renkema, 2004: Chapter 10). The other concerns the issue of presupposed knowledge contained in a text, its type, extent and content. These questions only illustrate some aspects that could be investigated. *Can you think of other issues to investigate?*

As stated above, discourse studies investigate the relationship between form and function. Among them, examples of analyses that would link cognitive processes and social matters could focus on the issue of presupposed (explicit and implicit) knowledge necessary for the reconstruction of coherence in political discourse. In particular, one could ask if there is a link between the type, extent and content of this presupposed knowledge, a political party's ideology, and the type of audience it tries to capture. In terms of presupposed knowledge, what are the characteristics of specific texts that have been given particular importance? Do "populist" parties and "elitist" parties differ nationally/transnationally in their strategies of textual composition? In other words and more generally, what textual strategies do political parties use in the composition of their political texts?

These studies can be pursued from different perspectives: nationally/transnationally, diachronically/synchronically. *What are the respective advantages/disadvantages of each option?* The type of analysis required by such projects is rather labor-intensive, and a qualitative approach would seem more appropriate at a first stage. *In these conditions, what type of corpus would you work on? How would you justify your choice on the basis of general criteria and of the socio-political phenomenon you are interested in?*

7. Practical relevance

The main practical purpose of studies on political discourse as defined above would be to shed light on textual characteristics that help parties get support among different segments of the population and reinforce their ideology in a covert manner. It is to be noted that the linguistic analysis is not sufficient in itself; it would need to be completed by a detailed study of the socio-political context.

When applied to a variety of texts and not just one category of discourse, this methodology could lead to the definition of indexes of linguistic, expertise and cultural readabilities. This would benefit the description of text types and the teaching of writing for specific purposes. Furthermore, these indexes would also be useful in defining textual levels of "intercultural readability." Readability can be affected by the contribution or lack of visual elements; the study of these elements would therefore need to be taken into account as well.

Conclusion

Presented as a possible solution to some practical difficulties faced by (critical) discourse analysts, this approach that provides a firm ground for other types of analysis is still, one should note, very time-consuming and labor-intensive. However, the model raises a number of interesting questions in varied domains of discourse studies, and its application has provided some valuable insights into formal textual characteristics and the function of media discourse in society.

Acknowledgments

I would like to thank my graduate students, Julia Babicheva, Rachel McGraw, Artëm Medvedev and Ksenia Svechnikova, for their very useful feedback on this chapter.

Assignment

The goal of this assignment is to provide a guided hands-on experience of how the model of coherence analysis works. From the pairs of elements in each sentence chosen for the coherence analysis above in "Research method," and using the three tables below, determine and explain the specific types of coherence relation that were established. Which types of knowledge (linguistic knowledge, domain knowledge, world knowledge) did you use to arrive at your conclusions? Was it explicit or implicit? Would you have reconstructed the coherence of this paragraph in another manner? If yes, does your automatically generated summary correspond to the global meaning you attach to this paragraph?

In the following tables, Hobbs' relations of expansion are indicated by an asterisk (*). P, p, p', a, A, b, B are elements belonging to sentence 1 (S1) or sentence 2 (S2) between which the relation of coherence is established.

Table 1. Relations of coordination

Units of analysis	Relations	Relations
1.	* *Elaboration*	* *Opposition*
S1	p(a)	p(a)
S2	p(a)	non-p(a)
2.	* *Parallelism*	* *Contrast*
S1	p(a)	p(a)
S2	p(b)	non-p(b)
	and $\exists \Sigma / a \subset \Sigma$ and $b \subset \Sigma$	and $\exists \Sigma / a \subset \Sigma$ and $b \subset \Sigma$
3.	*Parallelism*	*Contrast*
S1	p(a)	p(a)
S2	p(B)	non-p(B)
	and p(A) implied	and p(A) implied
	and $a \subset A$	and $a \subset A$
	and $\exists \Sigma / A \subset \Sigma$ and $B \subset \Sigma$	and $\exists \Sigma / A \subset \Sigma$ and $B \subset \Sigma$
4.	*Parallelism*	*Contrast*
S1	p(A)	p(A)
S2	p(b)	non-p(b)
	and p(B) implied	and p(B) implied
	and $b \subset B$	and $b \subset B$
	and $\exists \Sigma / A \subset \Sigma$ and $B \subset \Sigma$	and $\exists \Sigma / A \subset \Sigma$ and $B \subset \Sigma$
5.	*Parallelism*	W/O
S1	p(a)	
S2	p'(b)	
	and $\exists R / p\ R\ a$ and $p'\ R\ b$	
	and $\exists \Sigma' / p \subset \Sigma'$ and $p' \subset \Sigma'$	
	and $\exists \Sigma / a \subset \Sigma$ and $b \subset \Sigma$	

Table 2. Relations of subordination

Units of analysis		Relations	Relations
6.		* *Subordination*	*Contrast*
	S1	p(A)	p(A)
	S2	p(a)	non-p(a)
		and $a \subset A$	and $a \subset A$
7.		*Subordination*	*Contrast*
	S1	P(A)	P(A)
	S2	p(a)	non-p(a)
		and $a \subset A$ and $p \subset P$	and $a \subset A$ and $p \subset P$
8.		*Subordination*	*Contrast*
	S1	p(A)	p(A)
	S2	p'(a)	non-p'(a)
		and $a \subset A$	and $a \subset A$
		and $\exists \Sigma / p \subset \Sigma$ and $p' \subset \Sigma$	and $\exists \Sigma / p \subset \Sigma$ and $p' \subset \Sigma$

Table 3. Relations of superordination

Units of analysis		Relations	Relations
9.		* *Superordination*	*Contrast*
	S1	p(a)	p(a)
	S2	p(A)	non-p(A)
		and $a \subset A$	and $a \subset A$
10.		*Superordination*	*Contrast*
	S1	p(a)	p(a)
	S2	P(A)	non-P(A)
		and $a \subset A$ and $p \subset P$	and $a \subset A$ and $p \subset P$
11.		*Superordination*	*Contrast*
	S1	p(a)	p(a)
	S2	p'(A)	non-p'(A)
		and $a \subset A$	and $a \subset A$
		and $\exists \Sigma / p \subset \Sigma$ and $p' \subset \Sigma$	and $\exists \Sigma / p \subset \Sigma$ and $p' \subset \Sigma$

Explanation of mathematical symbols

$\exists$: "there exists"

$\subset$: "is included in"

Example: $\exists \Sigma / a \subset \Sigma$ and $b \subset \Sigma$ "There exists a set Σ such that 'a' is included in Σ and 'b' is included in Σ"

R : relation

Example: $\exists$ R / p R a "There exists a relation R such that 'p' and 'a' are linked by R"

"non-p(a)" is equivalent to "non p (a)" or "p (non a)"

Chapter 8

Implicit and explicit coherence relations

Maite Taboada
Simon Fraser University

Jan Renkema, in his *Introduction to Discourse Studies*, describes current research in coherence relations (also called rhetorical or discourse relations), and lists a few open questions in that area. One of the most important issues, from both a theoretical and applied point of view, is the signaling of relations, that is, the explicit marking of the presence of a relation. In this chapter, I question the existence of true implicit relations, those where there is no marking that indicates the presence of a relation. I present a number of open questions that can be used as starting points for course assignments and theses in this area.

1. Introduction

One of the fundamental issues in the study of discourse is the phenomenon of coherence. People perceive discourse as being coherent (or incoherent), but often fail to explain the source of that coherence. In discourse studies, coherence is often described as the way in which a discourse is sewn together, with pieces relating to other pieces. Mann and Thompson (1988) defined it as the absence of non-sequiturs, i.e., a coherent text is one where all the parts form the whole: "for every part of a coherent text, there is some function, some plausible reason for its presence, evident to readers, and furthermore, there is no sense that some parts are somehow missing" (Mann & Taboada, 2007). Renkema (2004: 103) indicates that coherence refers to "the connections which can be made by the reader or listener based on knowledge outside the discourse." Those connections are often captured in the form of coherence relations.

The relations I am concerned with here are referred to as coherence relations, discourse relations, or rhetorical relations. They are paratactic (coordinate) or hypotactic (subordinate) relations that hold across two or more text spans. When building a text or any instance of discourse, just as when building a sentence, speakers choose among a set of alternatives that relate two portions of the text. The two parts of the text that have been thus linked can then enter, as a unit, into another relation, making the process recursive throughout the text. Coherence relations have been proposed as an explanation for the construction of coherence in discourse. It is not clear how much speakers and hearers are aware of their presence, but it is uncontroversial that hearers and readers process text incrementally, adding new information to a representation of the ongoing discourse (e.g., Van Dijk & Kintsch, 1983).

There are many classifications and a variety of labels for coherence relations. Renkema (2004) proposes to divide them into additive and causal relations. Additive relations relate two spans of text (clauses, sentences, or larger portions) paratactically, i.e., through a form of coordination. For example, in (1), the relationship between spans 2 and 3 is one of Contrast. Span 1 is provided as additional context.[1]

(1) [1] Billy Bob Thornton is such a versatile actor. [2] He played character-driven supporting roles [3] and now he's lead in a black comedy.
(Epinions)

Causal relations, on the other hand, are hypotactic (or subordinating), relating a main and a subordinate part (sometimes referred to as nucleus and satellite), and express cause, reason, purpose, condition or concession. Example (2) shows a Purpose relation, with span 2 as the satellite, or less important part.

(2) [1] Indeed, Mike Myers recycled his entire CV of SNL characters [2] to create a Cat in the Hat that is unworthy of his name.
(Epinions)

Relations hold at all levels in a text, from the clause up. Typically, the clause is considered the minimal unit of analysis. In (2), the relation is between two clauses; in (1), between two sentences. In that example, there is a further relation between unit 1 and the unit made up of 2 and 3, which we could label as Evidence: Units 2–3 provide evidence for the claim in 1. A graphical representation of Example (1) is shown in Figure 1. Straight lines, such as those joining units 2 and 3, represent nuclei, and an arrow represents a satellite (the origin) attaching to a nucleus (the end point of the arrow). We can see that in this fashion, texts can be built recursively, with smaller units becoming part of larger units.

Throughout this chapter, I will be following Rhetorical Structure Theory, and its assumptions about discourse structure and coherence relations. Space precludes a more extensive discussion of the theory itself. More detail can be found in the original paper on RST (Mann & Thompson, 1988), a recent overview (Taboada & Mann, 2006a, 2006b), the RST website (Mann & Taboada, 2007), or in *Introduction to*

1. For a list of example sources, please see the Appendix.

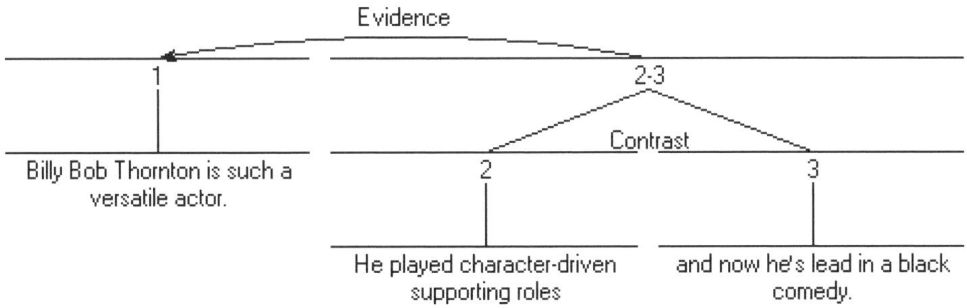

Figure 1. Structure of Example (1)

Discourse Studies (Renkema, 2004, Section 6.4). The types of relations I will be using will be hopefully self-explanatory from their labels (Evidence, Condition, Elaboration, etc.), but full definitions are available on the RST website.

2. The research challenge

One of the issues in the study of coherence relations is how to recognize them, both from the point of view of the analyst, and from the point of view of the hearer or reader. Some relations have cues that help identify them, such as conjunctions (*if, although, but*). These Renkema calls explicit relations (2004, Section 6.5). Many relations, however, do not contain clear indicators, and thus are implicit. The research challenge I present leads to questioning whether there are any true implicit relations.

The literature on coherence relations abounds with studies on signaling via cue phrases, also called discourse markers or discourse particles. For instance, in example (3), an invented example, one could easily interpret a causal relation between (3a) and (3b): The reason why Tom quit was that he was tired of the long hours. This can be made explicit through the marker "because," as in (4). A different marker can, however, indicate that there is no strong causal relation between the two sentences, as in (5). Long hours may have been a factor in Tom's decision to quit, but (5) seems to imply that there was another reason for the decision.

(3) a. Tom quit his job.
   b. He was tired of the long hours.

(4) Tom quit his job because he was tired of the long hours.

(5) Tom quit his job. He was tired of the long hours, anyway.

There are many other signaling mechanisms besides discourse markers: morphological, syntactic, semantic, and pragmatic. Morphologically, tense, for instance, helps mark temporal relations, guiding the reader in the interpretation of progressions or flashbacks in time. One syntactic mechanism is sentence mood (indicative, imperative, interrogative). Another mechanism is embedding, such as the use of a relative clause for Elaboration. Semantically, verb meaning can point to certain relations: *cause*, *trigger*, *provoke*, or *effect* can all indicate a causal relation. Pragmatically, phenomena such as implicature establish relations between propositions that are not explicitly present in the text, but are constructed in the minds of the speakers.

Few studies have considered all possible signals for discourse relations, and thus the perception is that signaling is low. Studies that consider only discourse markers usually show that over 50% of the relations are unsignaled. The analyses on the RST website (Mann & Taboada, 2007), a very diverse collection comprising 187 units, have about 72% of the relations unsignaled (by a discourse marker). In a study of two different corpora, I found that relations were signaled about 31% of the time in conversation, and 44% in newspaper articles (Taboada, 2006), again with reference mostly to discourse markers, although a few other signals are discussed in that paper (mood, finiteness and punctuation).

Many other signaling mechanisms remain understudied. One proposal that I have put forth (Taboada, 2006) is that expectations about how texts (and possibly conversations) proceed provide enough information to interpret higher-level relations. For instance, a reader may recognize the last few sentences of a text as a summary of the whole text because he or she is familiar with the general structure of texts, and knows that a conclusion or summary typically appears at the end.

My proposal here goes a bit further: It may be the case that all relations are indeed signaled, that is, that they are all explicit. The challenge lies in finding what the particular signal is in each case. If people truly interpret different types of relations with relative ease, they must be using signals to guide that interpretation. This leads to two different problems: establishing that relations are cognitively represented in the minds of hearers and readers; and, if indeed relations are cognitively plausible, discovering the cues used to interpret them.

In the rest of this chapter, I review some of the existing literature on relation signaling, and propose some research topics in this area. Section 3 presents examples of the different types of markers or signals for relations, and Section 4 a research method to explore different types of relation signaling, with a more detailed proposal in Section 5. Finally, Sections 6 and 7 present practical applications of the research, and further pedagogical resources.

3. Examples

Examples of signaling via discourse markers are widely discussed in the literature, and a summary of those studies can be found in Taboada and Mann (2006b). I am using the term "discourse marker" in a loose sense, to refer to any conjunction, adverb, adverbial phrase or other type of phrase that frequently links two or more units of discourse. Examples are *if, because, then, plus, on the other hand, in summary* or *it follows that.* Discourse markers and their functions are well-studied, within a coherence relations framework or not. Examples of relations signaled by discourse markers are frequently found in research on coherence relations, and some of the examples discussed here have appeared in print elsewhere (Taboada, 2004, 2006; Taboada & Mann, 2006b).

In example (6) below, in Spanish, the situation in (6b) is presented as a Result of the constraints in (6a): given that the speaker is busy at certain times, the result is that Friday at twelve is the best time to meet. This is marked with *por lo tanto*, "as a consequence" or "so."

(6) a. *Ah yo tengo clases el viernes de las diez a las once y de las dos a las tres,*
b. *por lo tanto si ⟨es⟩ tú me podrías ver a las doce, ese mismo día me parecería muy bien.*
Uh I have classes on Friday from ten to eleven and from two to three, / so if ⟨it's⟩ you could see me at twelve, that same day I would like that.
(ISL Corpus)

The next example, from the RST website (Mann & Taboada, 2007), shows a Condition relation between spans (7b) and (7c), signaled by the prepositional phrase "in the event that."

(7) [Copyright notice]
a. This notice must not be removed from the software,
b. and in the event that the software is divided,
c. it should be attached to every part.
(RST Website)

Lexical items may also be used to indicate a relation, such as the verb cause in a Causal relation, or concede, as in example (8) below, which in this case marks a Concession relation.

(8) [S] Some entrepreneurs say the red tape they most love to hate is red tape they would also hate to lose. [N] They concede that much of the government meddling that torments them is essential to the public good, and even to their own businesses.
(RST Discourse Treebank)

Sentence mood can indicate Solutionhood, as in example (9), where the relation between A's turn and B's entire turn is one of Solutionhood (there are further relations in B's turn), signaled by the interrogative mood in the satellite.

(9) A: *Qué dices. Que tienes entre las [pause] diez y las dos libre?*
B: *Sí. Tengo clase de dos a cinco. Así que entre las diez y las dos, o a la una y media, estoy libre.*

A: What did you say. That you are free between ten and two?
B: Yes. I have a class from two to five. So between ten and two, or at one thirty, I'm free.
(ISL Corpus)

Verb finiteness is sometimes the only indicator of a relation, as shown in example (10), from the LDC (Linguistic Data Consortium) corpus of Wall Street Journal articles (Carlson et al., 2002). The Circumstance relationship between spans 1 and 2–5 is signaled by the non-finite form of the verb insisting.

(10) [1] Insisting that they are protected by the Voting Rights Act, [2] a group of whites brought a federal suit in 1987 [3] to demand that the city abandon at-large voting for the nine-member City Council [4] and create nine electoral districts, [5] including four safe white districts.
(RST Discourse Treebank)

In Example (11), there is an Evaluation relation between segment 1 and 2. The author characterizes the narrator for the novel "The Wedding" as a character removed from the main protagonist, Noah, and therefore making the connection between narrator and protagonist quite indirect. The main indicator of this Evaluation relation is the semantic content of the word "indirect," an adjective conveying subjective content.

(11) [1] The first-person narrator of "The Wedding" is the son-in-law (Wilson) of Noah's daughter Jane. [2] ?????? Talk about indirect.
(Epinions)

In written text, punctuation is also used as a signal of certain relations. In example (12), there are two embedded Elaboration relations. The first one is signaled by a parenthesis, and elaborates on the first part of the news item. The second elaboration is signaled by a dash, and it elaborates on the title of the article quoted.[2]

(12) [N1] QUANTUM CHEMICAL Corp.'s plant in Morris, Ill., is expected to resume production in early 1990. The year was misstated in Friday's editions. [S1] ([N2] See: "Dividend News: Payout Stalled at Quantum Chemical Corp. — [S2] Firm Posts Quarterly Loss, Plans a Stock Dividend to Take Place of Cash — WSJ Oct. 27, 1989).
(RST Discourse Treebank)

2. For a tree representation of this example, see Taboada (2006: 585).

Example (13) provides another instance of embedded relations, in this case Elaborations. In the first relation, the satellite starts with "Recently, the boards…" and continues to the end of the paragraph, which is longer than displayed in the example here. The only possible signal that an Elaboration relation is present is the adverb *also* before the main verb *voted* in this satellite. The second Elaboration relation has that "Recently, the boards…" sentence plus the next sentence as nucleus. The satellite starts with "The transaction…" and continues for a while. This second satellite has no adverb, punctuation mark, or any other device that indicates an elaboration on what has gone before. Knowledge of the newspaper genre leads us to think that an article, unless other cues are present, proceeds in a series of elaborations.

(13) [N1] American Pioneer Inc. said it agreed in principle to sell its American Pioneer Life Insurance Co. Subsidiary to Harcourt Brace Jovanovich Inc.'s HBJ Insurance Cos. for $27 million. American Pioneer, parent of American Pioneer Savings Bank, said the sale will add capital and reduce the level of investments in subsidiaries for the thrift holding company. [S1] [N2] Recently, the boards of both the parent company and the thrift also voted to suspend dividends on preferred shares of both companies and convert all preferred into common shares. The company said the move was necessary to meet capital requirements. [S2] The transaction is subject to execution of a definitive purchase agreement and approval by various regulatory agencies, including the insurance departments of the states of Florida and Indiana, the company said. […] (RST Discourse Treebank)

The next example shows the use of word order in German to signal a Contrast relation. Units 2 and 3 are in a Contrast relation with each other, with the entire 2–3 span being Evidence for the claim presented in 1, that the deployment of the Army resulted in a sort of personal conflict for some members of the German Green party. The two spans that are in contrast, 2 and 3, have subject-verb inversion,[3] which is likely an indication of the contrast, conveyed in the English translation by the conjunction *while*. In addition, there is a "then versus now" contrast in the *nun* — *noch* pair.

(14) *[1] Es ist offensichtlich, dass dieser Bundeswehr-Einsatz bei vielen Grünen an die Wurzeln ihrer Identität rührt. [2] Konnte der Kosovo-Krieg noch mit dem Kampf für die Menschenrechte in Europa begründet werden, [3] geht es nun um die militärische Solidarität mit den USA in einem weit entfernten Dritte-Welt-Land.*

It is obvious that this deployment of the German Army touches, for many Greens, on the roots of their identity. While the Kosovo War could still be

3. Strictly speaking, the choice is only for span 2; span 3 would be ungrammatical with subject-verb word order.

justified by the fight for human rights in Europe, it is now about military solidarity with the U.S. in a far away Third World country.
(Potsdam Commentary Corpus, maz-ernsfall-9725)

4. Research method

The problem that I raise in this chapter can be explored using two different methods: corpus analysis and psycholinguistic experimentation. In this section, I provide general information on how to approach the research using these methodologies.

First of all, Corpus Linguistics is a well-known area of research for which general textbooks exist (e.g., Baker, 2006; Biber et al., 1998; Teubert & Cermakova, 2007). I assume that readers understand the need to carry out quantitative corpus research to find general linguistic trends. I will concentrate here on the particular issues around annotating and studying coherence relations in discourse.

In order to find out how relations are marked, one first needs to find the relations. This involves performing a full analysis of texts and annotating the relations. One can simply take pencil to paper and mark relations as they are found. More sophisticated methods involve the use of computer tools to mark the relations. In particular, within Rhetorical Structure Theory, the RSTTool[4] provides a graphic interface to annotate relations, indicating nucleus and satellite status and providing a label, which can be chosen from the standard RST set, or from a purpose-built one. The next step is to find particular cues for each of the relations. Unfortunately, this cannot be done automatically with RSTTool, and thus other tools are needed. A simple database could do the trick.

Obviously, the task of finding relation signals would be much easier if the relations had been identified for us already. This is precisely what existing corpora provide. The most frequently cited corpus is the RST Discourse Treebank (Carlson et al., 2002), a collection of Wall Street Journal articles annotated according to a version of RST. The corpus contains 385 articles published in the Wall Street Journal, a subset of the large Penn Treebank (Marcus et al., 1999). A portion of the articles was also annotated following a graph structure (Wolf et al., 2005). For German, Stede and colleagues have created a corpus of German newspaper editorials annotated according to RST (Stede, 2004).

Whether one annotates a corpus, or uses an existing one, an important issue is the lack of standards across annotations. Unfortunately, the field has not produced a consensus on what the annotation standard should be. Different researchers use

4. Downloadable from http://www.wagsoft.com/RSTTool. Mick O'Donnell is owed thanks and praise for creating the tool and for making it freely available to the research community.

varying inventories of relations, and even different definitions of minimal discourse units. Rather than accepting this as an unfortunate problem, researchers could take this issue up as a challenge. An important contribution would be the creation of a standard for annotation and the conversion of existing corpora to that new standard. Flexibility can be built into the proposal. For example, relation sets can be more or less detailed, as long as mappings between relation sets are always available (e.g., if a researcher wishes to distinguish Cause and Result relations, that is fine, as long as the new distinction can be easily mapped onto a more general Causal relation).

Reliability of the analysis is of foremost importance in any annotation effort. Even if the annotations are performed by a single person, they should be transparent and easy to reproduce. Better yet, a test comparison with another annotator with similar experience would lend validity to the annotation scheme. Reliability measures are well studied and widely applied, especially within computational linguistics (Carletta, 1996; Di Eugenio & Glass, 2004; Passonneau, 2004). Studies that specifically address reliability of rhetorical structure annotation are Den Ouden et al. (1998), Marcu et al. (1999) and Wolf and Gibson (2005).

Thus far, I have provided general information on how to find or create corpora and make sure that the annotations are reliable. The next task in such a project is the one that leads to its main focus: to find signals for discourse relations. My assumption is that, if an annotator reliably found a connection between two pieces of discourse, there must be something in those pieces that led the annotator to link them. As I mentioned in Section 3, discourse markers are the first line of action, because they tend to be the most obvious signals that a link exists. Syntactic information provides cues in a variety of cases: Reported speech and certain verbs indicate an Attribution relation (Redeker & Egg, 2006); relative clauses indicate Elaboration; interrogative mood signals Solutionhood; and non-finite clauses Circumstance (Taboada & Mann, 2006b). Lexical or cohesive chains may be indicators of an Elaboration relation. Punctuation and layout are also indicators of relations. Finally, genre-related structures probably play a role, in terms of the types of relations that are typically found in a particular text type, such as Preparation and Background in newspaper articles, and also in what relations are most frequent in each part of a text or conversation (Taboada, 2004).

The second method for finding markers for relations involves experimentation. Again, the assumption is that readers are able to recognize relations. If so, they must be using cues in the text. Previous research has shown a positive effect in comprehension when discourse markers are present (e.g., Degand & Sanders, 2002).

In all cases, one should bear in mind that there is probably no one-to-one mapping between a relation and any given marking. It remains to be seen how much ambiguity there is for most relations, and whether it is always resolved, or whether some instances of relations remain underspecified in the mental representation of the hearer or reader.

Beyond the signals already discussed in this section, psycholinguistic experimentation could be explored to discover other signals that we have not yet considered. For instance, if subjects shown two segments, one word at a time, make a connection between segment 1 and segment 2 at a particular point, we could infer something about the signals present up to that point.

Psycholinguistic experiments will also lend validity to findings from corpus studies. Following classical experiments, subjects can be shown the same text, but presented as an example of different genres. If the types of relations subjects find in the texts are different, then we can say that genre is a signal. Another avenue already partly explored is the use of eye-tracking devices to pinpoint the place where readers establish a connection (Mak & Sanders, 2008).

I have presented the research methodology assuming the study of a single language (e.g., English). A cross-linguistic study, albeit more complex, would shed light on different mechanisms to signal a relation. Fabricius-Hansen (2005), for instance, discusses the interesting absence of certain German connectives in English translation. If similar relations can be hypothesized in the English translations, then the relation must be signaled through other means. It would be valuable to undertake a similar study and, in general, other cross-linguistic work, whether on parallel corpora or not.

5. Recent research

Previous reports of relation signaling, including my own work, have given figures of up to 70% of relations without signals. I have already pointed out that most of this research considered only discourse markers. In fact, some lines of research study coherence relations only if they are signaled by a marker. In Section 3, I also discussed work that takes into account other sources of signaling.

Let's start with my own data. For my book (Taboada, 2004), I analyzed 30 conversations in English and 30 in Spanish, annotating them with rhetorical relations. On page 149, I present a table with each relation and the number of times a discourse marker was used to signal it. The summary is that relations were marked 30.86% of the time in English, and 45.88% in Spanish. My very narrow definition of discourse markers (p. 148) includes discourse connectives (*and*, *but*, *or*) and subordinating conjunctions (*because*, *so*, *if*). I excluded some elements that are elsewhere considered discourse markers, such as sentence adverbials (*also*, *on the other hand*). An extension of this work could involve studying those markers.

In Taboada (2006), I extended the types of markers considered, addressing punctuation, finiteness and order of segments. I also suggested that genre and other factors may play a role in the interpretation of relations. Current research aims at extending that study with all other cues mentioned in the previous section: punctuation, layout, syntactic cues, semantic relations, lexical and grammatical cohesion, and genre.

In this chapter, I have mostly focused on relation signaling for written discourse, including punctuation and paragraph breaks. Obviously, spoken language brings new types of signaling into play. Intonation, pauses and gesture are all potential indicators of relations. Cassell et al. (2001) found a correlation between posture changes and the boundaries of topics, with new discourse segments more likely to be accompanied by posture shifts. It is possible that posture also plays a role in signaling particular types of relations, not just a change in topic. Den Ouden (2004) found that pause duration and pitch were strong indicators of the RST structure of read-aloud texts.

6. Research proposal

The following is a proposal for a PhD dissertation that can be, of course, amended, shortened or expanded to accommodate different interests. The proposal combines corpus and psycholinguistic experimentation, but can be modified to emphasize one or the other. Other research topics can also be found on the RST website, under "Research Topics" (Mann & Taboada, 2007).

The first step in the project involves corpus research. This could be an existing corpus that has already been annotated, to which the PhD student can add further signals, or a newly created corpus. The goal is to annotate all the relations found in the corpus first, and then look for signals.

In previous sections I have discussed some of the signals studied in the literature, including lexical cues, syntactic structure, punctuation and layout. However, there is not, to my knowledge, any work that has explored, in one study, all the signals mentioned in the literature. This could be a valuable research initiative.

A slightly different version of the corpus research could involve searching patterns in corpora. For instance, consider the possible continuations to the first (invented) sentence in (15). The relation with one of the following alternatives is one of Sequence, indicated by the adverb *then*. However, the adverb placement is different in each of the three versions. Presumably, in (15c), the hearer or reader needs to wait longer to establish the connection. One possible project involves investigating the frequency of such patterns in large corpora. If one pattern is more frequent, it may be because it correlates with ease of processing.

(15) Sonia came home at five.
  a. Then we went out.
  b. We then went out.
  c. We went out then.

The next step in the project would then be to establish whether the corpus frequencies are replicated in psycholinguistic studies. Do subjects take longer to process (15c) than (15a)? Research along these lines, tying in corpus findings with experimental work, would be a valuable contribution to the field.

Another line of psycholinguistic-based research involves investigating order of acquisition of relations, and types of signaling, both in first and second language learners. It would be interesting to see if relations that are more unambiguously signaled are acquired earlier. There is some research in this area (Degand & Sanders, 2002; Pelsmaekers et al., 1998; Spooren, 1997), but further studies including more types of signaling are necessary.

It is important to point out, before closing this proposal outline, that many issues need to be solved before annotation or analysis can take place. Deciding on the number and type of relations, establishing a reliable annotation process, and even deciding on the representation of the relations (trees vs. graphs, for instance), are all contentious issues in the literature on discourse relations. For an overview, see Taboada and Mann (2006a; 2006b).

7. Practical relevance

Coherence is the basis of all communication, and coherence relations are a very important aspect of the perception of coherence in discourse. Understanding how coherence relations are signaled and processed has applications in many fields.

The corpus study proposed here will contribute to determining what the most frequent signals for coherence relations are. That knowledge can be put to use in writing and communication. Using the most typical signal for a given relation will ensure that there is no ambiguous interpretation of the relation.

One proposal within the clear language movement is to write in short sentences. Renkema (2004: 184) illustrates the trade-off between shorter sentences and signaling with the following example.

(16) a. If given a chance before another fire comes, the tree will heal its own wounds by growing new bark over the burned part.
b. If given a chance before another fire comes, the tree will heal its own wounds. It will grow new bark over the burned part.

The text in (16b) has been distributed into two sentences, conforming to a general guideline to write in short, concise sentences. The problem is that the Means relation that "by" is signaling in (16a) is now implicit and potentially more difficult to identify. The research proposed here could add to manuals on clear writing by emphasizing the need for explicit marking of relations, if that is indeed what both the corpus analysis and the experiments allow us to conclude.

The benefits from research on coherence relations and signaling extend to many other fields that rely on effective communication, from textbook writing to advertising and marketing and document design in general. Clear and unambiguous communication should also be the goal of any organization, including governments. This research could produce guidelines on how to clearly signal the coherence relations writers have in mind. Kamalski (2007), for instance, provides a very interesting study on the effects of coherence marking on the perception and persuasiveness of texts. Her study focused on discourse markers exclusively. Extensions to other types of markers and signals would further our understanding of the effect of signaling on readers' appraisal of texts.

Assignment

A challenge in the annotation of discourse relations involves subjective judgments about how to segment the text, which parts are more important (the nucleus-satellite distinction), and what relation to assign in any particular instance. The following is a text that has been analyzed in a number of ways. Try to annotate it using a standard set of coherence relations, such as the one available from the RST website (Mann & Taboada, 2007). After you have done so, examine the text again for signals of the relations that you have proposed. Take into account all signals, including discourse markers, other lexical, syntactic, semantic and typographic signals.

> Mother Teresa often gives people unexpected advice. When a group of Americans, many in the teaching profession, visited her in Calcutta, they asked her for some advice to take home to their families. "Smile at your wives," she told them. "Smile at your husbands." Thinking that perhaps the counsel was simplistic, coming from an unmarried person, one of them asked, "Are you married?" "Yes," she replied, to their surprise, "and I find it hard sometimes to smile at Jesus. He can be very demanding."
> (Extracted from Reader's Digest, January 1986, p. 117)

Appendix: Sources of examples

Examples marked "Epinions" are from a corpus of on-line reviews of movies, books, music and consumer products. Examples are reproduced verbatim, including any typos and grammatical errors. For more information on the corpus, see Taboada et al. (2006).

Examples marked "RST Discourse Treebank" are from the Linguistic Data Consortium corpus of Wall Street Journal articles annotated with RST relations (Carlson et al., 2002).

Examples with the label "ISL Corpus" are part of the Interactive Systems Laboratories Corpus of appointment scheduling conversations, and are described in Taboada (2004).

Examples labeled "RST Website" are from the Rhetorical Structure Theory site: http://www.sfu.ca/rst (Mann & Taboada, 2007).

The "Potsdam Commentary Corpus" examples are extracted from the corpus collected and annotated by Manfred Stede and colleagues. They are editorials from *Märkische Allgemeine Zeitung*, a German regional daily newspaper (Stede, 2004). Many thanks to Manfred Stede for permission to reproduce the examples.

Part V

Stylistics and Rhetorics

Chapter 9

Style and culture in quantitative discourse analysis

Martin Kaltenbacher
University of Salzburg

In the chapter on Style in *Introduction to Discourse Studies*, Jan Renkema (2004) argues that style can be theorized as "a choice of specific patterns" and that this choice is "partially dependent on the situation." In this chapter, I will argue that the national identity of an author and his membership in a particular cultural group can explain variation in the use of certain stylistic features better than traditional register based approaches. For substantiating such a claim, the qualitative analysis of a few selected texts is insufficient. Alternatively, I will suggest methods for quantitative discourse analysis that allow making claims about cultural style. For this purpose an Austrian and an American corpus of tourist websites will be analyzed for their exploitation of modal verbs of obligation (e.g., *must, have to*). The American tourist websites contain significantly more and stronger forms of obligation than Austrian texts. I will argue that this is a stylistic difference grounded in the authors' cultural backgrounds. Stylistic patterns in texts addressing potential tourists are therefore not dependent on the situation but on the cultural identity of the writer.

1. Introduction

Three fashionable approaches to the analysis of authentic text are Discourse Analysis (DA), Systemic Functional Linguistics (SFL), and Corpus Linguistics (CL). Among these disciplines strong interdisciplinary ties exist between SFL and DA. Many Systemic Functional linguists have published widely in the field of DA and vice versa. This can be seen, for instance, in the large amount of SFL-based contributions to the four-volume collection of essays on Critical Discourse Analysis (CDA), edited by Toolan (2002).

Ties between DA and CL on the one hand, and SFL and CL on the other hand, have so far been a little weaker. This is due to corpus analysis being a purely quantitative approach, looking at large collections of text, while DA and SFL are traditionally qualitative, looking at individual pieces of text of relatively small size. However, this seems to have started to change. In 2006 Thompson and Hunston (2006) published what they claim to be the first collection of papers devoted to exploring connections between SFL and CL, applying the methodology of the latter to the theoretical frame provided by the former. Likewise, recent years have seen a small but rising number of publications devoted to exploring similar connections between the disciplines of (C)DA and CL (for an overview, see Mautner, 2005). This development is not surprising. As Stubbs (1996: 158) points out, discourse embodies a "constellation of repeated meanings" whose "potential is used in regular ways, in large numbers of texts, whose patterns therefore embody particular social values and views of the world." It is particularly through the methods of CL that such "constellations of repeated meanings" can be identified. The benefits of quantitative research are highlighted by Mautner (2005: 815), when she claims that it enables researchers to "put analyses on a sound empirical footing, boost the credibility of both their evidence and the conclusions drawn from it, and thus counteract one of the criticisms perennially leveled at CDA, about the paucity, unrepresentativeness and supposedly agenda-driven selection of its data."

In the following, I will show how all three disciplines can be combined in an attempt to identify elements of cultural style in an international *corpus of tourist websites*. The data were collected in 2002 and 2003 and consist of tourist websites on regions and cities in Austria, Utah and Scotland. They originate from websites maintained by official tourist boards, private tourist companies, hotels and B&Bs (see Table 1). In particular, I will show how claims about stylistic discursive preferences can be established through qualitative discourse analysis and then tested through quantitative corpus analysis. That this is a feasible approach has been shown, e.g., by Kaltenbacher (2006, 2007, see below) and by Coffin and O'Halloran (2005), who undertook a Critical Appraisal Analysis of a newspaper article from the Sun and then checked their findings against the *sunnow* sub-corpus of the *Bank of English*, which led them to some unexpected conclusions.

Table 1. Categories and numbers of tokens in the corpus of tourist websites.

Town	Country/State	Hotels	Total
Salzburg city 146,108	Province of Salzburg 509,854	Austria 212,179	Austria 868,141
Salt Lake City 108,936	Utah 496,917	Utah 217,484	USA 823,337
Edinburgh 146,843	The Scottish Highlands 507,268	Scotland 209,679	Scotland 863,790

2. The research challenge

In *Introduction to Discourse Studies*, Renkema (2004: 145) claims that "the starting point for stylistic research is that the same content can be expressed in different forms." What follows from this, is that there must be other factors than content that determine a writer's choice on how to draft his text. Within traditional register based approaches to discourse these factors have been compiled in the so-called SPEAKING model (Hymes, 1972, discussed in Renkema 2004: 43ff.). This model lists sixteen different components which make up the discourse situation. The components comprise elements such as the *temporal* and *local setting* of a discourse, the *participants* in the discourse and their *relationship* to each other, the *tone* and the *ends* of the discourse, the *mode* in which it is performed, the *genre* in which it is manifested, etc. Useful as this model may be as a starting point for the analysis of a particular discourse, it does lack in comprehensiveness. Renkema (2004: 44), for instance, points out that differences in the participants' knowledge and attitude can likewise influence the discourse. Juliane House (1996: 359) has suggested that discursive differences may "reflect deeper differences in cultural preference and expectation patterns." This gives rise to the question whether the cultural background — and ultimately the national identity — of a writer may have a more decisive influence on the style of a particular text than the factors suggested by traditional register based approaches.

When talking about the influence of culture on style we first need to address the question how culture can be tracked down in a text. Hasan (1996: 192) maintains that "the assertion that specific cultures have specific semiotic styles is neither totally evident nor incontrovertible." She suggests that in order to identify differences in the semiotic styles we need to answer two questions: How do the linguistic systems employed by each culture differ from each other? And which resources are characteristically employed by which section of the speakers? Assuming that people from different countries talk and write differently about the same things, cultural differences would surface in contrastive analyses of texts that share traditional register variables but differ in the cultural background, i.e., the national identity, of the writer. If we analyzed musical show reviews, for instance, and if we found that reviewers of Broadway shows used significantly more superlatives than reviewers of London shows, we could conclude that we found a stylistic difference based on the cultural background of the authors.

However, if we do find stylistic differences in such analyses, how can we know that they are the results of the authors' cultural identity and not just of their idiolects? The answer to this question lies in the quantitative analysis of linguistic patterns. Only the stylistic analysis of large national corpora containing numerous genres and texts written by many different authors — all members of the same culture group — allows us to draw conclusions on whether particular linguistic patterns may be culture related or not.

3. Examples

Juliane House (1996) conducted a number of contrastive discourse analyses (qualitative) in which she identified five stylistic differences in the language of native speakers of German and English. House (1996: 358) attributes these differences to "language specific norms," which reflect the native speakers' cultural norms and preferences. The five differences are listed in Table 2. According to House, native speakers of German tend to follow principles on the left of this table, while native speakers of English follow the principles on the right.

Table 2. Cultural preferences in German and English (House 1996: 347)

German	English
Directness	Indirectness
Orientation towards Self	Orientation towards Other
Orientation towards Content	Orientation towards Addressee
Explicitness	Implicitness
Ad-Hoc Formulation	Verbal Routines

In this chapter, I want to challenge House's claim that native speakers of German are more direct than native speakers of English. In House's analyses it is the abundant use of the imperative in German that is seen as the prototypical instantiation of directness. There are, however, other means of being direct, for example, by using strong forms of obligation as instantiated in the modal verbs *must* or *have to*. Consider the following two examples presented in (1) and (2). Example (1) is taken from the Austrian sub-corpus, (2) comes from the American sub-corpus.

(1) … Every week a new program of activities is set for our guests in the area. Club Card holders are also entitled to reductions or no charge. Where do I get my Club Card? ***You must check in*** at your hotel, pension or bed and breakfast (a list of Club members will be sent on request). ***Then you take*** your check-in slip and a photo to the local tourist office where your card will be issued. The card is valid from …

(2) … Does my snowmobile ***have to*** be registered? ***Snowmobiles*** being operated or transported on public roads, trails, or lands ***must display*** a current snowmobile (OHV) registration sticker. If you are a nonresident visiting Utah, ***you must purchase*** a $30 nonresident snowmobile user permit from an authorized vendor. ***Mount*** them on both sides of the hood or pan. Base decals remain on your snowmobile until …

Both extracts are quite similar in certain respects, which suggests that underlying discursive strategies of this genre are used by Austrian and American writers alike. In both texts a question by an imaginary tourist instigates an answer that exerts some degree of authoritative directness over the reader. The Austrian text in (1) uses one strong form of obligation (*must*) followed by a sentence that directs the reader using a second person present tense (*then you take*). Though this is not technically an imperative, the interpersonal "tone" in this clause comes close to it so that we can argue that it represents the indirect speech act of an order. The American text contains four instances of obligation. The first one is part of the tourist's question and is an invitation for further obligations, which follow immediately. The second is an impersonal obligation (*snowmobiles must display a registration sticker*) and obliges the owners of snowmobiles indirectly. The third is a direct obligation (*you must purchase*) and the fourth is a direct command in form of an imperative. The degree of directness and obligation put on the reader is definitely stronger in the American text.

It would be easy to find numerous texts of this type of discourse in both corpora which contain either many or few of such instances of directness. The question of whether Austrians or Americans exploit these resources more systematically, however, cannot be answered with this type of qualitative analysis. This question can only be solved by looking at larger collections of text, hence by quantitative analysis through methods of corpus linguistics.

4. Research method

If the preliminary assumption underlying this chapter (i.e., differences in style are dependent on the cultural [national] identity of the author) is correct, we should be able to find evidence for this in all genres and registers of written and spoken discourse. One decisive factor for this is that the collection of relevant samples of discourse must be large enough to allow generalizations. There are a number of such collections readily available for analysis. Among the first electronic corpora compiled were the Brown corpus of American English, and the LOB corpus of standard written British English. Each of them consists of 500 texts comprising roughly 2000 words each, written in the same 15 genres, e.g., editorials, reports and reviews. The texts were all published in 1961. A quick search on the phrases *you must* and *you have to* reveals that the American Brown corpus contains 52 instantiations of these two phrases (in a total of 1,000,000 words), while the phrases can be found 74 times in the English LOB corpus. This allows us to formulate a fairly general hypothesis that British writers of the early 60s were more willing to oblige their readers than American writers were. This hypothesis would now need to be tested in detail in order to exclude that American writers used other linguistic means of obliging their readers.

Nowadays, it is fairly easy to compile one's own corpus with the help of the Internet. The *corpus of tourist websites* (see [1] above) was compiled by transforming websites maintained by official tourist boards, private tourist companies, hotels and B&Bs into text-files and feeding them into a database. What is important in such an enterprise is that the individual sub-corpora remain comparable in size and above all in genre and register distribution. Each corpus must contain a sufficient number of texts from different genres and by different authors, "which, when taken together, may be considered to 'average out' and provide a reasonably accurate picture of the entire language population in which we are interested" (McEnery & Wilson, 1996: 22). Once we have built a corpus, we have to identify lexical items for which to search. The selection of items depends on the research questions and the hypotheses to be tested. It often requires a fair amount of creative and strategic planning to identify those words that let you find the passages in a corpus that contain the answers to your research questions. There are three strategies how one can go about selecting such words.

The first strategy is to predict (guess) which words may be used to express the stylistic phenomenon one is interested in and then systematically search for them. When looking for instances of obligation, one can safely predict that *you must* and *you have to* will be phrases that come up in any corpus. More words with a similar meaning can easily be identified by looking up synonyms of *must* in a thesaurus. The Word thesaurus in Microsoft Office lists *have to, have got to, be obliged to, ought to, should* and *be required to* as synonyms. In addition to that we can predict that less direct forms of obligation will occur in phrases like *tourists/guests/visitors + must/have to/are obliged to ...*, where the reader is addressed in the third person as a potential member of an anonymous group of tourists.

A second, more subtle way of identifying suitable search words is by starting off with a qualitative analysis of several individual texts and then searching for each of the instances of obligation found. In the short extract listed in (3) all phrases that exert obligation over the reader have been marked in bold print.

(3) Backpackers **must** obtain a free backcountry use permit from a visitor center (fee charged at Canyonlands National Park). All garbage **must be** carried out or deposited in receptacles provided. Pets **must be** kept on a leash at all times and **are not allowed** on hiking trails, river trips, or in the backcountry. All plants and animals are protected; **it is against the law** to disturb them. Fishing is allowed with a Utah fishing license; hunting **is not allowed**.

The text in (3) contains some interesting phrases. First of all it is notable that there seems to be a difference in directness depending on whether or not *must* is used in the active or passive. Passive constructions like *garbage must be carried out* exert less direct obligation over the reader than *backpackers must obtain a permit*, while second person addresses as in *you must purchase a permit* as in (2) above are clearly the most direct. Noting this, it becomes clear that the cotext surrounding our search words holds vital clues to answering our initial research question. This cotext can be analyzed in respect to the "collocations," the "colligations" and the "semantic associations" that we find in the surroundings of our search words. Collocations are words that frequently occur together. Typical collocations of *must* in our data are *must have, must cancel, must see* or *you must, guests must, hikers must, audience must.* Colligations are the grammatical constructions that words typically occur in. *Must* clearly colligates with infinitives. An interesting question, however, is whether it prefers active infinitives (more direct) or passive infinitives (less direct). Semantic association is a relatively new term introduced by Michael Hoey (2005, 2006). Hoey (2006: 40) defines semantic association as the "semantic set or class" a word typically associates and often collocates with. Typical semantic associations here are *reservations* that *must be made* or *cancelled* or certain *attractions* that visitors *must see.* Furthermore, the passage in (3) contains two phrases that express negative obligation in the form of prohibition (*not allowed* and *against the law*). Therefore, we do not necessarily depend on the presence of a modal verb in order to express obligation. Thus analyzing a number of texts in detail, we can compile a list of relevant phrases, which we can then search for and analyze throughout our corpus.

A third possibility for identifying relevant search words is to refer to established lexical systems of linguistic analysis. In this respect, Systemic Functional Linguistics (SFL) is particularly suitable for corpus analysis, since it describes the lexico-grammar of a language as organized into systems made up by specific structures and words. Obligation in SFL, for example, is modeled as one of four categories within the system

Table 3. Values of modality in systemic functional linguistics (adapted from Halliday 1994: 357f.)

Value	**Modalization — indicative type**			**Modulation — imperative type**		
	Probability		**Usuality**	**Obligation**		**Inclination**
polarity yes		it is			do!	
high	certainly definitely	it must be	always	***required***	*must do* *be obliged* *be required*	determined
median	probably most likely	it will be could can	usually	***supposed***	*will do* *shall* *should* *would*	keen
low	possibly conceivably	it may be might	sometimes occasionally	***allowed***	*may do* *might* *want to* *be allowed*	willing
polarity no		it isn't			don't!	

of Modality. All four categories can be subdivided according to the strength (high, median, low value) of the modality expressed. An overview of modality is presented in Table 3.

5. Recent research

The methodology outlined in the previous section was fully developed in Kaltenbacher (2006, 2007). In Kaltenbacher (2007) the subject of analysis was how to track down exaggerations in websites of tourism. The analysis was based on Appraisal Theory and in particular on the functional system of Graduation as outlined by Martin (2004) and White (1998–2008). One of the search strings analyzed in Kaltenbacher (2007) contained the phrases: *in the whole, world-wide, in the world, of the world, world's, on earth.* Such phrases focus on the area of comparison in which evaluating items such as *best, largest, most famous* occur. They are typical for a particular lexical and grammatical environment which can be classified as follows: Phrases like *in the whole, world-wide …* prefer the semantic association of positive evaluations of size, age, quality, fame, etc. and colligate with superlatives. Therefore they typically collocate with words like *largest, oldest, best, most famous, most spectacular*, etc. American websites exploit these meanings considerably more often than Austrian and Scottish websites. Moreover, there are substantial differences in the types of the phenomena evaluated. The American corpus particularly highlights size through words like *largest, biggest* and *greatest.* Also, the representation of nature and outdoor sports through words like *natural, spectacular* and *magnificent* is salient in the American corpus. The Austrian corpus also evaluates natural phenomena, but in addition to that, it puts a focus on arts and culture through terms like *famous, leading* and *popular*. On the other hand, Austrian exaggerations are more objective, as they are more precise than American ones. It is easier to challenge an exact claim like *Eisriesenwelt Werfen — the world's largest ice cave* than a more subjective statement like *the Wasatch Mountains offer some of the best skiing in the world.*

In Kaltenbacher (2006), the main focus of analysis was on whether House's third claim, i.e., native speakers of German are more focused on content while native speakers of English are more focused on the addressee, can be supported by quantitative corpus analysis. It could be shown that the Austrian websites use affective verbs to a much greater extent than the American or the Scottish texts. In particular the use and the surroundings of the verbs *invite, enjoy* and *love*, which occur twice as often in the Austrian corpus, were investigated. The results — in contrast to House's (1996) findings — reveal a strong orientation of the Austrian writers towards their readers. The more frequent use of verbs of Affect with *you*, as in *if you are really romantically inclined, you will enjoy a horse-drawn sleigh ride*, demonstrates that native speakers of German do indeed focus on the addressee to a great extent. Such examples, however, also give evidence to a great degree of directness. This indicates a contradiction in House's classification: how can discourse be direct without being focused on the addressee? It seems that these two phenomena must naturally go hand in hand with each other.

Both studies (Kaltenbacher 2006, 2007) highlight strategies that meet the very research challenge this chapter is concerned with: how can cultural influences on style be tracked down in quantitative discourse analysis. Resuming the question whether German or English native speakers are more direct, the following section shall demonstrate how a research proposal along these lines can be taken up and explored quantitatively. In line with House's suggestion, the null hypothesis to be tested shall be: Austrian websites contain more instantiations of obligation than American websites and are more direct in addressing the reader with the second person pronoun *you*.

6. Research proposal

In a first attempt to test this hypothesis, the high value modal verbs that can be used to express obligation according to Halliday (1994: 357f.) should be investigated. These verbs should be enhanced by the modals *have/has to* and *have/has got to*, which serve as synonyms to *must*. Table 4 lists their numbers of occurrences in the Austrian and the American corpus of tourist websites.

It must be noted here, that many of these modals can also be used to express epistemic meaning. Leech (2004: 79f.) calls this "logical necessity" ("Modalization" in Halliday's terms). A typical example of this meaning is contained in the sentence *the streets are wet, it must have been raining*. Figures in the tables below may contain some instances of modal verbs used in this sense. This use, however, is quite rare in the tourism corpus. Within the first 50 concordance lines of *must* in the Austrian corpus, no single instance of logical necessity can be found. Instantiations of logical necessity

Table 4. Frequencies of high value modal verbs of obligation in the corpus of tourist websites

High value obligations	AUSTRIA	USA
must	168	403
have to/has to (without ...*offer*)	148	44
Subtotal #	***316***	***447***
have/has got to	2	1
required to	14	21
obliged to	8	–
Total #	**340**	**469**

can therefore be neglected for this corpus. In other corpora, however, instances of epistemic modality may be more frequent.

Table 4 reveals that Austrian high value modals of obligation make up only 72% of the numbers of strong obligations contained in the American corpus. The aggregates of the rarer phrases *have got to*, *required to* and *obliged to* are almost identical (24 occurrences in the Austrian, 22 in the American corpus). The following more detailed analysis in Table 5 will focus on the collocations and colligations for *must* and *have/has to*.

Table 5. Direct and less direct obligation.

Most direct		
you + obligation	**AUSTRIA**	**USA**
you must	8	72
you have to	22	8
subtotal #	***30***	***80***
Less direct		
guest(s)/tourist(s)visitor(s)/hiker(s) biker(s)/child(ren) must	9	28
guest(s)/tourist(s)visitor(s)/hiker(s) biker(s)/child(ren) have/has to	2	–
Subtotal #	***11***	***28***
Total	**41**	**108**

The figures in Table 5 confirm the tendency emerging in Table 4. Direct forms of obligation addressing the reader with second person *you* as well as indirect forms of obligation addressing the reader in third person are more than twice as frequent in the American corpus than in the Austrian texts, though both corpora prefer direct to less direct address. While figures are too small to establish collocates for the Austrian corpus, typical collocations and clusters in the American websites are *you must dial, be, turn, leave, include, use* and *you have to make*. Some examples are listed in (4).

(4) Obligations in the American corpus
In the Salt Lake area, ***you must*** *dial 322–3770 for camping reservations.*
You ***must have 20 or more people*** *to qualify for our group rates.*
To get to Baker Pass and Mount Raymond ***you must turn*** *left.*
Lounges and taverns sell beer only. ***You must be 21 years old*** *or older to enter.*

Table 5 lists the numbers of indirect obligations expressed in passive voice. In the Austrian corpus, clusters for *must/have/has to be* are *reservations must be made* (5 occurrences), certain forms *must be filled in/out* (4), certain fees *must/have to be paid* (6), and *reservations must/have to be guaranteed by credit card* (6). The passive clusters in

Table 6. Indirect obligations in passive voice

passive voice		
	AUSTRIA	USA
must be + past participle	56	130
have/has to be + past participle	39	1
total #	**95**	**131**

the American corpus include *cancellations must be made* (29 times), *guests under* xyz *inches in height must be accompanied by a responsible person* (24), *reservations must be made/confirmed/cancelled* (11), and the *audience must be seated by 9.15 a.m.* (9). One obvious qualitative difference here is that the American corpus contains passive clauses which have potential tourists (readers) as patient subjects, while the Austrian corpus does not.

Two striking differences can be observed in the results in Tables 4, 5 and 6. The first noticeable difference is the clear tendency of the American websites to contain more modals of obligation in all forms of address. This is illustrated in Figure 1. But while the general use of obligations in the American websites exceeds the Austrian numbers by only 38%, the American rate of the most direct form of obligation addressing the reader with *you* makes up 267% of the corresponding Austrian number. The number of less direct obligations where the reader is addressed indirectly with *guest*, *visitor*, etc. is 255% higher in the American corpus. As for the least direct forms of address where an obligation is expressed in passive voice the rate is down again to 138%.

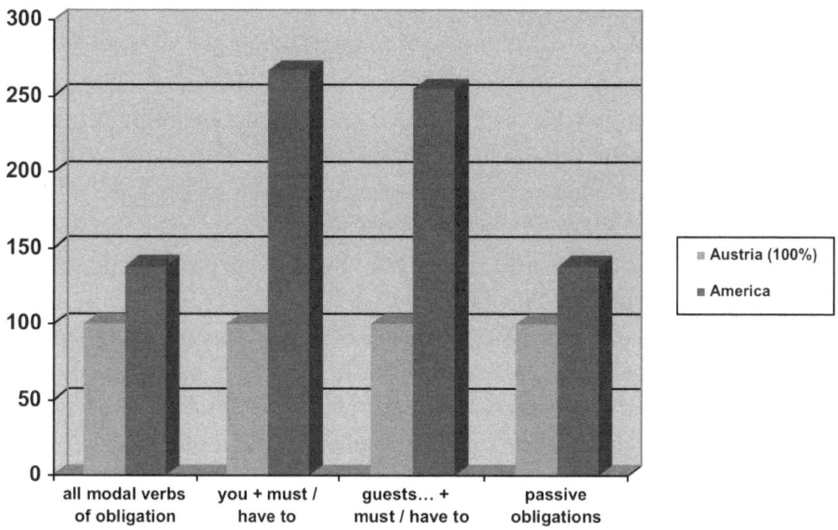

Figure 1. Cultural differences in directness of obligations in %.

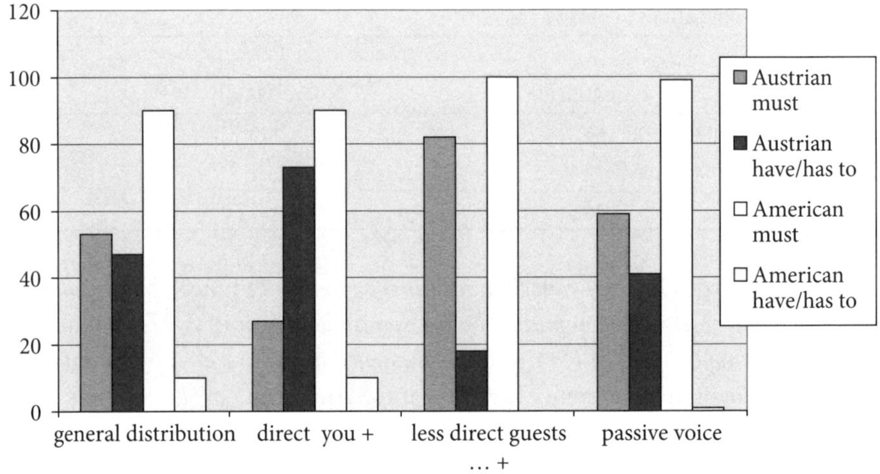

Figure 2. Distribution of *must* (speaker's authority) versus *have/has to* (external authority) in %

The second difference relates to the fact that the American corpus reveals a clear preference for the modal *must* (roughly 90%), while the distribution of *must* and *have/has to* in the Austrian corpus is 53% to 47% (see Figure 2). According to Leech (2004: 78ff.) there is an important difference in meaning between the two. Leech claims that the "usual implication of *must* is that the speaker is the person who exerts authority over the person(s) mentioned in the clause." In contrast to this, in a clause containing *have/has to* "the authority or influence of the speaker is not involved," but the obligation is derived from institutionalized authorities or through "the power of 'circumstances.'" Leech's claim gives further support to the general picture emerging. In the most direct form of address (*you*) 70% of the Austrian obligations are formed with *have/has to*, which means that the authors do not position themselves as the source of the obligation. In the American corpus 90% of the entries contain the stronger form *must* thus emphasizing the authors' authority. In the less direct passive constructions, the American authors emphasize their authority at an even higher rate (99%), while the Austrian writers use *must* in only 60% of these obligations.

Summarizing, we can conclude that in the Austrian corpus modal verbs of obligation have a clear tendency to colligate with passive clauses where administrative duties like making reservations, filling in forms, or paying fees are topicalized. When the reader is directly addressed, *you* collocates with *have to* in order to avoid the impression that the authority emanates from the speaker. The American corpus shows a preference for exercising speaker's authority through the modal verb *must*, which colligates with human subjects considerably more often. Whenever the readers are thus addressed, there is a clear preference for direct address with the second person pronoun *you*. In general, the way modal verbs of obligation are exploited in the two corpora shows that the American authors of tourist web-sites are far more direct in all respects than the Austrian authors. The hypothesis that Austrian websites are more direct in their use of obligation than American websites must be refuted.

But what about House's other claims about differences in the discourse of native speakers of German and English (orientation towards self/other, orientation towards content/addressee, explicitness/implicitness, ad-hoc formulations/verbal routines)? All these discursive preferences reflect nuances of style as manifestations of culture. All of them seem problematic, as they are derived from qualitative discourse analysis alone and lack any quantitative validation. Such validation could be provided fairly easily by research along the lines suggested in this chapter. It is important that such research is based on comparable samples of language collected in corpora of reasonable size. Systematic descriptions of meaningful lexico-grammatical resources as given by SFL can be useful in providing the theoretical framework that guides this kind of research.

7. Practical relevance

The results portrayed in the previous section show that Austrian and American websites reveal considerable stylistic differences in the use of modal verbs of obligation. House's (1996) hypothesis that native speakers of German differ from native speakers of English in five discursive (and stylistic) dimensions cannot be maintained in its original form. An immediate objection to her claim is, of course, that the distinction of discursive preferences into an all-English and an all-German style is far too broad. Naturally, there must be substantial cultural and stylistic differences between texts written by American, Australian, British, Indian, Irish, South African, etc. authors as well as among Austrian, German, Swiss, Transylvanian German, etc., writers. In fact, an analysis of obligation in the Scottish sub-corpus of tourist websites reveals different results again, of which some aspects are similar to the Austrian findings while others resemble the American results.

The type of research described above needs to be carried on and extended onto other linguistic systems across cultures. This can easily be done by building comparable corpora from texts available on the www. Stubbs (2006: 28) demands a "move from description to explanation, in particular an explanation of how cultural norms are reproduced by frequent phrasal units." The methodology outlined above offers a first step to meeting this demand. From a Systemic Functional perspective such research could include, for instance, detailed analyses of instantiations of *judgment* (the evaluation of human behavior), of the use of superlatives or other forms of *graduation*, of the distribution of process types (verb types), etc. Differences in process types in English and German travel guides have, e.g., been analyzed by Neumann (2003), who found that German travel guides contain significantly more material processes while English travel guides contain significantly more relational processes. Likewise, topics from more traditional or critical discourse perspectives can and should be investigated, such as the distribution of different types of speech acts, gender issues, representations of self- and otherness, etc. An interesting question which deserves more detailed discussion than is possible here is whether cultural styles can be described in such detail that it becomes possible to determine the cultural and national identity of authors by looking at the characteristics of their texts. If such an undertaking is feasible at all, it will only be so thanks to the probabilistic grammars made available through recent methods of corpus linguistics.

The significance of different cultural (and national) styles has already been recognized by international companies, though primarily with a focus on visual design. The official Austrian tourist board website (www.austria.info) offers 41 different national entry-pages to be selected according to the reader's country of origin. Members of the English language community, for example, can select between the following cultural versions: Australia, Canada, India, Singapore, UK & Ireland, USA, and one version for all the other countries that use English as a lingua franca. The individual entry pages differ according to the layout, the selection of visuals and the selection of topics and various menus and submenus. The texts do not differ, i.e., a text on skiing or on going to the opera is identical across the various versions, but it may be located higher up on the web-structure of one version than another.

It may well be that the recognition of different cultural styles may sooner or later lead to the integration of different versions of the verbal text according to the stylistic preferences of the target group. Should this come true, the writing of stylistically fine-tuned texts will first and foremost depend on such findings as have been described in this chapter.

Assignment

In this chapter, we have looked at positive manifestations of obligation through modal verbs. In contrast to these, there are also negative obligations which can be equated to lack of permission or prohibition. The most obvious instantiations of these are *may not, must not* and *not allowed*. There are, however, also other lexical means of expressing prohibitions. Compose a battery of words or phrases that can be used to express prohibition. What are your expectations for the frequencies of prohibitions in Austrian and American websites of tourism? In which contexts (semantic associations, collocations) do you think they will occur? Access one or two tourist board websites on the Internet and scan some of the texts to see whether your predictions are correct. Some tourist board websites, e.g., www.austria.info or www.utah.com, offer search tools that may facilitate your search.

Chapter 10

Devices of probability and obligation in text types

Xinzhang Yang
Xiamen University

Meanings of probability and obligation fall within the system of modality. According to Systemic Linguistics, the basic distinction that determines each type of modality is realized in the distinction between subjective and objective modality and between the explicit and implicit variants, as well as the value attached to the modal judgment. Every style has its own stylistic features. One of the tasks of discourse studies is to find out these features. The corpus-based approach can be an ideal method for investigating variations across registers. Based on the assumption that different registers differ in the use of devices of probability and obligation, a corpus-based study is conducted in this chapter to show that the distribution of modal verbs is different in academic writing and legal documents. The findings indicate that the nature of text types determines their use to form part of the stylistic characteristics. Similar work is also proposed in the hope that we can learn more about the patterns of discourse and that the research could be of practical value in language teaching and translation practice.

1. Introduction

Discourse is real language in use. Woods (2006) characterizes discourse as language plus context. Discourse analysts address a wide range of discourse phenomena, from the study of particular patterns of pronunciation, word choice, sentence structure and semantic representation, through the analysis of the structure of speech encounters, to the critical study of language-in-society.

Systemic Linguistics looks at language in a social semiotic perspective. According to Halliday, the way into the understanding of language lies in the study of texts. In this light, an instance of living language that is playing some part in the context of situation is called a text. The text is regarded as a semantic unit and thus an instance of meaning in a particular context. It is closely related to the social environment and the functional organizations of language. The context of a situation is interpreted by using the terms of *field*, *tenor* and *mode*. However, there is a correlation between the categories of the situation and those of the semantic system. The field is reflected in the ideational meanings, the tenor in the interpersonal meanings, and the mode in the textual meanings.

Halliday (1978) hypothesizes that there are three metafunctions of language: the *ideational* function, the *interpersonal* function and the *textual* function. Language is used to represent the speaker's experience of the real world, to enact social relations with the addressee, and to relate text to context. Each metafunction is realized by different aspects of the lexicogrammar. Ideational meaning is realized typically in the clause by transitivity, interpersonal meaning by mood and modality, and textual meaning by theme-rheme structure. Every clause is multifunctional in a text. The three strands of lexicogrammatical realization are interwoven in the wording of the clause. The clause simultaneously realizes these three types of meanings.

In daily life, it is very difficult for us to speak or write down something very objectively when communicating. Every utterance always contains the opinion, attitude or judgment of the speaker/writer. Modality is the area of meaning that falls in between yes and no, the intermediate degrees between the positive and negative polarity (Halliday, 1994: 356), like *sometimes* or *maybe*. Probability and obligation are part of the system of modality. Probability refers to the degree of likelihood of a proposition, while obligation refers to the degree of obligation in a proposal. In language, there are many devices for the expression of probability and obligation. Probability in English can be expressed by a modal verb, by a modal adjunct or by both together. They occur in the "information" clause. Obligation in English can be expressed by a modal verb or by an expansion of the Predicator. They occur in the "goods-&-service" clause. For example:

(1) That will be John. (probability, modal verb)

(2) That's probably John. (probability, modal adjunct)

(3) You should leave the building now. (obligation, modal verb)

(4) You are supposed to leave the building now. (obligation, expansion of the Predicator)

The modal verb is an important device to express meanings of modality. Biber et al. (1999: 73) divide English modal verbs into three types. There are nine central modal verbs, i.e., *can, could, may, might, must, shall, should, will, would*. In addition, there are marginal modal verbs like *dare (to), need (to), ought to, used to*. The third type consists of the semi-modals, which include *have to, (had) better, (have) got to, be supposed to*, and *be going to*.

2. The research challenge

Discourse analysts examine spoken, signed and written language and focus on any aspect of linguistic behavior. Renkema (2004: 1) defines discourse studies as "the discipline devoted to the investigation of the relationship between form and function in verbal communication."

One of the topics that concerns discourse studies is style. Style refers to the different ways to say the same thing. According to Renkema (2004), the concept of style is mainly studied with a focus on appropriateness that is mainly related to the situational context. From a stylistic viewpoint, there is no free variation in formulation. Each formulation has its own "stylistic" meaning.

In chapter 8 of *Introduction to Discourse Studies*, Renkema divides the numerous views on style into three categories. Scholars regard style as a possible form for a specific content, as a choice of specific patterns, or as a deviation from expectations. In speaking or writing, the speaker/writer has a number of different possibilities in phrasing what he would like to say. The style-as-choice approach is suitable for determining how the situation limits choice. On the other hand, judgment of good style is always very vague. We can judge someone's writing as "lucid," "blunt" or "objective," but it is unclear how these features are realized in wording. We can give students suggestions like "write naturally," and "write nouns and verbs," but we do not know how. Although there are suggestions for good style, Renkema lists several problems for a discourse studies perspective. The first problem is how these suggestions can be implemented in producing discourse and the second is what kind of stylistic devices a writer must avoid or use.

To solve these problems, the concept of *register* is a good help. A register is a concept of the kind of variation that goes with variation in the context of situation. The existence of registers is a fact of everyday experience. Every profession has its own way of speaking and writing: its own particular styles of language and its own convention for the construction of discourse (Woods, 2006). That is to say, it has its register.

As mentioned by Renkema (2004), the terms style and register can be used interchangeably in many studies. The term register is preferred when the formulation and the relation between language use and situation is discussed. Halliday (1978) uses the theory of register as a tool to understand what situational factors determine what linguistic features. Register is a configuration of meanings that are typically associated with a particular situational configuration of field, tenor and mode. It includes the expressions that have the function of indicating to the participants that this is the register in question. The choices that the speaker/writer makes under particular environmental conditions are realized in the form of grammar and vocabulary.

It should be noted that each register has its own registerial features. In addition, the speaker/writer always expresses his opinion, attitude or judgment in one way or another when he speaks or writes. Since devices of probability and obligation are the linguistic realizations of modality, we may ask whether the devices of probability and obligation are used in the same way across different registers. Modal verbs can be used to express the speaker/writer's opinion of and attitude towards a proposition or proposal. They can serve as devices of probability and obligation. This systemic description of modal verbs presents to us a general picture of the nature and function of English modal verbs, and reveals the general trend of their use in communication.

3. Examples

In order to distinguish modal devices of different kinds, Halliday (1994: 357–359) takes *orientation* as the basic distinction that determines how each type of modality is realized. He subdivides modality into four types based on the distinction between subjective and objective modality, and between the explicit and implicit variants, which can be seen in Table 1:

Table 1. Four types of modality

	Subjective	Objective
Implicit	Must	Certainly
Explicit	I'm certain that …	It is certain that …

Furthermore, three values can be attached to the modal judgement: high, median or low. See Table 2 below:

Table 2. Three values of modal judgment

	Probability	Obligation
High	certain	required
Medium	probable	supposed
Low	possible	allowed

(5) I'm certain Mary's left. (high value probability, subjective, explicit)

(6) Mary must have left. (high value probability, subjective, implicit)

In some cases, two or more devices may be used in a clause complex. For example,

(7) Surely it is required that money shouldn't go on being invested.

In (7), "surely" carries a high value objective probability and "is required" a high value objective obligation.

Modal verbs are subjective implicit devices of modality of probability and obligation with high, median and low values. Based on Halliday's (1994: 362) classification, *must*, *ought to*, *need* and *have to* are modal verbs of high value, *will*, *would*, *shall*, and *should* are modal verbs of median value, and *may*, *might*, *can*, and *could* of low value.

However, modal verbs, modal adjuncts and expansion of the Predicator are not the only devices of probability and obligation. Halliday uses the notion of "metaphor of modality" to refer to other phenomena. According to Halliday and Matthiessen (2004: 613–626), modality is an adjunct to a proposition rather than a proposition in its congruent form. The speaker's opinion of probability can also be coded as a separate, projecting clause. In the metaphorical variant, modality and proposition or proposal are realized by two clauses. The clause can serve not only as the projecting part of a clause nexus of projection, but also as a mood adjunct.

(8) I think Mary knows.

Here, the clause "I think" becomes the metaphorical variant of probability. It is not a projecting clause, but is regarded as a modal adjunct.

From these examples, we can see that different modal verbs can carry different modal values. They can serve as the starting point for us to investigate how their use is distributed across different registers in helping the writer/speaker to express his opinion, attitude or judgment.

4. Research method

Discourse studies often focus on language characteristics that extend across clause boundaries. When we examine whether the devices of probability and obligation are used in the same way across different registers, the corpus-based approach would be an ideal research method.

Systemic Linguistics is a theory of language. Language is viewed as meaning potential represented as a set of system networks. Any instance of language use is the outcome of choices from these networks. The actual frequency of occurrence in instances is taken as a realization of the potential options in the system.

The corpus-based approach is a methodology that can be aligned to any theoretical approach to language. As noted by Thompson and Hunston (2006), Systemic Linguistics is becoming concerned with methods of quantifying linguistic features, and Corpus Linguistics is intent on developing theories to account for its findings. Here, we find a natural synergy between Systemic Linguistics and Corpus Linguistics. The emergence of the corpus provides an analytical tool for the investigation of the occurrence of lexical and grammatical features. It is useful for studying how the speaker/writer uses the linguistic resources available to him. This approach exploits the information about language use in a large collection of naturally occurring texts from various registers and the descriptions that result from quantitative and qualitative research. The corpus-based approach can be used to address questions about register variation. We can begin by comparing the distribution of certain lexical and grammatical features across registers and then turn to more comprehensive register features. The way we use devices of probability and obligation to express our attitudes and judgments may differ from register to register. However, when it comes to the questions of how they differ in the use of these devices, we need to turn to corpus analysis.

As shown in the previous sections, registers are defined according to their situations of use. Mastery of a range of registers is very important for any competent speaker of a language. In real verbal communication, people choose from a range of options and select discourse forms appropriate in the particular context. We all speak and write a wide range of registers everyday. Depending on context, we switch among registers. The language that we use to write a research article is different from the language we use when talking to a friend.

Describing the characteristics of registers is an important area of study. With the help of the corpus, we can find that a certain register is characterized by the use of certain lexical or grammatical elements, and understand how the speaker/writer makes use of the resources of language and how words and structures occur in different contexts and serve different functions.

The corpus-based analysis is empirical. Biber et al. (1998) summarize four characteristics of the corpus-based analysis. First, it analyzes the actual pattern of use in natural texts. Second, it utilizes a large and principled collection of natural texts as the basis of analysis. Third, it makes extensive use of computers for analysis. Fourth, it depends on both quantitative and qualitative analytical techniques. However, the goal of corpus-based research is not simply to report quantitative findings, but to include qualitative, functional interpretations of quantitative patterns. A crucial part of the corpus-based approach is going beyond the quantitative patterns to propose functional interpretations explaining why he patterns exist. Corpus-based analysis is also complementary. Many research questions for corpus-based studies often grow out of other approaches. They are related to prior structural analyses, and theoretical frameworks.

There have been some corpus-based studies of the English devices of probability and obligation, especially modal verbs. Leech (2003) uses the LOB, Brown, F-LOB and Frown corpora, and finds that the English modal auxiliaries have declined in the frequency of use between 1961 and 1992. Semi-modals are gradually taking the place of the true modals. In spoken English, the decrease in the use of modals is more remarkable, and there is a sharp increase in the use of semi-modals. Smith (2003) uses LOB and FLOB to examine the use of semi-modals and modals in recent British

English. Smith finds that *have to* and *(have) got to* have risen in use significantly, while *must* has declined across all written genres. *Have to* is most used in the fiction and press genres and the rise of *need to* is well spread across the written British English corpora.

Based on corpus-based surveys, Gotti (2003) analyzes the recent uses of modal auxiliaries *shall* and *will*. *Shall* is relatively rare but appears more frequently in conversation and fiction. It can be used to express futurity, volition, and necessity. *Will* is the most frequent modal auxiliary, and appears in all registers, especially in conversation and news reportage. The functions of *will* are to make an inference, and to express volition, necessity, futurity, habit, and possibility. Gotti compares the recent use of these modal verbs with data of Middle English and Early Modern English, and indicates that *shall* has become less prominent and is mainly used to express prediction in spoken texts, and to convey obligation in written ones. *Will* has become more and more frequent, especially in its use to express futurity.

By using the International Corpus of English, Facchinetti (2003) focuses on the use of the modal *may* in current British English, and highlights the sociological and pragmatic factors that influence its distributions across different registers. It is shown that the most frequent uses of *may* are epistemic modality and existential modality. In spoken English, the analysis indicates that familiarity and confidence limit the need for *may*. For printed texts, *may* is most frequently used in Instructional Writing. Facchinetti also studies the relationship between the distribution of *may* and the sociolinguistic aspects of gender, age, and level of education. It is reported that people with university education tend to use *may* more often than those with secondary education.

However, when we are looking for linguistic patterns, conclusions cannot rely on intuitions or anecdotal evidence. As Biber et al. (1998) point out, it is a complex process because many different grammatical and lexical choices come into play. It can be very difficult to find patterns of use and analyze the contextual factors. We need to analyze a large amount of language collected from many sources, but it is time-consuming to carry out the analyses. In this event, the corpus-based approach provides a means of handling a large amount of language and keeping track of many contextual factors at the same time.

5. Recent research

I (Yang, 2006) carried out a corpus-based study to explore the distribution and semantic features of central modal verbs in English legal texts and academic texts. I established a corpus of legal texts of 236,378 words and a corpus of academic texts of 182,902 words. The search results of the nine central modals are shown in Table 3.

Table 3. Search results of nine central modals

Modals	Academic texts		Legal texts	
	occurrence	percentage	occurrence	percentage
May	273	12.11	1034	39.46
Might	125	5.55	8	0.31
Will	454	20.14	110	4.20
Would	347	15.39	182	6.95
Must	219	9.72	266	10.15
Shall	59	2.62	915	34.92
Should	217	9.63	38	1.45
Can	381	16.90	59	2.25
Could	179	7.94	8	0.31
Total	**2254**	**100**	**2620**	**100**

We can see that the prominent feature of legal texts is the use of *may* and *shall*. They make up 39.46% and 34.92% of all the central modals respectively. The occurrence rate of *might* and *could* is the lowest. In academic texts, the occurrence rate of *will* is the highest, constituting 20.14% of all the central modals. It is obvious that our attention should focus on the use of *may* and *shall* in the legal text on the one hand, and *will* in the academic text on the other hand.

The legal text is to prescribe legal obligation and duties in an authoritative tone. The concordance line shows that 79.67% of the modal verb *shall* can express the meanings of obligation and permission. When used with a negative element, *shall* express a strong degree of prohibition. 20.33% of *shall* in the legal corpus is used this way. When used in the legal text with the modal meanings of obligation and permission, *shall* is a high value modal verb. The modal verb *may* expresses permission and possibility and explains the rights authorized by the law. It is a low value modal verb. In the legal document, *may* expresses prohibition when used with a negative element, but its modal value is lower than that of *shall*. In the academic text, the writer/speaker expresses his academic views and exchanges his research results. He uses *will* to indicate his personal willingness and predication of future events. Besides, the speaker/writer always needs to illustrate his personal opinion and judgment, and to avoid giving the impression of imposition. Thus, low value modal verbs *can*, *would* and *may* are used.

Shall is a low value modal verb in academic texts but a high value one in legal documents. *May* expresses probability in academic texts, but carries the modal meanings of permission and prohibition in legal documents. *Shall* and *may* have the highest occurrence rate in the legal text, while *will*, *can*, *would* and *may* occur more often in the academic text.

6. Research proposal

In the previous section, we have seen that the use of central modal verbs in different registers represents the choices made by the speaker/writer, and is constrained by the context of situation. Thus, the use of modal verbs can constitute one of the prominent features of the registers of academic texts and legal documents. Alternatively, they can be said to be one of the stylistic features of texts.

As a technical term in Systemic Linguistics, register is often used to refer to discourse occurring in a particular context. Comparisons between registers may take broad groupings, such as texts in newspapers, or texts in academic contexts. Alternatively, we can compare research papers in contrasting academic disciplines or the different parts of research papers in a single discipline. In addition to analyzing the language use patterns for a linguistic structure, studies of language use can focus on the language of a text or a group of speakers/writers.

An adjunct is typically realized by an adverbial group or a prepositional phrase. Modal adjuncts are interpersonal in metafunction and are classified under the two sub-headings of mood adjunct and comment adjunct (Halliday & Matthiessen, 2004). When speaking or writing, we tend to comment on a fact or entity and express their opinions. We can use the explicit way of expressing our opinions directly, e.g.,

(9) I tell you frankly that Kris didn't want to know.

(10) I presume that Alison has bought a new car.

Yet, we can also choose to use the implicit way of expressing our opinion. We can choose to avoid mentioning the speaker, e.g.,

(11) Frankly, Kris didn't want to know.

(12) Presumably, Alison has bought a new car.

Comment adjuncts are an important lexicogrammatical resource for the speaker/writer to convey his/her attitude towards part or the whole of a proposition. The academic text is the place where the writer expresses his/her points of view. It plays an important part in social progress and administration. Thus, we can work out a research proposal to analyze comment adjuncts in English academic texts and primary school textbook texts, by using the corpus-based approach. The purposes of this research are to explore the use and functions of comment adjuncts in these two registers and to illustrate the close relations of comment adjuncts to academic texts.

To conduct this kind of research, we can, first of all, give an overview of the previous studies on this topic. Knowing what other scholars have done can help the reader identify the place of the present research in relation to other studies. Biber et al. (1999: 130–132, 874–875) use the term *stance adverbial* to refer to those adverbials that typically express the attitude of the speaker/writer towards the form or content of the message. According to their discourse functions, stance adverbials are multifunctional in discourse. They can convey epistemic meanings, attitudinal meanings, style meanings, and so on. In Quirk et al. (1985: 615), the concept of *disjunct* is similar to comment adjuncts. Disjunct is subdivided into style disjunct and content disjunct. The former conveys the speaker's comment on the style and form of what he is saying. It involves the speaker's comment on modality and manner (e.g., *truthfully*, *if I may say so*), and respect (e.g., *personally*, *in broad terms*). The latter, also known as *attitudinal disjunct*, makes observations on the actual content of the utterance and its truth conditions. It involves degree of or conditions for truth of content (e.g., *really*, *certainly*) and value judgment of content (e.g., *understandably*, *wisely*). To Quirk et al., disjunct can be realized by adverbs, prepositional phrases, adjectival groups and clauses.

Semantically, the speaker can choose to use the adjunct to make comments. Explicit disjunct can be a process adjunct. Thus, the explicit disjunct of "frankly" in "Frankly, I am tired" is "I tell you frankly." In questions, the disjunct *can* have several meanings. For instance, the explicit disjunct of "frankly" in "Frankly, is he tired?" may be "I ask you frankly." It can also be "Tell me frankly." In formal style, comments can be realized by subordinate clauses, such as "*If I may say so without offence*, your writing is immature."

In Systemic Linguistics, comment adjuncts are a type of modal adjunct. In Halliday's (1994: 83) view, comment adjuncts express the speaker's attitude to the proposition as a whole. They can construe the modal meanings of opinion, admission, persuasion, entreaty, presumption, desirability, reservation, validation, evaluation and prediction (Halliday, 1994: 49). Halliday and Matthiessen (2004: 129–131) extend the scope of comment adjuncts and classify them into two types: comment on the proposition or on the subject and comment on the particular speech function. The propositional type occurs only with declarative clauses and the speech functional type occurs with either declarative or interrogative clauses. Comment adjuncts are usually realized by adverbs or propositional phrases. They can occur at the beginning of the clause as a separate information unit or in the final position as afterthought. They can also occur medially after the item that is prominent.

Propositional comment adjuncts that involve the proposition as a whole are claims and signals of naturalness, obviousness, sureness, prediction, presumption and desirability. Those that involve the subject construe the meanings of wisdom and morality. The speech functional type carries the meanings of assurance, concession, factualness, validity, honesty, secrecy, individuality, accuracy and hesitancy.

Thus, we can see that the disjuncts in Quirk et al. and stance adverbials in Biber et al. include words, groups and phrases and even clauses, and are similar to mood adjuncts and comment adjuncts in Halliday (1994). Yet, Halliday's classification is specific and delicate semantically. We may want to use the systemic classification of comment adjuncts to examine their distribution in the two registers.

To characterize registers more thoroughly, we can bring the concept of register and use the corpus to study the ways in which comment adjuncts are distributed in the two registers. So, what we have to do next is to use existing corpora or establish new corpora of our own to search the features of patterns. Based on the actual distributions of linguistic features in a large corpus of texts, we can identify the occurrence patterns, and then compare the results. The concordance line will show that different types of comment adjuncts have different distributions. Some features are more prominent and others are less prominent. One of my recent studies shows that academic texts uses comment adjuncts of factualness, naturalness, validity and obviousness frequently (Yang, 2007).

Following this, we can explain and interpret why some comment adjuncts occur more frequently than others. Then we can come to a conclusion. We may want to point out that the prominent features of certain comment adjuncts constitute an aspect of the characteristics of the register under study. Understanding these characteristics is useful for such practical fields such as language teaching and translation.

7. Practical relevance

The study of modal devices is of great practical relevance to language education and translation. As an approach in linguistics, corpus-based analysis provides a new perspective on language use. The findings of corpus-based studies show that there are strong, systematic patterns in the way language is used. Of course, it is very difficult to measure style. As mentioned by Renkema (2004), an analysis based on these quantitative elements cannot produce a full-fledged description of the style. Quantitative analyses are not sufficient in themselves.

Thus, qualitative interpretations are necessary to examine the functional bases of underlying patterns of linguistic features. It has been shown that linguistic features from all levels have patterned differences across registers. As mentioned above, our research results will show the different distributions of different comment adjuncts in English academic texts and primary school textbook texts. We can find some prominent features.

Corpus-based research is not only useful for our academic understanding of language function and use. Through the corpus-based analysis, we can document such patterns, providing the information needed for more information and helpful language instruction and material development.

In language education, textbooks play an important part in enhancing learners' awareness of register. The findings of corpus-based studies could help improve textbooks in two ways. First of all, books could emphasize those linguistic features most commonly found in the target register. Textbooks can teach the type of comment adjuncts that students are most likely to encounter, given their communicative goals. Second, students can be given explanations of when to use different comment adjuncts. In writing and composition teaching, knowledge of the use of comment adjuncts can facilitate the process of register acquisition.

In translation practice, understanding the registerial features is very important. The features of a register in one language can be different from those in another language. Different languages may differ in the use of modal verbs in expressing the meanings of probability and obligation. For example, the high value modal verb *shall* expresses the meaning of obligation in English legal documents. Yet, in Chinese this meaning is realized by *yingdang* (should) or *bixu* (must). Thus, when people translate the English *shall* in legal documents into Chinese, *yingdang* or *bixu* should be used, to keep registerial consistency.

A wide range of studies are possible. Many additional investigations could be done in terms of related research questions by applying similar analytical techniques. For instance, we might be interested in tracking the use of other kinds of linguistic features, such as nominalizations, transitivity structures, clause types, discourse markers, stance markers, metadiscourse devices. We might be interested in registers used in every aspect of life and investigate public speeches, textbooks, reports, or the relationship between e-mail as a register and other interactive registers.

As more corpus-based studies are carried out, we should be able to learn more about patterns of discourse that hold across texts and registers.

Assignment

Text 1 is an extract from an academic journal article, in which the author is giving his conclusion from his previous discussion. Text 2 is chosen from the British Prevention of Terrorism Act 2005. Analyze the use of central modal verbs in these two texts and explain what kind of modal meanings is attached to them. Then, build a corpus to examine the use of adjuncts in English legal documents and in the part of General Introduction to the University in university websites. Use the Internet to collect the texts you need for analysis.

Text 1

As a starting point, I would suggest that subject experts and terminologists should be encouraged to begin living up to their social responsibility by ensuring that any new terms that are created in this (or indeed in any) subject field are created in a gender-sensitive way. I would also suggest that recommendations for gender sensitivity be included in any new guidelines that are developed for term formation and use. Then, as a further step, perhaps some of the existing insensitive terms can be gradually re-examined and replaced. The work presented here can also be extended beyond the field of terminology proper, which is concerned primarily with lexical units, to include studies that investigate the role of discourse and metaphor in the construction of gender in LSPs — for instance, metaphors that present women as resources to be exploited, as expressed by terms such as *egg harvesting* or *egg mining*.

Text 2

(5) A non-derogating control order must specify when the period for which it is to have effect will end.

(6) The Secretary of State may renew a non-derogating control order (with or without modifications) for a period of 12 months if he —
  a. considers that it is necessary, for purposes connected with protecting members of the public from a risk of terrorism, for an order imposing obligations on the controlled person to continue in force; and
  b. considers that the obligations to be imposed by the renewed order are necessary for purposes connected with preventing or restricting involvement by that person in terrorism-related activity.

(7) Where the Secretary of State renews a non-derogating control order, the 12 month period of the renewal begins to run from whichever is the earlier of —
  a. the time when the order would otherwise have ceased to have effect; or
  b. the beginning of the seventh day after the date of renewal.

(8) The instrument renewing a non-derogating control order must specify when the period for which it is renewed will end.

(9) It shall be immaterial, for the purposes of determining what obligations may be imposed by a control order made by the Secretary of State, whether the involvement in terrorism-related activity to be prevented or restricted by the obligations is connected with matters to which the Secretary of State's grounds for suspicion relate.

Chapter 11

Analysis and evaluation of argumentative discourse

Frans H. van Eemeren and Bart Garssen
University of Amsterdam*

Among the dominant theoretical approaches to argumentation, there is a paradigmatic division between rhetorical approaches, concentrating primarily on problems of analysis, and dialectical approaches, focusing more emphatically on problems of evaluation. By methodically integrating relevant insights from rhetoric in a theoretical framework that is basically dialectical, the pragma-dialectical approach links the analysis and the evaluation of argumentative discourse in a systematic way. This chapter explains what the pragma-dialectical approach amounts to and illustrates its theoretical and practical significance.

1. Introduction

Although Renkema's *Introduction to Discourse Studies* (2004, chapter 12) provides a useful introduction to the study of argumentation, this brief account does not provide a full characterization of the field. Among the dominant approaches to argumentative discourse, a general distinction can be made between dialectical approaches, which view argumentation from a critical perspective as aimed at establishing the tenability of the standpoints at issue, and rhetorical approaches, valuing its practical effectiveness. A prominent example of a dialectical theory that is missing in Renkema's overview is "formal dialectics," initiated by Hamblin (1970); an influential rhetorical theory that should certainly be added is the "new rhetoric" developed by Perelman and Olbrechts-Tyteca (1958/1969). In addition, a recent innovation that must be considered is the integration of rhetorical insights in a dialectical approach proposed in "pragma-dialectics" (Van Eemeren & Houtlosser, 2002).

* This contribution is partially based on Van Eemeren and Houtlosser (2000) and Van Eemeren, Houtlosser and Snoeck Henkemans (2008).

Because a full-fledged theory of argumentation should deal not only with the factors determining the effectiveness of argumentation in practice but also with the critical standards argumentative discourse should comply with to be reasonable, the study of argumentative discourse is part of a special branch of pragmatics that we refer to as "normative pragmatics" (Van Eemeren, 1990). In Section 2, we introduce a major research challenge by explaining what the normative pragmatic theory of argumentative discourse entails that is developed in pragma-dialectics. In Section 3, we quote some examples of challenging argumentative texts. In Section 4, we sketch our research method by explaining how including rhetorical insights in the pragma-dialectical framework creates a more refined tool for reconstructing argumentative discourse. In Section 5, we introduce recent pragma-dialectical research by showing how both the analysis and the evaluation of argumentative discourse benefit from integrating dialectical and rhetorical insights. As an illustration, Section 6 discusses a research proposal directed at the use of authority argumentation in a medical context. Section 7 highlights the practical relevance of this type of research. Section 8 presents an assignment that can be used for lecturing.

2. The research challenge

In pragma-dialectics, argumentation is viewed from a communicative perspective as a complex speech act aimed at resolving a difference of opinion by critically testing the acceptability of the standpoint at issue. Because argumentation is not just an empirical phenomenon but should also be judged for its quality, argumentation research has a normative as well as a descriptive dimension. Pragma-dialecticians make it their business to connect these two dimensions systematically with the help of a comprehensive research program that combines well-considered normativity with explanatory description. The name *pragma-dialectics* expresses this methodical combination of empirical research of actual communication (pragmatics) and critical regimentation (dialectics).[1]

In combining pragmatic and dialectic insights, pragma-dialecticians rely on four meta-theoretical principles, which serve as their methodological starting points: "functionalization," "socialization," "externalization," and "dialectification." Functionalization is achieved by using the fact that argumentative discourse occurs through —

1. The dialectical conception of reasonableness is inspired by critical rationalists and analytic philosophers, such as Popper, Albert, and Naess, and by formal dialecticians and logicians, such as Hamblin, Lorenzen, Lorenz, Barth and Krabbe. The pragmatic conception of argumentative discourse as consisting of making regulated communicative moves is rooted in Austin and Searle's ordinary language philosophy, Grice's theory of rationality in discourse, and other studies of communication by discourse and conversation analysts.

and in response to — speech act performances. Identifying the complex speech act of argumentation and the other speech acts involved in resolving a difference of opinion makes it possible to specify the relevant "identity conditions" and "correctness conditions" of these speech acts.[2] In this way, for instance, a specification can be given of what is "at stake" in advancing a certain "standpoint," so that it becomes clear how the argumentative discourse is organized around this context of disagreement. Socialization is achieved by identifying who exactly take on the discussion roles of protagonist and antagonist in the collaborative context of argumentative discourse. By extending the speech act perspective to the level of interaction, it can be shown in which ways positions and argumentation in support of positions are developed. Externalization is achieved by identifying the specific commitments that are created by the speech acts performed in a context of argumentative interaction. Rather than being treated as internal states of mind, in a speech act perspective notions such as "disagreement" and "acceptance" can be defined in terms of discursive activities. "Acceptance," for instance, can be externalized as giving a preferred response to an arguable act. Finally, dialectification is achieved by regimenting the exchange of speech acts aimed at resolving a difference of opinion on the merits in an ideal model of critical discussion.

In a critical discussion, the protagonist and the antagonist of a particular standpoint try to establish whether, given the point of departure of the parties, this standpoint is tenable in the light of critical responses. To be able to achieve this purpose, the dialectical procedure for conducting a critical discussion cannot deal only with inference relations between premises (or "concessions") and conclusions (or "standpoints") but should cover all speech acts that play a part in examining the acceptability of standpoints. In pragma-dialectics, the concept of a critical discussion is given shape in a model that specifies all stages the resolution process has to pass, from confrontation and opening to argumentation and conclusion, and all speech acts instrumental in these stages. Because in actual argumentative discourse a great many speech acts are performed implicitly or indirectly, in practice, a great variety of speech acts may fulfill a constructive role in the resolution process.

In pragma-dialectics, the critical norms of reasonableness authorizing the performance of speech acts in the various stages of a critical discussion are accounted for in a set of dialectical rules. In a critical discussion, the protagonists and the antagonists of the standpoints at issue not only go through all stages of the resolution process, but they must also observe in every stage all the rules that are instrumental in resolving a difference of opinion (Van Eemeren & Grootendorst 1984, 2004). The rules of the pragma-dialectical procedure for critical discussion state all the norms that are

2. For a definition of argumentation as a complex speech act, see Van Eemeren and Grootendorst (1984: 39–46; 1992a: 30–33). For the distinction between identity conditions and correctness conditions, see Van Eemeren and Grootendorst (1992a: 30–31).

pertinent to resolving a difference of opinion on the merits and cover the entire argumentative discourse. Each of the rules constitutes a distinct standard or norm for critical discussion and any move constituting an infringement of any of the rules, whichever party performs it and at whatever stage in the discussion, is a possible threat to the resolution of a difference of opinion and must therefore be regarded as fallacious (in this particular sense). Thus, the use of the term *fallacy* is systematically connected with the rules for critical discussion and fallacies may range from preventing each other from expressing any position one wishes to assume in the confrontation stage to unduly generalizing the result of the discussion in the concluding stage.

As a matter of course, the way in which ordinary argumentative discourse is conducted will usually differ a lot from the way in which it is portrayed in the ideal model of a critical discussion. The research challenge pragma-dialecticians are confronted with therefore is to connect their theoretical insights in the analysis and evaluation of argumentative discourse with the predicaments of argumentative reality.

3. Examples

Argumentation is used in all spheres of life and argumentative discourse can be encountered in an enormous variety of contexts. In the analysis and evaluation of argumentative discourse, the context in which the argumentation takes place should be duly taken into account. If we concentrate, for example, on the analysis and evaluation of medical advertisements in the United States in which products such as pain relievers, sleeping pills and vitamins are recommended, an important contextual constraint is that the Federal Trade Commission prescribes that such advertisements must be truthful and non-deceptive. In the following examples of advertisements for sleeping pills it may even not be immediately clear that they are argumentative.

(1) Amazing Insomnia Relief
Fall asleep fast with Amazing Insomnia Relief guaranteed!
Amazing Insomnia Relief™ has ended insomnia and provided an amazing night sleep for thousands of people in the United States, in Canada, United Kingdom, Australia, India, and many countries around the world! The question is…
Are YOU next?

Here, precise and verifiable claims are avoided. Nevertheless, an analysis should make clear that implicitly the standpoint is put forward that Amazing Insomnia Relief cures insomnia and that this standpoint is defended by referring to the number of people in several countries who benefited from this drug. Our next example contains similar problems of implicitness.

(2) Tylenol Simply Sleep
If you're losing sleep, you're not alone. One in three adults experiences occasional sleeplessness. Simply Sleep is the non-habit forming sleep medicine with nothing more than what helps you sleep. It's for those nights when you simply want to sleep.
While everyone has different sleep needs, the National Sleep Foundation recommends that most people get 8 hours of sleep per night. And it's not just the number of hours that counts — it's also the quality of the sleep. It's important to get an uninterrupted, restful night's sleep.
You're probably not getting the sleep you need if you:
Feel groggy and lethargic in the morning
Feel drowsy during the day
Need more than 30 minutes to fall asleep
Wake up frequently during the night and have trouble getting back to sleep

Our argumentation research should enable us to answer questions like: what are the standpoints that are put forward in these advertisements, how exactly are they defended, and in what way does the context in which they are presented play a role in the analysis and evaluation of such pieces of argumentative discourse?

4. Research method

Recently, Van Eemeren and Houtlosser (2002) have explained that for making an analysis of argumentative discourse that is as refined as is required for a fair evaluation, insight from rhetoric should be included in the theoretical framework for analysis and evaluation. In their view, the existing separation between dialectic and rhetoric can be remedied by realizing that, in principle, the two theoretical perspectives are not incompatible, but complementary. In analyzing argumentative discourse, the arguers' rhetorical attempts to have things their way may be considered incorporated in their efforts to realize their dialectical aspiration of resolving a difference of opinion in accordance with the standards pertaining to a critical discussion. Viewed pragma-dialectically, in every stage of the resolution process the parties are not only going for the optimal rhetorical result at the stage they are going through, but may at the same time also be presumed to hold to the dialectical objective of that discussion stage. Thus, the dialectical aim of each of the four stages of the resolution process may be taken to have its rhetorical analogue. To reconcile the simultaneous pursuit of these two different aims, the arguers make use of *strategic maneuvering* aimed at diminishing the potential tension between the two endeavors.

In pragma-dialectics, an analytic distinction is made between three basic aspects of strategic maneuvering. First, there is making an expedient selection from the "topical potential," i.e., choosing from the options that are open in a certain discussion stage: in the confrontation stage, for instance, the standpoint will be chosen that seems most suitable to the arguer; in the opening stage, the premises that can be helpful starting points of the discussion; in the argumentation stage, the reasons that seem most appropriate for defending the standpoint; in the concluding stage, the best possible outcome. Second, there is framing one's contribution in accordance with "audience demand," i.e., adapting one's moves in each of the four stages to the specific expectations and preferences of the listeners or readers. Third, there is using the most effective "presentational devices," i.e., exploiting the various stylistic means of conveying a message.

In practice, argumentative discourse takes place in argumentative "activity types" that are to a greater or lesser degree institutionalized, so that certain practices have become conventionalized. Unlike theoretical ideal models based on analytic considerations,[3] such as the pragma-dialectical model of a critical discussion, activity types — and the speech events associated with them — are empirical entities that can be identified by careful observation and understanding of argumentative practice. In the various activity types, the conventional preconditions for argumentative discourse may differ to some extent and these differences have an impact on the possibilities for strategic maneuvering.[4]

Activity types can be defined argumentatively by characterizing them, and the specific preconditions for argumentative discourse they create, in terms of critical discussion. In activity types that belong to a context of adjudication, for instance, the initial situation is a dispute that is to be decided by a third party, whereas in mediation the third party has no jurisdiction to decide the disagreement. In the activity types of adjudication, the starting points are largely explicit codified rules and explicitly established concessions whereas in those of mediation there are implicitly enforced regulative rules and hardly any explicitly recognized concessions, and in those of negotiation there are changeable sets of explicit concessions. While argumentation in adjudication is based on evidence and the interpretation of legal rules, in negotiation it is incorporated in exchanges of offers and counteroffers. The outcome in adjudication is not a resolution of the difference by a decision of the parties, but a settlement of the dispute by a sustained decision of the third party, and in negotiation the activities end in either a mutually accepted agreement or a return to the initial situation.

Although the realization of rhetorical aims can go well together with the pursuit of dialectical objectives, this does not mean that in strategic maneuvering there is always a perfect balance between the two. If parties allow their commitment to a critical

3. Such models aim to provide the most pertinent representation of the constitutive parts of a problem-valid procedure for carrying out a particular kind of discursive task.

4. Apart from posing constraints on the strategic maneuvering they may also open up special opportunities.

exchange of argumentative moves to be overruled by their persuasive aims, so that their moves are no longer in agreement with the critical norms of the pragma-dialectical rules, their strategic maneuvering gets "derailed." The criteria for determining whether a rule for critical discussion has been violated may vary according to activity type — in a law case, for instance, the criteria for appealing to an authority are different from those in political debate.

In the type of strategic maneuvering that consists of defending a standpoint by advancing an "argument from authority" — a variant of "symptomatic argumentation" — the transition of acceptance is brought about by introducing in the premise an external source that has a certain kind of knowledge or expertise and then referring to this source when drawing a conclusion dependent on such knowledge or expertise. Using arguments from authority is potentially a sound type of strategic maneuvering, but in argumentative practice it can also derail. An appeal to authority may not be justified in a particular case because one or more of the "critical questions" that need to be asked to check if the criteria applying to the activity type concerned have been fulfilled cannot be answered satisfactorily so that the argument violates the *Argument Scheme Rule* and must be considered an *argumentum ad verecundiam*.[5] In different activity types, different criteria may apply for complying with the soundness norm incorporated in the argument-from-authority variant of the Argument Scheme Rule.

There are various kinds of authority argumentation and some of them are typical of specific activity types. In adjudication, for instance, both eyewitness reports and expert opinions are used to sustain certain claims and in some political activity types it is common to refer to scientific authorities (e.g., environmental studies). The procedures for critically testing the validity of these appeals to authority are different in each case: with regard to an eyewitness, a critical question is whether this person is in any way related to any of the parties (i.e., is this witness unbiased), but in the case of the expert opinion of a scientist this question is not relevant. The evaluation of authority argumentation is an intersubjective matter, but what the intersubjective evaluation procedure involves must be specified according to the activity type and the kind of authority at hand.

Generally, carrying out a pragma-dialectical analysis of argumentative discourse amounts to interpreting the discourse systematically from the theoretical perspective of a critical discussion.[6] Such an analysis is pragmatic in viewing the discourse as essentially an exchange of speech acts in context and dialectical in viewing this

---

5. To mark the important distinction between non-fallacious and fallacious strategic maneuvering as clearly as possible, we use the traditional names of the fallacies, such as *argumentum ad verecundiam*, exclusively for the fallacious cases.

6. In practice, the first question always is whether, and to what extent, the oral or written discourse that is to be analyzed may be regarded argumentative.

exchange as a methodical attempt to resolve a difference of opinion on the merits. By pointing out which speech acts are relevant in the various stages of the resolution process the model of a critical discussion has the heuristic function of indicating which speech acts need to be considered in the analysis.

For obvious reasons, argumentative reality seldom resembles the ideal of a critical discussion. According to the model, for example, in the confrontation stage antagonists of a standpoint must state their doubts clearly and unambiguously, but in practice doing so can be "face-threatening" for both parties so that they will have to operate circumspectly.[7] In order to be able to give a sound evaluation, a reconstruction of the discourse is needed that results in an *analytic overview* of all those, and only those, elements that are potentially relevant to the resolution of a difference of opinion. The analytic overview recapitulates the difference of opinion at issue in the confrontation stage and the positions of the participants; it identifies the procedural and substantive premises presented in the opening stage that serve as the starting point of the discussion; it surveys the arguments and criticisms that are — explicitly or implicitly — advanced in the argumentation stage, the argument schemes that are used, and the argumentation structures that are developed; and it determines the outcome that is reached in the concluding stage. The concepts referred to in the analytic overview, such as "type of difference of opinion," "unexpressed premise," "argument scheme," and "argumentation structure," are all defined from the pragma-dialectical perspective of a critical discussion.[8]

The reconstruction that takes place in the analysis amounts to making explicit all elements that remain implicit in the actual discourse but are relevant to the resolution process ("addition"), reformulating in an unequivocal way those speech acts whose function would otherwise be opaque ("substitution"), rearranging in a more insightful way speech acts whose order does not reflect their function in the resolution process ("permutation"), and leaving out of consideration all speech acts that do not play a part in the resolution process ("deletion") (Van Eemeren & Grootendorst, 2004: chapter 5).[9] In *Reconstructing Argumentative Discourse*, Van Eemeren, Grootendorst, Jackson and Jacobs (1993) emphasize that it is crucial that the transformations carried out in the analysis are indeed justified. They must be faithful to the commitments that may be ascribed to the participants on the basis of their contributions to the

7. Expressing doubt may also go against the "preference for agreement" that governs normal conversation. See Van Eemeren, Grootendorst, Jackson, and Jacobs (1993: chapter 3).

8. These terms and concepts are explained in Van Eemeren, Grootendorst and Snoeck Henkemans (2002). See also Van Eemeren and Grootendorst (1992) and Van Eemeren (Ed., 2001).

9. These reconstruction transformations are carried out in a cyclic process, proceeding in as many stages as necessary to achieve an adequate analytic overview.

discourse. In order not to "over-interpret" what seems implicit in the discourse, the analyst must be sensitive to the rules of language use,[10] the details of the presentation, and the contextual constraints inherent in the speech event concerned. To go beyond a naïve reading of the discourse, empirical insight concerning the way in which oral and written discourse are conducted, including the way in which strategic maneuvering develops, is to be used to augment the analyst's intuitions with the help of the results of such empirical research, both qualitative and quantitative (See Van Eemeren, Grootendorst, Jackson & Jacobs, 1993: 50–59). Only then, the reconstruction can lead to an analytic overview that is a sound basis for carrying out an evaluation in which any fallacies occurring in the discourse can be fairly displayed.

5. Recent research

In recent research, the theoretical tools developed in the integrated pragma-dialectical approach are used for the analysis and evaluation of argumentative discourse in specific argumentative activity types in the legal, the political, and the medical sphere. An example is the following brief analysis of an "advertorial" that appeared in a great many American magazines at the time that in the United States public attitudes toward smoking had started to shift dramatically (Spring 1984). Part of a call for Congressional hearings to consider further restrictions on the advertising of cigarettes was the argument that tobacco companies were advertising to children to replace the growing number of adult smokers who were quitting or dying. Among R.J. Reynolds Tobacco Company's responses was the following advertorial:

(3) Some surprising advice to young people from R.J. Reynolds Tobacco.
Don't smoke.
For one thing, smoking has always been an adult custom. And even for adults, smoking has become very controversial.
So even though we're a tobacco company, we don't think it's a good idea for young people to smoke.
Now, we know that giving this kind of advice to young people can sometimes backfire.
But if you take up smoking just to prove you're an adult, you're really proving just the opposite.
Because deciding to smoke or not to smoke is something you should do when you don't have anything to prove.

10. An integration of the Searlean speech act conditions and the Gricean conversational maxims in a set of "rules of language use" is proposed in Van Eemeren and Grootendorst (1992a: 49–55, 2004: ch.4).

> Think it over.
> After all, you may not be old enough to smoke. But you're old enough to think.

Although an advertorial is an activity type that is, in spite of having the form of an editorial, an advertisement with a commercial rationale, it is not supposed to contain assertions that are not true, and any argumentation that is used may be seen as a serious attempt to defend a standpoint. It is against the background of these institutional constraints that we are going to analyze the case made by R.J. Reynolds Tobacco Company. For the sake of brevity, we shall focus only on the strategic maneuvering with topical selection in the argumentation stage.[11]

After the announcement preceding the text has created the "surprising" perspective desired by Reynolds, the text begins with the pronouncement "Don't smoke." This pronouncement initiates the confrontation stage by expressing — by way of a rather paternalistic advice — the normative standpoint that Reynolds, viewed dialectically, is expected to defend in the text. A reconstruction of the structure of the argumentation put forward by Reynolds in defense of their standpoint looks like this:

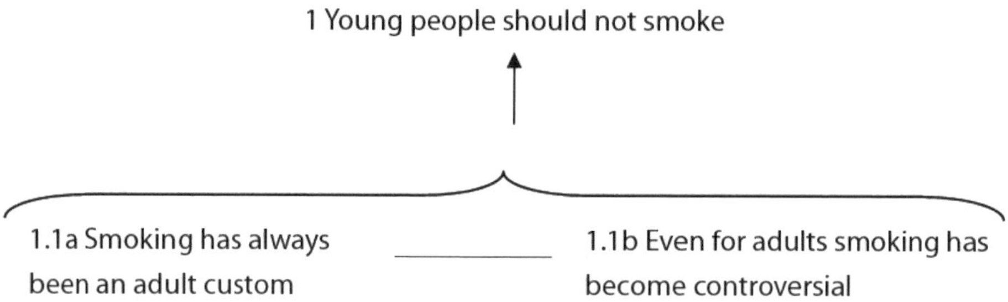

Figure 1. Reconstruction of the argumentation

What observations can be made concerning the topical choice made in this strategic maneuvering in favor of the standpoint that young people should not smoke? Paradoxically, it is already clear from the start that the arguments that are advanced will not appeal to young people. It is more than doubtful — to say the least — whether convention and age will be decisive reasons for young people to decide not to smoke. It is more likely that to the average young person the conventional presupposition that smoking is the privilege of adults will be an occasion to go against that. And that smoking has become "controversial" will make it only more interesting to the young. An even more striking property of Reynolds's topical choice is that they leave conspicuously unmentioned the readily available arguments, which are both more obvious and much stronger, that smoking can become an addiction and causes cancer. The

11. This analysis is based on Van Eemeren and Houtlosser (2000); see also Van Eemeren, Grootendorst, Jackson and Jacobs (1997).

reason for not mentioning these arguments will be clear: if the firm would commit itself to them, this would leave Reynolds with an awkward dialectical inconsistency. The health argument would strongly undermine the credibility of the standpoint that adults should be allowed to smoke. This standpoint may not be expressed in the text but, as a tobacco company, Reynolds is, of course, committed to it.

The arguments advanced for the standpoint that young people should not smoke seem — in a perverse way — selected for their *incapacity* to contribute to the defense of the official standpoint that young people should not smoke. By advancing arguments that so evidently do *not* support the disputed standpoint satisfactorily, Reynolds evokes the *topos* "If there are only *bad reasons* for not doing something, then there are *no good reasons* for not doing it." The reasoning toward the desired conclusion suggested to the young readers can be reconstructed in the following way (unexpressed steps are put in parentheses):

(1) (There are no good reasons for young people not to smoke)
1.1a–b Smoking has always been an adult custom and even for adults smoking has become controversial
(1.1a–b′) (These are the only reasons why young people should not smoke)
(1.1a–b″) (They are bad reasons)
(1.1a–b‴) (If there are only bad reasons for refraining from doing something, then there are no good reasons for not doing it)

It is evident that Reynolds intends to convey standpoint (1) — that there are no good reasons for young people not to smoke — through implication without committing themselves to this standpoint. It can be left to the young readers to draw this conclusion for themselves.

After having thus "argued" why young people should not smoke, viewed analytically, Reynolds returns to the opening stage of the discussion to acknowledge a concession: "We know that giving this kind of advice to young people can sometimes backfire." On the face of it, this acknowledgement is followed by a move aimed at preventing the dreaded effect from occurring: "But if you take up smoking just to prove you're an adult, you're really proving just the opposite." On closer inspection, however, a different effect must be aimed for, because it is obvious that this warning will not be very effective. Although Reynolds may suggest that young people who take up smoking only do so to prove that they are adults, strictly speaking, they say that those who take up smoking *only to prove that they are adults* prove exactly the opposite. In other words, there is no problem when you take up smoking *for some other reason* — let us say because you happen to like smoking. In that case, you *do not* prove that you are not an adult. The addition of "just" even allows for taking up smoking to prove that you are an adult as long as you *also have other reasons* for smoking.

In this analysis, we concentrated on topical selection in strategic maneuvering rather than audience adaptation and stylistic devices. Taking these other aspects into account can further strengthen the analysis. Take, as a case in point, the presentational choice of the word "controversial" when Reynolds stated that smoking was controversial even for adults, thus suggesting that the matter is still *undecided* and that there is something to be said *both* for the positive and the negative view of smoking, so that smoking might, after all, be acceptable. In this and other ways, R.J. Reynolds Tobacco Company's text is pervaded with efforts to get young people to reject rather than accept Reynolds's case.

We have made plausible that the strategy Reynolds followed here is, in fact, aimed at being *counter-productive*. Thus, our analysis of the advertorial not only shows that a pragma-dialectical analysis and evaluation become stronger and more pertinent when rhetorical insight is incorporated, but also that a rhetorical analysis of argumentative discourse is more meaningful when it takes place in a dialectical framework that defines the range of reasonableness and sets limits to the strategic maneuvering that is allowed.[12]

6. Research proposal

In medical advertisements published in the United States, usually the claim is defended that the health product that is advertised (pain relievers, vitamins, etc.) is effective. While the ultimate goal is to get the reader to buy the product, the advertisers are constrained in their methods of persuasion by the advertising code imposed by the Federal Trade Commission. In arguing to convince the readers of the effectiveness of the product, they will have to take these constraints into account. A type of argumentation that can often be found in this activity type is the argument from authority. In such arguments, a trustworthy person or agency (often a medical doctor or someone who has experience in using the product) is claimed to guarantee the effectiveness of the product, so that it becomes clear that it is worth buying. The proposed research is aimed at finding out (1) when the strategic maneuvering by means of arguments from authority in these medical advertisements can be considered reasonable and when fallacious, and (2) to what extent the readers of these advertisements are able to identify these arguments and to evaluate their reasonableness. For this purpose, a corpus will be used of American medical advertisements.

12. Assimakis Tseronis, Dima Mohammed, Corina Andone, Yvon Tonnard, Bilal Amjarso, Marcin Lewinski, Constanza Ihnen, Roosmaryn Pilgram, and Lotte van Poppel are currently carrying out PhD projects in which further pragma-theoretical instruments are developed to deal with other medical and political argumentative activity types.

7. Practical relevance

The partial analysis of the Reynolds advertorial we have given in Section 5 is exemplary for how pragma-dialecticians go about when dealing with argumentative discourse. Of course, a well-balanced evaluation of the discourse is possible only after the analysis has been completed. All the same, the analysis we provided already enables us to observe that Reynolds, because they advance arguments that are from the outset unlikely to convince, violates in a special way the *Relevance Rule* for critical discussion, stating that standpoints may not be defended by non-argumentation or argumentation that is not relevant to the standpoint (Van Eemeren & Grootendorst, 2004: 194), so that they are guilty of committing a strategic variant of the relevance fallacy of *ignoratio elenchi* (Van Eemeren & Grootendorst, 1992: 205). Thus, the pragma-dialectical method of analysis and evaluation opens up the possibility for a critical treatment of the strategic maneuvering taking place in the various kinds of activity types in which argumentative discourse plays a part. In this way, pragma-dialectics proves at the same time its scholarly and its practical significance.

Assignment

Students are asked to apply the pragma-dialectical method we have explained to the strategic maneuvering carried out by KLM in an advertorial in defense of their actions regarding the killing of 440 squirrels. Carrying out this assignment can be a useful preparation for conducting research regarding the strategic maneuvering performed in other argumentative activity types. Apart from focusing on problems of topical selection, this research could also concentrate on problems concerning the adaptation to audience demand or the exploitation of presentational devices — or a combination of each of these — and the fallacious derailments that may occur in such maneuvering.

In the advertorial below, KLM apologizes for its involvement in a tragic incident. KLM not only apologizes but also argues in order to clear its name. Indicate how KLM maneuvers strategically to minimize the damage to its public image. Focus on the topical selection of standpoints in the confrontation stage, starting points in the opening stage, and arguments in the argumentation stage. Explain what kind of strategic maneuvers KLM employs.

KLM APOLOGIZES FOR DESTROYING SQUIRRELS

In April 1999 the airline company KLM was in the news because it had finished off 440 North American banded ground squirrels after it had been ordered to do so by the national agency for the inspection of cattle and meat. The required exportation and health documents were lacking, and the squirrels were not adequately packaged. The animals were put through a chopper alive. The squirrels came from Beijing and were on their way to Athens. The sender in Beijing did not want to take the squirrels back and no country outside Europe volunteered to receive the animals. The chopper in which the squirrels came to their end was a destroyer that is also used in the bio-industry to cut up cocks. Cocks, however, are substantially smaller than squirrels, and with cocks one can make sure that the head goes first. With the ground squirrels, whose size equals that of three hands, this was not feasible. In the press release below, KLM accounts for having destroyed the squirrels.

PRESS RELEASE

KLM sincerely apologizes for having been forced to have 440 squirrels destroyed, last Monday in the KLM Cargo animals' hotel. KLM has acted in a way that is formally justified, but admits that an ethical assessment mistake was made. KLM fully endorses the criticisms that have been voiced by the public and the various organizations.

The airline company has decided to start a thorough investigation into what exactly happened at the reception of the package in Beijing. The events in the KLM Cargo animals' hotel will also be investigated.

Pending this investigation and in view of the emotions that these events have aroused, the Board of KLM has deemed it desirable that the employee concerned will stay home for the period of this investigation.

On Sunday April 11, 1999, KLM has received orders from the Department of Agriculture, Environmental Management and Fishing (AEMF) to destroy the animals. KLM is of the opinion that this order, in this form and without feasible alternatives, was unethical.

The Board of KLM holds, however, that the KLM employee concerned has acted formally correct in this matter by promptly following the directives of the Department of AEMF, but also acknowledges that this employee has made an assessment mistake.

KLM once more emphasizes that the company regrets the course of events and offers its sincere apologies to all animal lovers and all those who have been hurt by the events.

KLM has informed the Animal Protection Society, the AAP Foundation, the Worldwide Fund for Nature, the Cites Netherlands Foundation, the Foundation for the Relief of Squirrels in The Meern, the European Association of Zoos and Aquaria, and the Dutch Association of Zoos of the above and has invited these organizations to come to a consultation on how to avoid deplorable situations of this kind at a short term.

Part VI

Discourse and Cognition

Chapter 12

Embodied cognition, discourse, and Dual Coding Theory

New directions

Mark Sadoski
Texas A&M University

This chapter introduces new, alternative views to explaining cognition in discourse for both text comprehension and text composition. The perspective taken here is that cognition is inherently *embodied*. That is, all mental representations and processes derive from the concrete experience of our sensory modalities (vision, hearing, etc.) and retain some modality-specific information in memory. The embodied perspective can be contrasted with perspectives derived primarily from artificial intelligence in which the mind is modeled as a computer that processes abstract, computational representations through equally abstract programming rules. Currently, the most thoroughly developed embodied theory of cognition is Dual Coding Theory which explains all cognition through the interaction of two mental codes: the verbal code and the nonverbal code. The verbal code deals with language in several sensory modalities, and the nonverbal code deals with images in all sensory modalities. Connections within and between the codes are a powerful explanatory vehicle for discourse and its effects.

1. Introduction

The study of cognition in discourse is an area that has seen new and exciting developments lately. These include new theoretical insights into the evolution of discourse, the nature of discourse in human cognition, and consequent implications for research and education. Many of these ideas have fascinating historical roots as well. In this chapter, I will briefly discuss some of these issues and summarize the challenge that they pose for current theories of cognition in discourse.

One of the most enduring theories of the evolution of discourse is that it evolved from gestures, including vocal gestures, specifically intended to refer to concrete objects and events in the world. Years ago, Sinclair (1944: 113) stated this position simply:

> Speech is simply gesture made audible. Speech is simply gesture that can be listened to, instead of watched. Speech is an extensively complex system of more or less standardized and conventionalized noises, and writing is an even more highly standardized and conventionalized system of visible marks upon a surface, but, in principle, speech and writing are as much gesture as is pointing the finger.

Current evolutionary theorists make new and compelling arguments that language in all its forms grew from a nonverbal base of bodily sensation and expression and remains connected to it (e.g., Armstrong & Wilcox, 2007; Paivio, 2007).

The form that this movement takes in cognitive theory is *embodied cognition*. This emerging viewpoint maintains that all cognitive representations and processes are based in the body's physical interactions with the world. Contemporary proponents of this view include Lakoff and Johnson (1999), who proposed three central tenets derived from current cognitive science: (1) the mind is inherently embodied, (2) thought is mostly unconscious, and (3) because direct sensory experience is concrete, abstract concepts are largely metaphorical (e. g., time is a journey with the past behind and the future ahead).

In her review of theories of embodied cognition, Wilson (2002) found that a common claim is that unconscious cognition is body-based. That is, many internal, allegedly abstract cognitive activities employ sensorimotor representations and processes in a covert way. Wilson (ibid: 632–633) explained:

> Consider the example of counting on one's fingers. In its fullest form, this can be a set of crisp and large movements, unambiguously setting forth the different fingers as counters. But it can also be done more subtly, differentiating the positions of the fingers only enough to allow the fingers to keep track. To the observer, this may look like mere twitching. Imagine, then, that we push the activity inward still further, allowing only the priming of motor programs but no overt movement. If this kind of mental activity can be employed successfully to assist a task such as counting, a new vista of cognitive strategies opens up. Many centralized, allegedly abstract cognitive activities may in fact make use of sensorimotor functions in exactly this kind of covert way.

In discourse, sensorimotor functions might underlie the comprehension and composition of rhetoric including exposition, narration, description, and argument. Consider, for example, the vocal intonations and gestures of speakers that are converted to boldface or italics in print, or to video montage and sound effects in multimedia presentations. These have obvious sensorimotor appeal, but deeper levels of cognition may be based in embodied mental representations and processes in a more covert way.

2. The research challenge

To explain how all cognition is embodied, we can turn to established theories of cognition that emphasize sensory experience as the basis of knowledge and thought. Dual Coding Theory (Paivio, 1971, 1986, 2007; Sadoski & Paivio, 2001, 2004, 2007) is currently the most empirically established, fully embodied theory of cognition. Dual Coding Theory (DCT) explains all cognition through the interaction of two mental codes that derive from sensory experience: the verbal code and the nonverbal code. The verbal code deals with language in several sensory modalities (e.g., hearing spoken language, seeing written language, or touching the raised dots of Braille), and the nonverbal code deals with images in all sensory modalities. Connections within and between the codes account for meaning and memory, and they are a powerful explanatory vehicle for discourse and its effects. For example, concrete language that evokes sensory images (e.g., *stained glass window*) is better understood and recalled than abstract language that has less access to images (e.g., *theory of semiotics*).

Opposing contemporary theories come mainly from artificial intelligence (e.g., Kintsch, 1998). In these models, the mind is an abstract information processor, whose perceptual connections to the outside world are of little theoretical importance. The mind's deeper abstract mechanisms, usually described as abstract schemata and propositions, are to human cognition precisely what programming is to computers: the abstract structure of thought without any content, empty computer programs awaiting data (i.e., instantiation). The form of the incoming data is of little or no consequence once it has been converted into a common computational code by these mechanisms. Chapter 5 and chapter 13 in Renkema's (2004) *Introduction to Discourse Studies* cover several such abstract theories with their general explanation of discourse production and comprehension. Such theories differ basically from theories like DCT in which cognition is based on bodily experience and its modality-specific mental representation.

The differences between the theories are more than academic. They have real-life consequences in the effective composition and comprehension of messages in a variety of discourse forms. The scientific study of discourse effects involves tests of competing theories of discourse processing. A general approach to testing these differing theories of discourse processing is to compare the effects of discourse that is based in objects, pictures, and concrete language against discourse that is designed to address abstract cognitive structures regardless of the use of objects, pictures, or the concreteness of the language employed. If knowledge could be shown to retain a sensory basis, abstract theories are challenged and new directions emerge. Applicable research approaches will be discussed in more detail later in this chapter.

3. Examples

For our purposes in this section, let us focus on persuasive or argumentative discourse. Sadoski (1992) provided an extended explanation of the DCT account of persuasive and argumentative discourse with examples, and the interested reader should consult this reference for a full explanation. A briefer explanation will suit our purposes here.

Recall that Lakoff and Johnson (1999) proposed that because direct sensory experience is concrete, abstract concepts are largely metaphorical. The experiential basis of argument metaphors has been summarized by Jenson (1983). Such metaphors include journeys (e.g., we are "led to" conclusions), edifices (e.g., an argument is "well grounded" in evidence), physical conflict (e.g., we "stand our ground" in a debate), artefacts (e.g., "turn the tables" on the opposition), natural phenomena (e.g., "weed out untruths" from the rhetoric), and so on. Such metaphors are not simply colorful language; they may be the body-based stuff of thought and feeling. Dodd (1990), an expert trial lawyer and legal consultant, suggested externalizing such metaphors in trial proceedings as a way to win a jury. The principle is to make a case so vividly real to the five senses that the jury naturally accepts it as true.

For example, he advocated using actual measuring sticks rather than verbal metrics in showing distances to juries. In fact, the preferred measuring stick was the heavy two-by-four, a piece of lumber. Dodd (1990: 41) reported a case in which one was used:

> A brilliant young lawyer in Washington, D.C., effectively used a 9-foot two-by-four in front of the jury in her closing argument to demonstrate that the 5-foot 4-inch defendant, even standing on tiptoe, could not reach up and unscrew a light bulb attached 9 feet up the wall. Instead of asking the jury to imagine the defendant failing to reach up 9 feet, or trying to show how impossible this was using a tape measure, she demonstrated that the defendant could not reach up to touch the top end of a 9-foot two-by-four. The jury acquitted the defendant of rape because the victim's description of what happened had included his reaching up and unscrewing the light bulb, and this demonstration dramatically impeached her testimony.

Dodd provided other examples of where sensory objects or pictures of them could be used to make an argument even better than the concrete language used to describe them verbally. He noted that demonstrative evidence is legally defined as evidence which is addressed directly to the senses without interpretive testimony. He concluded from many court cases that appeals to relevant sensory experiences often carry more weight with juries and judges than the use of abstract, logical argument structures.

4. Research method

Direct tests of the predicted effects of differing discourse theories can be accomplished using established scientific means such as randomized experiments. Researching this issue need not involve actual objects and pictures although they have been used and their effects have been established. In fact, Paivio (1971, 1986, 2007) established that pictures are recalled better than concrete language which is recalled still better than abstract language. However, let us deal with language alone for now.

A direct, discourse-level method is to test the comprehension and recall of concrete language passages that directly evoke sensory memories against more abstract but similarly structured discourse passages. According to computational theories, differences should be minimal — the abstract structure of the passage should rule over the sense-evoking qualities of the language because abstract discourse schemata would be accessed and the sense-evoking qualities of the language would be lost when mentally coded into propositional form. According to embodied theories like DCT, concrete language should still have an effect where discourse structure is similar because of the direct appeal to sensory information in memory.

Likewise, in researching the composition of discourse, a similar method would be to test the use of a concrete prompt for composing versus more abstract or general prompts that were similar in appeals to abstract cognitive structure. For example, a study might assign writing extended definitions of both concrete terms and abstract terms that were similar in category membership, number of attributes, or other abstract structural characteristics. Computational theories would again suggest that compositions should be similar on measures such as the quantity and quality of writing because abstract memory propositions and schemata would be employed in composing. Embodied theories would suggest that concrete language should still have an effect where structural attributes are similar because of the appeal to sensory information in memory. Studies of comprehending and composing using these methods have been conducted. I next review examples of those studies.

5. Recent research

Text comprehension

In an experimental study of text comprehension and recall using the methodology suggested in the last section, Sadoski, Goetz, and Rodriguez (2000) tested whether passages that shared a common general structure but differed in their language concreteness also differed in their effects on reading. Persuasive texts were used along with narrative, expository, and literary texts. Two sets of passages for each genre differed in the rated concreteness of their language but were otherwise matched for length and readability. The general structure of the persuasive texts was similar for both the concrete and abstract passages — a thesis statement followed by several supporting arguments. Here is an example of an abstract passage used in the Sadoski et al. study:

> Character cannot be summoned at the moment of crisis if it has been squandered by years of compromise and excuses. The only testing ground for the heroic is the mundane. The only preparation for that one great decision that can change a life is those hundreds of half-conscious, self-defining, seemingly insignificant decisions made in private.

Here is an example of a concrete passage used in that study:

> Think twice before buying another kitchen "convenience." Grandmother's kitchen had a pan, a spoon, and a knife. It produced a Sunday dinner of roast chicken, potatoes, salad, vegetables, and apple pie. The kitchen of today contains a food processor, blender, laser-cut knife system, and a 20-piece cookware set that produces a Sunday dinner of microwave pizza.

Results of participants' ratings for text comprehensibility and their amount of immediate gist recall were striking. For the persuasive texts, participants rated the concrete texts as significantly more comprehensible than the abstract texts, and their gist recall of the concrete texts was *twice* that of the abstract texts. Therefore, the concreteness of the language was a factor well beyond the general discourse structure of the texts. This same pattern held for the expository, narrative, and literary text passages as well.

Text composition

In a series of studies of written composition, Sadoski and colleagues have tested the effects of composing written definitions of concrete terms versus abstract terms (Goetz, Sadoski, Stricker & White, 2007; Sadoski, Goetz, Stricker, & Burdenski, 2003; Sadoski, Kealy, Goetz, & Paivio, 1997). Definitions are critical in all aspects of discourse, particularly legal, argumentative discourse.

In these several studies, concrete and abstract words to be defined were variously equated for abstract, structural features including familiarity, meaningfulness, categorizability, and number of attributes as well as word length. Examples of abstract words to be defined were: *pride*, *theory*, *time*, *science*, *mind*, and *truth*. Examples of more concrete words to be defined were *library*, *aisle*, *ceremony*, *scene*, *hotel*, and *picture*. The results of all the studies showed that written definitions of concrete words used more words and were higher in rated quality. In addition, participants began writing definitions of concrete words sooner and reported the conscious use of a mental imagery strategy during composing them much more. These results are consistent with DCT, but difficult for competing theories to explain.

6. Research proposal

The foregoing sections suggest several directions for research, and the inventive student can probably imagine many more. Much research has been done on the effects of concreteness on composing and comprehending discourse, but the picture is far from complete.

From a DCT perspective, a needed program of research is to determine the extent to which verbal discourse components work either additively or interactively with the effects of language concreteness. Recall that DCT proposes contributions to comprehension and memory from two mental codes: the verbal code and the nonverbal code. Cognitive effects derive from one of these two sources or from both.

Verbal aspects of discourse typically take some form of context. For discourse to be discourse it needs to have a degree of verbal context — a random arrangement of words and sentences would not qualify. In extended discourse, verbal organizational cues provide one overt form of contextual organization. Such cues may take various forms depending on the type of discourse (e.g., logical: "if…then"; chronological: "earlier…later"; cause-effect: "because…as a result"; comparison-contrast: "either… or"). Many more subtle forms of discourse context have also been detailed (Halliday & Hasan, 1976). Context is truly a many-splendored thing.

Nonverbal aspects of discourse take the form of appeals to mental imagery through the use of concrete language, as described earlier, or the use of pictures, videos, or physical objects such as the two-by-four described earlier. In DCT, these effects are assumed to be additive. That is, verbal effects and nonverbal effects are independent in their contributions to comprehension and memory. Recall that the study by Sadoski et al. (2000) showed just that: The use of concrete language doubled the amount of gist recall when contextual variables such as discourse structure and readability were similar. The two qualitatively different mental encodings appear to be twice as good as one.

However, many aspects of context could be tested individually where concreteness was kept similar, or where concreteness was varied orthogonally, to determine their respective effects. An interesting set of experiments from the DCT perspective was conducted by Maes (1997). He studied the effect of the concreteness of referents on establishing and maintaining text coherence with anaphora (i.e., pronoun antecedents). In one experiment, technical school students were given a first sentence and asked to complete a second sentence given only a first word. The referent in the first sentence could be either concrete or abstract, and the second sentence began with either a demonstrative "pointing out" pronoun or a non-demonstrative personal pronoun. For example, the first sentence, *The little pin causes an increase in pressure in the cylinder*, was followed by the incomplete sentence starters *This*_____ or *It*_____. The participants used both types of pronouns to continue a concrete referent (e.g., *pin*), but they generally avoided continuing an abstract referent (e.g., *pressure*). Two other experiments confirmed the pattern. Maes concluded that abstract referents are more difficult to refer to in writing than concrete referents because of their lower cognitive accessibility and the greater mental effort required to maintain reference to them.

Maes' (1997) findings are consistent with DCT, and serve as an example of how contextual variables at all levels can be varied together with concreteness. Many such studies need to be done to untangle the effects of various aspects of context separately from, or in addition to, the effects of concreteness.

7. Practical relevance

The relevance of embodied theories of cognition for discourse is evident. Using concreteness in discourse in various ways has been shown to have powerful effects both the comprehension and composition of texts. Sadoski and Paivio (2001, chapter 8) reviewed many applications in educational settings including many of the studies described earlier.

A recent study can be seen as a direct theoretical application of embodied DCT principles. Block and her colleagues have developed a method called Comprehension Process Motions (CPM) for teaching young readers to learn reading comprehension processes (Block, Parris, & Whiteley, 2008). CPM lessons teach students gestural hand placements and movements that symbolize comprehension processes such as main idea, inferring, drawing conclusions, clarifying, making predictions, and so on.

For example, recognition of a main idea is symbolized by holding one hand horizontally, palm down, while the other hand is extended vertically below it with the fingertips touching the extended palm in a series of right-to-left motions. The main idea, when recognized, is symbolized by the horizontal hand like a table top. The number of supporting details is symbolized by the vertical strokes like table legs. CPM lessons are designed to help children grasp comprehension processes, not through verbal definition and drill, but through dual-coding, embodied strategies that provide children with overt gestures that stand for them.

In an experimental study, a group of primary grade children were taught to use CPMs. A control group was taught the same comprehension strategies verbally without the assistance of the CPM teaching aids. Students were tested on standardized, norm-referenced comprehension tests and specific criterion-referenced tests of several comprehension strategies including recognizing a main idea and its support. The experimental group significantly outperformed the control group on every measure. For example, the mean score for the main idea test was 80 out of a possible 100 for the CPM group but 52 for the control group. This amounts to more than a 50% increase in achievement for the CPM group over the control group, and an effect size in standard deviation units of $d = 4.71$. This a huge effect size, perhaps among the largest in all reading comprehension strategy instruction. Embodied DCT principles explain these research results directly and provide one powerful example of their application in education.

Assignment

The concept of embodied cognition is growing in many directions. The way this concept applies to one cognitive theory, DCT, has been touched upon here. In particular, the effect of concrete language that appeals to the senses over more vague, abstract language was noted.

An entertaining exercise is to do an Internet search of "jargon generators" and "gobbledygook." Jargon generators produce meaningless but meaningful-sounding phrases, sentences, and longer texts by grammatically combining vocabulary items that are highly abstract. For example, the Postmodernism Essay Generator (www.elsewhere.org/pomo/) provides entire, meaningless postmodern essays in academic discourse format! The striking thing about jargon generators and gobbledygook is that the language, while legal in grammar and discourse structure, is almost entirely abstract.

As an assignment, go the Plain English Campaign website (www.plainenglish.co.uk) and click on "Examples." One choice will be "Before and After" rewrites of gobbledygook text. Find the simpler, more concrete rewrites of these examples of gobbledygook on the website:

1. High-quality learning environments are a necessary precondition for facilitation and enhancement of the ongoing learning process.
2. Your enquiry about the use of the entrance area at the library for the purpose of displaying posters and leaflets about Welfare and Supplementary Benefit rights, gives rise to the question of the provenance and authoritativeness of the material to be displayed. Posters and leaflets issued by the Central Office of Information, the Department of Health and Social Security and other authoritative bodies are usually displayed in libraries, but items of a disputatious or polemic kind, whilst not necessarily excluded, are considered individually.

The answers to these two are provided in the answer key. Many other real examples of excessively abstract, abstruse language are provided on this official website, complete with suggestions to address the problem at various levels of discourse. This exercise is an entertaining way to demonstrate how language should "make sense," that is, conform to the real world of embodied experience.

Chapter 13

The cognition of discourse coherence

Ted Sanders and Wilbert Spooren

This chapter focuses on the cognition of coherence relations, that is, relations like *Cause-Consequence*, *Contrast*, and *Enumeration*. Understanding the coherence relations between utterances in a discourse is a crucial aspect of verbal communication. If readers and listeners have not inferred the coherence relation, they have not understood the text fully. We argue that all possible relations that connect discourse segments share certain conceptual properties. For example, we can distinguish between positive relations like *List* (*and*) and *Cause-Consequence* (*as a result*) and negative relations like *Exception* (*unless*) and *Concession* (*but*). The basic claim of our *Cognitive approach to Coherence Relations* (CCR) is that all relations share a limited set of conceptual properties, and that this set is cognitively basic: Humans use them while interpreting and producing discourse. We discuss evidence from the lexicon of connectives in several languages, from language acquisition, to discourse processing and representation.

1. Introduction

Discourse is often considered a crucial notion for understanding human communication, or, as Graesser, Millis, and Zwaan (1997: 164) put it, "Discourse is what makes us human." A central objective of discourse studies is to characterize discourse connectedness. Consider the following example from a Dutch electronic newspaper, which we have segmented into (1a) and (1b):

(1) a. *Greenpeace heeft in het Zuid-Duitse Beieren een nucleair transport verstoord.*
Greenpeace has obstructed a nuclear transport in the South German state of Bavaria.
b. *Demonstranten ketenden zich vast aan de rails.*
Demonstrators chained themselves to the rails.
(*Telegraaf*, April 10, 2001)

This short electronic news item does not create any interpretation difficulties. Nevertheless, in order to understand the fragment correctly, a massive amount of inferencing has to take place. For instance, we have to infer that the nuclear transport was not disturbed by the *organization* Greenpeace, but by members of that organization; that the protesters are members of the organization; that the nuclear transport took place by train; that the place where the protesters chained themselves to the rails is on the route the train took; that the time at which the protesters chained themselves to the rails coincided with the time of the transport; and that the obstruction of the transport was *caused* by the protesters chaining themselves to the rails.

Some of these inferences are based on world knowledge, for instance, that organizations consist of people and that people, but not organizations, can carry out physical actions. Others are based on discourse structural characteristics. For example, people reading news texts expect to get explanations for the phenomena described. When one event in the text can be interpreted as an explanation for another, readers will infer a causal link between them.

What we see from such a fragment is that readers work hard to make a coherent interpretation of the information in a text. This coherence may, but need not, be signaled explicitly in the text. That is why we advocate a *coherence* approach: The connectedness is a characteristic of the mental representation of the discourse rather than of the discourse itself. Although coherence phenomena are of a conceptual nature, their reconstruction is often based on linguistic signals in the discourse itself. These linguistic expressions are considered "processing instructions" to language users. For instance, connectives (*because, however*) and (other) lexical markers of coherence relations, such as cue phrases (*On the one hand... on the other hand*) and signaling phrases (*The problem is... A solution might be...*) make the meaning relations between discourse segments explicit. In fragment (1), the causal relation between (a) and (b) could have been signaled through a connective like *because*.

The relation between the linguistic surface code on the one hand (so-called cohesion phenomena), and aspects of the discourse representation on the other hand (coherence), has become a crucial research issue in the interdisciplinary field of discourse studies.

2. The research challenge

This chapter focuses on the cognition of coherence relations, that is, relations like Cause-Consequence, Contrast, Enumeration. Understanding the coherence relations between the utterances in a discourse is a crucial aspect of verbal communication. Inferring coherence relations between the segments of a discourse is a prerequisite for understanding the discourse: If a reader has not inferred the coherence relation, s/he has not understood the text fully. Consider the following examples:

(2) (i) Mart likes lollypops. (ii) Willem prefers licorice.

(3) (i) It was the end of a long day at work. (ii) Jan was exhausted.

(4) (i) Daan and Anneke aren't in. (ii) Their car isn't in the driveway.

In order to understand the mini-texts in these examples, the reader must infer the coherence relations between (i) and (ii): Contrast, Cause-Consequence, and Claim-Argument, respectively. That these are the relations involved follows if we look at the semantics of the connectives and cue phrases that can be used to make the relation explicit: *but*, *as a consequence*, and *because*, respectively.

In the past, theories have been proposed that make an inventory of the kind of relations that can be found in different types of discourse (written or spoken). Rhetorical Structure Theory (Mann & Thompson, 1988; Taboada & Mann, 2006; Taboada, chapter 8 of this volume) is among the most influential ones. It generated a host of publications (see the RST website, http://www.sfu.ca/rst/, for an up-to-date bibliography) in different areas such as natural language generation, discourse analysis and (text) linguistics. An issue that we have raised in previous work (Sanders, Spooren & Noordman, 1992; Sanders & Spooren, 2007) is to what extent such inventories (that can consist of large or even infinite numbers of relations, see Hovy & Maier, 1995) are more than just an analytic tool for text analysts. If coherence relations are part of the cognitive representation that a reader makes of a text, they should have a cognitive status. What evidence is there for such a claim? A second issue is how we can investigate the alleged cognitive status of coherence relations. In this chapter, we will provide an answer to both questions.

By way of preview to our answers: We will argue that all possible relations that connect discourse segments share certain conceptual properties. For example, we can distinguish between positive relations like List (*and*) and Cause-Consequence (*so*) and negative relations like Exception (*unless*) and Concession (*but*). Our working hypothesis is that we can come up with a limited set of such properties, and that it is this set that is cognitively basic: Humans use them while interpreting and producing discourse. This hypothesis constitutes the heart of the Cognitive approach to Coherence Relations (CCR).

3. Example

The following is a "letter to the editor" in a Dutch monthly. We will analyze the coherence relation structure of the letter.

[S1a] *Het stukje van Inge van den Blink over het boek "Gewiste sporen" van Annelies Nolet*
[S1b] *(Opzij, november)*
verbaast mij wat.
The piece by Inge van den Blink about the book "Erased traces" by Annelies Nolet
[S1b] (*Opzij*, November)
is something of a surprise.

[S2a] *Zij geeft aan dat het even duurt*
She indicates that it takes a while

[S2b] *voordat ze wist wie wie is.*
before she knew who is who

[S3] *Daar had ik geen enkel probleem mee.*
I didn't have any problem with that.

[S4] *Het is na twee minuten lezen volstrekt helder.*
It is completely clear after two minutes of reading.

[S5] *Ik heb erg genoten van het boek.*
I enjoyed this book very much.

[S6] *Deze wijze waarop de hoofdpersoon heen en weer pendelt tussen "onze werkelijkheid" en "haar werkelijkheid" en uiteindelijk volledig in "haar werkelijkheid" blijft, wordt prachtig beschreven.*
The way in which the main character moves between "our reality" and "her reality" and ultimately stays completely in "her reality" is described beautifully.

[S7a] *Het taalgebruik is erg helder,*
The use of language is very clear

[S7b] *waardoor de gevoelens die bij dit proces spelen, op een intelligente wijze bij de lezer worden opgeroepen.*
as a result of which the feelings which play a role in this process are evoked in the reader in an intelligent way

[S8] *Het is een ontroerend en daardoor boeiend boek.*
It is a moving and consequently captivating book.

Tilburg, B.J.M. Staffhorst
(*Opzij*, January 2000, p. 8)

First, something about the segmentation into units. All complete sentences of the text are separate units. Also, some of the clauses have been taken as separate units: that does not hold for restrictive relative clauses ("in which … in 'her reality'") nor for the complex noun phrase in S8 ("a moving and consequently captivating book"), but it does hold for the adverbial clause in S7 ("as a result of which … intelligent way"). An in-between case is the adverbial phrase in S2 ("before she …who"), which in a narrow sense is part of the direct object clause "that it takes a while … is who"), but that is elaborated to such a degree that it seems reasonable to consider this a separate unit.

In the analysis, as a rule we work top-down: from larger units to smaller units. For instance, in this text there is a separation between S1–S4 and S5–S8. S1–S4 gives the response of the author to the piece by Van den Blink. This makes it a background for the own judgment by the author in S5–S8. This leads us to the following analysis:

Segment	Relation	Connective
[S1-S4]–[S5-S8]	Background	–
[S1]–[S2-S4]	Evidence	–
[S2]–[S3-S4]	Contrast	–
[S3]–[S4]	Evidence	–
[S5]–[S6-S8]	Evidence	–
[S6]–[S7]–[S8]	Enumeration	–
[S7a-S7b]	Cause-Consequence	*waardoor*

This analysis is visualized in Figure 1.

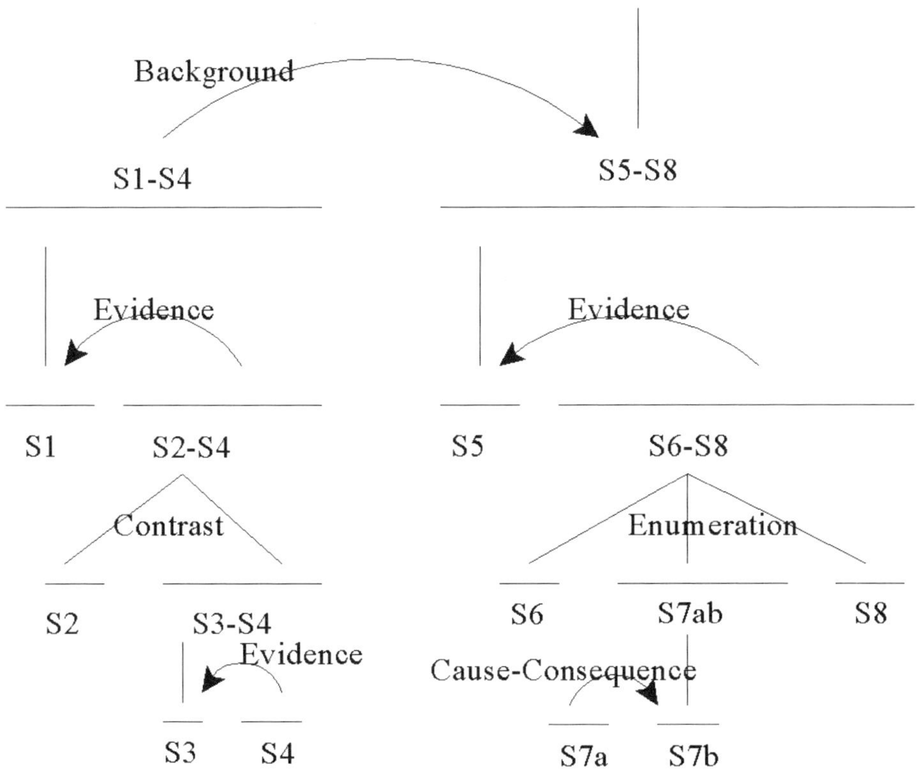

Figure 1. Analysis of coherence relations in example text

According to this analysis, segment S5 is the core of the text: One way or the other all other text parts are linked to this segment (all arrows in Figure 1 point to this text segment). By this analysis, we make an estimate of the intentions of the author. Not everybody has to agree with this estimate, but at the very least it is defensible.

The analysis shows, by the way, that coherence relations can exist both between smaller segments (separate sentences and clauses) and between larger segments (collections of sentences, like S1-S4 and S5-S8). They can even hold between paragraphs, sections and complete chapters. Coherence relations can therefore be used locally and globally (see Taboada, chapter 8 of this volume, for more details).

4. Research method

For the analysis of our text example we used a variety of different relations. In the original RST proposals, a total of 23 (Mann & Thompson, 1986) of such relations were mentioned. However, Hovy and Maier (1995) made an inventory of relations mentioned in the literature and presented a profligate list of relations, which may even be infinite in principle. In fact, the recent accounts of RST, which are widely used in computational analyses (Carlson, Marcu & Okurowski, 2001), present 78 relations. As much as such numbers may be useful for descriptively adequate analyses, CCR claims that only a limited number of primitives determine the cognitively relevant categories of relations. In other words, it is not so much the relations themselves that are cognitively real, but rather the basic distinctions that can be used to classify all relations. CCR has been formulated as a classification of relations (Sanders, Spooren & Noordman, 1992). The starting point of our classification consists of four basic relational concepts. These are four properties common to all relations. We have set out to define the "relations among the relations," relying on the intuition that some coherence relations are more alike than others. Fur the purposes of demonstration we sketch two of these properties. For a full description, see Sanders et al. (1992).

Basic operation: Additive versus causal relations

The Basic Operation refers to the intuition that discourse segments can be either connected strongly (in causal relations) or weakly (in additive relations). In additive relations, there is a relation of conjunction between the two segments, see example (2). In causal relations, the basic operation is implicational. For instance, as much as the relations in (3) and (4) differ, they also have something in common: causality. A type of physical causality is involved in (3), which could be expressed by "That is why" or "as a consequence," but there is also a causal implication relation involved in the reasoning expressed in (4), where the speaker concludes something on the basis of an observation. This type of Conclusion/relation can typically be expressed by connectives like *because*.

Source of coherence: Content, epistemic and speech act relations

In a content relation, the link involves a real world connection: The relation involves the propositional or ideational content of the related segments (example 3); in an epistemic relation, the connection involves the level of reasoning and concluding (example 4). In a speech act relation, the connection is at the level of illocutions (example 5) (cf. Sweetser, 1990).

(5) Does anybody need to go to the restrooms? Because we are leaving in a minute.

How can the cognitive status of coherence relations be investigated?

The central hypothesis is that, together, the principles in CCR account for coherence relations and connective use, and play a pivotal role in explaining the processing and representation of discourse. We believe that this hypothesis can be tested through empirical study of the use of language. Below, we summarize examples of such research. We will first explore the role of two of the basic categories underlying coherence relations, namely basic operation and source of coherence, as they show up in categorization tasks like sorting cards. Second, we compare the use of connectives in different languages. Third, we investigate the role of causal connectives and relations in discourse processing and in language acquisition.

5. Recent research

Categorization of relations

In CCR, distinctions like content-epistemic-speech act and causal versus additive are claimed to play a crucial role in a cognitive account of causal coherence. Is there any empirical evidence for their relevance? The evidence for the psychological plausibility consists of data gathered in different experimental tasks, such as labeling relations and sorting tasks.

In a labeling experiment, reported as Experiment 1 in Sanders et al. (1992), a set of 34 sentence pairs along with ten filler pair items were presented to 13 experts on discourse analysis (researchers and advanced students). The sentence pairs were chosen from Dutch newspaper articles, advertisements and the like and represent two examples of each coherence relation listed in the experiment, along with ten filler items. In an instruction phase, the participants were asked to read carefully through a list containing the names of 17 relations along with their definitions. After the training session the participants labeled the 34 relations, plus 10 fillers. It was expected that the participants agree to a considerable degree with our classification, specifically at the level of categories like causal/additive and content/non-content. To test this expectation, an analysis of the participants' responses was carried out: What type of labels did participants choose?

It turned out that for 238 out of 285 possible causal labels (83.5 %), the participants chose a causal label. For 114 out of 126 possible additive labels (90.5 %), the participants chose a label for an additive relation. Similarly, for 118 out of 181 possible content relation labels, participants chose a content label relation (65.2 %); for 198 out of 230 possible non-content relation labels participants chose a non-content (i.e., epistemic/speech act) relation label.[1] All these agreement scores were well above chance level, although agreement for content relation labels was lowest. From this we concluded that analysts use distinctions like causal/additive and content/non-content to carry out the labeling task. These data allow for two types of conclusions. First, there is substantial agreement among language users concerning relation categorization (people tend to agree on the use of categories like causal and non-causal). Second, if there is disagreement, then this disagreement is systematic in that it can be described in terms of the categories proposed. Both conclusions support the psychological validity of relation categorization in the Cognitive approach to Coherence Relations (CCR).

Cross-linguistic study of connectives

Distinctions as source of coherence have also been used in many linguistically oriented studies. Some of these studies have a purely theoretical nature, others have included the analysis of naturally occurring language material (so-called corpus studies). What do these studies show? Consider the following examples.

(6) It was a hot day. *So* Noortje went swimming.

(7) The temperatures were below 0 for weeks. *So* the pond was frozen.

(8) Their car is not there. *So* the neighbors are not at home.

(9) We are having a party. *So* what do you want to drink?

All these causal relations can be expressed in English with one connective, *so*. It is possible to use one connective *dus* in the Dutch equivalents, but this would lead to different interpretations (see Sanders, Sanders & Sweetser, ms, for more details). Especially the content interpretation seems no longer to be available. The Dutch lexicon of causal

1. In our 1992 analysis we did not make a distinction between epistemic and speech act relations.

connective and cue phrases enables speakers to be very specific on the exact type of causality they intend to express. The clearest example is *daardoor* ("as a result"), which cannot possibly be used to express speech act (9) or epistemic relations (8).

(6)' *Het was een warme dag. Daarom ging Noortje zwemmen.*

(7)' *De temperatuur was al weken onder 0. Daardoor was de vijver bevroren.*

(8)' *Hun auto staat er niet. Dus de buren zijn niet thuis.*

(9)' *We hebben een feestje. Dus wat wil je drinken?*

A recurrent finding in corpus studies is that Dutch connectives like *doordat* ("as a result") and *daarom* ("that's why") express predominantly content relations and that connectives like *dus* ("so") specialize for more subjective, i.e., epistemic and speech act relations. Recently, major findings were replicated in large scale, automatic analyses (Bestgen, Degand & Spooren, 2006). Section 6 continues on a research proposal for this subject.

Processing

If categorizations of coherence relations have real cognitive significance, they should prove relevant in areas such as discourse processing and language development. Much suggestive evidence already exists and additional studies are on their way. For instance, there is substantial evidence from processing studies demonstrating the psychological relevance of causality as a conceptual category at the discourse level. Causal relations result in better memory representations than additive relations (see Noordman & Vonk, 1998; Sanders & Noordman, 2000). It remains to be seen what the precise explanation is for the relatively fast on-line processing of causal relations.

But how about source of coherence? There is not too much experimental work on this distinction. Studying on-line text processing, Traxler, Bybee and Pickering (1997) focused on the difference between content and epistemic causal relations and concluded that content relations are processed quicker than epistemic ones. Noordman and De Blijzer (2000) arrived at similar conclusions.

Another type of evidence for the cognitive relevance of content versus non-content categories was recently reported by Kamalski, Lentz, Sanders and Zwaan (2008). They investigated the processing and representation of causal connectives and cue phrases in persuasive texts. Fragments including epistemic markers like *Therefore* in (10) and content markers like *As a result* in (11) were compared to their implicit equivalents — that is, to identical fragments, but without the causal connective and cue phrase. Text fragments (10) and (11) are taken from larger persuasive texts on genetic manipulation.

(10) (…) *Therefore*, there is only one clear answer to genetic manipulation: stop eating genetically manipulated food. Biological foods are safer for the environment…

(11) Extra genes are introduced. *As a result*, the organism changes.

The experimental texts were manipulated at several places, so that four versions could be compared: content implicit, content explicit, epistemic implicit and epistemic explicit.

Readers were asked whether they considered the author convincing. It turned out that the content explicit text versions were considered most convincing, whereas the epistemic explicit versions were considered less convincing. When asked to judge the author's intentions, participants appeared to consider epistemic explicit versions most "persuasive." Perhaps even more interestingly, on-line processing results show that epistemic and content markers result in different ways of processing. Reading times indicated that readers slowed down at the end of the sentence in the epistemic explicit condition, but not in the content explicit condition. Kamalski et al. suggest that epistemic marking in persuasive text leads to a so-called *forewarning effect*: readers resist the author's message because this author is very clearly present ("on stage"), making an argument in favor of his own claims.

Children's language

We expect the different conceptual categories to show a different pattern in acquisition. We will also consider whether the data predict differences in cognitive complexity: Do they allow for conclusions on the *relative order* of acquisition?

Most children build their first multi-clause discourse before the age of three; instead of uttering one clause at a time, they start producing combined clauses (cf. Clark, 2002). At first, the coherence relations between these clauses remain implicit. Later, children learn how to use connectives to make relations explicit. Both naturalistic and experimental studies of first language acquisition indicate that additive relations are acquired before causal relations, and that additive connectives are acquired before causal connectives (Spooren & Sanders, 2008), which appear around age two. More precisely, Bloom (1991) reports that English children follow the same route in acquiring coherence relations:

(12) additive < temporal < causal < adversative

Studying the speech data of twelve Dutch-speaking children, Evers-Vermeul & Sanders (2008) show that the first causal connective (as in their example 13) does not appear before an additive connective (as in 14) has occurred.

(13) *Kim is een meisje.* ***En*** *jij bent een jongetje he?* (Thomas, 2;8.23)
Kim is a girl. And you are a boy, aren't you?

(14) *Ik heb (een) beetje griep.* ***Want*** *ik ben laat gaan slapen.* (Abel, 3;3.8)
I've got a touch of flu. Because I went to bed late.

In the field of acquisition, many research challenges rise, too. We will continue on this subject at the end of the following section.

6. Research proposal

This section continues on the recent studies that have been introduced in Section 5.

Categorization of relations

Research of the categorization of relations produced inspiring results: First, there is a high amount of agreement on the use of certain relations, such as causal/non-causal. Second, any occurring disagreement is systematic in that it can be described in terms of the proposed categories.

These fundamental issues call for new empirical investigations. In the meantime, several new studies are already on their way.

Cross-linguistic study of connectives

From cross-linguistic study of connectives, we conclude that the categories identified in connective use show a strong resemblance to those identified in the coherence tradition. This should not come as a surprise, since connectives are the linguistic counterpart of coherence relations. The picture sketched here should be filled in, by elaborate corpus studies that allow more languages to be compared.

Processing

The cognitive status of differences in subjectivity appears relevant across genres. The cross-genre and even cross-media comparisons of coherence phenomena are an important research are for future discourse studies.

Childrens' language

Children use an additive connective before they begin to use causal connectives. Still many research challenges rise in the field of acquisition. One major issue is the role of parental input, and the question how this relates to theories of inherent complexity: is it because of differences in complexity that children acquire the connectives in this order, or does the input they receive play a decisive role?

7. Practical relevance

How does the analysis of coherence relations in terms of CCR help us in matters of practical importance? To answer this question, we have to take a step back from the principles expressed in CCR to the use of coherence relations and connectives in actual language use. The principles are mainly of interest for a psychologically plausible model of text processing. That means that their interest is mainly of a theoretical, fundamental nature. To apply these principles, we must consider the importance of coherence relations and the way they are marked for how language users make a representation of the information in the text. We will give two examples.

The benefit of connectives in natural reading situations

In a very recent study (Sanders, Land & Mulder, 2007), we have investigated the experimental effect of coherence markers on text comprehension in a so-called ecologically valid, i.e., natural, reading situation. We compared the reading of two text versions, one explicit, with coherence markers like connectives and cue phrases signaling important relations in the text, and another, implicit one. Furthermore, we compared the reading of these two text versions in two situations: a "classical" laboratory context and a natural context. In the latter case, readers were unaware they were taking part in an experiment while reading. Sitting in a business meeting, they read a text that was directly relevant to the decisions that had to be taken. In this natural context, readers of the explicit version performed better on text comprehension questions than readers of the implicit version. We consider this an important finding. It suggests that reading in a laboratory context is not that different from reading in a natural situation, at least when the interpretation of important coherence relations is concerned.

In a second study, poor readers in the second grade of pre-vocational secondary education, turned out to benefit from coherence signaling. When texts were presented with coherence markers present, they performed better on a text comprehension task than when these markers were lacking. Leading textbooks, especially developed for these pupils, often do not contain text characteristics that stimulate the construction of a coherent text representation. Rather, these text books show an attempt to minimize cognitive load: fragmented presentation of textual information in short sentences that are not explicitly connected. Our research has shown that this strategy is not beneficial to this group of readers. This corroborates Beck et al.'s (1991) conclusion that many school texts are difficult to understand.

Still, several crucial questions remain for the further development of a cognitive approach to discourse representation and document design. All the markers used in these experiments seem to have at least one thing in common: they enable readers to make better text representations. Still, a first key question is: can we generalize over all these different linguistic markers of coherence? In the experiments, we used several types of relational markers, varying from causal connectives to lexical cue phrases, which make enumerations explicit. These various types of coherence markers are likely to have varied effects on the processing and representation of discourse. For instance, content causal connectives have a different influence on on-line processing and text representation than epistemic markers that express the arguments of the author. Further research on the differences of the various markers is imperative.

A second key question is: how do we explain this effect of coherence markers on comprehension? The literature suggests that the effects of connectives and lexical markers of coherence relations depend on reader characteristics and that they only lead to better comprehension under average conditions: when texts are not too difficult and when readers are not too knowledgeable. For instance, reader's prior background knowledge has been shown to interact with coherence marking: High knowledge readers were found to perform worse on comprehension questions after reading a signaled text version, whereas low knowledge readers performed better after reading an explicit text version (McNamara & Kintsch, 1996). Several researchers have suggested that a very explicit text causes high prior knowledge readers to process the text superficially because they "get lazy" and they do not make many inferences, resulting in lower understanding (Gilabert, Martinez & Vidal-Abarca, 2005).

At the same time, it is of the highest importance to conduct additional studies of the cognitive processes involved: What is the influence of the markers on the on-line reading process of the low proficiency readers? Are there indications that markers speed up the reading process, as they do in highly skilled readers (Sanders & Noordman, 2000)? The experimental set-ups required in order to answer these questions are new challenges for ecological validity. Modern experimental technology is likely to help out here: Present-day eye tracking devices allow for less intrusive measurements during reading.

Automatic summarization

The amount of information available to us is gigantic. A recent estimate puts the size of the web at over 45 billion pages (www.worldwidewebsize.com, consulted on March 4, 2008). What a valuable tool an automatic summarizer of that amount of information would be! If you have ever used Microsoft Word's Auto summary tool to summarize your document, you know that it works very poorly. The cause is in the way it works: It looks for the sentences containing the most frequent words in your document, because it thinks that those sentences must be the core sentences in the text. It then puts the sentences containing the most frequent words in the summary.

This procedure fails for several reasons. A summary (see Hahn & Mani, 2000, for an accessible description of the state of the art of automatic summarization):

1. **The summarizer should know what the text is about.** Writers like to vary. They use synonyms and paraphrases. The summarizer must know that in the case of a paraphrase the text is still about the same concept.
2. **The summarizer must know what the structure of the text is**. A sentence in the text can be about the main topic of the text or about a detail. Sentences about the main topic are more important, and consequently should be in the summary; sentences about the details shouldn't.
3. **The summarizer must have an idea about the writer's goals with the text.** One and the same piece of information can be used for very different purposes. "With the arrival of the oil pipeline from Rotterdam to the Ruhr area the situation changed. Now it was no longer necessary to transport the oil in long liner trains. That made the construction of the so-called Betuwelijn superfluous." In a text about the developments in the Rotterdam harbor since 1945, the first sentence will be central one, because it sketches the new situations. In a text about the causes of the failure of the Betuwelijn project, the final sentence is most important. In order to decide on the structure of the text you need to know the writer's intentions.
4. **The summarizer should know what the genre of the text is.** In a news story, the most important information is put in the first paragraph. In a scientific article, the most important information is in the introduction and the conclusion. In an ad, the most important information invariably is "Buy me," and in a novel, all parts are equally important. To be able to decide what the most important information is, the summarizer must know what the genre of the text is.
5. **The summarizer must be sensitive to different information modalities.** Modern day texts are multimodal: information in texts is given in words, in pictures, and sometimes even in other modalities (such as sounds, etc.). A good summarizer should be able to deal with the multimodal character of modern documents.
6. **The summarizer must be able to formulate.** Nobody accepts a summary that consists merely of words that are a repetition from the original text. The summaries produced by Word are of this kind. They are what Hahn and Mani (2000) call *extraction summarizers*. But to qualify as a good summary, a summary must be a reformulation of the original text. Hahn and Main (2000) call such formulating summarizers abstraction summarizers.

These requirements are far from met in today's available summarizers. To know what the text is about and what the genre of the text is, the program needs access to world knowledge. For other issues it needs textual knowledge. Some computational linguists claim that recent increase in computing capabilities will allow producing summaries on the basis of purely statistical information drawn from the text. However, it is difficult to see how such approaches will be able to deal with issues of text structure. This is where coherence relations come in. Taboada and Mann (2006b) give an overview of RST-based approaches to summarization. The basic tenet of these approaches is that the summary of the text consists of all the core segments in a texts (i.e., segments to which the arrows in the analysis point). Furthermore, since a coherence relation analysis gives an indication of the hierarchical level of the text, it is possible to distinguish formally between central parts of the text (the higher level elements) and details (the lower level parts in the text). It remains an unresolved issue to what extent coherence relation analyses can be done automatically. Much of the work in the discourse community revolves on this issue.

Assignment

1. Do you consider the following examples content, epistemic or speech act relations? Motivate your answer.

   (1) a. Bill Hamers (aged 20) is the murderer of his father.
       b. Witnesses saw him at the crime scene.

   (2) a. The United States produce more grain than needed for internal consumption.
       b. That is why they export the surplus.

   (3) a. I am the chairman of this meeting.
       b. You are out of order.

2. Connectives play an important role in this chapter. Connectives can make coherence relations explicit, but not every connective can be used for every relation. Below you find on the left side a number of relations taken from RST (Mann & Thompson, 1986) and on the right side a number of connectives. Which relation can be expressed with which connective?

Background
Condition
Contrast
Restatement
Goal
Evidence
Cause-Consequence
Temporal Sequence
Elaboration

and
if
because
after
so
although
but
since
in order to
as a result
in other words

3. Relational coherence can be established by different kinds of connectives: Subordinating conjunctions (*because, if, although*), coordinating conjunctions (*and, but*), conjunctive adverbs (*so, therefore, yet*) and conjunctive adverbial phrases (*as a consequence, in contrast with this*). Find the connectives in the following fragment and identify the subtype:

   If you want to make the best use of this book, you should note the following. This book can be used either as a straightforward handbook for its recipes, or as a full course in modern vegetarian cookery, because the recipes are all described in enough detail for anyone with only a little cooking experience to be able to follow them. In addition, we have tried to anticipate, and provide remedies for, any snags which might occur.

Chapter 14

A computational psycholinguistic algorithm to measure cohesion in discourse

Max M. Louwerse and Patrick Jeuniaux
University of Memphis

An important aspect of discourse and discourse comprehension is the organization of the linguistic materials in the discourse as well as the organization of the interpretation arising from those materials in the mind of the comprehender. We use the term *coherence* for the representational relationships in the mind of the comprehender and *cohesion* for the discourse cues that coherent representations should build. Cohesive cues in discourse typically facilitate how coherent representations should be built in the mind of the hearer/reader. The computational psycholinguistic technique Latent Semantic Analysis (LSA) is able to determine the semantic relatedness between words, sentences and paragraphs, and is therefore useful in measuring cohesion and coherence.

1. Introduction

Discourse is a two-way instrument for speakers and hearers, writers and readers (Renkema, 2004). In order for this instrument to be used successfully, its components need to be organized. On the one hand, the organization can be made explicit in the discourse itself through various linguistic cues, and on the other hand, the organization can emerge in the mind of the hearer/reader. We have used the term *coherence* for the representational relationships in the mind of the hearer/reader and *cohesion* for the discourse cues to the comprehender that coherent representations should be built. In a nutshell, cohesion emphasizes discourse-as-product, and coherence emphasizes discourse-as-process (Louwerse, 2002).

Examples of cohesive devices are connectives that link clauses together, pronouns that refer to noun phrases, and semantic overlap that links two semantically related concepts (see Sanders & Spooren, chapter 13; Taboada, chapter 8 of this volume).

A sentence like *My neighbor plays saxophone, because the man loves the sound of the instrument* links *man* to *my neighbour*, *instrument* to *saxophone*, and marks a causal relationship between the two clauses with the connective *because*. Cues like these help the hearer/reader build a coherent mental representation. But cohesion is neither necessary nor sufficient for coherence. That is, the absence of specific cohesive cues can still bring about coherence (e.g., *My neighbor plays saxophone. He loves the sound* can be made coherent without these cohesive cues). Similarly, the presence of cohesive cues does not guarantee coherence (*My neighbor plays saxophone, for the reason that the organism likes the subjective sensation of hearing the single-reed woodwind with a conical bore*). In other words, a text should be as cohesive as needed for a reader to make a coherent representation.

Many psycholinguistic studies have shown that cohesion generally facilitates coherence (Graesser, Gernsbacher & Goldman, 2003; Traxler & Gernsbacher, 2007; Zwaan & Radvanksy, 1998). For instance, semantic similarity between sentences or paragraphs facilitates the construction of a mental representation of the events described by the text, compared to sentences that do not share such semantic content. Similar findings with regards to the use of referential, temporal, spatial, and causal relations have been reported.

To study the impact of cohesion on coherence, psychological experiments have carefully manipulated one variable (e.g., the connective), while keeping other variables constant (e.g., the two clauses). On the one hand, it can be argued that this creates unnatural texts perhaps useful for experiments but problematic for general text comprehension. On the other hand, identifying all cohesion relations in an actual text (novel, newspaper, etc.) requires a painstaking linguistic analysis with many variables to consider. Coders could mark connectives, pronouns, repetitive nouns and similarity in semantic content between sentences and/or paragraphs, and count the number of occurrences for each cohesion category, but such an exercise is not very practical and limited to a very small number of texts. Computational linguistic algorithms offer a solution to this problem in that they can be applied to natural texts and imply a minimal intervention of human judges.

2. Research challenge

Computational linguistic algorithms can help in determining how cohesive a text is. In fact, commonly used readability formulas like the Flesch-Kincaid scores and the Flesch Reading Ease (Klare, 1974–1975) have done this successfully over the last few decades. For instance, the Flesch Reading Ease formula reads as follows:

(1) Flesch Reading Ease = 206.835 – (1.015 × ASL) – (84.6 × ASW)
where:
ASL = average number of words per sentence
ASW = average number of syllables per word

However, whereas these readability formulas only focus on surface features, cohesion takes into account a variety of deeper features involving semantic and grammatical factors. Moreover, traditional readability scores and cohesion scores sometimes operate in opposite directions: adding a connective typically increases cohesion, but the sentence becomes longer, thereby decreasing the Flesch Reading Ease score. Similarly, repeating noun phrases typically increases cohesion compared to an ambiguous pronoun, but it adds to the average number of syllables per word, thereby lowering the Reading Ease score. Finally, readability formulas cannot inform about the structuring of the text. For instance, if three sentences are presented in random order, thereby presumably decreasing cohesion and coherence, readability scores will remain the same.

But how can computational algorithms measure cohesion if it is not uniquely identifiable in terms of surface features? In this chapter, we will focus on using the meaning of words, sentences and paragraphs to measure cohesion and coherence. This is not a trivial task. Indeed, how can computers understand the meaning of a text? How would a computer know that the meaning of *neighbor* is more similar to *man* than to *saxophone*?

Moreover, there is an additional research challenge we would like to address. In addition to finding a computational linguistic algorithm that helps to determine the cohesion of a text by using semantic information, it would be desirable that such algorithm would have realistic characteristics from a psycholinguistic perspective. The advantage of a computational psycholinguistic algorithm is bi-directional: the computational findings could be tested experimentally and shed light on psychological processes, and the psychological hypotheses could be tested with the algorithm and help improving it. In fact, a sub-domain of computational linguistics is devoted to this issue. The domain of computational psycholinguistics aims to build theories of psycholinguistic processes using computational models (Lewis, 2003). Not only do the computational algorithms have to be successful, they also need to have psychological validity.

In sum, the extent to which a text is cohesive is important for determining to what extent coherent mental representations can be built in the reader's mind. Identifying these cohesion relations computationally would be very useful. Moreover, it would be beneficial if computational linguistic algorithms that allow for identifying cohesion relations also have psychological validity. How could such a computational psycholinguistic algorithm be designed?

3. Examples

A common way to determine whether a computational linguistic algorithm can capture cohesion is by comparing cohesive texts to obvious non-cohesive texts using a random reordering of sentences (Hovy, 1988; McNamara, Cai & Louwerse, 2007). For example, consider the first sentences of Section 1.3 (p5) of Renkema's *Introduction to Discourse Studies* (2004), as presented in Table 1.

Table 1. Sample from Renkema (2004)

Original
1. The material in this book has been organized to serve as a first introduction to discourse studies at University level.
2. Inherent in the interdisciplinary nature of the field of discourse studies is the fact that each phenomenon can be looked at from different viewpoints.
3. Moreover, the danger exists of trivializing theoretical concepts as they are taken out of their disciplinary context.
4. Special attention will therefore be paid to the origins of key concepts in discourse studies.
5. Inter- or multidisciplinary discourse studies arose during the 1980s.
6. However, it is rooted in classical rhetoric and language philosophy and classics psychological and social article studies from both the Anglo-American and European traditions.
7. It is for that reason that relatively much attention is given to classic or impressive landmarks in the field of discourse studies.
Random reordering of sentences
1. It is for that reason that relatively much attention is given to classic or impressive landmarks in the field of discourse studies.
2. However, it is rooted in classical rhetoric and language philosophy and classics psychological and social article studies from both the Anglo-American and European traditions.
3. Moreover, the danger exists of trivializing theoretical concepts as they are taken out of their disciplinary context.
4. The material in this book has been organized to serve as a first introduction to discourse studies at University level.
5. Special attention will therefore be paid to the origins of key concepts in discourse studies.
6. Inter- or multidisciplinary discourse studies arose during the 1980s.
7. Inherent in the interdisciplinary nature of the field of discourse studies is the fact that each phenomenon can be looked at from different viewpoints.

Intuitively, the original text seems more coherent than the manipulated text. But why? Note that a readability formula cannot capture the differences in texts, and neither can an algorithm that counts the number of connectives or pronouns. So what computational linguistic algorithm, or better computational psycholinguistic algorithm, should be considered?

4. Research method

Looking at the Renkema example from the previous section, we likely need an algorithm that investigates semantic associations between text units. Latent Semantic Analysis (LSA) is a technique used to approximate just that. The input of LSA is a corpus of texts, and one possible output of this algorithm is a set of numbers between −1 and 1, representing the semantic similarity between each word of those texts. The underlying mechanism is roughly as follows (see Deerwester, Dumais, Furnas, Landauer & Harshman, 1990, for a mathematical introduction). The texts are segmented in contexts (e.g., sentences or paragraphs). The frequency of occurrence of each word in each context is computed. The resulting matrix of co-occurrence contains lots of zeros since many words only appear in a few contexts. A mathematical compression technique transforms this matrix and "infers" the relation between each word and each context, even in the cases in which the word does not occur in the context. That is to say, that LSA goes beyond the simple unit-context frequency matrix. Words are not only similar because they appear in the same context (which is what the unit-context frequency represents), but because they occur in *similar* contexts (i.e., contexts with similar words). In LSA, words are represented by long vectors of numbers that define a high dimensional space. The similarity of any two words can be assessed by computing the cosine between their vectors (a method that will be used in our study). These vectors can be used to represent sets of words (e.g., sentences or paragraphs). It is therefore possible to compute the similarity between sentences, paragraphs, and so on, which is helpful to measuring cohesion.

In fact, LSA is able to capture semantic relations quite well. Take, for instance, Table 2, which presents the semantic relations between six words. As the table shows, based on word co-occurrences in a large body of text, LSA is able to show that *neighbor* has more semantic association with *man* than with *instrument*, whereas for *saxophone* the opposite is true.

Table 2. Example of LSA similarity values between six words

	neighbor	played	saxophone	loves	sound	instrument
neighbor	1	.17	−.02	.29	.10	.04
played	.17	1	.29	.26	.21	.33
saxophone	−.02	.29	1	.11	.46	.51
loves	.29	.26	.11	1	.05	.13
sound	.10	.21	.46	.05	1	.31
instrument	.04	.33	.51	.13	.31	1

When we compute the similarity values between the five adjacent sentences of the original text and five adjacent sentences of the randomized text that we used in Table 1, it turns out that the average similarity value for the original text is .22 (SD = .05) and the randomized text .17 (SD = .05). In other words, the order of sentences in a text matters to its overall "similarity" — which can be taken as an index of its cohesion. This example of course does not allow general conclusions. First, the small number of sentences considered do not allow enough degrees of freedom to generalize these findings. Second, and related to the previous point, there are maximally 120 ways of constructing a text from 5 sentences, but many of these are almost identical to the original version (e.g., only one sentence pair differs), also in part because of the symmetry of the similarity relation (sentence 1–2 and sentence 2–1 are equally similar). Third, the example is limited to one section from one text. In order to generalize the findings, more texts are needed.

To account for these problems, six sources were selected (Table 3). In addition to Shakespeare's *Hamlet* and Tolstoy's *Anna Karenina*, we used the Switchboard Corpus (Godfrey & Holliman, 1993), a collection of 2,400 two-sided random topic telephone conversations taken from 543 speakers from all areas of the United States, and the Santa Barbara Corpus (Du Bois, Chafe, Meyer & Thompson, 2000), a collection of natural speech recordings taken from people across the United States. Finally, the New York Times and Wall Street Journal corpora consisted of all articles from those newspapers from 1996 (Graff, 1996).

Table 3. Means (SD) of original and manipulated texts average sentence-to-sentence (top) and paragraph-to-paragraph (bottom; italics) similarity values for six sources

Source	Anna Karenina	Hamlet	New York Times	Wall Street Journal	Switch Board	Santa Barbara
Year	1877	1601	1996	1996	2000	1997
Words	358,689	32,756	29,560,931	17,956,625	464,932	3,702,166
Genre	Literature	Literature	Newspaper	Newspaper	Dialogue	Dialogue
original	.09 (.18) *.09 (.18)*	.09 (.18) *.09 (.18)*	.09 (.16) *.15 (.17)*	.08 (.16) *.19 (.20)*	.08 (.19)	.12 (.19)
rand1	.02 (.11) *.03 (.12)*	.04 (.12) *.04 (.13)*	.01 (.08) *.02 (.08)*	.01 (.08) *.04 (.11)*	.018 (.10)	.072 (.15)
rand2	.02 (.11) *.02 (.11)*	.04 (.12) *.04 (.13)*	.01 (.08) *.02 (.08)*	.01 (.08) *.04 (.10)*	.022 (.11)	.071 (.15)

Text cohesion can be measured at the local level (the level of the sentence) and at a global level (the level of the paragraph). The cohesion of each six sources was analyzed at both levels. First, LSA similarity values were computed for all adjacent sentence pairs in their original order, and in ten randomizations of the original sentence order. The means and standard deviations of the cosine values of the original and of two randomized versions (instead of 10, for the sake of space) are presented in Table 3 (number on the first line). Without exceptions, similarity values for original versions were almost twice as high as those for randomized versions. In fact, when all original versions were compared with all randomized versions, significantly higher values were obtained for original versions than randomized versions ($t(124)=20.47$, $p<.001$). These results show that LSA can reliably distinguish locally cohesive from non-cohesive texts, where non-cohesive is defined as those texts with a randomized sentence order.

The second question is whether LSA can reliably distinguish cohesive and non-cohesive texts at a global level. The same sources were used, but now the order of paragraphs was randomized. As with the local cohesion analysis, ten randomized texts were created. Again, all similarity values were considerable higher for original than for randomized versions ($t(82)=15.19$, $p<.001$), as presented in Table 3 (numbers at the bottom, in italics). To sum up, these analyses show that LSA can distinguish between cohesive and non-cohesive texts from large corpora of a variety of genres, both at the local and global levels.

5. Recent research

Several arguments can be made against the evidence that LSA can distinguish between cohesive and non-cohesive texts. First, one could say that the randomization of the order of sentences and paragraph did not yield non-cohesive texts but unnatural texts. Secondly, one could argue that LSA similarity values do not tell us anything about cohesion because cohesion implies human interpretation of the text and LSA does not come close to human interpretation. We will address these two arguments next. The argument that randomized orders do not yield non-cohesive texts but unnatural texts is problematic. First, non-cohesive texts are by definition unnatural, since authors generally aim to help the reader in constructing a coherent mental representation, rather than to impede reading. Secondly, the texts with randomized sentence order are not necessarily perceived as unnatural. Take for instance example 1 taken from Anna Karenina and example 2 taken from the Santa Barbara Corpus.

(1) **Anna Karenina**
He muttered recalling everything that had happened.
She had not seen him since his abrupt departure from Moscow and she sent her elder son to bid him come to see her.
He could not believe that what gave such great and delicate pleasure to him and above all to her could be wrong.

Then remembering his brother Nikolay he resolved to himself that he would never allow himself to forget him that he would follow him up and not lose sight of him so as to be ready to help when things should go ill with him.
She knew as certainly as if he had told her that he was here to be where she was.
She saw that they felt themselves alone in that crowded room.

(2) **Santa Barbara Corpus**
.. You know.
.. I mean,
.. Oh —
I mean I trim horses,
and stuff like that,
but I mean,
I'm not like,
I'm not uh,
I don't know how to say it.
But you know,
they do it for a living.
you know,
… most people that you would get to trim your horse do it .. all the time.
and I'm not… that good or,
… very strong.

Although the first example will look more natural than the second to some readers, it may come as a surprise that the first example is actually taken from a sentence-randomized version of Anna Karenina while the second comes from one original turn of one speaker in the Santa Barbara corpus. Though these examples are obviously snapshots, they do show that determining what is natural and what is not is not necessarily easier for humans than for computers.

Despite their practical utility, the argument can be made that LSA similarity values do not tell us anything about cohesion because cohesion requires human interpretation. Contrary to this view, theories behind models like LSA have claimed to provide a solution to the psychological problem of how humans observing a relatively small set of events can construct knowledge representations that are adaptive in a large, potentially infinite variety of situations (Landauer & Dumais, 1997). LSA's mapping of initially meaningless words into a high dimensional semantic space can be seen as simulating cognition. Like language comprehension, memory for the initial local associations (surface structure) becomes memory for more global representations (latent meaning). Such a claim is controversial (Glenberg & Robertson, 2000; Sadoski, chapter 12 of this volume), but Louwerse (2007), and Louwerse & Van Peer (2006) have shown that there is evidence to support this claim.

6. Research proposal

In order to determine how cohesive cues in the text facilitate coherence in comprehenders it is helpful to computationally measure cohesion. Various computational linguistic techniques are able to do this, but techniques like LSA have proven to be particularly successful. LSA measures the semantic relatedness between words, sentences, paragraphs or even texts.

Because it measures semantic relatedness, the technique reaches highest performance with lexical items. One possible research question might target the other kind of cohesion devices (for example, similarity in terms of syntactic structure) and examine how they are involved in the perception of coherence, along with the vocabulary-driven cohesion.

Moreover, different cohesion strands have been differentiated: referential, spatial, temporal and causal. An interesting study would be to determine their relative importance in the computation of text cohesion.

Because LSA is able to compute the relatedness between different sizes of text units (e.g., clauses, sentences, paragraphs, chapters), it can cover a smaller or larger scope of the text. Another possible research focus would be to study how the relative importance of these different scopes in determining the coherence of the text as a whole. For instance, is local coherence (i.e., at a sentence level) more important than global coherence (i.e., at a paragraph level)?

A variety of distinctions can be considered in relation to text cohesion. For instance, texts can be distinguished in terms of the discourse register (spoken versus written, monologue versus dialogue, narrative versus expository) and one can ask what register is more cohesive in terms of semantic similarity. Another possible distinction could be the target audience of the text (children's books vs. texts for older readers).

7. Practical relevance

Since 1990, LSA has been used in a variety of applications. Initially it was used for information retrieval purposes (Deerwester, et al., 1990). To test LSA's knowledge of synonyms, Landauer and Dumais (1997) tested how well LSA would pass the Test of English as a Foreign Language (TOEFL) test by the Educational Testing Service that every foreigner at an American University needs to take. On 80 multiple choice test items, an LSA space of approximately 2000 pages scored 64% correct, compared with 33% correct for word-overlap methods, and 64% correct for the average student taking the test. But LSA can do more than identifying synonyms in language. Landauer, Foltz and Laham (1998) trained LSA on introductory psychology textbooks and tested how well it would identify the right answer in multiple choice questions given by the textbook publishers. Performance was not outstanding, but compared to class average, LSA would receive a passing grade. When Landauer et al. (1998) created on LSA space of textbook and student essays they found that LSA correlated better with expert graders than these graders did with each other. The success of LSA in grading essays has led to the Intelligent Essay Assessor (IEA), now a commercial product that is commonly used. The IEA computes content, style, and mechanics of an essay as well as self-validation, confidence and counterfeiting measures.

Kintsch (2002) also applied LSA to identify the theme and subthemes of a text. By comparing the propositions of a text, LSA was able to construct the macrostructure, and thereby the theme, of the text. Louwerse (2004) applied LSA to literary texts to determine the style of the author (idiolect) and groups of authors based on gender and literary period (sociolect). Where simple keyword algorithms failed, LSA was able to classify texts in terms of idiolect and sociolect on the basis of lexical consistency. Louwerse et al. (2006) classified literary texts on the basis of the semantic characteristics, making it possible to cluster texts according to their literary period solely on the basis of semantic content. Louwerse, Lewis and Wu (in press) classified Shakespearean plays in their different genres, based on the assumption that plays within a genre (e.g., comedy) have lexical content in common different from plays from another genre (e.g., tragedy). Louwerse and Zwaan (in press) showed how LSA can predict geographical information, like longitude, latitude, and population size of cities. Louwerse (2007) and Louwerse and Van Peer (in press) illustrated how cognitive phenomena attributed to embodied cognition, can also be modeled using the typically non-embodied technique of LSA. Finally, LSA is an important component of Coh-Metrix (Graesser, McNamara, Louwerse and Cai, 2004), a web-based tool that analyzes texts on over 50 types of cohesion relations and over 200 measures of language, text, and readability. In Coh-Metrix, LSA measures the semantic relatedness between sentences, paragraphs and texts.

In sum, LSA has been widely used in a variety of applications, ranging from text analysis, metaphor comprehension to problem solving. In most of these cases, the application simulates what a human would do otherwise. The practical relevance of computational psycholinguistic algorithms like LSA goes well beyond academics. Clearly, from an academic point of view it is important to develop cognitive models that simulate human performance, and computational tools that help researchers on a particular coding task. But knowing to what extent a text is cohesive is not only helpful for researchers. It can also help researchers conducting experiments who want to control for the various variables under investigation. It can help publishing houses who want to ensure that texts are readable for particular groups of readers. It can help teachers who want to know whether their textbooks are appropriate for their students.

And it can help readers themselves who may want to know the readability in terms of cohesion.

Assignment

As we have shown earlier, LSA computes semantic associates in similarity ranging from −1 to 1. A similarity of 1 corresponds to the idea that the two words can be found in very similar contexts (like synonyms). A similarity of −1 corresponds to the idea that the each word will be found in contexts very dissimilar from the contexts in which the other word is found. A similarity of 0 corresponds to words which are semantically unrelated.

Go to http://lsa.colorado.edu. Click on *Matrix Comparison*. Choose your corpus by specifying the topic space (or leave it to the default option). Make sure that the default option for comparison type, term to term, is selected. Now type in a handful of words, one at a time with a white line in between and click on the "Submit texts" button.

(1) To understand better the meaning of the similarity values, enter semantically related terms (e.g., *fruit* and *vegetable*), synonyms (e.g. *car* and *automobile*), antonyms (e.g., *black* and *white*), unrelated terms (e.g., *saxophone* and *neighbor*). What do you find? Can you explain these results?

(2) Based on the findings at the word level, now try comparing sentences that have anticipated LSA cosine values of 1, −1, and 0. Can you explain the results? What are the words in the sentence LSA performs on well? What are the words in the sentence LSA has difficulties with? Why do you think this is the case?

(3) As we have shown earlier, some have argued that LSA can be seen as a computational model of human cognition (Landauer & Dumais, 1997). If any, what are the limitations of LSA as a model of human cognition (think of the contribution in this volume by Sadoski)?

Part VII

Discourse and Institution

Chapter 15

Chinese questions and power relations in institutional dialogue

Jinjun Wang
Yunnan University

The turn-taking model proposed by Sacks et al. (1974) has made a great contribution to our understanding of conversational activities. However, there have been some objections raised against it, which partially have been discussed in Section 9.2 of *Introduction to Discourse Studies* (Renkema, 2004). This chapter, from the perspective of Critical Discourse Analysis, intends to introduce another challenge to the model, that is, its failure to take power relations into consideration. In the turn-taking model, participants are regarded as equal and cooperative and have equal rights to take turns and exchange speech roles. In fact, this is not always the case in the empirical study, in particular, in institutional dialogue. On the basis of the collected data concerning three subgenres of Chinese institutional dialogue, i.e., news interview, medical encounter and classroom encounter, I try to claim that Chinese questions are an important means to exercise power in institutional dialogue by way of exploring turn-taking, topic control and the distribution of question types.

1. Introduction

In the 1960s and 1970s, a group of American sociologists, like Harvey Sacks, Emanuel Schegloff and Gail Jefferson, have concentrated on conversational activities and developed the ethnomethodological approach to conversation. To them, conversation analysis is a branch of enthnomethodology. Ironically enough, the founding work in conversation analysis has been done by sociologists instead of linguists. Among concepts and mechanisms concerning conversation, the turn-taking model by Sacks, Schegloff and Jefferson (1974) is highlighting. The turn-taking system shows that there are two possibilities when a turn is transferred. The first is that the current speaker can select the next speaker by way of using vocatives, gaze, posture or asking a listener questions and so on. The second possibility is that the next speaker may self-select. Within the turn-taking system, only one person speaks at a time and speaker change recurs. It seems that conversation is a generative mechanism which keeps speakers taking turns.

The model indicates that participants in conversation are regarded as equal and cooperative and have equal rights to take turns and exchange speech roles. However, the model has been criticized by many scholars in one way or another. Kress and Fowler (1979: 63) point out that "in conversation, any appearance of intimacy, solidarity and co-operation is generally illusory. Speakers act out their socially ascribed roles in contending for attention, for the right to initiate new segments of the conversation, to introduce new topics, and to 'hold the floor.'" Eggins and Slide (1997) suggest that conversation is always a covert struggle over power, which is disguised by the apparent equality. Some scholars have criticized Grice's Cooperative Principle (CP in short) for its basis on the equal, symmetrical and cooperative conversation. Harris (1995) argues that Grice's CP as a universal pragmatic principle is questionable as it does not take into consideration power and inequality in communicative contexts.

In fact, the turn-taking model overlooks power and inequality in communicative contexts. In casual conversation, power and inequality are covert or not easy to scrutinize. However, in institutional dialogue, power is more or less overt and is easy for people to scrutinize owing to its highly conventionalized structure. Obviously enough, the turn-taking model fails to take power into consideration, whether in casual conversation or in institutional dialogue.

Although the turn-taking model has made a great contribution to our understanding of conversational activities, it has some defects and has encountered some objections against it, which partially have been discussed in Section 9.2 of *Introduction to Discourse Studies* (Renkema, 2004). Challenging the model from the perspective of Critical Discourse Analysis, I intend to show that the turn-taking model should involve in the factor of power relations between participants in conversation by ways of exploring Chinese questions and power relations on the basis of the collected data on Chinese institutional dialogue. It is held that Chinese questions in institutional dialogue exercise power through turn-taking and topic control, and different question types have their own ways to exercise power.

2. The research challenge

Many Chinese scholars like Lü (1982), Shao (1996), and others, believe that Chinese questions in general can be divided into two types, that is, general questions and special questions, and two other types like disjunctive questions and tag questions are derived from general questions. Similar to their classification, Li and Thompson (1981) divide questions into four types: interrogative-word question, particle question, disjunctive question and tag question. In general, these four types of questions are determined by particles, conjunctions and interrogative words in sentences. Interrogative-word questions or special questions are identical to English "Wh"-questions as they contain Mandarin interrogative-words like 谁 (who), 什么 (what), 怎么 (how), 几个 (how many), 为什么 (why), 哪一个 (which), etc. For example,

(1) **谁**要和我一起去？
Who wants to go with me?

(2) 他要买**什么**呢？
What will he buy?

A disjunctive question is presented with a choice between two options. Generally speaking, it is composed by two declarative sentences joined by "or," which is frequently expressed by Chinese conjunctions "---还是" and "是---还是---." For example,

(3) 你学英语，**还是**学俄语？
You learn English or Russian?

(4) 你**是**要辣的，**还是**不要辣的？
You want it spicy or not spicy?

A tag question is composed of a statement followed by an "A not A" form. For instance,

(5) 他**去不去**？
Will he go there or not?

(6) 老师今天**能不能**来？
Can the teacher come today or not?

A particle question or general question is a question signaled by the presence of a question particle in sentence-final position. Question particles are "吗" (ma), "吧" (ba), "啊" (a), etc.

(7) 我们也去北京**吗**？
Shall we also go to Beijing?

(8) 我还来得及**吧**？
Do I have enough time?

It is often believed that casual conversation or informal talk occurs in informal settings, such as talk between friends or family members, while institutional dialogue takes place in institutions, such as medical encounters, classroom encounters, news interviews, etc. The dichotomy between formal talk and informal talk, and casual conversation and institutional talk, frequently associates with the division between equality and inequality, and symmetry and asymmetry. According to Drew and Heritage (1992), an ordinary conversation is an unmarked and predominant form of interaction, while institutional dialogue consists of "role-structured, institutionalized, and omnirelevant asymmetries between participants in terms of such matters as differential distribution of knowledge, rights to knowledge, access to conversational resources, and to participation in the interaction" (1992: 49). Thornborrow (2002: 4) generalizes institutional dialogue as "talk which sets up positions for people to talk from and restricts some speakers' access to certain kinds of discursive actions." The central concern of institutional dialogue is its asymmetry, which derives from the asymmetry of the overall organization and the asymmetry of power and status. In particular the question/answer sequence in institutional dialogue is very highlighting and distinctive, which makes institutional dialogue distinguished from casual conversation.

3. Examples

Chinese institutional dialogue bears all the characteristics of institutional dialogue. The following medical encounter[1] can be regarded as one sample of Chinese institutional dialogue.

1. 病人: 医生。
   Patient: Hi, Doctor.
2. 医生: 吃了药以后好点没有？
   Doctor: Do you feel better after you've taken the medicine?
3. 病人: 好一点。
   Patient: Feeling better.
4. 医生: 好一点啦。现在还有哪里不好？
   D: Better. Where are you still feeling not well with?
5. 病人: 现在有点担心，我这个病是中期，好是好不了了。现在大便好解一点了。
   P: I'm a bit worried. My illness has been in the middle stage. It's difficult to recover completely. Now I have a better bowel movement.
6. 医生: 大便好解了吗？
   D: You've got a smooth bowel movement?

1. The excerpt was recorded in the Outpatient Department of Bai Ethnic Group Autonomous Prefecture Hospital in Dali, Yunnan, China at 15:15 to 16:20 September 24, 2007 with the permission of both the doctor and the patient and was transcribed according to the conventions of the written language.

7. 病人: 嗯，好解了。
   P: Yes, I have.
8. 医生: 躺在床上去。(医生指了指检查床)
   D: Lie on the bed. (The doctor is pointing to the inspection bed)
   病人: (躺在床上)
   P: (Lying on the bed)
9. 医生: (看了看腹部的皮肤) 现在还痒吗?
   D: (Inspecting his abdomen skin) Is it itching now?
10. 病人: 不痒了。
    P: No.
11. 医生: 燥热的东西不能吃，吃了要发病的。
    D: Don't eat dry and hot food, which will lead to a relapse.
12. 病人: 嗯，燥热的东西不能吃。这个病还要治多长时间？
    P: Ok, I'll keep away dry and hot food. How long will the treatment last?
13. 医生: 可能还要吃四、五个礼拜的药。
    D: Perhaps you have to take the medicine for four or five weeks.
14. 病人: 四、五个礼拜的药？
    P: Take the medicine for four or five weeks?
15. 医生: 嗯。(写病历，开处方。然后递给病人药方)
    D: Yes. (The doctor is describing the case on the medical record, making a prescription and then handing it to the patient)
16. 病人: 好，谢谢。
    P: Thanks.
17. 医生: 嗯。
    D: Ok.

In this medial excerpt, the doctor has altogether 9 turns and the patient has 8 turns. Among the doctor's 9 turns, there are 4 questions including 3 particle questions and 1 interrogative-word question, and 1 command. All the questions are used to diagnose the patient. The excerpt displays prominent features of interactional domination on the part of the doctor, who controls the organization of the interaction by asking questions. Turn-taking is mainly under the doctor's control and the patient only takes turns when the doctor directs a question to her. Although the patient asks two questions, they are mainly used for confirming the illness. The doctor's domination of the interaction is also reflected by his control of the topics. It is mostly the doctor who shifts topics from the patient's present condition to bowel movement then to abdomen skin, etc. Topic control is also realized by the selective way in which the doctor takes up the responses of the patient to previous questions.

4. Research method

Power is the central concern of Critical Discourse Analysis. Fairclough (1989: 46) points out that "power in discourse is to do with powerful participants controlling and constraining the contributions of non-powerful participants." Van Dijk (2001) defines social power as control and holds that groups have power if they are able to control the acts and minds of other groups. Therefore, power accrues to verbal interaction and is determined by institutional role and speakers' socio-economic status, gender or ethnic identity, etc.

Questions or questioning have been recognized by many scholars as a way of exercising power. Linell (1990: 159) points out that "asking questions is a well-known dominant strategy (unless we are faced with submissive questions, by which a party, often a subordinate one, shows deference and respect by suggesting that the other party talk)." Sacks (1995) holds that questioning is a kind of power or the ability to control and the person who asks the questions seems to have first rights to perform an operation on the set of answers. Wang (2006: 539–543) suggests that

> English questions are a prominent means to exercise power in institutional dialogue in that notably unequal distribution of questions produces the unequal allocation of turn-taking, dominant questions controls both local and global topics and Yes/No questions and Wh-questions exercise power in different degrees.

In order to verify the status of Chinese questions in institutional dialogue, the statistics have been made on the basis of the data collection concerning three subgenres of Chinese institutional dialogue, namely, the news interview, the medical encounter and the classroom encounter. The question ratios of all participants and special and general question ratios of powerful participants in three speech genres have been figured out. As the number of questions by the less powerful participants is very limited, their special and general question ratios are not considered.

All the medical encounters were recorded in the Outpatient Department of Bai Ethnic Group Autonomous Prefecture Hospital in Dali, Yunnan, China from 15:15 to 16:20 on September 24, 2007 and from 9:50 to 11:30 on September 26, with the permission of both doctors and patients. The interviewing data come from China Central TV (CCTV in brief), a daily program named Focus Interview, from October 20 to October 22, 2006, whose scripts were published on http://news.cctv.com. The classroom encounter data were recorded at 8:20 to 9:00, September 12, 2007 in the math class of Class 3, Grade 5 of Zhonghua Elementary School, Kunming, China. All the recordings were transcribed in accordance with the conventions of the written language. The following table indicates the question ratios of all participants, and in particular special and general question ratios of powerful participants in three speech genres.

Table 1. Question ratios in three speech genres

Speech genres	Participants	Special question ratio (%)	General question Ratio (%)	Question ratio total (%)
News interview	Interviewer	39	61	98
	Interviewee			2
Classroom encounter	Teacher	34.8	65.2	97.9
	Student			2.1
Medical encounter	Doctor	25	75	78.3
	Patient			21.7

The statistics show that among the three speech genres, question ratios of interviewers, teachers and doctors are higher than those of interviewees, students and patients, that is, 98%, 97.9% and 78.3% respectively. Therefore, the great difference of question ratios exists between two participants in news interviews, classroom encounters and medical encounters, that is, 96%, 95.8% and 56.6% respectively. As in institutional dialogue, participants' right of asking questions is restricted by institutionality, questioning is dominated by the powerful participants, interviewer, teacher and doctor.

In institutional dialogue, questions not only control initiating turns, they also control the whole structure to a certain degree. As asking a question is just like claiming a topic or a local topic, questions in a sequence develop a series of local topics, which lead to a global topic in the end.

Compared with the statistics shown in Wang (2006), which are based on the English data, the present Chinese data have some differences. First, the Chinese question ratios by teacher and student are 97.9% and 2.1% respectively, whereas the English question ratios by teacher and student are 56% and 44%. One reason for the large difference between the figures is that the present data is on the elementary school basis, while the former figures were on the university basis. In the elementary schools in China, teachers' asking questions in the classroom is regarded as a main teaching method. Second, concerning questions in medical encounters, it is found that patients' questions in the present statistics take 21.7%, which is higher than the 9% found by West (1984), and the 6% that Wang (2006) found, but lower than the 38.7% found by Ainsworth-Vaughn (2001). Patients' increasing question ratio to a certain degree shows that China is practicing a medical reform, which gives patients a chance to choose the doctors they want. As the medical reform to some degree improves the relationship between doctors and patients, it also helps to increase the question ratios of patients. Third, general questions are frequently used by the powerful participants, interviewer, teacher and doctor. Their general question ratios are 61%, 65.2% and 75%, which mean that the general questions take the higher percentages than the special questions. Interviewers, teachers and doctors tend to use general questions more often for the sake of restricting and constraining the less powerful participants, i.e., interviewees, students and patients. In particular, teachers tend to ask frequently tag questions with "是不是" (yes or not), "好不好" (OK or not), "能不能" (possible or not; able or not) and "对不对" (right or not), etc. Look at the following sample tag questions of a teacher from the recorded classroom encounter:

(9) 教师：现在剩下的**是不是**都是对角线？
Teacher: Now the remaining lines are all diagonal lines, aren't they?

(10) 教师：也就是说对角线的数目一定比边的数目要少3，**对不对**？
Teacher: That is to say, the number of the diagonal lines must be 3 less that that of the sides, is it right or not?

Tag questions are often used to ask for confirmation, information or help, which are considered as quite a friendly or polite way of making a request. However, in the classroom encounter, the teacher's tag questions are intended to ask for confirmation or information but mainly to guide and direct the students. Therefore, the teacher restricts the students by asking questions to a great degree.

5. Recent research

Many scholars have had interests in discovering the differences between casual conversion and institutional dialogue, and in particular much attention has been paid to the research into institutional dialogue. Much work centers on the comparison between casual conversation and institutional dialogue from different aspects, such as person reference, lexical choice, grammatical construction, turn-taking and institutionally specific inferences, etc.

Since 2002, I have tried to explore questions and power relations in English spoken discourse from the perspective of critical discourse analysis. I have published related articles in Chinese and international journals and one monograph on a critical analysis of English questions in spoken discourse. These publications tend to explore that English questions are an important means to exercise power in all verbal interactions, whether in casual conversation or in institutional dialogue. On the basis of the collected data, it is proved that questions are a latent powerful means in casual conversation and a prominent powerful means in institutional dialogue. Furthermore, the immediate allocation of turn-taking and the temporary topic control result in the latency of questions as a powerful means in casual conversation. Comparatively, the prominence of questions as a powerful means focuses on three factors. That is to say, unequal distribution of questions produces the unequal allocation of turn-taking;

dominant questions control both local and global topics, and Yes/No questions and Wh-questions exercise power in different degrees.

Recently, my interest has been concerned with comparing the differences between Chinese questions and English questions in institutional dialogue. I intend to contrast questions in both Chinese and English in institutional dialogue from two main aspects, namely their form and function. Among many subgenres of institutional dialogue, I have chosen three, that is, classroom encounter, medical encounter and news interview. Concerning questions and power relations in institutional dialogue, three levels are taken into consideration, that is, the lexico-grammar level, the conversational structure and the generic structure. The lexico-grammatical level is concerned with two parts, that is, lexis and grammar. On the lexical level, more attention is paid to the lexis in questions, such as vocatives, modality, appraisal lexis, etc. As question-answer is viewed as a typical exchange and a classic adjacency pair, the answer is also an element to be considered. On the grammar, I mainly deal with the different grammatical forms in both Chinese and English institutional dialogue and their pragmatic meaning and different ways to exercise power. On the level of conversational structure, I intend to compare and contrast the conversational structures of questions in three different institutional dialogues in both languages. On the level of generic structure, the main focus is to find out the generic structures of three subgenres of institutional dialogues in two languages. My research tends to dispose the relationships between the generic structures and power, and what roles questions play.

6. Research proposal

It has been proven that power is overt in institutional dialogue and that questions are a prominent means to exercise power. Much work has been done on the English questions. In fact, it is possible to analyze questions and power relations in other languages than the English language, such as my present research on the Chinese questions.

When we try to make a critical analysis of questions in institutional dialogue in other languages than English, we can follow the same procedures with those adopted in analyzing the English questions in institutional dialogue.

First, it is necessary to collect enough data although the data can not be exhaustive. Second, data transcription is needed and certain transcribing conventions should be followed. If you intend to deal with the phonological features of questions, specifically speaking intonation, the related marks should be labeled. If you will not analyze the phonological features of questions, you can just transcribe the recordings in accordance with the conventions of the written language.

Third, you can figure out the question ratios and the turns that participants take, and recognize the characteristic sequential dynamics of institutional dialogue.

Fourth, you can explore the institutional authority and control by way of analyzing the turn-taking system, topic control, pragmatic implicature, lexical choice, institutional inference, etc. Through the related analysis, it is possible to reveal institutional asymmetry, ideology, power relations in institutional dialogue.

Except for questions as a prominent powerful means, other possible means may be explored to exercise power, such as lexical resources, grammatical patterns, conversational structures and generic structures.

It is suggested that power in institutional dialogue can be analyzed from the three levels, that is, the lexico-grammatical level, the conversational structure level and the generic level. The three-layer framework is founded on the stratified or systemic tradition in functional linguistics. According to Systemic Functional Linguistics, a system is a paradigmatic set of choices available in a certain environment, which can be realized by syntagmatic structures. Following the Hallidayan tradition, the linguistic strata are classified as genre, register and language, and language is further organized into three separate levels, namely phonology, lexico-grammar and discourse. Analyzing the different levels will be useful to disclose the unequal power relations between participants and how power is negotiated and negotiable in institutional dialogue.

As lexical items are an important device to express different attitudes and stance of participants, and to construct social identity and status, appraisal systems proposed by Martin (2000), Eggins and Slide (1997) and others, will be very useful and practical. In general, appraisal lexes include three kinds, i.e., evaluative lexes, modal expressions, vocatives and technical terms. Evaluative words are used to evaluate attitudes of participants and to expose their respective ideology. Moreover, analyzing evaluative lexes is beneficial to establish social identities and reveal power relations between participants. Modality is considered to be related to the degrees of politeness and to the hierarchy of power relations as well. Fairclough (1989: 3) points out that "power exists in various modalities" and modality can be regarded as a discursive device to police or mobilize people, and as an effective device that a group of people use to exert power over others. Therefore, modality is not only a matter of the relation between participants in a verbal interaction, but also a matter of their social relations. Vocative and technical terms are also evaluative devices to construe social identity and social distance.

Concerning grammatical patterns of participants, the three patterns except questions are imperatives, declaratives and exclamatory, and imperatives are most worth exploring. As imperatives are often related to order and command, it is possible to deal with imperatives in different subgenres of institutional dialogue, such as courtroom cross-examination, medical encounter, classroom encounter, etc. Their pragmatic implicatures can be taken into consideration when imperatives are coped with.

Regarding the conversational structure level, Eggins and Slide (1997) have made an elaborate analysis of the conversational structure of casual conversation, which will be beneficial to the analysis of institutional dialogue. The conversational structure primarily deals with the analysis of turns and the analysis of moves or speech functions. By way of analyzing turns and moves taken by different participants, the role relations between participants can be detected.

A genre is a schematically structured and goal-oriented social process. A dialogue is often schematically structured and its participants have to take various steps to achieve the goals. According to Hasan's (1985) generic structure potential, which prescribes obligatory and optional elements of a genre, a generic structure analysis can include the analysis of stages that speech functions take and the analysis of roles that speech functions play in combination with the conversational structure analysis. By way of the generic structure analysis, it is possible to find out how participant relations are constructed and how social power is distributed.

Although the three levels are suggested to be considered for disposing power in institutional dialogue, whether one or all the levels are considered in your analysis depends on your writing purpose and a proposed length of your article. In addition, the number and the choice of speech genres of institutional dialogue also depend.

7. Practical relevance

Through the exploration of questions and power relations in Chinese institutional dialogue, it is found that some participants dominate the position of asking questions, while some participants have very limited opportunity to ask questions due to institutional roles and identities. As a matter of fact, power is overt in institutional dialogue and power relations are greatly influenced and constrained by the characteristics of institutions or organizations. It is proved that Chinese questions are a prominent and important means for the powerful participants to exercise power. The data analysis shows that the unequal distribution of questions produces the unequal allocation of turn-taking; dominant questions control both local and global topics and special questions and general questions exercise power in different degrees. On the one hand, Chinese institutions endow some participants with power to ask questions. On the other hand, Chinese institutions deprive of or constrain some participants' opportunities to ask questions and force them to answer questions as their responsibilities and obligations.

The present study also has practical relevance. At the present time, China is constructing and promoting a socialist harmonious society. The core of harmonious society is to establish harmonious interpersonal, social and ethnic relations. As language is an important part of social life, a harmonious society needs harmonious linguistic activities. The construction of a linguistically harmonious society plays a crucial role in social stability and solidarity. Harmony is not equal to being identical, however it is the coordinate unity composed of different parts. Harmonious society also means fair and mutual-beneficial interpersonal relationships. From the perspective of a harmonious society, the present study indicates that different institutional roles constitute a kind of social harmony as everyone has a role in different institutions. Some participants are endowed with power by institutions to ask questions, whereas some are deprived of power and forced to answer questions. Their different speech acts are closely connected with their social roles. The institutional roles represent obligations and responsibilities. The obligations and responsibilities and the corresponding linguistic activities lead to a kind of social harmony.

The present study also shows that participants in institutional dialogue perform and pursue their respective institutional tasks and goals by way of using different linguistic resources. Among all the linguistic resources, questions or questioning are the most prominent and most powerful way for the powerful participants to exercise power. As one performs different roles in a society, s/he has to realize his/her own role and identity in different contexts by adopting the corresponding linguistic activities.

Acknowledgement

I'd like to thank Miss Wenling Li, a postgraduate at the School of Foreign Languages, Yunnan University, for her very helpful work in collecting and transcribing the medical encounter data.

Assignment

Many scholars have recognized questions or questioning as a way of exercising power in institutional dialogue. Questions are the prominent and main means for the powerful participant to exercise power in institutional dialogue, and questioning is also a dominant strategy for the powerful to control topics and turn-taking. However, the less powerful are restricted to ask questions or only ask questions when invited. Therefore, the dominating questions control the less powerful to a great degree. Comparatively speaking, in casual conversation participants are mostly peers, friends or family members, which are conceived as equal due to their intimacy, solidarity and the minimal social distance. It seems that all participants have the right to ask questions. Can it be concluded that casual conversation is a power-free communicative activity and questions can never be regarded as a means of exercising power? Please illustrate your point of view.

Chapter 16

Towards a process view of preformulation in press releases

Geert Jacobs and Tom van Hout
Ghent University

Within the field of media discourse, it has been shown that press releases constitute an important and interesting genre. In particular, previous discourse-analytic work (Jacobs, 1999) has demonstrated that they are heavily preformulated, i.e., through a number of metapragmatic features like self-quotation and third-person self-reference they can easily be copied by journalists in their own news reporting. The present chapter sets out to further explore this notion of preformulation by presenting an innovative mix of linguistic ethnography and computer-assisted writing process analysis on how press releases are being written at the PR department and rewritten at the news desk. Drawing on preliminary fieldwork data collected in various institutional settings (including Kim Sleurs' work at a major Belgian financial institution as well as Tom van Hout's work at a Belgian Dutch-language quality newspaper), we will point to the wide range of practical as well as political concerns that have been glossed over in previous work on the topic. We will also discuss the practical implications of these findings both for PR and media professionals.

1. Introduction

Ever since their origins in the 1970s, media discourse studies have predominantly focused on what can be generally seen as news products, first on the (written) texts that are published in newspapers and magazines, later also on the (oral) interactions that are broadcast on radio and TV. Broadly speaking, while the former continue to be the subject of critical, often quantitative scrutiny focusing on lexis and discourse representation practices (starting with Fowler & Kress, 1979), the latter have predominantly given rise to ethnomethodological, CA-inspired studies detailing the mechanics of turn-taking, repair and pause length (most prominently, Heritage & Clayman, 2002).

It is not difficult to see why news products have been so popular: to begin with, they are highly accessible, making it easy for scholars to get hold of the data for empirical, corpus-based research; in addition, even before discourse analysts started to look at news products, scholars in the field of mass communication had been examining their impact on readerships and viewing audiences and it had become clear that the media played a major role in a lot of people's lives: hence news products were not just highly accessible; they also constituted socially relevant objects of investigation (e.g., the notion of agenda-setting).

Over the last few years, the rise of technology (including, of course, the Internet) has reinforced this interest in news products: with increasing numbers of media websites now boasting large-scale on-line archives, news data have become even more accessible and their impact has only increased. At the same time, technological innovations have led to the creation of interesting new types of news products, often combining features of orality and writing and thus strengthening the movement towards multimodal discourse studies, which had been started off by researchers within the critical tradition of media studies (Kress & Van Leeuwen, 2001); not surprisingly, these new types of news products have become the subject of more research (e.g., Thornborrow & Fitzgerald, 2002, on dealing with e-mails in radio phone-ins).

While news products will no doubt remain centre stage, recently the scope of media discourse studies has started to gradually broaden to include the complex discursive practices that lie at the heart of the news production process. Instead of just focusing on the products (and what they lead to in terms of response), various researchers have started to get interested in what comes before: surely, if — say — newspapers are so influential, it must be worthwhile investigating how they are produced. For one thing, it is the growing interest in institutional discourse that has led discourse analysts to pay attention to such specialized workplace settings as the newsroom and the corporate PR department. In addition, thanks to the new technology, it is not just the news products that have become more easily accessible: crucial ingredients of the news production process too are now being opened up to researchers, with corporate websites starting to parade massive press release archives and Internet-based news agencies and e-mail distribution services spreading breaking news in real time to whoever is interested.

Interestingly, even before the rise of institutional discourse studies and the start of the Internet it was sociologists and mass communication specialists who first drew attention to the news production process and who, in investigating how political and economic relationships underpin the media business, came up with useful concepts like pro-active news management and gatekeeping. Some of these studies have unmistakable titles, including Tuchman's *Making News: a study in the construction of reality* (1978) and Fishman's *Manufacturing the News* (1980), and they are part of a long and wide-ranging tradition from Boorstin's 1961 concept of pseudo-events and Galtung and Ruge's pivotal 1973 article on newsworthiness to John B. Thompson's more recent work on mediazation (1995). Crucially, relatively little has been done on the micro-level textual practices, the linguistic nitty-gritty, of the news production process. More than fifteen years on, Allan Bell's book on the language of news media (1991) continues to be the main reference here as far as the discursive analysis of journalists' professional newsmaking routines is concerned. In focusing on so-called "preformulation" in press releases, the present chapter sets out to document the rise and development of one strand of discursively oriented research on the news production process (see www.ntt.ugent.be for information on the Ghent University NewsTalk&Text research group dedicated to the analysis of news production processes).

2. The research challenge

Even if discourse analysts have only started to show an interest in them very recently, there can be no doubt that press releases have long played a major role in the news production process. It is generally assumed that back in the 1880s US congressman Benjamin Butler was the first to send journalists his "self-prepared opinions." Ever since, all sorts of would-be news sources — from companies and political parties to even private persons — have been writing press releases in order to see their views and words reproduced in news reporting. Instead of waiting for journalists to invite them for an interview, press officers of all kinds are now trying to pro-actively "manage" the news by issuing press releases or calling press conferences.

While the study of press releases is a welcome addition to the analysis of the news production process, it is interesting — and perhaps ironic — to note that so far they too have almost exclusively been examined from a product perspective. Jacobs' book-length study (1999), for example, is based on four corpora: the press releases issued by Exxon Corporation in the wake of the 1989 oil spill at Valdez, Alaska; the press releases received by the business editors of the Belgian Dutch-language quality newspaper *De Standaard* over a period of two and a half months; the press releases received by Belgium's Belga press agency over a period of three months; and, finally, the press releases issued by the so-called BEL 20 companies (i.e., Belgium's top 20 companies quoted on the Brussels stock exchange) over a period of more than two years. Similarly, Lenaerts (2002), in trying to find out to what extent press releases find their way into the media, sticks to a corpus-based approach, comparing six political press releases on a language policy-related crisis in Belgium with the newspaper articles that report on it. Pander Maat (2007) finally looks at how the promotional elements in 43 press releases issued in the aviation industry have been edited in daily newspapers, subscription-based travel magazines and free Internet publications.

W. P. Carey & Co. provides Carrefour $91 million in net lease financing deal
Sale-leaseback transaction includes purchase of eight state-of-the-art warehouse facilities

New York, March 28 2002 — *W. P. Carey & Co. LLC (NYSE: WPC), a leading real estate investment banking firm, announced today that it has acquired and leased-back eight warehouse facilities from Carrefour (Paris: CARR.PA), France's largest retailer, for approximately US $91 million (euro 104 million).*

Under the terms of the sale-leaseback agreement, the facilities will be leased to Carrefour under nine year net leases. The properties, totalling more than 3,460,000 square feet, are state-of-the-art facilities with average floor to ceiling heights of 32 feet or more and are located in Paris, Lille, Caen, Nancy, Le Mans, Agen, Bourges and Lyon. The facilities were purchased on behalf of Corporate Property Associates 14 Incorporated, a member of the $3 billion W. P. Carey Group of publicly held non-traded real estate investment trusts (REITs). To date the W. P. Carey Group has acquired 16 properties, net-leased to eight tenants in 12 cities throughout France.

"This sale-leaseback transaction will free up $91 million for Carrefour to fund corporate initiatives that focus on the company's core business," said Anthony S. Mohl, Senior Director of W. P. Carey. "The tightening of today's global credit markets is making a sale-leaseback the preferred choice of financing for companies seeking to grow and expand their business."

"The transaction was structured with a loan from DePfa/Aareal Bank," said Chantal Gautier, General Director of DePfa/Aareal Bank. "DePfa Bank/Aareal Bank was pleased with closing the financing on this portfolio of 8 facilities leased by Carrefour France. We hope that the strong relationship we built with W. P. Carey over the course of this transaction will allow us to conduct many deals in the future as we appreciated the professionalism and efficiency of Anthony and his team in getting this deal done."

Founded in 1973, W. P. Carey & Co. specializes in corporate real estate financing through the corporate net lease, or sale-leasveback structure. The firm and its affiliates continue to be the leading lessors of net leased corporate real estate in the United States. As the largest publicly traded limited liability company in the world, the company owns and/or manages more than 450 commercial and industrial properties throughout the United States and Europe comprising of more than 55 million-square-feet of space. The firm is headquartered in Manhattan and has offices in London and Paris.

Figure 1. Press release.

Crucially, from these corpus-based studies it is clear that, in order to facilitate reproduction in the media, press releases are already prefabricated in an appropriate news style. The typical so-called "preformulating" features of press releases are illustrated in the press release in Figure 1. They include the use of powerful, newspaper-like headlines, followed by a comprehensive "lead" paragraph as well as a number of special metapragmatics, most prominently third-person self-reference ("W.P. Carey and Co." and "the company" instead of "we") and (pseudo-) quotation as in the third and fourth paragraphs (cf. Jacobs, 1999).

While such preformulation is a very interesting discursive strategy in its own right, the central purpose of this chapter is to go beyond product analysis and to show how the concept of preformulation in press releases can be subjected to a further, empirical study in which we work towards taking into account the institutionalized media and PR setting. In particular, we would like to examine what role preformulating concerns actually play in the news construction process. In doing so, we will take a diachronic, natural-history view of the news since we believe that what gets published in the papers and broadcast on radio and TV is the result of a complex so-called entextualization process, one in which discourse is rendered "extractable" and writers of press releases "help" journalists "[lift stretches of linguistic production] out of [their] interactional setting" (Bauman & Briggs, 1990: 73).

3. Examples

So what kind of textual puzzles are we hoping to solve? What are some of the data that we set out to deal with? We'll give two very different examples here.

First, here are two Dutch-language extracts that are the result of fieldwork conducted by Kim Sleurs. They are taken from a press release issued by a major Belgian bank (BB) telling the complex story of their sponsoring involvement in an educational website KS (see Sleurs & Jacobs, 2005).

> *Niet overtuigd? Breng dan snel zelf een bezoekje aan www.ks.be. Jim, de BB-kantoordirecteur, en Jack, de burgemeester van KS, zullen u graag verwelkomen in hun virtuele stad, die nu ook haar eigen BB-bank- en verzekeringskantoor heeft.*
>
> Not convinced? Then quickly pay a visit to www.ks.be. Jim, the BB office manager, and Jack, the mayor of KS, will be happy to welcome you in their virtual city, which now also has its own BB bank and insurance office.
>
> *Ongetwijfeld verneemt u vanwege de initiatiefnemers van KS meer over deze verjaardag.*
>
> No doubt you will hear more about this birthday from the initiators of KS.

What is special about these extracts is that they do not conform to the standard preformulating requirements spelled out above. Indeed, based on previous corpus-based research (Jacobs, 1999), it has become clear that direct, second-person reference to the reader is typically avoided in press releases. The reason is that, if press releases are meant to be read both by the journalists and then — after they got copied verbatim in the media — by a more general readership, it is not clear who "you" refers to: is it the journalists or the public? Surely, so it has been argued, it cannot normally be both, which means that we have a problem in terms of preformulation. The question can therefore be raised where the two "you's" in BB's KS press release come from. If we only look at the product, we are bound to get stuck. So this is where the fieldwork conducted by Kim Sleurs comes in. As we have shown in Sleurs & Jacobs (2005), a close look at the writing process can help us out by foregrounding some of the practical as well as political concerns involved. Take the first extract. What we seem to conclude here from our fieldwork is not that preformulation does not seem to be on BB's press officers' minds. Instead, it seems to have gone lost in the kind of copy-paste operation which turns out to have been a major part of writing this press release. More generally speaking, it looks as if writing this press release was a highly intertextual business, intertextuality with reformulating concerns clashing with the genre's preformulating requirements and real-life institutional writing practices turning out to be a lot more messy than a product-oriented approach would have made us believe. As for the second "you," our fieldwork data demonstrate that it is an intriguing textual hiccup, a meaningful trace left behind in the fierce behind-the-scenes power struggle between BB and KS that no researcher working on the text data only could have imagined.

Of course, it's not always anomalies in the news products that lie at the basis of this kind of research. Here's a translated transcript of an extract from a story meeting attended by Tom van Hout at the business newsdesk of a major Dutch-language

244.	TRE:	Pieter- xxx Pieter on his cartoons xxx
245.	AMT: →	there's also erm-
246.		(*laughter*)
247.	HOM:	gosh, are you already doing that now?
248.	GRI:	yeah, that's incre[dible that xxx that's going to become a xxx or something
249.	AMT: →	[the signing of the new management agreement between the Flemish government and erm the V I B and IMEC they're getting 20% [more money
250.	GRI:	[what? two months?
251.	TRE:	three
252.	GRI:	three months and he's already putting him in front of the [tv]?
253.	ONL:	[woohahaha]
254.	AMT: →	[should attention be paid to this?]
255.	LRN: →	[60 line-] 60 lines on eco 4, no? if they get more money
256.	AMT: →	yes 20 procent [xxx]
257	TRE:	[xxx]
258	TRA: →	what's that AMT, the Flemish government and?
259.	AMT: →	v i b and Imec are getting more money
260.	HOM:	from Fientje?
261.	AMT:	from Fientje
262.	LRN:	that's biotechnology [and (1.1)
263.	HOB:	[xxx so biotechnology]
264.	LRN:	(*jokingly*) c'mon, you still don't know this? goddammit??? time and again I've xxx

Figure 2. Transcript.

quality newspaper in Belgium, in which a senior reporter (AMT) tries to introduce the story of increased government funding of one of Flanders' most prestigious biotechnology research institutes VIB. This time, both VIB's press release and AMT's newspaper article based on it look perfectly normal but again our fieldwork data shed new light on preformulation.

As the transcript begins with some playful banter about parenting between three other senior reporters, AMT tries to address his desk chief LRN (line 245) but his initial attempt drowns in group laughter. In line 249, AMT mentions the VIB story by first referring to the pseudo-event of the signing of the agreements and then by adding the more newsworthy detail of the budget increase.

249	AMT: →	[the signing of the new management agreement between the Flemish government and erm the V I B and IMEC they're getting 20% [more money

Figure 3. Transcript excerpt

This double-edged pitch shows how AMT (re)entextualizes the VIB story: shifting into a more formal, nominal register typical of story summaries ("the signing of the new management agreement"), AMT clearly echoes — almost ventriloquizes — the opening paragraph of the VIB press release:

Press Release from Fientje Moerman, Vice-Minister-President of the Flemish Government and Flemish Minister for Economy, Enterprise, Science, Innovation and Foreign Trade

08-03-2007

More than 400 million euro for biotech and nanotech

Today Flemish Minister for Science and Innovation Fientje Moerman has signed the new management agreements (2007 – 2011) for VIB and IMEC. The Flemish government reserves more than 400 million euro in the coming five years for research in these two top institutes. The budget of operation of both institutes increases with 20%.

Figure 4. VIB press release.

AMT's (re)entextualization of "Today Flemish Minister for Science and Innovation Fientje Moerman has signed the new management agreements (2007–2011) for VIB and IMEC" illustrates a social function of preformulation to draw LRN's attention.

Previously, preformulation was conceived of as a textual property of press releases. This excerpt, however, illustrates a previously unheard of social function: AMT draws on the press release in order to promote the VIB story to his desk chief LRN (see also van Hout & Jacobs, 2008).

4. Research method

In order to investigate the wide range of discursive PR and newsroom practices in general and the actual process of writing and rewriting press releases in particular, we combine two methods: on the one hand, we propose a linguistic ethnographic approach to the PR and news businesses, in which — broadly speaking — we hope to gather information about what the people who are actually involved in writing and rewriting press releases really think and do (Rampton et al., 2004); on the other hand, we recommend computer-assisted writing process analysis, which should allow for a closer, micro-level reconstruction, analysis and interpretation of the discursive PR and news routines at hand (Levy & Ransdell, 1996). It is beyond the scope of this chapter to expand on the methodological challenge posed by this unusual combination of mentalistic or cognitive-psychological and socio-cultural traditions (see Sleurs et al., 2003, for a preliminary discussion). Let's just briefly go into some detail about the two methods used here.

Our linguistic ethnographic approach, to begin with, implies weeks, if not months, of fieldwork in the middle of the public relations and newsroom action: attending meetings, observing writing practices, overhearing telephone conversations, taking part in a wide range of informal face-to-face interactions, reading cc-ed e-mail messages and conducting semi-structured interviews with the main actors on the scene. Hence, our research corresponds to Agar's definition of ethnography in that it involves "long-term association with some group, to some extent in their own territory, with the purpose of learning from them their ways of doing things and viewing reality" (1996: 58).

In contrast with the holistic, context-oriented approach of linguistic ethnography, computer-assisted writing research allows for a fine-grained reconstruction of the complete writing or rewriting process for a single press release, letter by letter, revision by revision. This is done through on-line registration of the writing process. To this end, two software applications are used: Inputlog and Camtasia Studio. Inputlog is a Microsoft Windows based logging tool which records keyboard strokes and mouse movements and generates datafiles for statistical, text, pause and mode analyses (Leijten & Van Waes, 2006). Camtasia Studio is an online screen registration tool which can be used to make screenvideos of the observed writing processes; these videos enable easy and immediate playback of the recorded writing process data during retrospective interviews. Both applications can be used to record, reconstruct and

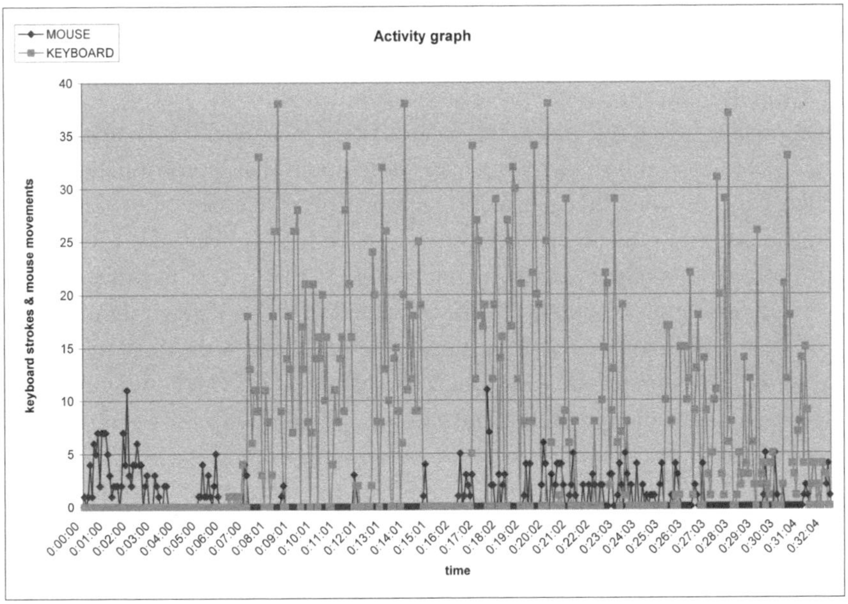

Figure 5. AMT's writing process for the VIB story

analyse writing processes. They generate a wide range of descriptive statistics and they allow the researcher to plot the writing process in various activity graphs. Figure 5 is a very simple example, which nevertheless sheds interesting new light on the role of press releases in this journalist's writing process. Based on a five-second-period linear log file generated by Inputlog, it graphically represents AMT's writing process for the VIB story referred to above by plotting temporal data (in absolute time) against process data, i.c. keyboard strokes and mouse commands.

The graph shows four distinct phases in AMT's writing process: a preparatory phase (0'00"–7'00"), two text construction phases (7'00"–16'01" and 17'02"–24'03") and a revision phase (at the end). The preparatory phase consists of mouse movements (scrolling through emails and opening attachments), while the text construction phases show a high number of keyboard movements (text insertion and deletion) as well as mouse movements (cursor movement, switching and resizing computer windows, looking for online information). Here, we know, AMT was drawing heavily on VIB's press release, with preformulation almost visibly facilitating a smooth writing flow. During the final, revision phase AMT edits his text.

Of course, on-line registration of the writing process can be combined with concurrent and retrospective protocols: the researcher can ask the writer to think aloud and explicate whatever he is doing in the course of the writing process. Alternatively, immediately afterwards we can replay some of the extracts of the on-line registration and invite him to explain certain choices he made in writing or rewriting the press release.

5. Recent research

Based on the preliminary research that we have conducted in this area, it seems like preformulation plays a real role in writing and rewriting press releases. To begin with, Sleurs et al. (2003) have shown that there can be no doubt that preformulation is on the PR officers' minds when they are writing up their press releases. Focusing on the design and function of quotes, it is perfectly clear, both from what the PR officers say and from the details of the actual writing processes, that quotes in press releases are typically pseudo-quotes made up by the press officer because they might well be reproduced by the journalists who want to use the press release in their own news reporting. As we have seen above, Van Hout & Jacobs (2008) provide similar evidence of the impact of preformulation on the journalists' writing process.

At the same time, the picture turns out to be a lot more complicated than we had assumed. Sleurs et al. (2003), for example, show that it's not just the views of the organization's own leaders but also the would-be words of all sorts of third parties that qualify to be included between quotation marks in press releases. Those third parties range from famous business analysts, whose sound bites turn out to be for sale, to representatives of other organizations that are involved in the events reported in the press release. As for the newsroom, we have indicated above that preformulation should not only be conceived of as a textual property; apparently, it seems to play a social role as well (Van Hout & Jacobs, 2008). From this point of view, preformulation and press releases should be seen as part of a wider sourcing spectacle, with multiple social actors "[assigning], and [struggling] over, authority, ownership and control over the text" (Peterson 2003: 193).

More generally speaking, we have seen that zooming in on preformulation in press releases offers a helpful way of exploring what would otherwise be an extremely difficult writing process to monitor.

6. Research proposal

While there can be no doubt that the type of PR and newsroom ethnographies referred to above are shedding interesting new light on the writing and rewriting processes for traditional, paper press releases, we believe it is high time to start examining the impact of digital technology. This research proposal follows up on our interest in the discursive aspects of news production processes by exploring the use of press releases on the Internet (also called e-releases). As it is, press releases seem to be finding themselves in a crucial phase of their discursive development. As Public Relations expert Zhenya Gene Senyak says in a contribution to one of the many Internet newsgroups on the topic, "the press release is dead and thriving" (www.clickz.com).

Perhaps not surprisingly, it is the rise of the Internet that has led to this rather unusual condition of what are commonly called e-releases. In Senyak's words: "The Internet has changed the very reason we prepare and distribute press releases. And it doesn't have much to do with news." With the Internet rapidly expanding access to press releases beyond the circles of professional journalists, the question can be raised to what extent preformulating practices are being affected. Interestingly, while the impact of the Internet on public relation practices has recently drawn quite some attention in the PR literature, little or no interest has been shown in how the new technology has affected press releases, let alone the language of press releases.

In order to try and address this research question, it is necessary to reach a deeper understanding of how press releases are being used on the Internet through participant observation and fieldwork in a number of selected PR and news communities. Since we are essentially talking about on-line communities here, we are calling for what Hine (2000) has labeled "virtual ethnography." What distinguishes virtual ethnographies from the classical linguistic ethnographies that we are used to is that they are time- and space-shifted. This means that the ethnographers and their participants are not sharing the same time or space frame, thus challenging the traditional conceptualization of ethnographic authenticity. Secondly, virtual ethnographies are bound to be focused on digital, written texts, which seems to clash with a romantic legacy in ethnography treating speech as the primary mode of communication. Finally, virtual ethnographies are highly reflexive, with the ethnographers' private on-line interactions taking up centre stage.

At the PR end of the e-release spectrum, we expect a virtual ethnography of customized websites and on-line press release distribution services offering "long-term residual exposure" for press releases through archived pages that are indexed by the major search engines and that often come up high in the listings for relevant keyword queries. If press releases are no longer primarily for journalists to copy in the media, the question can then be raised if there is any point left in writing them in an impersonalized style the main purpose of which is that it requires little or no reworking on the journalists' part. E-releases could well constitute a hybrid mix of the traditional preformulated features of paper press releases (like headline and lead, third-person self-reference and pseudo-quotes) and a more direct kind of discourse reminiscent of direct mail from which preformulation is being phased out (including superlatives and other persuasive features, direct reader address, imperatives and emphatic all-capital typography).

As for the way e-releases are taken up in the on-line media, it is reasonable to assume that the Internet is creating a new location for PR to play its mediating role in. One question that can be raised here is to what extent on-line news remains tied in with traditional media. We can also think here of on-line press conferences, with journalists logging in from their PC at the newsdesk, monitoring the proceedings in real time and asking questions through e-mail. It should be interesting to investigate what this unusual participation framework implies in terms of access to the interactional arena and in terms of the balance of power among the parties involved.

7. Practical relevance

We believe that the research presented in this chapter should be practically relevant in various ways. Put very simply indeed, there are three parties involved in the broad news production process, viz. first, those who have an interest in managing what gets published in the papers, broadcast on radio and TV and posted on the Internet (headed by the various branches of the PR business of course), second, the journalists and third and finally, the general public. Since there can be no doubt that it must be very relevant for all three to get to know what the others are doing, what our research promises to contribute in this respect is an improved understanding of how PR officers write press releases and how journalists rewrite them.

To begin with, it would pay off for PR practitioners to learn more about how journalists reproduce their nicely preformulated copy and it would probably pay off even more for them to find out why they often don't. A frequently heard complaint from journalists is that PR practitioners don't seem to have a clue of what's happening inside the newsroom. This type of research can help do something about this and it would make sense to integrate some of our future research findings in PR training programs.

The same can of course be said about would-be journalists: few of them have any idea about the mechanics of journalistic writing and the role of sources (including press releases) in it. In fact, it could even be argued that it would be good for practicing, even experienced journalists to have their writing processes monitored and analyzed along the lines we have suggested above. It would certainly allow them to take a distance from the daily routines in the newsroom.

Finally, there's the general public. Hardly any of us are aware of the practicalities of news management and newsmaking. We believe that an increased understanding of how the news gets made and managed would help us become more critical news consumers. But it would also no doubt encourage us to question our own role in the media business.

Assignment

The mix of linguistic ethnography and computer-assisted writing process analysis which we have described in this chapter implies that the researcher follows a story in real time and as close to the action as possible. It is therefore by definition difficult to apply the approach described above by means of a desk analysis of PR and news data acquired through the Internet only. The main reason is that this would imply the kind of retrospectivity which makes it impossible to collect data for writing process analysis or to engage in fieldwork. However, what we can do is start out from either an interesting press release archived on a corporate website or an interesting news article that refers to a press release and try and explore from there what happened next or what happened before, i.e., we can use news products to reconstruct the news production process. Of course, this can never replace the kind of full-fledged analysis of the news production process which we have called for in this chapter, but at least it gives us some idea of what happens to a press release once it's been issued.

The reader is therefore invited to look for an interesting story in the form of a press release that was issued about it or of a news article that refers to a press release. As far as the press release is concerned, it should be newsworthy enough to generate media attention. The next step is to look for one or more news articles based on the press release or to try and find the press release that the news article is based on as well as one or more news articles in other media, and to determine to what extent preformulation seems to have played a role in the journalist's writing.

Chapter 17

Media discourse

Kenneth C.C. Kong
Hong Kong Baptist University

This chapter examines how discourse analysis can offer insights as to why news is written the way it is. It will start with a review of some key works in the study of news discourse. An emerging genre in news reporting, known as property transaction reports is then discussed with examples. The genre is problematic because it has the characteristics of both news reports and advertisements. The mixing is more successful than advertorials, the promotional stance of which can be easily recognized because of its full-blown label of "advertisement" and its one-sided focus on a product/service. It is argued that the new genre should be best studied by analyzing its specific move structure instead of the generic moves of news stories. Practical implications will be drawn and some thought-provoking questions will also be raised at the end.

1. Introduction

Media discourse has attracted enormous attention from linguists and media communicators because it is important for several reasons (Garret & Bell, 1998). The first reason is the easy accessibility of media discourse. Second, the use of media "influences and represents people's use of and attitudes towards language in a speech community." (Garret & Bell, 1998: 3). Third, many social and cultural stereotypes and meanings are projected and constructed through language.

News stories, as one of the most prevalent discourses in everyday life, have been studied particularly for the way in which they are structured (Van Dijk, 1998). Based on the classical narrative model of Labov (1972), Bell (1991, 1998) proposes a framework for analyzing news structure, in which a news story mainly consists of three key components: *attribution*, *abstract* and *story*. Attribution includes information such as the name of the news agency and the journalist's by-line. The abstract includes information such as the headline and lead. The story is the most complicated component and can be subdivided into *episodes* and *events*. In each event, there are attribution, actors, action, setting, follow-up, commentary, and background. Background refers to the events that occurred before the current event in the framework. Commentary refers to the journalist's or news actor's observations and evaluative comments on or expectations of the events as "commentary," and may provide context to help readers understand the news story. Follow-up, consisting of verbal reaction by other parties or non-verbal consequences, covers any action after the main action of the event. Bell also compares the discourse structure of news stories and the chronological structure of the news event. The temporal sequence is usually not followed in news reports, which are instead organized in terms of the perceived news value, such as recency and negativity, giving rise to the inverted-pyramid structure or top-down principle which ignores chronological sequencing and arranges events in terms of importance.

In addition to Bell's inverted-pyramid structure, Ungerer (2000) studies the structuring of hard news and sports news stories and proposed that the use of extracted topicality and the package approach has constantly been replacing sequential structuring or main-event-based structuring. Newsworthy events are still selected on the basis of well-known news values — recency (or immediacy), negativity, proximity, lack of ambiguity, novelty, personalization and eliteness of the news actor, size and quantity, reference to elite persons, predictability, continuity (Bell, 1991; Ungerer, 2000). Nevertheless, Ungerer argues that as newspapers are at a disadvantage when competing with other media in terms of the most important attribute — recency — journalists have begun to use *extracted topics and the package approach*. Instead of topicalizing and reporting the news story directly through the Main Event, which is probably known to the public from other media such as TV news or the Internet, journalists enter the event frame through other non-central elements, such as Consequence and Reaction, which also carry a strong potential of newsworthiness. In addition to the shift of topicalized event lines, newspapers try to "package" the news event in a more fragmented manner, usually offering a wider angle of seeing the event from different perspectives to make the story more attractive. For example, details of the Main Event can be found in photographs and their captions that are placed beside the main reports or background information in factual articles. By offering the use of extracted topicality and the package approach, newspapers have been able to compensate for the loss of recency as a news value.

2. The research challenge

A quote from *IDS*:

> The challenge of the media discourse approach is to prove from discourse analysis and research into production and perception to what extent news stories are biased, in what way this is caused by the opinions of the journalists and to what extent this influences readers or listeners. Discourse analysis of the media is an extended stylistic analysis. It includes the study of content (which topics are selected or excluded?), the structure (what is put in the lead of a story and what kind of information is located at important places, at the start of a paragraph?) and the wording: the structuring of the information and lexical choices. (Renkema, 2004: 267)

Property transaction reports are an emerging genre in property magazines, and are particularly common in Hong Kong. As Hong Kong is a geographically small place with high population density, land is scarce and expensive. While many people are living in the housing estates provided by the government, most want to own their own apartments. Nevertheless, this decision does not come easy as Hong Kong's apartments are among the most expensive in the world. The high price of apartments is coupled, like any commodity, with price fluctuations that are caused by many factors both internal and external to the local economy. Hence, when someone buys a property in Hong Kong, it can involve a long process of research and consideration. Besides people who want to live in their own flats, there are also people who buy properties for investment — long term (for leasing the apartment so that rent can be "earned") and short term (for buying and selling quickly with a view to making profit). These two groups of people (as users of properties and as investors) form the largest audience for property magazines in Hong Kong. Of course, there are also owners who want to sell their properties but are not sure when they should do so to maximize their profits.

There are two property magazines in Hong Kong: the *Property Times* and the *Property Browser*. Both of these are published weekly on Saturday when people are relatively free to do what they cannot do during the rest of the week. The magazines come as free supplements to two newspapers, the *Hong Kong Economics Times* and the *Sing Tao Daily*, but both are also sold separately as stand-alone magazines. The structure and content of the magazines are very similar although they may not have the same sequence of content. There are four main types of content. The first type is feature articles on a particular issue related to properties in Hong Kong. These can range from the promotion strategies of a new property to property price forecasts. The second type of content is estate agency advertisements, which comprise almost half of the overall content. The third type of content is features on home decoration and furniture. These are sometimes accompanied by buying guides. The fourth type of content that concerns us here are the so-called "transaction reports." Other miscellaneous types of content include bank mortgage rate comparisons and the telephone numbers of public utilities and institutions that are related to property buying and selling.

Transaction reports, on surface, seem to be a simple genre of reporting. What the audience wants to know about are the latest transactions so they can make the "right" decisions. However, compared with the feature articles, which closely resemble news reports and have clearer boundaries of journalistic and other voices, transaction reports are a "possibility for advertisers to exploit news media" (Ungerer, 2004) because they not only report what has been sold and bought, but also provide the background and additional information that can motivate potential buyers and sellers to make decisions. The information is usually one-sided and is provided by property agents. The voices of the protagonists who were involved in the transactions (the seller, the buyer or even the estate agent involved) are all missing. Journalists are only responsible for organizing and presenting the information provided by the estate agent, playing what Goffman (1981) calls the role of animator but not the principal.

This "hybrid" genre, in other words, embodies what is traditionally labeled as news reports and advertisements. Advertisements, as a form of promotion, have been regarded as the colonizers of other genres that are increasingly promotional, such as those that take a hard sell approach by adopting advertisement-like language and style. One of the "colonized" genres is the news report, which increasingly integrates the promotional elements of advertisements to increase the desire of the audience to consume. News reports are seen to benefit less from this colonization than advertisements, because they have to adopt an advertisement-like style but the same is not true vice versa (Ungerer, 2004). Advertisements have also "invaded" other types of discourse (such as the "advertorial," a kind of advertisement that uses a semi-editorial style that is one-sided). The more dynamic role of intertextuality in re-negotiating or recontextualizing a new reality is usually downplayed by assuming that one of the genres is superimposed and the other is embedded and parasitic. In this connection, intertextuality should be seen as "a matter of recontextualization — a movement from one context to another" (Fairclough, 2003: 51). In other words, intertextuality is neither a matter of who gains more or less, nor which genre is a colonizer or colonized, but it is a more interactive phenomenon through which a text producer and recipient engage in the making of meaning. A genre that imitates another genre can be resisted as unacceptable. While one genre is integrated with another genre, taking the advertorial as an example, people will be ready to judge the credibility of the source by looking at whether it is a real news report or just an imitated one. On the other hand, advertorials reinforce the credibility of news reports, keeping their boundaries intact.

In other words, it is less meaningful to examine genre imitations that are already accepted or recognized than to examine genres that are more integrated with the voices of more than one genre. Transaction reports are good candidates to examine this phenomenon because most of them subtly integrate the two genres in question. To use the example of advertorials again, they are easy to detect because they repeatedly use certain brand names or sometimes carry an explicit label of "promotional material" or even the full-blown label of "advertisement" through which newspapers and magazines tend to distance themselves and avoid legal responsibility. Transaction reports, however, are more subtle in the sense that no such labels are used and no brand names are mentioned (the name of individual estate agent and their agency can be found but they are disguised as sources of the news). Of course, the genre is as promotional as advertisements because it only gives one-sided opinions and can be fully integrated with advertisements to achieve what an advertisement is meant to do. This issue is made even more complicated by the lack of a consistent reporting style in Chinese.

This chapter has two main objectives: to examine how transaction reports draw on resources, particularly the structural elements of news reports and advertisements to accomplish their goals; and to examine the degree of usefulness of the prototypical categories established in discourse analysis to identify genres.

3. Examples

The following is a typical example of a transaction report taken from the *Property Times*.

(3) 沙田中心 摸貨獲利$11.8萬
中原蔡創文表示，區內一名投資者以「確認人」身份，斥資$123.8萬購入沙田中心A座中層H室，面積356呎，呎價$3,478；單位原業主為一名區內資深的投資者，於本年3月以$112萬「摸入」單位，是次轉售帳面獲利$11.8萬，單位於2個月內升值逾一成。(PT)

A mortgagor sold a property in Shatin Centre and gained $118,000.
Choi Chong Man, from Centraline, indicated that an investor from the district bought a middle-floored flat H of Block A in Shatin Centre for $1.238 million as a confirmor. The flat is 356 sq. ft. and sold for $3,478/sq.ft. The original owner of the flat was an experienced investor in the district and bought the flat from a mortgagor at $1.12 million in March this year. This resale brought the owner a profit of $118,000. The property value has risen by over 10% in two months.

There are at least three features here that I would like to discuss briefly. In terms of length, most transaction reports are rather short, ranging from 68 to 331 characters, with an average of 150 characters. The language is semi-formal with occurrence of technical jargon, such as "摸入," which means the acquisition of a property from a mortgagor who has not yet completed the original transaction. There are some informal words but the language is mostly based on standard written Chinese, instead of Cantonese (a more local variety of Chinese). There are reporting verbs throughout, but the boundaries of the voices are not distinctly marked. The report reads like a piece of continuous prose created by one single person. Second, although the source of the information is clearly stated, "中原蔡創文表示" ([Representative] of [Property Agency] indicated), the journalist's by-line is missing. The writer of the news is taken to be the magazine at large. This is perhaps surprising to English speaking readers but the omission of the by-line is more common in Chinese newspapers. The third general feature worth discussing here is the fact that most of the ideas of the reports are not from the journalist or magazine but from the property agency. This can be identified easily by comparing two magazines in terms of reports about the same transaction. Eight transactions were reported in both magazines. A report on the transaction discussed above also appeared in *Property Browser*.

(4) 沙田中心「摸售」賺11.8萬
中原地產沙田中心高級分行經理蔡創文表示，區內一名投資者斥資123.8萬元購入沙田中心A座東寧大廈中層H室，單位面積356方呎，每方呎價3,478元；單位原業主同為一名區內資深投資者，於本年3月以112萬元「摸入」上述單位，是次轉售帳面即時獲利11.8萬元，單位於2個月內升值逾10%。該單位擁優質的開揚景致，飽覽東南河景，乃用家喜愛之類別，故該名投資者因此甚為看俏其後市升幅，於未曾參觀過現樓的情況下，即斥資購入單位作投資用途。蔡氏補充，沙田中心於本月交投持續有不俗的走勢，截至5月22日錄得約15宗成交，預計本月可望衝擊30宗成交紀錄。(PD)

A mortgagor sold a property in Shatin Centre and gained $118,000
Choi Chong Man, Senior Branch Manager of the Shatin Centre Branch of Centraline, indicated that an investor from that district spent $1.238 million to buy a middle-floored flat H of Block A at Chesterfield Mansion in Shatin Centre. The flat is 356 sq. ft. and sold for $3,478/sq. ft. The original owner of the flat was an experienced investor in the district; s/he bought the above-mentioned property from a mortgagor at $1.12 million in March this year. This resale brought an immediate profit of $118,000; the property value has risen by over 10% in two months. The flat provides a high-quality, spacious view, and embraces the south-east river view. These kinds of flats are owners' favorites. The investor had a good prospect of the property's future value, and therefore bought the property for investment, even without visiting the flat. Choi added that Shatin Centre sustained a pretty good transaction record this month. By 22 May, about 15 transactions were recorded, and it was expected that there would be about 30 transactions in the month.

The second report contains almost exactly the same information as that which was reported in the first report, not only in terms of the information but also the words that are used to describe the main event. Of course, there are some minor differences in terms of description, and the second report contains more information and elaboration than the first (which will be explained below). However, both reports are very similar because the information is taken from the same property agency, not from the people involved such as the seller or buyer. The view is purely one-sided, unlike what someone would expect in a normal news report, in which the content will be very different across different newspapers even though the event reported is the same.

What the analysis above tries to explain is that the journalist, without a clear display of identity, mainly draws on the voices of the property agency (not even the agent who was involved in the transaction). In one *Property Times* feature, the journalist explained how the system works. He said that he received many emails from property agencies every day and he would select some and write up the transaction reports. It can be deduced from the comparison above that the journalists of both magazines used mainly the words of the agency representative, with only minor modifications. Nevertheless, the boundaries between the journalist's words and the representative's voice are not clearly marked by quotation marks ("xxx" if using a more westernized approach, or 「xxx」 using the more traditional approach in Chinese). In other words, the property agency provides the information and the journalist selects what is included and then gives it a final structure. The agenda of the estate company is obviously to arouse people's desire to sell and buy properties, which is why the language is promotional and only focuses on the positive side of the transactions. In contrast, the journalists represent the interests of both the magazines for which they work and the property agency, which is a major buyer of advertising space. Hence he or she has to borrow the voices of property agencies to serve at least two functions: first, to forge the objectivity that is expected in news reporting, and second, to distance themselves and avoid responsibility that may arise from any mistaken or misleading information. This emerging genre is situated in an activity in which magazine journalists and property agency representatives have to work together to perform their jobs — one for promoting and the other for distancing. In the following, I will compare the reports with the prototypical structures of news events and advertisements.

4. Research method

The data that are used in this paper are transaction reports selected from two local property magazines in Hong Kong — the *Property Times* (a supplement of the *Hong Kong Economics Times*) and the *Property Browser* (a supplement of the *Sing Tao Daily*). The texts were collected on the same date (28 May 2005) to compare how certain events were reported differently in the two magazines. Eighty-three reports were collected — 51 from the *Property Times* and 32 from the *Property Browser*, encompassing all of the reports of the particular date.

Initially they were compared with the prototypical structure of news reports using the model of news stories that Bell (1991) developed. The various components that are unique to news reports were identified and counted in terms of their occurrence in each report and total occurrence (including recurrence) in all of the reports. The purpose was to examine the extent to which these reports were similar to typical news reports.

5. Recent research

The 83 texts were analyzed using Bell's model of news structure (1991, 1998), which identifies the following main components: *Abstract* (including Headline and Lead), *Source Attribution*, *Event* (including Orientation, Evaluation, Action and Resolution), *Background*, *Commentary* and *Follow-up*. In general, the structure of the corpus is very close to Bell's framework, in terms of the occurrence of the main elements,

Table 1. Sample analysis (1): News structure (Source: the *Property Times*)

TEXT	MOVES
凱帆軒 業主勁賺$141.4萬 The owner of a property at Hampton Place made a substantial profit of $1.414 million	Headline
利嘉閣封重動表示， Mr Fung Chung Fan from Ricacorp Properties Limited indicated that,	Source Attribution
近日錄得凱帆軒2座高層C室，面積608呎，擁全海景觀，以$335萬成交，呎價$5,510。 the company recently recorded a transaction of a high-level flat C of Block 2, 608 sq. ft, having a complete sea-view, sold for $3.35 million or $5510/sq. ft.	Main Event
據悉，原業主於03年4月以$193.6萬買入上址， It is reported that the original owner bought the above-mentioned flat for $1.93 million in April 2003,	Background
現帳面勁賺$141.4萬離場。 now making a big profit of $1.414 million.	Consequence
買家為外區長線投資客，睇好凱帆軒未來升值潛力， The buyer was an "out-of-district" long-term investor, with a good prospect of the future appreciation value of Hampton Place,	Event-Actor
故購入該單位收租。 [and therefore bought the flat for rental.]	Main Event
現時凱帆軒租盤盤源只有12個，平均呎租$20至$25，客源不乏中環上班客，故出租率極快。 At present, the number of flats in Hampton Place available for rental is only 12. The average rent is $20-$25/sq. ft., with workers in Central as the main source of tenants. The rental rate is therefore extremely high.	Commentary

except for the Follow-up move. According to Bell, the first element of a news story should be the Abstract. However, in our corpus, due to the length of the texts, none of them use a lead. The Headline — representing the Abstract — summarizes the whole text and appears as the first element. The source of information starts the body of the report. After attributing the information source, the transaction and the evaluation of the property comprises the Main Event, followed by the Background, which is the information on the seller (i.e., original owner) of the flat. Consequence, instead of being the result of the main happening, which is usually negative in news stories, here refers to the effect of the transaction on the seller: that is, whether the seller gains a profit or suffers a loss. The category "Event-Actor" is a subcategory of the element Main Event in Bell's model since in our corpus, the viewpoint of the buyer and/or the seller towards the transacted property and the property market is always reported separately from the Main Event. Commentary is usually the last element, quoting the additional comments of the agents on the housing estate in which the flat sold is located, such as the availability of similar flats. The following is an example of analysis, based on a text from the *Property Times.*

Several things should be noted before we move to further discussion. It is rare to find all of the elements in each report; some of them have a very low percentage of occurrence. It is also not common to find the elements in the same order as shown in Bell's framework. This will be further explained in the following section. One category that is not included in Bell's framework is identified in some of the texts, i.e., Eye-catcher. This usually appears after the Headline, and its function will be further discussed in the later part of this section.

Another element that is not captured in the sample analysis above is the occurrence of the element "Main Event 2." Most of the time, only one transaction is presented in each report. However, some of the texts describe two transactions. As journalists sometimes report more than one event in a news story, writers of the transaction

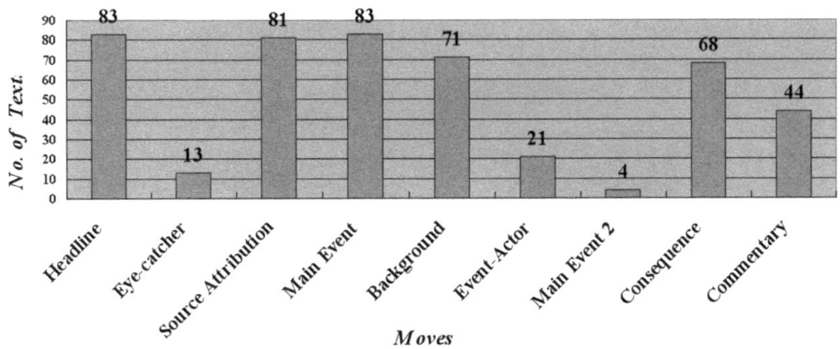

Figure 1. Occurrence of moves (excluding recurrences), with reference to moves found in news stories.

reports may also provide information on more than one deal at a time. In other words, in addition to the "central" Main Event, the reporters can provide information about a property located in the same estate as another Main Event, or about another transaction of the seller of the property of the Main Event.

By analyzing the occurrence and recurrence of the elements of transaction reports, we aim to investigate the extent to which they are realized in the configuration of news stories. The following bar chart shows the total number of occurrences of the elements among the 83 texts in our corpus. The elements are only counted on their first occurrence, excluding any recurrences.

It is clear that Headline and Main Event are present in every text. Almost all of the texts include Source Attribution (although none of the texts carry a by-line), with the exception of 2. Other frequent moves include Background and Consequence. Commentary is found in about half of the corpus (44 texts). As mentioned above, some moves were found more than once in a report. They were counted in calculating the percentage of occurrence below. The following pie chart shows the overall percentage of the occurrence of each move among the total number of moves (i.e., 498). The percentage is calculated by:

$$\frac{\text{Number of occurrences (including the recurrence) of a particular element.}}{\text{Total number of occurrences of all the moves in all the texts (i.e., 498)} \times 100\%}$$

The most frequent element is Main Event (20.88%), followed by Headline (16.67%), Source Attribution (16.27%), Background (16.06%), Consequence (13.65%), Commentary (8.84%), and the sub-category of Event-Actor (4.22%). Other elements account for less than 3% the total occurrence. In other words, the occurrence of elements is highly predictable from Bell's model of the prototypical news structure. Particularly

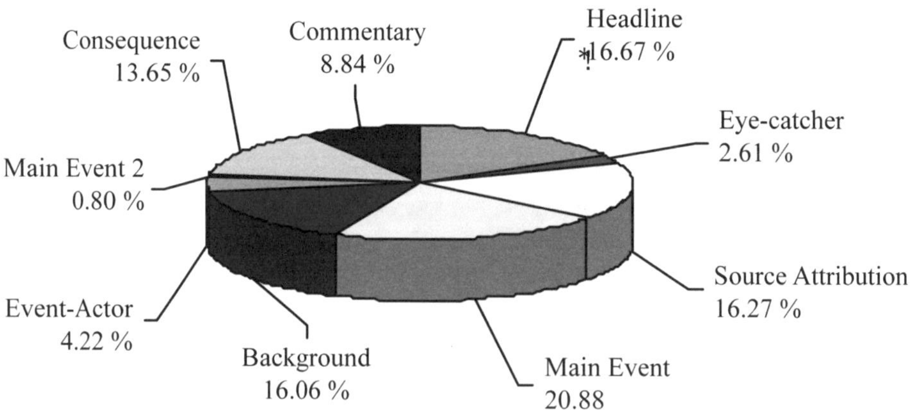

Figure 2. Overall occurrences of moves, with reference to moves found in news stories.

interesting is the high importance attached to the Main Event, which is less important in current news reporting because newspapers are slower than other media to report "current" events. Readers may know of the event already (through other media such as the Internet, TV news) by the time that they read the news. Newspapers tend to focus on other elements such as Consequence and Commentary on the people involved (Ungerer, 2000). There are at least two reasons for the pattern found in the data. First, transaction reports are different from news reports in the sense that readers usually do not have any information about the transaction through other means. As a result, they want to know the details of the Main Event of the transaction. The second reason is related to the function of a prototypical news structure in forging objectivity in news reporting. In this respect, the prototypical structure of a genre can be employed as a device to increase the persuasive power of a message.

Another equally frequent element is Headline. As most newspaper and magazine articles contain a headline, its presence can also enhance the credibility of the transaction report. However, it should be noted that the headline is more than simply a summary of the transaction. Many of them contain highly evaluative lexes, commenting on the positive side of the transaction, whether someone has made a big profit, or other desirable attributes of the transaction.

(3) '凱帆軒 業主勁賺$141.4萬' (PT)
Owner of Hampton Place made a substantial profit of $1.414 million

(4) 巴富大廈 高市價20%轉手 (PT)
A flat in the Perth Building was resold at 20% higher than the market price

(5) 慧景軒 單位升值43.8% (PT)
A flat at Vianni Cove rose by 43.8%

(6) 德福花園 則王閃電獲承接 (PT)
A flat with the "best sketch" [good design] of Telford Gardens was resold swiftly

However, some headlines highlight the negativity of the event by showing that the owner has cut the price to an attractive level.

(7) 翠湖花園 勁減$25萬放售 (PT)
An owner at Garden Vista cut the price substantially by $25,000 for the sale of a property

(8) 都會軒 低市價2%轉讓 (PT)
A flat at Metropolis Residence was resold at 2% lower than the market price

(9) 雍景臺「筍盤」840萬易手 (PD)
A "best-valued" flat at Robinson Place was resold for $8.4 million

Although these headlines suggest the negative aspect of the property transaction to the owner, this is portrayed as a reason for buyers to take action quickly. Another important function of headlines is to arouse the attention of readers, which is one of the most important functions of advertisements. This will be followed up in the discussion on the specific moves of transaction reports and their promotional functions.

Source Attribution is the third most frequent element, with an occurrence percentage of 16.27%. Understanding that buying a property is a big decision to make, especially in Hong Kong where land is scarce and housing is relatively expensive, people are not likely to make a decision to purchase a flat just because of hearsay or property advertisements (Cheng, 2001). The source of information is important, and almost all of the texts (81 out of 83) contain this move. As the move that claims authority and reliability, Source Attribution is usually at the very beginning of the texts, immediately after the Headline. Interestingly, the sources of information are property agencies, which have profit-making as their main goal. The information that they provide is usually regarded as "biased" or "one-sided" by customers, but here is disguised as "authority" in the configuration of a news report. The structural order of the information source is: the name of the property agency → (position) → name of the representative → reporting verb.

(10) 美聯物業山頂南區分行高級營業經理唐志傑表示…(PD)
Tong Chi Kit, Senior Branch Manager of the South of the Peak Branch of Midland Property **indicated** that…

(11) 中原地產海逸豪園分行經理王淑儀透露…(PD)
Wong Shuk Yee, Laguna Verde Branch Manager from Centraline, **disclosed** that…

(12) 美聯杜漢祥表示…(PT)
To Hong Cheung from the Midland Property **indicated** that…

(13) 利嘉閣周德龍指出…(PT)
Chow Tak Lung from Ricacorp Properties Limited **pointed out** that…

As illustrated in the third and fourth examples above, the institutional position of the representative is not always mentioned, so it is regarded as an optional element. Other elements are regarded as essential. The most common reporting verbs found in the corpus in order of frequency are 表示 (indicate), 透露 (disclose) and 指出 (point out). These are all neutral reporting verbs in Chinese. No reporting verb that displays a writer's negative attitude, such as "聲稱" (claim without evidence) was found. Another interesting feature, as mentioned above, is the unclear boundaries between the voices of the journalist and the quotes, as no quotation marks are used in the reports.

(14) 利嘉閣地產黃榮城透露,一名 YOHO Town炒家因銀行加息而心怯 …(PT)
Wong Wing Shing, from Ricacorp Properties Limited, disclosed that a short-term investor in YOHO Town was concerned about the increase in interest rates…

In the reporting culture of Chinese news writing in Hong Kong, unmarked boundaries can mean either direct or indirect quotes. By comparing the same event in the two magazines under study, it can be concluded that the words are direct quotes of the property agent. It can be argued that the use of quotation marks may signal maximal distance between the journalist and the quote, which is not intended by the writers of transaction reports, who try to create objectivity with a reasonable amount of distance because too much distancing may jeopardize the creditability of the quotes. Quotation serves at least two important functions (cf. Bell, 1991). First, the quote is "a particularly incontrovertible fact because it is a newsmaker's own words." The second function is "to distance and disown to absolve journalist and news outlet from the endorsement of what the source said" (Bell, 1991: 207–8). The writers of transaction reports seem to balance these two functions by, on the one hand, portraying the voice as a coherent whole of the event (by not using quotation marks), and on the other hand by giving enough distance to the voice to avoid responsibility (by using neutral reporting verbs).

The Actor is an important element of information in a news report. People want to know who is involved and what happens to them in an event. This is particularly the case for transaction reports, in which a great deal of attention is paid to the actor (particularly the buyer) in a transaction. Twenty-one of the reports so prominently elaborate on this particular piece of information that it deserves to be identified as an individual element instead of a sub-element under Event.

(15) 買家則為同區換樓客，認為單位間隔四正、光猛開揚，而且交通方便…(PD)
The buyer was a trade-in buyer of the district. He/She perceived that the unit was well-designed, well-lit and spacious, conveniently located…

(16) 買家為外區投資客，無懼加息影響，認為加息幅度比預期小… (PD)
The buyer was an out-of-district investor. Not worried about the effect of increase in interest rates, he perceived that the increase was smaller than expected…

(17) 一名篤信風水的買家聽從風水師指點，認為單位可有助財運及健康…(PT)
A buyer who devoutly believed in Feng Shui followed the instructions of a geomancer. The buyer believed that the property could help improve his/her wealth and health…

(18) 一租客本身租住大埔區物業，並一直有意自置居所，故無懼近日銀行加息風險，加上房屋署建議縮短居屋自由轉讓的年期限制，令居屋屋苑再受市場注意，該租客亦認為居屋物業造價吸引，單位質素理想… (PD)
A tenant had been renting a property in Tai Po, and longed to buy his/her own flat. Therefore, the tenant did not worry about the risk of increases in interest rates. Besides, the proposal of the Housing Authority to shorten the time limit on the resale of Home Ownership Scheme flats has attracted market attention to Home Ownership Scheme estates. The tenant also perceived the Home Ownership Scheme properties as attractive in price and ideal in quality…

(19) 一名孝順子購入上水順欣花園予父母居住… (PT)
A filial son bought a flat in Sheung Shui Sunningdale Garden for his parents…

Many of the examples above carry highly evaluative lexes. Instead of giving background information about the buyer, the description focuses on why the buyer made the final decision of acquiring a property. However, this is only from the perspective of the property agency and it is never clear whether it is accurate. Yet these evaluative descriptions or reasons for buying are important to neutralize the resistance of potential buyers.

The analysis above points to the complex structure of transaction reports, which cannot be fully understood from within the prototypical structure of news reports. Some elements are so salient in transaction reports that they should be examined in a different framework. The use of the Actor element as a move in itself is a good example of analytic modification to capture what is going on in a hybrid genre. There are also other elements that should ideally be singled out.

6. Research proposal

Although the generic news model can be applied to transaction reports, there are many important elements that lose their identities if we keep the model intact. As pointed out earlier, the Actor is an important element that should not be treated as sub-component under Event. It plays a crucial role in persuading people to take action and entails what we can call the desirability element of an advertisement. Indeed, the category of "Actor" is still not adequate because an actor can be a seller or a buyer. Equally important is information such as the size and view of the properties. Similar to information about the actor, they can also stimulate the desire of readers to buy a property. As a result, 14 moves were identified in the reports; however, they do not exist in entirety and in a fixed sequence, and some of them could recur. The following examples show how some of the moves are realized.

Table 2. Sample analysis (2): Generic structure (Source: the *Property Times*)

TEXT	MOVES
康怡花園 業主降價$8萬沽售 Owner of a property of Kornhill reduced the price by $80000 and sold his/her flat	Headline
減價 Price reduction	Eye-catcher
利嘉閣丁培鴻表示, Mr Ding Pui Hung from Ricacorp Properties Limited indicated that,	Source of information
康怡花園F座低層13室 a low-level flat 13 of Block F of Kornhill,	Address
錄得成交, was transacted.	TRANSACTION
單位748呎, The flat is 748 sq. ft.,	Additional information
業主降價$8萬將就買家, The owner reduced the price by $80000 for the buyer,	Seller
最終以$302萬 and, finally at $3.02 million,	Price
售出單位, sold the flat,	SELLS
呎價$4,037, 低市價2%, The price per sq. ft. is $4,037 — 2% lower than the market price.	Price
承接買家為區內換樓客。 The buyer was a 'trade-in' buyer of the district.	Buyer / Purpose
據悉, 原業主於89年以$120萬購入上址, It is reported that the original owner bought the above property at $1.2 million in 1989.	Background
現時單位售價雖以較低價錢售出, 但帳面仍勁賺$182萬。 Although s/he now sold the flat at a lower price, s/he still earned a big profit of $1.82 millions.	Profit

Some of the moves bear resemblance to those in the model of news structure such as headlines, commentary and background. However, most of the moves are specific to the genre in question. As mentioned, a total of 14 moves were identified, including headlines, but not all of them can be found in a single report. For example, the above reports already show a different pattern of moves. Both of them carry essential information such as price, address and profit. However, the first report begins by referring to the transaction explicitly ("錄得成交," literally meaning "recorded a transaction"). The transaction was then reported from the perspective of seller, and then from that of the buyer. In the second report, the transaction was reported without the use of the

Table 3. Sample analysis (3): Generic structure (Source: the *Property Times*)

TEXT	MOVES
慧景軒 單位升值43.8% Value of a property of Vianni Cove rose by 43.8%	Headline
中原黃海表示， Mr Wong Hai from Centraline indicated that,	Source of information
一名區內投資者 an investor in the district	Buyer / Purpose
以$210萬 at the price of $2.1 million	Price
購入 bought	BUYS
慧景軒2座高層F室， a high-level flat F at Vianni Cove.	Address
單位面積902呎， The property is 902 sq. ft.	Additional information
呎價$2,328， The price per sq. ft. is $2,328.	Price
單位每月租金料達$7,500，租金回報率料達4.3厘。 The monthly rental of the flat was expected to reach $7,500; the rental profit rate was expected to reach 4.3%.	Commentary
據了解，原業主於03年以$146萬購入上述單位， It is reported that the original owner bought the above-mentioned flat at $1.46 million in 2003.	Background
業主帳面獲利$64萬，單位升值43.8%。 He/she made a profit of $0.64 million. The value of the flat rose by 43.8%.	Profit

meta-label of "transaction," and the transaction was only reported from the perspective of the buyer.

The following bar chart shows the total number of unique occurrences of the elements amongst the 83 texts, disregarding any recurrences.

The elements Headline, Address, Additional information and Price occur in all of the texts. They can be regarded as the obligatory moves of transaction reports. However, some of the moves recur with a fairly high frequency, and recurrence is also taken into account by using the following formula:

$$\frac{\text{Total number of occurrence of a move (in 83 texts)}}{\text{Total number of texts (i.e., 83)}}$$

If the figure is more than one, then the move has recurred. The higher the figure, the more frequent the recurrence.

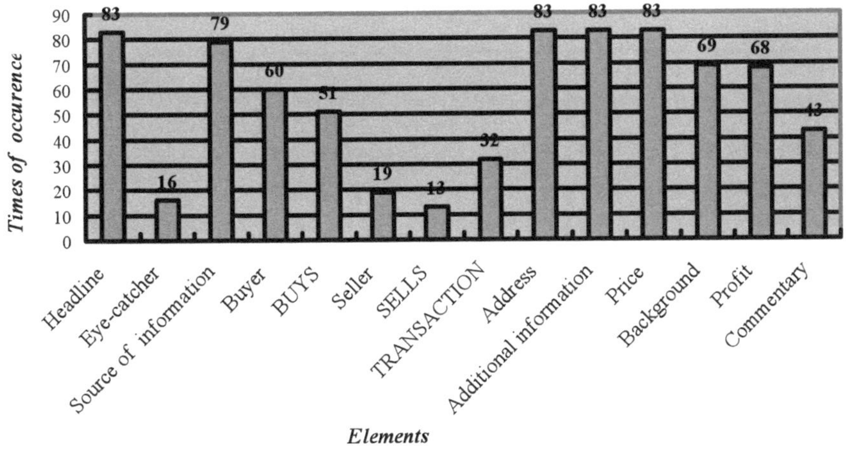

Figure 3. Occurrence of generic moves.

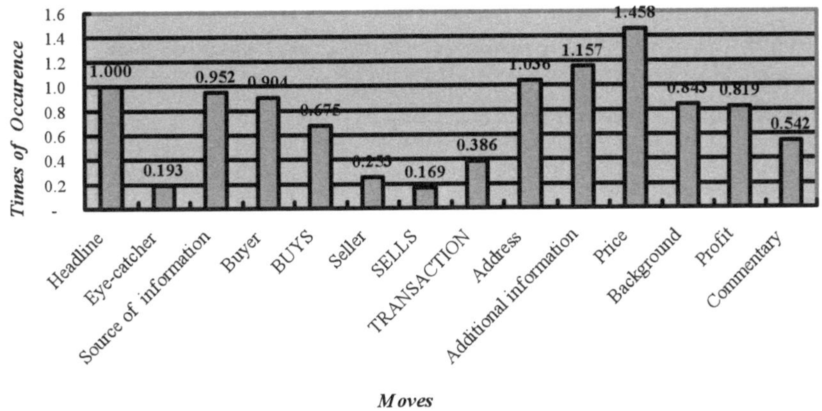

Figure 4. Recurrence of generic moves.

As every report has only one headline, it has the value of 1. Three moves — Price, Additional Information and Address — have recurrence rates higher than 1 but less than 2, meaning that they occur more than once in some reports. Other elements do not appear in every text. This notion of recurrence is very useful for identifying the prominence of the elements.

Each move can be assigned to the 4 main promotional functions of attracting attention and arousing interest, stimulating desire, creating conviction and getting action. Attracting attention and arousing interest are combined because "the obvious way of catching the reader's attention is to show him or her that what the product has to offer is of interest to him/her" (Vestergaard & Schroder, 1985: 58):

Table 4. Promotional functions of moves in transaction reports

MOVES	Promotional Functions
Headline	Attract attention and arouse interest
Eye-catcher	
Source of information	Create conviction
Buyer/Purpose OR Seller/Purpose	Stimulate desire
BUYS or SELLS or TRANSACTION	
Address	
Additional information	
Price	
Background	Create conviction
Profit	Stimulate desire
Commentary	Get action

It can be seen that the most important function of transaction reports in terms of promotion is that of stimulating desire, which has been argued to be the single most indispensable element in any advertisement. In other words, transaction reports accomplish what most advertisements are trying to perform.

7. Practical relevance

If one has to address the initial question of whether the genre in question is a news report, an advertisement or a new genre, there are at least two different explanations, following the standard practice of uncovering intertextuality in genre analysis. On surface, property transaction report is a promotional genre, i.e., advertisement in the configuration of a news report, which is type of embedded intertextuality. But through a detailed analysis as demonstrated above, property transaction reports are not "just" in the configuration of a news report, and it is plausible to say the genre is mainly a news report but it carries subtle elements of promotion, having the characteristics of a "hybrid genre" (Bhatia, 2005). In other words, both the elements of news reports and advertisements are present in the genre and the communicative functions of the genre are to inform as much as to persuade. Although the combination of these two communicative functions may not qualify the genre as a new genre, this mixing is more subtle and sophisticated than "advertorials" in which advertisements and "objective" editorial contents are merged together, carrying easily-recognizable traits of promotional texts. However, it may not be the final shape of the genre which is the most interesting, but it is the activity in which the genre is created which should draw more attention.

The genre in question is embedded and situated in an activity in which two "communities of practice" (Lave & Wenger, 1991) have to accommodate, synchronize and coordinate their practices. The intertextual links are not something invented or used "consciously" by the journalists. Instead, they are products of the synchronization of two practices. In other words, intertextuality is not a product of conscious mixing, but a product of an on-going negotiation of three parties at least — the journalist, the property agencies (who are the major sponsor of advertising space) and the readers (who are the potential patrons of those agencies). Property transaction reports qualify as "boundary objects" (Star, 1989; Wenger, 1998) in promoting and reporting. Of course, at the receptive end, readers can also "attend to one specific portion of the boundary object" (Wenger, 1998: 107) while ignoring others. The intertextual analysis here points to the need to situate a text or genre in wider context of analysis. The definition of genre as "a class of communicative events" (Swales, 1990) also has to be rethought. Genre is situated in a much wider context than is presumed. If one has to define a genre by communicative events, then it should be a multiple class of communicative events that are not restricted by a single set of homogeneous rules.

From a diachronic perspective, transaction reports can be seen as a further development of the advertorial, which is losing its original appeal and is now widely considered as a kind of advertisement. People are looking for further ways of using language to promote products or images. As illustrated in the analysis, the dependent relationship between journalists and property agents is not obvious in the reports. On the surface, journalists are simply reporting what is transacted. However, the income of these magazines comes largely from property agency advertising. Moreover, they certainly have a common interest in promoting the property market so that both of them can benefit (property agents gain by earning commission and the magazines gain by increasing their sales volume). To a certain extent, transaction reports have almost become another venue for promotion and have lost their identity as reports. They have successfully suppressed the contradictions that are inherent in the discourses and established "particular insulations between them" (Chouliaraki & Fairclough, 1999: 119). However, "when different discourses are worked together in interactions these contradictions may re-emerge" (1999: 119). This explains why there is a continuing push to invent new genres for promotion. When one form dies, it is replaced by another.

As mentioned above, intertextuality is a kind of recontextualization for interactional purposes, rather than simply mixing elements for sake of mixing. The main advantage of seeing intertextuality as recontextualization is that it can allow us to focus on the "locus of occurrence" (Forstorp, 1998). Users may not be aware of the labels or the consequences of mixing styles or registers. The prototypical categories are "little more than tools. We set up categories in order to better understand the world around us" (Ostman, 2004: 437). Prototypical categories are useful in the sense that some notions of the genre in question are needed for us to understand how resources are drawn on and then mobilized. As shown in the analysis, although property transactions reports are shaped in the configuration of a news report, they have other own generic structure that has to be understood to better understand their promotional characteristics. In other words, discourse analysts have to be flexible with any tools that they are employing. Prototypicality is something that does not bid users, but can be turned as a device for negotiating another reality.

Part of this chapter is adopted from Kong, K.C.C. (2006). Property transaction report: News, advertisement in a new genre. *Discourse Studies, 8*(6): 771–768.

Assignment

1. Compare the move structure of the following two different property transaction reports of the same event. The boundaries of the moves have been identified for you.

Text A

1. 麗港城 成交勁跌五成 **1. Big Drop of 50% in Transactions of Laguna City**
2. 利嘉閣張木強表示， 2. According to XXX of Ricacorp,
3. 麗港城36座中層E室 3. Flat E of Middle Floor, Block 36
4. 錄成交， 4. had a transaction.
5. 單位面積861呎， 5. The area of the flat is 861 square feet.
6. 成交價$316萬，平均呎價$3,670，屬合理市場價。 6. The deal is $3.16 million, which is a reasonable market price.
7. 上址原業主03年11月以低價$201萬購入上址， 7. The original owner bought the flat at a low price of 2.01 million in November 2003.
8. 是次帳面勁賺$115萬離場。 8. The transaction made a big profit of 1.15 million.
9. 過去的周六、日，麗港城睇樓量下跌兩成，5月份至今成交量有22宗，較上月同期勁跌五成。 9. The last weekend recorded a 20% drop of potential buyers' appointments. There were only 22 transactions in May, a 50% drop compared with last month.

Source: *Property Times* (28 May 2005)

Text B

1. 麗港城業主轉手賺 115萬 **1. An Owner of Laguna City makes a big profit of 1.15 million**
2. 利嘉閣地產東九龍區域經理張木強表示, 2. According to XXX, the District Manager (East Kowloon) of Ricarcorp Properties,
3. 觀塘麗港城第36座中層E室 3. Flat E of Middle Floor, Block 36
4. 最近獲得成交, 4. recently had a transaction.
5. 單位面積861方呎, 5. The area is 861 square feet.
6. 作價316萬元, 每方呎價3,670元, 屬合理市場價。 6. The deal is 3.16 million (3,670/sq feet), which is a reasonable market price.
7. 原業主之前態度極之強硬, 鐵價不二叫價335萬元, 但由於近日加息, 7. The original owner was very firm in the former deal price of 3.35 million. But because of recent increase in interest rate,
8. 故買家還價316萬元便立即成交, 8. the offer of 3.16 million by the buyer resulted in the deal.
9. 而他在03年11月以低價201萬元購入上址, 9. The original owner bought the flat at a low price of 2.01 million in November 2003,
10. 是次帳面勁賺115萬元離場。 10. Making a big net profit of 1.15 million.
11. 張木強表示, 剛過去的周六、日, 麗港城睇樓量下跌20%, 截至5月24日成交量22宗, 較上月同期勁跌50%, 平均造價每方呎3,300元, 呎價較上月的3,500元下跌4%。張氏指出, 加息後放盤量增多5%, 目前有333個放盤, 平均叫價每方呎3,280元, 下調3%, 反映業主對後市信心不足。 11. XXX claimed that there was a drop of 20% in the potential buyers' appointments. As at 24 May, there were 22 transactions, a 50% drop compared with last month. The average transaction is 3,300 per square feet, a 4% drop of 3,500 of last month. XXX claimed that after the rise of interest rate, there was a 5% increase of flats available for sale. There are 333 flats available for sale at the moment, with an average price of 3,280 per square feet, a drop of 3%, which shows the owners lack confidence in the market.

Source: *Property Browser* (28 May 2005)

Additional ideas for research

2. Collect news reports on the same event from different sources (tabloid versus spreadsheet, local versus international, printed versus the Internet version, etc.). Compare their move structure and explain the discrepancies.

3. Identify any new or unfamiliar reporting genres in the Internet. Study their move structure and the extent of influence by other similar genres.

Part VIII

Discourse and Culture

Chapter 18

Critical Discourse Analysis

Theo van Leeuwen
University of Technology, Sydney

This chapter introduces "social actor analysis," a method of discourse analysis developed in the context of Critical Discourse Analysis (cf. Renkema, 2004: 282–285). After introducing Critical Discourse Analysis and clarifying its aims and methods with reference to a classic study by Tony Trew (1979), the chapter explains Social Actor Theory as a systematic socio-semantic framework of the way humans can be represented in English. Because it also details the way its various categories are realized, the framework provides a clear tool for the analysis of a range of issues in Critical Discourse Analysis. And because it has a socio-semantic basis, it can also be applied to other languages. The chapter ends by applying the method to a corpus of texts from two British newspapers, *The Times* and the *Sun*, to show the relevance of the method for critical discourse analysis.

1. Introduction

Critical Discourse Analysis (CDA) is based on the idea that text and talk play a key role in maintaining and legitimizing inequality, injustice and oppression in society. It uses discourse analytical methods to show how this is done, but without restricting itself to one particular discourse analytical approach. Many have followed Fairclough (1989) in drawing on the linguistics of Michael Halliday (1989). Others use other methods, for instance argumentation strategies (Wodak & Matouschek, 1993), narrative analysis (Mumby, 1993), or conversational analysis (Ehrlich, 1998). As Van Dijk has said, CDA is methodologically eclectic: "[it] chooses and elaborates theories, methods and empirical work as a function of their relevance for the realization of socio-political goals" (1993: 252).

Critical Discourse analysts do not just use discourse analytical methods, they also work with Critical Social Theory. Fairclough in particular has consistently explored ways of grounding Critical Discourse Analysis in Critical Social Theory (see, e.g., Chouliaraki & Fairclough, 1997). Strongly influenced by Marx and Gramsci, he also engages with Foucault, Bourdieu, Habermas, Harvey and Giddens, to mention just a few theorists. But again, there is no theoretical orthodoxy in CDA. Van Dijk (1993: 258; 1998), for instance, sees "ideology" as the "worldviews" that constitute "social cognition": "schematically organized complexes of representations and attitudes with regard to certain aspects of the social world, e.g., the schema (…) whites have about blacks," while Fairclough has a more Marxist view of ideology in which ideologies are "constructions of practices from particular perspectives (…) which iron out the contradictions, dilemmas and antagonisms of practices in ways which accord with the interests and projects of domination" (Chouliaraki & Fairclough, 1997: 26). But this has not led to divisions within CDA. What unites Critical Discourse analysts is neither methodology nor theoretical orthodoxy, but a common goal: the critique of dominant discourses and genres that effect inequalities, injustices and oppression in contemporary society.

As can be seen in the pages of journals such as *Language and Politics* and *Critical Discourse Studies*, CDA is no longer of interest only to linguists and discourse analysts, but used by social scientists from a wide range of fields. On the other hand, some linguists have strongly criticized CDA, and these critiques are often included in collections of CDA papers (e.g., Toolan, 2002) and in the prescribed reading lists of university courses in linguistics departments. In one of the most widely quoted critiques, Widdowson (1995), for instance, argued that it is the business of discourse analysis to describe formal patterns "above the sentence" and that Critical Discourse analysts confuse discourse analysis with textual interpretation. In a similar vein, Stubbs (1997) has called the analyses of Critical Discourse Analysis "textual commentaries." Like Widdowson, Stubbs mainly targeted Fairclough, conveniently ignoring the wide range of Critical Discourse work published over the years in the journal *Discourse and Society* and elsewhere. The texts analyzed in Fairclough (1989), which are in fact pedagogic examples to demonstrate methods of analysis in what is essentially a textbook, are, according to Stubbs, "fragmentary" and "insufficient" because they do not constitute a representative sample and they do not involve the kind of large scale quantitative work in which many linguists are now engaged. Above all, these critics took offense at the explicit social and political goals of CDA. Widdowson, for example, argued that texts are differently interpreted by different readers and that Critical Discourse analysts unfairly privilege their own interpretations. From the point of CDA, traditional sociolinguistic and stylistic approaches to the study of language in social life may have succeeded well in describing patterns of language use and patterns of language change, but they have not explained them. They have treated them as more or less meaningless conventions or autonomous evolutionary processes. Critical Discourse analysts are seeking to explain why texts are the way they are and why they change the way they do, and, following Halliday, they look for the answers to these questions in the social, economical and political world. They are aware that their work is driven by social, economical and political motives, but they argue that this applies to all academic work, and that CDA at least makes its position explicit. And they feel no need to apologize for the critical stance of their work. On the contrary, by writing about issues that are of crucial importance to society, they continue the tradition of reasoned debate that has been fundamental to democratic societies since Antiquity.

2. Research challenge

As discussed in the introduction, Critical Discourse analysts investigate how important social issues are constructed in discourse by powerful agencies. Their main challenge is to do so on the basis of linguistic arguments. A Critical Discourse analyst may, for instance, study a newspaper text or corpus of newspaper texts about a particular industrial issue and discover a pattern in which different saying verbs are used for the different parties in the industrial conflict, so that, for instance, Unions are much more frequently said to "claim" and employers to "state" or simply "say." Now people may differ in how they think about Unions, but, Critical Discourse analysts would argue, if they are speakers of the English language, they will have to agree that the verb "claim" lends less credibility to an utterance than the word "state" and therefore that the newspaper in question lends less credibility to Unions than to employers, and this without providing any arguments, but merely by labeling their utterances differently.

3. Examples

I will attempt to explain the aims and methods of Critical Discourse a little further by means of a few classic examples. They come from the early days of Critical Discourse Analysis, when CDA was known as "Critical Linguistics." Critical Linguistics started at the University of East Anglia in the mid 1970s (Fowler et al., 1979; Hodge & Kress, 1993). Halliday's Systemic Functional Linguistics provided the fundamental insight that made it possible to move linguistic analysis beyond formal description and use it as a basis for social critique (1989: 101):

> Grammar goes beyond formal rules of correctness. It is a means of representing patterns of experience (…) It enables human beings to build a mental picture of reality, to make sense of what goes on around them and inside them.

Critical Linguistics added two further steps. The first was inspired by Marx. The "patterns of experience" Halliday refers to, they argued, are not necessarily neutral. They are patterned the way they are to suit the needs and interests of those who use them, and if such interests include domination, they can fairly be called ideological. The second was inspired by Benjamin Whorf (1956), who studied the way different languages embody different "patterns of experience." If this is so, Critical linguists argued, then different uses of one and the same language can perhaps also encode different "patterns of experience" — and different ideologies. Following Halliday, they felt that this is not just done through different vocabularies, of the well-known *freedom fighter* vs. *terrorist* type, but also and especially through different grammatical structures. Grammatical structures, they argued, construct agency and causality with respect to the actions and events they embody. A typical active clause has both an Agent (an element responsible for the action) and a Patient (an element to whom or which the action is done):

Rhodesian police /	killed /	thirteen unarmed Africans
Agent	*Action*	*Patient*

But there are at least three ways in which agency, responsibility for an action, can be obscured:

- By representing what is going on as an event, something that just happens, rather than as an action done by someone or something:

Thirteen demonstrators /	died /	when police opened fire
Patient	*Event*	*Circumstance of time*

In this example, the action of the police is represented as a "circumstance," something that just happened to go on at the same time, rather as the cause of death.

- Through *passive agent deletion*. In passive clauses, the agent in fact becomes a circumstance, and circumstances can be left out without making the sentence ungrammatical — "Thirteen demonstrators were killed" is, grammatically, a perfectly acceptable clause, even though it has no Agent.

Thirteen demonstrators /	were killed /	by the police
Patient	*Action*	*Passive Agent*

- Through *nominalization* and the use of "process nouns." In nominalizations, actions are made into nouns, represented as things. Neither Agent nor Patient are grammatically required (although they may occur, in the form of pre- or post-modification), and the nominalization can then be used to make all kinds of assertions about the event. The nominalizations below are italicized:

> The *rioting* in Salisbury townships on Sunday, and the *shooting* by police, were typical of dozens of such incidents.

"Process nouns" also express actions or events, but they are not directly derived from verbs by means of the *-ing* form, as with the italicized nouns below:

> A political *clash* has led to *death* and *injury*.

In this example, all traces of what actually happened have disappeared and the event has been recast as a "Tragic Sunday" (this was the headline of the article from which the example was taken).

These examples come from a classic article by critical linguist Tony Trew (1979), that detailed how the British and African press reported an event in what, in 1975, was still Rhodesia. The Harare police had fired into a crowd of unarmed people and shot thirteen of them. Immediately after the event, *The Times* carried the headline "Rioting Blacks Shot Dead By Police" (passive clause), while the more leftwing *Guardian* wrote "Police Shoot 11 Dead in Salisbury Riot" (active clause). In Africa, the *Rhodesia Herald* wrote the sentence I already quoted, "A political clash has led to death and injury," while the *Tanzanian Daily News* wrote: "Rhodesia's white supremacist police (…) opened fire and killed thirteen unarmed Africans." Different ways of wording the same event represent different interpretations of the event, and different political views, Trew concluded. With work of this kind, Critical linguists took the fundamental step of interpreting grammatical categories as potential traces of ideological mystification, and broke with a tradition in which different ways of saying the same thing were seen as meaningless stylistic variants.

4. Research method

Social Actor Theory

In my own work, I tried to extend CDA by starting, not so much from specific grammatical processes such as "passive agent deletion" and "nominalization," but from broader discourse-semantic issues such as "exclusion" — the exclusion of social actors from the representation of actions and events in which they in fact took part. Below I set out a framework for answering the question *How can we represent social actors (with a language like English)?*, which includes exclusion as well as other aspects of the representation of social actors, some well-known in the CDA literature, some less so. This framework can then be used to look at the way social actors are represented in specific texts or kinds of texts, as I will demonstrate in the next section of this chapter.

Exclusion

Some social actors who are in reality part of an action or event or practice, may be left out, and remain unrepresented, excluded. Such *exclusions* may be "innocent" — "details" the reader is assumed to already know or which are deemed irrelevant in the context — or problematic, preventing a full understanding of what happens or has happened. Systematic exclusions are always of interest. In studying the representation of schooling (Van Leeuwen, 2008), I found for instance that fathers are radically excluded from texts written for teachers, but included in many children's stories, even if only briefly.

Role allocation

As we have already seen, social actors may be "activated," given an Agent role, or "passivated," given a Patient role. In the first of the two examples below, children are Agent, while television is Patient. In the second example, it is the other way around. Who is right? It is difficult to say. For the Critical Discourse analyst, it is more important to ask *why* the two discourses represent this relationship differently.

> Children seek out aspects of commercial television as a consolidation and confirmation of their everyday lives.
>
> Television affects children's sex role attitudes.

Generic and specific reference

In the case of *generic reference*, social actors are generalized, referred to as *classes* of people rather than as specific, identifiable individuals. In English, generic reference is usually realized by the plural without article:

> Non-European immigrants make up 6.5 per cent of the population.

Generic reference plays a large role in establishing "us" and "them" groups, for instance "us, Europeans," and "them, non-European immigrants" (cf. Wodak, 1997).

Assimilation

Social actors can be "individualized," represented as individuals, or "assimilated," represented as groups, in which case a "they're all the same" effect may occur. I distinguish two types of *assimilation*, "aggregation" and "collectivization." Aggregation is realized by definite or indefinite quantifiers, as in this example, where "critics" as well as "immigrants" are "aggregated," though in different ways:

> A number of critics want to see our intake halved to 70,000.

Aggregation is a powerful tool of social control. Opinion polls, surveys, marketing research, etc., all create aggregations which are then used to regulate social practices and manufacture consensus opinions, even though they are presented as factual documentation.

In the case of collectivization, groups are referred to by means of words that express group identities, e.g., *crew*, *staff*, *community*, etc.

Association and dissociation

Associations are groups formed for the purpose of engaging in a common activity or pursuing a common interest. Often they are impermanent, lasting only as long as the joint activity, and in texts they may form and un-form as the text proceeds. They are realized by co-ordinated nominal groups, as with "politicians, bureaucrats, and the ethnic minorities" in the example below:

> They believed that the immigration program existed for the benefit of politicians, bureaucrats, and the ethnic minorities, not for Australians as a whole.

Association may also be realized by what Halliday calls a "circumstance of accompaniment" with the preposition "with," as in:

> They played "higher and higher" with the other children

Indetermination and differentiation

Indetermination occurs when social actors are represented as unspecified, "anonymous" individuals or groups whose identity does not matter. It is realized by indefinite pronouns such as *somebody*, *someone*, *some*, *some people*, etc., or, as in this example, by "they," referring to unknown others who are never specified:

> They won't let you go to school until you're five years old.

Differentiation explicitly differentiates an individual social actor or group from a similar actor or group, again creating an "us" and a "them," as in the following example from a middle class Australian daily:

> And though many of the new migrants are educated high achievers from places like Singapore and Hong Kong — "uptown" people in American terminology — others are "downtown" people from places like Vietnam, the Philippines and Lebanon.

Clearly, the readers of this newspaper are addressed as "uptown" people who do not want any "downtown" people to settle in their neighborhood.

Nomination and categorization

Social actors may be represented in terms of their unique identity, by being *nominated*, or in terms of identities and functions they share with others (*categorization*). In stories, nameless characters tend to fulfill passing, functional roles, and do not become points of identification for the reader or listener. The same applies in many other contexts.

Nomination is of course realized by proper nouns, which can be formal (surname only, with or without honorifics), semi-formal (given name and surname), or informal (given name only). Items other than proper names can also be used for nomination, especially when, in a given context, only one social actor occupies a certain rank or fulfills a certain function. Nominations of this kind in fact blur the dividing line between nomination and categorization. They are very common in stories for young children (e.g., *The Little Boy*, *The Giant*), and may even be used in vocatives:

> Turkish Sultan, give me back my diamond button.

Nominations may be "titulated," either in the form of "honorification" — the addition of standard titles, ranks, etc., such as *Dr.* or *Lt.-Col.* — or in the form of "affiliations" — words that indicate a personal or relationship term (*Auntie Barbara*, *Comrade Bukowski*). Press journalists often use categorizations as unique identities, in phrases like *controversial cancer therapist Milan Brych*. As in standard titles, the definite article is absent in such pseudo titles.

Functionalization and identification

I distinguish two key types of categorization, *functionalization* and *identification*. In the case of functionalization, social actors are referred to in terms of an activity, for instance an occupation or role. It is typically realized by nouns formed from verbs with the aid of suffixes such as *-er*, *-ant*, *-ent*, *-ian*, and *-ee* (e.g., *interviewer*, *celebrant*, *correspondent*, *guardian*, and *payee*), by nouns which denote something closely related to an activity and which have suffixes such as *-ist* and *-eer* (e.g., *pianist*, *mountaineer*, etc.), or by adding "man," "woman," or "person" to such nouns (e.g., *camerawoman* and *chair-person*).

Identification occurs when social actors are defined, not in terms of what they do, but in terms of what society (or some sector of society) believes them to *be*, unavoidably and more or less permanently. I have distinguished three types: *classification*, *relational identification* and *physical identification*.

In the case of classification, social actors are represented in terms of the major identity categories of a given society or institution, e.g., age, gender, provenance, class, wealth, race, ethnicity, religion, sexual orientation, and so on. Each is realized by a closed set of nouns which form rigid, bony-structured categories in which all people must fit, even if in reality many people do not, or not easily, e.g., age terms such as *child* and *adult*.

Relational identification represents social actors in terms of their personal, kinship or work relation to each other. It is realized by a closed set of nouns such as *friend*, *aunt*, *colleague*, etc., typically with a possessive pronoun (*my friend*, *my daughter*, etc.) or a genitive (*the child's mother*) or postmodifier with *of* (*a mother of five*).

Physical identification represents social actors in terms of physical characteristics which uniquely identify them in a given context. It can be realized by nouns denoting physical characteristics (*blonde*, *cripple*, etc.), or by adjectives and/or postmodifications (e.g., *a little girl with a long, fair pigtail*). Physical identification often invokes stereotypes such as the "dumb blonde."

Finally, social actors can be represented by means of words that denote a value judgment only, e.g., *the darling*, *the bastard*, *the wretch*, *the thug*. I have called this "appraisement."

Personalization and impersonalization

The categories discussed so far *personalize* social actors, representing them as human beings. But social actors can also be *impersonalized*, represented by abstract nouns, or concrete nouns whose meaning does not include the semantic feature "human." I distinguish two kinds of impersonalization: *objectivation* and *abstraction*.

Objectivation occurs when social actors are represented by means of reference to something closely associated either with their person or with the activity they are represented as being engaged in. This may be a place ("spatialization"), as in:

> Australia is generous to a fault.

It may be the instrument with which an activity is carried out ("instrumentalization"), as in:

> A 120 mm mortar slammed into Sarajevo's marketplace.

It may be the utterance of a social actor, rather than the actor him- or herself ("utterance autonomization"), as in:

> The survey showed that the level of support for stopping immigration altogether was at a postwar high.

Or it may be that actors are referred to by means of reference to their body, or some part of it, as in *I need a hand* ("somatization").

These categories can often be important diagnostic tools in CDA. Instrumentalization, for instance, is widely used to avoid assigning responsibility to human agents, e.g., in bureaucracy, and somatization is widely used to refer to women as sexual objects.

In the case of abstraction, social actors are referred to by means of qualities they supposedly have, e.g., the quality of being "problematic," as in the following example, where immigrants are referred to as "problems":

> Australia is in danger of saddling itself up with a lot of unwanted problems.

Overdetermination

My work on the representation of social actors includes one further category, *overdetermination*. Overdetermination is particularly common in fictional representations. It includes, for instance, *anachronism*, setting a story in a distant past or future, even though it deals with contemporary issues. This is often used to express views that cannot be said straightforwardly because of political or other censorship. For reasons of space, it is not possible to discuss overdetermination in detail here, and interested readers are referred to Van Leeuwen (1996).

5. Recent research

The representation of "ordinary people" in **The Times** *and the* **Sun**

In this section I use "Social Actor Analysis" to investigate how two British newspapers, *The Times* and the *Sun*, represent "ordinary people." *The Times* is a conservative middle class newspaper, and the *Sun* is a working class newspaper which has often been taken to task for its sensationalism, sexism and prejudiced representation of minorities (e.g., Van Dijk, 1991). The category "ordinary people" is taken from Bell (1991). It excludes politicians, celebrities, sports people and so on, but includes ordinary people whose doings and sayings are reported in relation to their work, e.g., airline crews, policemen and nurses. The example is taken from a study I conducted in 1995, but never published. I used just the news pages of one issue of each newspaper (February 7th, 1994), so that the study formed a kind of snapshot. The news pages of the relevant issue of *The Times* contained 1300 references to ordinary people, those of the *Sun* 859. As *The Times*' news pages contained 28,000 words and those of the *Sun* 11,000, it is clear that the *Sun* proportionally refers more often to ordinary people than *The Times*.

For reasons of space, I will focus on three aspects of the way these papers represented ordinary people: nomination, assimilation and categorization:

Nomination

Both newspapers used all the types of nomination discussed in the previous section: formalization (e.g., "barmy birdman *Miller*"), semi-formalization, (e.g., "supercool *Chris Boyd*"), informalization (e.g., "computer wizard *Chris*"), honorification ("*Mr. Hollis*, 43") and affiliation (e.g., "*Auntie Barbara*," "*Comrade Bukowski*"). The *Sun* used many pseudo-titles such as "Pal Tony, a businessman from Swindon, Wilts."

The Times named ordinary people less often (10%) than the *Sun* (18%) did. This is because *The Times* only nominated ordinary people who were in the news because of their work. Police*women* were named, policemen were not. Soldiers who had *left* the Army were named, soldiers who still served were not. This was not the case in the *Sun*.

In *The Times*, 38% of the named people had titles, mostly "Mr" and "Mrs"; in the *Sun* only 0.7%. Ordinary people were "Chris" and "Sue" in the *Sun*, not "Mr." and "Mrs." Also, as shown in Table 1, *The Times* formalized 40% of nominations, the *Sun* only 8.5%. And while *The Sun* informalized 62% of nominations, *The Times* informalized only 18%, and this in three distinct kinds of instances, (1) in attributions, when somebody was *quoted* as referring to someone else by their first name, (2) in reference to women in the roles of "wife" and "nanny" (the 7 February issue carried a long article on the trials of finding a good nanny) and (3) in references to children. The *Sun*, on the other hand informalized everyone, including ministers of religion, BBC reporters, millionaires and doctors, murderers, thieves, victims of murderers and thieves and so on. Class was not recognized. Everyone was equal, even royals, as can be seen from the following corresponding headlines:

> *The Sun*: Charles: 1000 years of breeding saved me
> *The Times*: Protester tries to attack Prince

Table 1. Formalization

Formalization	**The Times (N=128)**	**The Sun (N=151)**
Formalization	40%	8.5%
Semi-formalization	42%	29.5%
Informalization	18%	62%

Clearly, in the *Sun*, identity is private identity. You are who you are to your wife, your husband, your son, your daughter, your friend, your neighbor — regardless of whether you are a murderer, a murderer's victim, a lottery-winner, a "squaddie," a millionaire, or a supermarket worker.

In *The Times*, on the other hand, private identity is reserved for wives, nannies and children. Identity is public identity. You are who you are to strangers. And murderers, murderer's victims, lottery winners, squaddies, millionaires and supermarket workers could never be part of your circle.

Assimilation

Both newspapers used all the forms of assimilation discussed in the previous section. Aggregation was common, e.g.:

> *A number of Muslims and evangelical groups* have expressed interest.
> In 1993 the army lost *8,482 people*.
> *33 per cent of voters* said they would be delighted.

Collectivization was frequently used:

> *Passengers* said the jet was badly equipped.
> We need better protection for *staff*.
> *The team* are under the watchful eye of championship organizer Judy Phillips, 50.

And association was also common:

> *David and Shaun Harris and their parents, Adrian, 25, and Kim, 27,* were taken to Fort Bovisand Underwater Centre.
> *Miss Dover, with three colleagues*, arrested Sams in his Newark workshop.

The Times assimilated and associated people more often (37%) than the *Sun* (20%), and therefore seemed more preoccupied with the group identity, and less with the individual identity of ordinary people. This is because *The Times* discussed social problems such as teenage delinquency in objectivating and abstract ways. The people involved — teenagers, victims, parents, social workers, etc. — became statistics or were generalized as "teenagers with behavior problems," etc. The *Sun* conveyed such issues through stories of the concrete experiences of individuals such as the victims or the parents of the delinquents. Table 2 shows the types of assimilation used in the two papers:

Table 2. Types of assimilation/association

	The Times (N = 483)	The Sun (N = 36)
Collectivization	78%	64%
Aggregation	17%	21%
Association	5%	15%

Many of the aggregations in *The Sun* were in fact cases of two or three friends who did something together and were then referred to, for instance, as "the two," or "the three," which is in many ways closer to association. In other words, in the *Sun* the emphasis was on individual people doing things together, rather than on undifferentiated group identity.

To sum up, in the *Sun*, ordinary people were more often given individual identity, and where their identity derived from belonging to a group, individuality was less often submerged in the whole. In *The Times*, ordinary people were more often given collective identity, without individuals being differentiated.

In *The Times*, collective identity revolved around publicly visible work roles, especially those of comparatively low status (policemen and women, ambulance workers, nurses, air crews). Victims, too, were more often collectivized. In the *Sun*, on the other hand, collective identities derived most often from client roles (consumer, pensioner, viewer, tourist, student, claimant) and from private roles generally.

Categorization

The Times categorized people a little more often (45%) than the *Sun* (39%). More striking differences emerge from Table 3.

Table 3. Types of categorization

Types of categorization	The Times (N=600)	The Sun (N=342)
Functionalization	44%	32%
Classification	42%	40%
Relational identification	12%	16%
Physical identification	0%	3%
Appraisement	2%	8%

Clearly, *The Times* functionalized ordinary people more often, mostly in terms of their occupation and in terms of their roles as clients of major social institutions (passengers, home buyers, pupils, etc.). Together these two types account for 87% of the functionalizations in *The Times*.

The Sun, on the other hand, placed more emphasis on relational identification, on people as wives, husbands, friends, colleagues, and neighbors. It also contained a fair amount of appraisement (people were called "yobs," "rats," and "monsters") and physical identification, mostly in relation to the physique of women.

Table 4, finally, shows the kinds of classification which occurred in the two newspapers.

Table 4. Types of classification

Types of classification	The Times (N=254)	The Sun (N=138)
Gender	31%	22%
Age	25%	35%
Place of residence	11%	20%
Nationality	6%	4%
Regionality	2%	0%
Ethnicity	0%	4%
Rank	12%	0%
Affiliation	6%	10%
Education	3%	0%
Class	2%	4%
Religion	1%	0.5%
Marital status	0.5%	0.5%

In conclusion, rank and function are clearly of fundamental importance in *The Times*, whose way of representing social actors is deeply class-related, despite the lack of overt references to class. The *Sun*, on the other hand, has an egalitarian stance and places more emphasis on relational identity — on people's identities as husbands and wives, parents and children, friends and neighbors.

Finally, gender is problematic in *The Times*: women in traditionally male roles are always explicitly identified as women. In the *Sun*, women are almost always related to men, and their occupation or role, if mentioned at all, is added casually and separately. Physical identification and appraisement is common, e.g., "stunning blond singer Toby Bishop."

6. Research proposal

The examples below indicate the kind of projects that could be undertaken with the help of social actor analysis:

(1) Choose a contemporary conflict, for instance the on-going war in Iraq, and compare the soldiers of the different warring parties are represented in two contrasting publications, for instance an Arab and an American publication, or a fictional and a non-fictional account.

(2) Choose an issue relating to teenagers (e.g., teenage pregnancy, teenage delinquency) and compare how the social actors involved (the young mothers and fathers, the parents, the teachers, the doctors, etc.) are represented in a publication aimed at teenagers and in the mainstream press.

7. Practical relevance

Clearly, Social Actor Analysis can bring out patterns — habits of representation — some of which do, and some of which do not accord with preconceived notions. This is one important aspect of its relevance. The other is that it can provide the basis for critical evaluation, for identifying the positive and negative aspects of particular discourses. Before I undertook the small investigation reported in the previous section, I did not expect I would have something positive to say about the *Sun*. Now I find myself just as much inclined to deplore the excesses of objectivation, functionalization, anonymization and collectivation of ordinary people in *The Times*, as I find myself inclined to deplore the excesses of depoliticization, sexism and racist prejudice in the *Sun*. If only *The Times* had a little more of the sense of community and of the individual worth of each person that the *Sun* conveys. And if only, in the *Sun*, that community could include more people and a greater diversity of communal life.

Assignment

In the following article from *The Daily Mail Onlin*e (May 29, 2008):

- Which social are actors are "nominated", which remain anonymous, and why?
- How is Lord Turner represented and why?
- How are "immigrants" represented and why?
- How is the "native" British population represented and why?
- How is the Labour Government represented and why?
- Which process are nominalized and why?
- How can the article be said to legitimate (or de-legitimate) inequality, injustice or oppression?

The article:

> **We don't need any more immigrants, says senior Labour adviser**
> Britain does not need any more immigrants, one of the Government's most senior advisers has warned.
> Predicting unaffordable house price and a risk of overcrowding, Lord Turner attacked Labour's "economically illiterate" case for mass migration.
> He accused ministers of using arguments, knowing they do not stack up, to justify the influx of newcomers against a possible "racist backlash."
> Lord Turner is a former CBI director who headed Gordon Brown's Pension Commission.
> His intervention is a blow to the Home Office, which has justified the unprecedented number of arrivals from overseas — increasing the foreign-born population by 865 a day — on economic grounds.

But Lord Turner said: "In general, the language of an absolute 'shortage' of workers, of a 'need' for immigrants to fill gaps in the labour market, plays little useful role in the immigration debate and in most cases is simply economically illiterate.
"If we had fewer immigrants, the average wage rate of an office cleaner might be a bit higher, and businesses would either pay the extra charge, clean the office less frequently or use more efficient vacuum cleaners.
"But we would not have offices cleaned precisely as now and others not cleaned at all."
He added: "The idea that we 'need' higher fertility or immigration to cope with the burden of a rising dependency ratio is therefore simply wrong, a polemic argument rather than a reasoned and fact based contribution to the debate.
"We do not 'need' babies or immigrants to support an ageing population. It is wrong to say we need more immigrants, and it is clearly wrong to say that everyone gains from immigration.
"The simple answer to the question 'Do we need more immigrants and babies?' is therefore 'No'."
Lord Turner, Chairman of the Committee on Climate Change, said a stable, rather than increasing population, would be more favourable for residents.
He argued that welfare issues linked to a growing population, such as disappearing green spaces, housing shortages and transport congestion will have a greater impact than the economic benefits of immigration.

Warning that the English population could rise by 30 per cent by 2050, and by more in the South East, he said: "These are significant changes over just half a typical lifespan, with major implications for how crowded an already highly populated region will feel."

Shadow Home secretary David Davis said: "This is yet another authoritative argument for a policy of controlling immigration much more effectively.
"Lord Turner is right to point out the serious dangers of following the Government's current path."
Sir Andrew Green, chairman of Migrationwatch UK, said: "This is an extremely important intervention by a very influential figure.
"It is high time that the Government listened to the growing groundswell of opinion in favour of a better balance of migration."
The Home Office said migration contributed about £6 billion to the economy in 2006, but that there "are wider impacts too."
The Migration Impacts Forum had been set up to provide independent advice on how migration affects communities, it added,
Lord Turner's comments were made to the House of Lords Economic Affairs Committee, which is looking at immigration impact.

Chapter 19

Gendered discursive constructions of bank manager positions

Conflicting social identities

Inger Lassen
Aalborg University

Human beings are notorious categorizers with a predilection for defining, labeling and evaluating. By referring to categories such as sex, age, religion and occupation, we construct social roles for ourselves and for our fellow human beings; we thereby develop identities that give us a sense of security. However, such membership categorization at the same time functions as a system of social control because stereotyped perceptions (Pickering, 2001; Schneider, 2004) about who we are (our identities) and what we can do (our actions) tend to constrain our range of freedom. This chapter subscribes to the social constructionist view that identities are discursively constructed and negotiated in social encounters. This will be illustrated on the basis of two sets of data obtained from focus group interviews. In the first set of data, female employees in a Danish bank, "the Bank," discuss their prospects of obtaining management positions in the financial sector. In the second set of data, male colleagues discuss the same issue. My analysis will explore how social roles are stereotyped and evaluated (Martin & White, 2005) by participants in two focus group interviews.

1. Introduction

The research area presented in this chapter has its origin in a gender imbalance in management positions observed in a specific bank in Denmark, henceforth referred to as "the Bank." Like in most other European countries, by far the vast majority of managers in the Bank are men, and the study described below illustrates the societal problem of women being underrepresented in management positions. With historically low unemployment figures in Denmark in 2006 and 2007, and driven by a need to build a positive image, the Bank seems to have realized that cutting-edge competition on the labor market makes it necessary to appeal to both men and women when advertising for new managers. Over the past few years, the Bank has tried to redress the situation by selecting talented employees for a career track, male as well as female.

However, as we shall see later, stereotyping, understood as *exaggerated or reduced beliefs associated with specific categories of people*, seems to thrive among staff members in the Bank, and it therefore seems relevant to discuss stereotyping as a possible obstacle to women wishing to climb the career ladder. From a gender perspective, a relevant research question to be asked is therefore: *How might stereotyping affect female employees' possibilities of obtaining management positions in the Bank?* Answering this research question would provide more insight into the lack of success faced by the Danish financial sector in recruiting female managers, a problem that is shared with most of the banking sector across Europe (Crompton, 1997: 140, in Linstead, Fulop & Lilley: 59; see also Williams, 1995: ibid).

The case is situated in the broad domain of discourse studies — more narrowly defined within the field of Critical Discourse Analysis (CDA). For my approach, I have been inspired by Fairclough (1989, 1992, 1995, 2003), while at the same time paying attention to the critique against CDA launched by Widdowson (1998: 143; 2000: 22) and his call for analysis of authentic text and for the need to pay attention to both text production and consumption. A brief overview of CDA is offered in Renkema (2006: 282–284), who highlights the notions of *power relations* and *ideology* as central to CDA where "reality" is presented by those who hold power. In Renkema's words (ibid: 283), "discourse is seen as a constitutive factor of social relations and belief systems." In other words, discourse represents and reproduces social relations and belief systems, and the role of the analyst is then to de-naturalize power relations and ideologies that prevent the reader or listener from perceiving reality in unbiased ways. The Faircloughian approach to CDA is a three-dimensional, scalar approach subsuming the levels of text, discourse and social practice. I have argued elsewhere (Lassen, 2004) that CDA and Systemic Functional Linguistics (SFL), a social semiotic approach developed by Halliday and his colleagues in Australia, go well together. This point of view is shared by Renkema (2006: 284), who recommends using SFL for a more systematic description of discourse, and Young and Fitzgerald (2006), who combine CDA and SFL in their approach to analyzing power in language. (For descriptions of language as a social semiotic, see, e.g., Halliday 1978, 1994. See also Matthiessen, 2004; Martin, 1992; Martin & White, 2005).

2. The research challenge

In chapter 15 in *Discourse Studies*, Renkema (2004: 286) raises the issue of gender and discourse, pointing to the many studies on gender difference and dominance and the role played by discourse in this field. However, as observed by Renkema (ibid: 288), it is uncertain whether the discourse phenomena found can be characterized as gender-bound, and he thus opens up to some of the complexities present in gender studies as also described in Linstead et al., 2004. In management theory, competing perspectives on gender can be identified, of which I shall briefly comment on two, viz: Gender in Management and Gendering Management. In the Gender in Management perspective, advocated by Judy Rosener (1990, cited in Linstead et al., 2004: 72), men and women have different management styles because they are socialized differently. Rosener (ibid) refers to the male managerial approach as a *transactional* approach, which uses rewards, punishments and positional authority as guiding mechanisms. The female managerial approach, on the other hand, is referred to as a *transformational* approach, which is based on motivation, persuasion and encouragement. The female approach is thus seen to foreground personal qualities rather than positional authority. In the Gender in Management perspective, a person's identity as male or female follows the person's biological sex. By contrast, the Gendering Management perspective perceives of male and female identities as discursive constructs, and according to Alvesson and Billing (1997: 218, cited in Linstead et al., 2004: 78) gender identities are thus not "an inevitable product of biological sex" and there is no "automatic relationship between body, specific processes of social constructions and a set of characteristics/orientations." The corollary is that gender identities may be discursively constructed as gendered identities, through what gender literature commonly refers to as masculine and feminine values.

In Western society, commonly recognized masculine values include being rational, objective, self-confident, competitive, aggressive and unemotional, whereas female values are the softer values of caring for others, showing empathy, being emotional, and encouraging or empowering others. In this perspective men are seen as *doers*, while women are constructed as *carers*. In Caldas-Coulthard and Van Leeuwen (2002, cited in Renkema, 2004: 286) examples are given of differences in the representation of gender based on texts about toys, in which the Barbie doll is constructed as static and given the identity of a woman without control. By contrast, the Action Man, who is also described in the example, is constructed as a dynamic man, who is in control of his own life. Both figures are discursively constructed on the basis of commonly recognized male and female values and thus reproduce societal expectations of "normal" male and female behavior.

Gender values and identities may be studied by looking at texts like the ones analyzed by Caldas-Coulthard and Van Leeuwen. But as observed by Renkema (2004: 286) such analysis does not tease out important information about how men and women construct gender identities through discourse, although their re-semiotized form as Barbie and Action Man may indicate that gender values are reproduced through an intertextual chain of actions moving from talk to text to product. To obtain more information about how such values are being internalized and reproduced, it is important to study how men and women talk about their gender identities.

3. Examples

Because the Bank is interested in obtaining more knowledge about some of the barriers prospective female managers are facing, focus group interviews were conducted during 2007, and the stereotypes offered below are from these interviews. The male participants saw men as possessing features that would qualify them for a management job. These features included statements such as "men are influential," "men are focused and competitive," "they want to be in control," "they are self-confident," "they do not give priority to their families and children" and "they are tough guys." But while stereotyped assumptions about men were predominant and seemed to foreground what is perceived as characteristic masculine values in the branch of management literature that subscribes to ideas of "difference," there were also dissenting voices that stressed men's sometimes unspoken needs for support and comfort. When commenting on women's leadership abilities, the men interviewed did not find those convincing although one of the interviewees saw women as strong competitors. The general perception was that female managers are competent, but that they often suffer from perfectionism. In addition, according to the men, competent female managers are strategic and dangerous, and although women are generally good at listening and caring for others, they do not belong in the old boys' network where they would rather be a disturbing element. In fact, some of the men doubted that their female colleagues were genuinely interested in getting a management job and saw them as lacking ambition.

In a similar vein, the focus group consisting of women constructed rather stereotypical images of both men and women as human beings and as leaders. Interestingly, the women constructed their own gender as possessing management skills that would be beneficial to the Bank. Women generally described their own gender as "human and emotional," "caring," "possessing empathy," "straightforward" and "not afraid of admitting errors." On a more negative note, though, they also described themselves as "timid," "vulnerable," "lacking self-confidence" and "obsessed with inabilities rather than abilities." Moreover, they seemed to have taken over the generally accepted belief in society that women cannot work long hours because they have the responsibility for their children. Unlike the relatively positive way in which the women constructed their own gender, the women described their male colleagues as "conflict-averse," "unemotional," "strategic," "afraid of admitting errors," "afraid of showing vulnerability," "having no conscience," and "being inclined to discriminate against women when appointing staff for management positions." However, on the more positive side, men were at the same time seen as "having a drive and self-confidence," "being goal-oriented" and "focusing more on abilities than inabilities." These stereotypical values closely match masculine values described in management literature, and seem to reproduce values commonly defined in society as characteristic of the male gender. Interestingly, however, the focus group participants seemed to agree across the two genders that men are self-confident and assertive while women often lack these qualities. As the issue of self-confidence was a salient point in the focus group interviews, example 1 has been included to show how the issue is discussed by a group of women (original Danish texts are to be found in the appendix).

(1) Voice 1: And again, there is this problem of being a woman. We are *a bit* vulnerable, are we competent *enough*, and are we good *enough*, this is something I work on a lot.
Voice 2: But this is very interesting because you say, are we *good enough*!? Where you *sort of* look at it from the point of view of women. You know, this is rather interesting, because don't you cover yourself up that way? By thinking … *sort of* …..are we good enough as women?
Voice 1: Some cultural inheritance, *I think*!
Voice 2: Yes, it *might well* be…. Well, but it struck me a little for I agree with you, for I also look at my own standards, but I cannot help but feel it as part of being a woman, in one way or the other….
Voice 3: Also today and the people I associate with where it is very clear, isn't it — I mean many of them, if only they would step forward by 80% of what a similar man would do. In some ways, men are not nearly as competent as women. But they [men] just have more clout. They have more drive. But of course it also matters who is capable of doing things; that goes for everybody, I mean it matters who has courage to do things. But men are just more, they have….
Voice 1: *I think* they have, at least part of what they have is that they focus on what they can do, where we focus a lot on what we cannot do. Where they blow up their huge egos and we prefer to take a back seat, generally speaking.[a]

For comparison, example 2 illustrates how the male participants constructed themselves as self-confident, while they saw women as non-assertive, timid and preoccupied with detail. A discussion of the two examples follows in Section 4.

Example 2: Stereotypical statements about assertiveness and self-confidence in men (underlined).

(2) Voice 1: Now tell me what's the use of having women in the network?
Voice 2: [....] It IS a good idea to get as much of the crap as possible sorted out right from the start so that way it is a good idea to discuss any objections. This is where I really benefit from having some girls, you know. They are often damn professional. But they may not express it the same way.
Voice 3: Well, they are more focused on detail than we men.
Voice 4: We are quicker at making a deal. Damn, this will do, let us move on. We are probably less critical, I think.
Voice 3: It is perhaps this thing about us men being more goal-oriented. I mean, never mind about this battle, it is the war we want to win.
Voice 5: I don't know really. Well, I have sometimes noticed that things are being more nuanced when there are both men and women, but I sometimes think that it gets bloody more complicated and that I do not always see why things must be done in a particular way. Why do we have to make this or that detour, and I also think, and this is my assertion, I think that women are more strategic than we are. They also do certain things for personal gain and if we have a group of two or three women, then you will often find that one of them would do something to place one of the others in an unfavorable light. I have the impression that we men are more like ..... Then we will go out and kick nuts if we disagree over something.
Voice 2: But is this the way it is, or is it just something we say?
Voice 5: Perhaps, again it is this macho image; we want to show that we are tough guys.[b]

4. Research method

As discourses and social situations are being reproduced, people develop and maintain beliefs about the world. These beliefs constitute what Fairclough (2003: 82) has referred to as "common-sense" assumptions, which are assumptions that people use in discursive interaction without being conscious about their effect. As we have seen, common-sense assumptions may lead to stereotyped value judgments and generalizations with possible adverse consequences for social practice. We therefore need a theory capable of uncovering stereotyped value judgments in the discursive construction of gender, and for this purpose the Appraisal framework, developed within SFL, proves useful (see Martin & White, 2005).

This field of exploration succinctly combines essential elements from CDA and SFL while drawing on social science theory. Stereotyping, more recently referred to as "othering," has been studied for quite a number of years. Lippman introduced the notion of stereotyping in the 1920s and another well-known scholar, Tajfel (1963, 1981), has published widely on social identity theory, which is a closely related concept. (See Pickering, 2001 for an excellent overview of theories of stereotyping). Even if a combination of the theories introduced above will take us a long way towards answering some of the questions at stake in the social construction of gender, a case-study illustrated through a few examples is by its very nature reductionist and could not possibly draw a complete map of stereotyping and the effect this has on gender identity.

Stereotyping, as explained above, invariably has strong elements of value judgment as it builds on common-sense assumptions about typical ways of being and doing. To obtain deeper insights into the nature of stereotyping, I propose to apply a model suitable for revealing some of the elements that are essential in the judgment of people and their actions, and the Appraisal framework (developed by Martin & White, 2005) seems to be suitable for that purpose. Grossly simplified, the Appraisal framework embraces resources available in language to speakers or writers for expressing stances, sharing feelings or normative assessments, positive or negative (2005: 1). The resources used for these purposes are interpersonal and originate in the register dimension tenor as described in Halliday's early work (e.g., 1978). In an overview of Appraisal resources, Martin and White (2005: 35ff.) include Engagement, Attitude and Graduation. Engagement subsumes various kinds of modality, negation and attribution, which in various ways open or close dialogue. Attitude incorporates the three value categories of Affect, Judgment and Appreciation. Affect is an umbrella term for resources that describe emotions such as security/insecurity, happiness/unhappiness or satisfaction/dissatisfaction. Judgment covers resources for assessing and categorizing people and their actions according to societal beliefs about generally accepted moral principles. Sub-categories under Judgment are Normality, Capacity, Tenacity, Veracity and Propriety. Appreciation is concerned with resources for assessing things, but as this category is hardly relevant in gender stereotyping, with the exception of stereotyped statements about appearances, I shall make no further comment on it here. The third appraisal category, Graduation, is a resource available for amplifying or toning down attitudes and voices of engagement and thus cuts across the other categories. It is important to notice that people (and things) may be evaluated in implicit (evoked) or explicit (inscribed) terms. A simplified overview of the Appraisal framework is offered in Figure 1, Appendix 1.

Examples 1 and 2 illustrate discursive interaction among women and men respectively. In both text extracts there are many examples of what is immediately identifiable as stereotyping (underlined). In example 1, three female voices judge women negatively as being timid ("we are a bit vulnerable, are we competent enough, are we good enough") and without confidence in themselves ("we focus a lot on what we cannot do" and "we prefer to take a back seat") in spite of the stereotypical statement also present in the interview, namely that women have high levels of competence ("In some ways, men are not nearly as competent as women"). These assumptions stand in stark contrast to men who are constructed as being self-confident and full of drive ("Men just have more clout. They have more drive"). In appraisal terms the women judge their own gender negatively and the male gender positively as regards *tenacity*; women are stereotyped as lacking courage and drive while they find this feature typical of their male colleagues. However, the women at the same time assess themselves positively and the male gender negatively when it comes to *capacity*. They see women as more capable than men in many situations, but never boast about it. The examples are all inscribed Judgment; however at a subtler level it is possible to identify what may on the surface be seen as negative Judgment of tenacity as being instead an example of evoked positive Judgment of women's *propriety*. This calls without a doubt for further explanation: In the particular culture that prevails in the part of Denmark where "the Bank" is located, modesty is highly valued as good moral behavior. So when the women interviewed refer to their own gender as not possessing courage and clout, while being competent, they at the same time evoke a token of high moral standards in not boasting about their competences.

What we have been looking at could be said to be the level of content. However, if we were to look at the level of expression, the women's stereotyped attitudes about female *tenacity* seem to be underscored by the way in which they engage with the topic under discussion. In example one we find many examples of graduated statements ("*a bit* vulnerable," "competent *enough*," "we prefer to take a back seat," "*sort of*"), which mostly tone down the force or focus of the statements. There are also some examples of modality ("I think," "it might be"), where the speaker expands dialogue by inviting other attitudes into the discussion. All of these elements contribute to constructing women as a gender with limited self-confidence.

In example 2, slightly diverging opinions are voiced as five different voices participate in the discussion. Women are stereotyped in negative terms as they are said to have a predilection for unimportant detail ("they are more focused on detail than we men" and "it gets bloody complicated"). This way women's *tenacity* is being negatively appraised as they are seen as being too meticulous and not goal-oriented at all. However, opinions vary as women are appraised positively for their *capacity* ("damn professional") and indirectly for their critical sense ("men are less critical"). However, while the male discussants judge women as competent, one of them blames the female gender of being strategic ("women are more strategic than we are") and deceitful ("one of them would do something to place one of the others in an unfavorable light"), which are features characteristic of negative *veracity* in women, who are thus constructed as less credible and manipulative. By contrast, the male discussants use positive appraisal about the male gender. Men are "quick at making a deal" (inscribed positive judgment of *capacity*), men are "goal-oriented" (inscribed positive judgment of *tenacity*), men are "probably less critical" (evoked positive judgment of *capacity*), men do not set up strategic traps, but "go out and kick nuts" (inscribed positive judgment of *veracity*), even if one participant suggests that this may be because men generally want to build a "macho image" (evoked negative judgment of *propriety/veracity*). Based on example 2, the impression of the male participants' attitudes about men is that they construct the male gender in positive terms as self-confident and capable. It is interesting to see whether it is possible to identify traits of self-confidence both at the level of content and at the level of expression. In example 2, the use of swear words is much more pronounced than in example 1, which makes for a much more blunt style. We also find fewer examples of graduation in example 2, where statements are hardly toned down at all. However, there is quite a lot of modality in example 2 such as "they *may* not express it," "we are *probably* less critical, *I think*," "it is *perhaps* this thing," "I sometimes *think* that," "*I think* that women are more strategic," "*perhaps, again it is this macho image*." By using epistemic modality as illustrated, the men use a style that expands dialogue by inviting voices into the text. They thereby construct a male image that is slightly less self-confident than suggested by the content of some of the statements.

It is of course not possible to draw a general conclusion on the basis of the limited number of texts discussed; however, the examples suggest that each gender seems to appraise its own category more favorably, even if there seems to be consensus that men have more confidence in themselves than do women. This gives the two gender different scores on the *tenacity* scale, women scoring low and men scoring high, which may have consequences for their future possibilities of taking up management positions.

5. Recent research

Quite a lot of research has been done within the field of gender studies, (see, e.g., Tannen (1994), who studied differences in involvement [cited in Renkema, 2004: 287]). However, recent research has paid more attention to the role played by the social practices in which men and women engage. In a chapter on language and gender, Young and Fitzgerald (2006: 36) refer to recent research which suggests that the way people speak is determined by who they are and what they do rather than by their gender. Most recent research on gender and discourse as well as on gender and management follows this line of thought and subscribes to the idea that gender is socially constructed in interaction instead of being a predetermined category based on biological sex (see, e.g., Holmes & Meyerhoff, 1999, see also Alvesson & Billing, 1997).

At Aalborg University in Denmark a research team, *Communication and Culture in Professional Settings*, are exploring a number of questions relating to the issue raised above, viz: that very few women occupy management positions in the Danish bank sector. As explained earlier, this is a common problem across Europe, but so far it has not led to major changes in recruitment. However, the corporate sector is gradually beginning to show interest in gender issues as there is mounting evidence that companies with women executives often produce better financial results. The Aalborg group works from a social constructionist position and focuses on aspects of language and discourse situated in context. Much of this work on how prospective male and female managers, respectively, construct, negotiate and reproduce social identity is still in progress, but the group is now in the process of writing up first drafts for publication. In addition to the project on stereotyping explained above, the group explores how politeness is used to create solidarity and rapport among group members and whether politeness strategies may help employees pursue career opportunities (Strunck, work in progress, building on Cameron, 1998; Holmes, 1995, 2006; Litesseliti, 2006; Mills, 2003 and Scollon & Wong-Scollon, 2001). Further approaches study gendered discourse in context and how men and women may adopt both similar and different discourses. This research, which quotes among others Charteris-Black (2004), Holmes (2006), Litosseliti (2006) and Mullany (2007), focuses on metaphor and other discursive features as they are used in various communities of practice to allow men and women to take up particular gendered subject positions. (Holmgreen, work in progress). A slightly different approach is found in a study that discusses job advertisements issued by the Bank in the light of male and female managerial styles. An initial analysis of a job advertisement is compared to a focus group analysis of the same job advertisement to explore how potential readers would react to the wording and style. The purpose is to explore to what extent the Bank should change their discourse strategies to appeal to women when advertising for new bank managers. The analysis is based on Critical Discourse Analysis and gender management theory (Askehave, work in progress). The final example of research I shall touch upon looks at bank directors' discursive construction of gender equality, leadership and recruitment in the Danish financial sector; however, additional purposes are to study top management in terms of a gendered, hierarchical organization and how their construction of gender equality add meaning to gender. Answering these questions might contribute to a broader debate on how contexts may contribute to breaking down or reproducing gender hierarchies and gendered norms. The study quotes theorists such as Acker (1990), Billing (2005), Kanter (1977) and Fiig (work in progress). Against this background, there still seems to be a widespread need for exploring how some of the barriers to equal opportunity in job recruitment in the financial sector may be broken down.

6. Research proposal

Seeing that male and female social roles seem to be discursively constructed stereotypical images reproduced by both genders, and seeing that most of these seem to disqualify women as managers, if not as leaders, it is hardly surprising that women meet numerous obstacles on their way to management positions. As noted by Brewis and Linstead (2004: 78), identity perceptions are "the powerful result of discourse," where roles are created for individuals "to live up to." The possibilities open to us as men or women are therefore restrained by our own discourses. This would imply that because bank management positions are usually occupied by men, women would have to adopt masculine values leading to rational, self-confident, direct and unemotional management styles. This would be a paradox, though, as gendered feminine values such as being emotional, intuitive, creative and oriented towards dialogue, are seen as more effective in terms of producing healthier workplaces. Management theories have therefore argued in favor of introducing gendered feminine values into organizations under masculine control in order to obtain a more balanced view of values (see, e.g., Frenier, 1996, cited in Linstead et al., 2004: 83; see also Alvesson & Billing, 2000: 149). Moreover, according to results published by the American research group Catalyst (2007), women in management positions are found to enhance corporate success, and companies with female executives in the boardroom produce better financial results than those without. While it is not clear whether the positive results are due to changing management styles in terms of companies having adopted more feminine values or there might be other explanations, the report opens up to interesting questions about the stability of feminine and masculine values and beliefs across gender, and it would therefore invite the following research questions:

> To what extent are management styles in the financial sector gender specific?
>
> To what extent do masculine values prevent women from acquiring management positions in the financial sector?

It would require a lot of time and effort to answer these questions for the financial sector across Europe for instance, and it would therefore be necessary to narrow the scope to a specific sector in a specific country. To sharpen the focus of the study, it might be rewarding to compare it to a similar study already undertaken for a different country. To be able to observe any discursive changes, I suggest a so-called diachronic study of genres written by companies within a specified sector over the past 10 or 20 years. Examples of genres could be job advertisements, vision and mission statements, personnel handbooks, annual reports, etc. Studying these kinds of corporate documents might reveal changing discursive constructions of management values. As a supplement to the diachronic study, the topic might be surveyed by organizing focus group interviews with a number of male and female managers as well as potential job applicants. The purpose of these interviews would be to learn more about how leaders in management positions construe gender in management and how job applicants "consume" the documents. As an alternative to the focus group interviewing technique, a representative survey of the topic might be undertaken, administering questionnaires to a wide range of male and female managers as well as male and female job applicants in a given sector. This might then be followed up by semi-structured interviews with selected managers, male and female.

Focal themes might be stereotyping and the construction of social identities. This would entail looking at common-sense assumptions, beliefs and ideologies resulting from organizational culture or gender differences, which might be identifiable in the stylistic and rhetorical choices made in the texts and communicative events studied. The project would thus be inter-disciplinary and eclectic, combining socio-cultural theory (management theory, gender theory, cultural theory) with discourse analysis.

A relevant approach for teasing out implicit meaning and common-sense assumptions is offered by Critical Discourse Analysis and Fairclough's three-dimensional model, which looks at the three meta-redounding scales of text, discursive practice and social practice. This would entail studying socio-cultural aspects (e.g., overarching ideologies, organizational culture and stereotyping), discursive practice (orders of discourse, genres) and text (various characteristic types of documentation), and how these layers of discourse interact to produce generally accepted beliefs and assumptions. An important element in CDA is the study of discursive change and how discourses have power to reproduce or change long-established patterns of behavior.

The study methodology, based on mixing qualitative and quantitative methods, would be inductive and data-driven, as data would be obtained from a text corpus as well as from a survey (focus group interviews and/or a questionnaire survey).

7. Practical relevance

The results obtained from the project described under point 6 would be an important contribution to understanding some of the mechanisms at play in the corporate sector's recruitment of top managers. As explained in point 3, there is a strongly felt need across Europe to remove some of the barriers that have sometimes been referred to as "the vertical glass ceiling," and one of the arguments in favor of change is that female values seem to play a role for more positive psychological atmospheres in companies and — perhaps as a result — also pave the way for enhanced results on the bottom-line. Finding an approach to changing the stereotyped construction of men and women in the workplace would have wide-ranging consequences for society. First of all, the results might influence the ways in which corporate documents such as job advertisements are designed. Moreover, a foregrounding of what is commonly known as the soft and caring approach characterizing feminine management style would rub off on the overall tone used in companies; this would mean less psychological pressure on everybody and perhaps, as a consequence, a reduction of the national bill on therapy. It would mean motivated staff and better overall performances. It might mean improvement of the mutual respect and equality of men and women and perhaps lower divorce rates. However, there is still a long way to go before all of these goals are accomplished.

Assignment

In an article titled "Do women make better managers?" the authors focus on gender issues, managerial skills and the problem of breaking the glass ceiling. (A web link is provided in endnote C; a scanned version of the article is offered in Appendix 2). On the basis of the text, try to answer the questions asked in the following assignment.

1. On the basis of the article, please discuss whether the gender perspective displayed is a *gender in management* or a *gendered management perspective*.
2. Then write up a list of female stereotypes and male stereotypes found in the article.
3. Using the Appraisal framework, try to analyze stereotyping in the article. What are the different linguistic features used to produce the stereotypes?

Appendix 1. The Appraisal system

Main categories	Sub-categories	Further delicacies	Further delicacies (a gloss)	Examples
ENGAGEMENT	monogloss			
	heterogloss	contract	deny	No, didn't never
			counter	Yet, although, amazingly, but, etc.
		expand		Possible, probably, I think, it may be, etc.
ATTITUDE	Affect	Un/happiness		Sad/happy
		In/security		timid/confident
		Dis/satisfaction		Fed up/absorbed
	Judgement	Social esteem	Normality (how special?)	Normal, familiar, predictable or odd, unpredictable, peculiar, etc.
			Capacity (how capable?)	Powerful, gifted, competent or weak, helpless, incompetent, etc.
			Tenacity (how dependable?)	Brave, meticulous, resolute or timid, weak, disloyal, etc.
		Social sanction	Veracity (how honest?)	Honest, credible, direct or deceitful, manipulative, blunt, etc.
			Propriety/integrity (how far beyond reproach?)	Good, ethical, caring, altruistic or immoral, arrogant, selfish, etc.
	Appreciation	Not relevant	Not relevant	Not relevant
GRADUATION	Force	Intensification		Slightly, very, etc.
		Quantification		Small, few, etc.
	Focus	sharpen		A true father
		soften		An apology of sorts

Source model adapted from Martin and White (2005).

Appendix 2. Do women make better managers?

FT FINANCIAL TIMES

Do women make better managers?

As women gained traction in the workforce, gender differences among senior and junior staffers have turned up in every workplace, from offices to factory floors to fighter planes. Now that women are involved in the boardroom and launching their own companies the number of women firms has increased tremendously in the past 10 years.

Studies show that both male and female styles of leadership can be effective. But when compared side by side, the female has the edge. Researchers are discovering physiological variations in the brains of men and women. For example, male brains are about 10% larger than female brains. But women have more nerve cells in certain areas. Women also tend to have a larger corpus-collusum (the group of nerve fibres that connects left and right hemispheres). That makes women faster at transferring data between the computational, verbal left half and the intuitive, visual right half. Men are usually left-brain oriented.

As girls and boys grow up, of course, they're also molded by differing sets of social rules and expectations. Gender obviously colours behaviour, perception and just about everything else.

Gender matters

"Women managers tend to have more of a desire to build than a desire to win", says Debra Burrell, regional training director of the Mars-Venus Institute in New York. "Women are more willing to explore compromise and to solicit other people's opinions." By contrast, she says, men often think if they ask other people for advice, they'll be perceived as unsure or as a leader who doesn't have answers.

- Women are better than men at empowering teams and staff.
- Women encourage openness and are more accessible.
- Women leaders respond more quickly to calls for assistance.
- Women are more tolerant of differences, so they're more skilled at managing diversity.
- Women identify problems more quickly and more accurately.
- Women are better at defining job expectations and providing valuable feedback.

Men tend to be more speedy decision-makers, compared to women. Male managers are also more adept at forming what management psychologist Ken Siegel calls "navigational relationships," or temporary teams set up to achieve short-term goals.
How do such "female" traits translate into better business management?

In today's lean workplace, when employees have multiple jobs and fleeting loyalty, when technology enables even tiny companies to compete in global marketplaces, the ability to make staff feel charged up, valued and individually recognized is a definite competitive edge.

"Some companies succeed while others don't," says Jeffrey Christian, CEF of Christian & Timbers, a well-known Cleveland search firm. "It's not about production ... it's about talent. Whoever has the best team wins."

Money is not the primary reason talented people stay on the job or jump. Rather, they stay predominantly because of relationships. "Women get that," says Christian.

Generally, women delegate more readily and express their appreciation for hard work more often. "Women ask questions, men tend to give answers," says author, consultant and career coach, Terri Levine. By communicating company goals more readily and expressing appreciation more often, women tend to be better at making staffers feel valued and rewarded. That translates into cost-effective recruiting and being able to operate with stable, loyal employees - or, as Christian puts it, the best talent.

Besides generally being credited with better communication and relationship skills, women are lately demonstrating higher levels of traditional "hard" or "male" skills as well. Some investigators suggest that many women workers had such skills for a long time, but that male bosses either overlooked or misperceived them. Others think that the cumulative years of experience for women are broadening their skills.

More glass ceilings to break
Obviously, there are still very few women running Fortune 500 companies and, in the corporate VP ranks, roughly three men to every woman. So if women have the managerial edge, how come you don't see more of them in positions of power?

Here's my speculation; Men are used to running the show and, for the most part, don't reward "female" style management because they see it as weak. Women have had to prove that their way of managing works, over and over again. Then, too, women have only gained the independence and skills to ascend in the latter half of the last century. No doubt, their rise will continue.

For owners of small and mid-sized businesses, being able to keep staffers and stakeholders enthusiastic as you steer the company forward may be the most important factor in building success.

The upshot for chief executives should be to move over to the "female" side of management, whether you're a thoroughgoing left-brainer or woman manager who may be trying to manage the "male". As it turns out, girls do it better.
(Courtesy - McQuire Rens & Jones (Pvt) Ltd)

Back to Top « Back to Business

| Front Page | | News | | Editorial | | Columns | | Sports | | Plus | | Business | | Mirror Magazine |
| TV Times |

Appendix 3. Endnotes

A. Example 1: Stereotypical statements about lack of self-confidence in women (underlined)

Voice 1: Ja, og så det der igen med at være kvinde. Man er *lidt* skrøbelig, kan vi *nu nok* og er vi *nu nok*, det er sådan noget jeg arbejder meget med.
Voice 2: Men det er jo *lidt* interessant fordi du siger, er vi gode nok!? Hvor du sådan ser det på kvinderne, på kvindesiden. Det er jo *lidt* interessant, fordi ligger du dig ikke lidt bagved så? At du tænker *sådan lidt* er vi gode nok, som kvinder?
Voice 1: Noget kulturarv tror jeg!?
Voice 2: Ja, det kunne det godt være … Nå, men den ramte mig bare *lidt* for jeg er enig med dig for jeg ser jo også på mine egne standarder, men jeg kan ikke lade være med at føle det i fællesskab med kvinder, på en eller anden måde…
Voice 3: Også i dag de mennesker jeg omgiver mig med, hvor det er så tydeligt ikke også, altså mange af dem, hvis de ville — hvis de trådte bare 80% så meget frem som en tilsvarende mand. På nogle områder der når mændene ikke kvinderne til sokkeholderne i kompetencer. Men de er bare bedre til at manifestere sig på den måde. De har et andet drive. Men altså selvfølgelig har det da også noget at gøre med hvem der kan det, det har det hele vejen rundt, altså hvem der tør det. Men mændene de er bare mere, de har …
Voice 1: *Jeg tror* de har, i hvert fald noget af det er de har det er det store fokus på det de kan og hvor vi har det store fokus på hvad vi ikke kan. Hvor de pudser deres store ego op og vi *putter os selv lidt ned*, sådan generelt.

B. Voice 1: Fortæl mig så hvad der kan betale sig ved at have de kvinder med.
Voice 2: [….] Det er altså en god ide at jo mere vi kan få sorteret fra fra starten jo bedre og der er det altså en god ide lige at have de der indvendinger vendt. Der har jeg altså stor glæde af at bruge nogle piger ikke. De er ofte pisse dygtige. De får det måske bare ikke trykket ud på samme måde.
Voice 3: Ja de er mere detalje orienterede end vi mænd er

Voice 4: Vi laver hurtigere en deal. Det er fandeme godt nok det her lad os komme videre. Vi er nok sådan mere ukritiske tror jeg.

Voice 3: Det er måske den der hvor vi har lidt mere målrettethed. Altså skidt nu med det her slag, det er krigen vi vil vinde.

Voice 5: jeg ved sku ikke. Jo nogle gange har jeg den oplevelse at det bliver mere nuanceret når der er både mænd og kvinder, men nogle gange har jeg sgu også den oplevelse, at det bliver langt mere kompliceret og jeg kan ikke altid lige gennemskue hvorfor vi skal gøre tingene. Hvorfor skal vi lige den vej omkring og jeg tror også, det er som påstand, at kvinder er lidt mere udspekulerede end vi er som mænd. De gør også nogle ting for egen vindings skyld også hvis vi har en gruppe hvor der er 2 kvinder eller der er 3 kvinder, så kan du sagtens komme i at den ene gør noget for at stille den anden i et dårligt lys. Der er det mit indtryk at vi mænd er sådan mere, så kan vi gå ud og sparke nosser om det hvis vi ikke er enige.

Voice 2: Jamen er det reelt eller er det noget vi bare siger

Voice 5: Det er måske igen det der macho, at vi gerne vil vise at vi er hårde.

C. http://lakdiva.org/suntimes/030914/ft/16%5D.htm

Chapter 20

The semiotics of racism

A Critical Discourse-Historical Analysis

Ruth Wodak
Lancaster University

This chapter presents salient dimensions of the Discourse-Historical Approach (DHA) in CDA while analyzing visual argumentation strategies from a recent Austrian election campaign, in February 2008. The posters are deconstructed by applying pragmatic means and by investigating the topoi and fallacies employed in such a multimodal genre. Moreover, the history of the DHA is briefly summarized. Frequent criticism brought forward against work in CDA by prominent scholars is discussed and refuted in detail. The DHA also offers a precise and retroductable step-by-step methodology; this is elaborated while presenting a possible example for further and future analysis.

1. Introduction

Due to space constraints, this chapter introduces aspects of the Discourse-Historical Approach (DHA) in Critical Discourse Analysis (CDA) in a necessarily simplified way.

The DHA is one of many theoretical and methodological approaches in CDA (see Wodak, 2001, for extensive overviews). This approach focuses on multiple genres, large data corpora and on argumentative, rhetorical and pragmatic interdisciplinary analysis, while integrating multiple layers of socio-political and historical contexts in order to theorize dimensions of social change and identity politics. Thereby, the DHA differs, for example, from the socio-cognitive approach of Teun van Dijk, who focuses on the impact of media on the (re)production of racism (apart from theorizing important concepts such as knowledge, context and ideology), and the dialectical-relational approach of Norman Fairclough, who employs Functional Systemic Grammar in mainly analyzing relevant aspects of neo-liberal ideologies on British political developments.

Three concepts figure indispensably in the DHA and in all CDA: the concepts of *critique*, of *power*, and of *ideology*. The DHA adheres to the socio-philosophical orientation of Critical Theory. As such, it follows a conception of social critique that analytically embraces three interconnected aspects (see Reisigl & Wodak, 2001: 43ff.):

(1) *Text* or *discourse immanent critique* aims at discovering inconsistencies, contradictions, paradoxes and dilemmas in the structures internal to the text or discourse.

(2) *Socio-diagnostic critique* is concerned with demystifying the — manifest or latent — (possibly persuasive or "manipulative") character of discursive practices. Here, the analyst makes use of her or his background and contextual knowledge and embeds the discursive event in a wider frame of social and political relations, processes and circumstances. On this level, we also draw on social theories to interpret the discursive events. This indicates that the DHA is inherently interdisciplinary (see below, theory of context).

(3) *Prognostic critique*: This form of critique contributes to the transformation and improvement of communication (for example, by developing guidelines against sexist language behaviour or in order to reduce language barriers in hospitals, schools, and so forth).

In sum, the DHA elucidates the object under investigation. It should also theoretically justify why certain interpretations of discursive events seem more valid than others. And, of course, normative positions come into play when interpreting texts and discourses, which need to be made explicit within their respective contexts.

In the DHA, I view ideology as an important means to establish and maintaining unequal power relations. I take particular interest in the ways in which language mediates ideology in a variety of social institutions. Even with differing concepts of ideology, "critical theory" seeks to create awareness in agents of how they are deceived about their own needs and interests. This was, of course, taken up by Pierre Bourdieu's concepts of *violence symbolique* and *méconnaissance* (Bourdieu, 1989). One of the aims of the DHA (and of all CDA) is to "demystify" discourses by deciphering ideologies.

Language is not independently powerful — it gains power through the use that powerful individuals make of it. This explains why the language use of those who have power and thus access to important institutions and public spheres can be studied by employing the DHA. Power is signaled, for example, by grammatical forms within a text or a text's genre. It is often exactly within the genres associated with given social occasions that power is exercised or challenged (for example, who is interviewed in the media, whose opinions are quoted, etc.).

The DHA therefore integrates different approaches, and proceeds multi-methodically based on a variety of empirical data as well as background information (see, for example, Wodak et al., 1990, 1999; Heer et al., 2008). The specific choices depend on the problem in question — in this chapter, on aspects of visual racist propaganda.

2. Research challenge

Much criticism has been voiced about CDA in recent years (see Renkema, 2004: 284). Especially Widdowson (2004) has pointed to — what he labels as — a lack of systematic analysis and representative data. While this criticism might be justified in relationship to some studies, it can certainly not be generalized for the entire CDA paradigm. In the following, I briefly engage with some of Widdowson's critiques, as stated in his book *Text, Context, Pretext* (2004; see also Wodak, 2006).

In promoting his definitions of "text, context, pretext," Widdowson attempts to distinguish himself *inter alia* from more sociolinguistic approaches (Chafe, Firth, Hymes), from Pragmatics (Grice, Sperber & Wilson), from Functional Systemic Grammar (Halliday, Hasan), from CDA (Fairclough, Van Dijk, Wodak), from Corpus Linguistics (Stubbs), from Critical Linguistics (Fowler, Kress), and others. If one looks at the huge range of research he challenges, it is unfortunate that he includes very little recent research, no research in languages other than English, and that he also neglects relevant research in related fields like text linguistics. The criticism of CDA seems to have been a prominent part of Widdowson's agenda for years.

At several stages in his book (2004), he emphasizes how much he still admires the prominent proponents of CDA, while, later on, he accuses them of being "unserious scholars":

> Now the proponents of CDA can be regarded as activists in that they are critical, but as discourse analysts they are academics. They work in university departments, write papers in learned journals in the accepted scholarly idiom, and in general lay claim to the authority of academic scholarship: That being so, it seems reasonable to be critical of their work, as discourse analysis, where it appears not to conform to the conventions of rationality, logical consistency, empirical substantiation and so on that define that authority… (ibid: 173)

Widdowson continues at this point that students need to be taught a methodology:

> [i]f students are not taught principles and procedures that they can apply for themselves, they have no means of questioning the ideas and interpretations they are presented with, and these then, carrying the imprimatur of higher authority, simply become "naturalized," confirmed as unquestionably valid… To the extent that CDA does not provide for independent initiative, its practices as discourse analysis are not only incompatible with its ideological purpose, but flatly contradict it (ibid: 173).

Widdowson seems to neglect the vast array of recent books on methodology in CDA (for an extensive overview, see Wodak & Meyer, 2001, 2003, in press). Indeed, he bases most of his criticism on his interpretation of one single book — Titscher et al. (2000/1998) (ibid: 139ff.), an *overview* of 14 qualitative and quantitative methods of text and discourse analysis. This book, however, does not provide thorough examples of analysis due to the book's genre and scope.

Other critics of CDA have also not read much of the more recent research, as well as research published in languages other than English. Otherwise, they would have come across large studies with a great deal of data from multiple genres, which are analyzed very systematically in both qualitative and quantitative ways.

The following example, which is a pilot study due to space restrictions, presents a systematic research program (Reisigl & Wodak, in press). The *challenge* — in responding to Widdowson's critique about the lack of systematic methodologies in CDA — consists in *systematically* approaching visual data from a recent election campaign by a right-wing populist party (see below), which carries many persuasive, ideological elements and frameworks. Following a detailed description, I will contextualize the data and interpretations, and present and justify the methodology, the "tools" of analysis, and the selected interpretations. Moreover, social theories on right-wing populism need to be consulted.

In the context of this challenge, it is necessary to state a *caveat*; thus, all possible systematic readings should be considered and interpretations should not be deduced from the outset.

It is important to distinguish between dichotomizing, racist/discriminatory exclusionary rhetoric, and differentiated debates about integration, inclusion and exclusion that put forward various reasoned arguments with pros and cons. Hence, it is certainly legitimate according to many political scientists to propose greater integration of EU member states before continuing with enlargement (Stråth, 2006). In analyzing debates on inclusion/exclusion, we therefore need to pay attention to the immediate and broader contexts of such persuasive discourses, to its many functions, and to the linguistic-pragmatic-argumentative choices that are made. Obviously, the form of these discourses is important, as is the choice of arguments and topoi, and their possible fallacies. Hence, it is the aim of this illustrative pilot study to present a theoretical framework and methodology, which relates different discursive forms of inclusion and exclusion, which I have elaborated elsewhere, to each other (Wodak, 2007a, 2007b).

I assume that many theoretical contradictions come into play when shifts in inclusion and exclusion are suggested by the various heterogeneous governing elites in politics, the media, and so forth. These contradictions imply, *inter alia*, value conflicts (between tolerance, democracy, etc.), conflicts of differing ideologies and beliefs, conflicts of interests, and power conflicts. I furthermore assume that the public management of "inclusion" and "exclusion" is a question of "grading" and "scales," ranging from explicit legal and economic restrictions to implicit discursive negotiations and decisions. Such multifaceted processes necessarily call for an interdisciplinary approach. Thirdly, I assume that "inclusion/exclusion" of groups, people, nation states, migrant groups, and so forth changes due to different criteria of how insiders and outsiders are defined in each instance. Thereby, various *topologies* are discursively constructed, i.e., group memberships, which sometimes include a certain group and sometimes do not, depending on socio-political and situational contexts.

Thus, a specific migrant status (coming from a certain host country) may serve as a criterion for exclusion; sometimes however, language competence is defined as salient. Furthermore, a specific job qualification may mean inclusion, even if the respective migrant comes from an otherwise excluded host country; in other cases, religion and gender are regarded as criteria which discriminate against specific groups. The mere use of certain labels, for example, already manifests the fluidity of definitions and membership categories (see nomination and predication strategies, Section 4).

3. Examples

In December 2007 and January 2008, traditional exclusionary discourses suddenly appeared in the public sphere, triggered by three primary factors: the expansion of the Schengen area (border controls between Austria, Slovakia, the Czech Republic, Hungary, and Slovenia were abolished on December 21st, 2007), the possible EU-accession of Turkey, and new and very strict immigration laws in Austria and in other EU member states.

New xenophobic slogans from the rightwing populist party, FPÖ (*Freiheitliche Partei Österreichs*), such as "*Lieber Schweinskotelett statt Minarett*" ("Rather pork cutlets than minarets"), "decorated" the streets of Vienna. In the city of Graz, which voted for a new city council in early 2008, much exclusionary racist rhetoric was posted by the BZÖ (*Bündnis Zukunft Österreich;* www.sauberesgraz.at), which focused on the term "*säubern*" (to clean/cleanse), an obvious allusion to Nazi propaganda from the 1930s and 1940s and ideology of "cleansing cities of Jews" — a euphemism for ethnic cleansing and genocide ("*Säuberung von Juden; Judenrein*"). The photos below illustrate this exclusionary rhetoric and the many negative ethnic, religious, and national stereotypes which are (re)produced in this way, i.e., stereotypes of the "Poles as thieves" and the "drug-dealing African":

Figure 1. "Wir säubern Graz!"
("We are cleansing Graz" say Peter Westenthaler and Gerald Grosz, from the BZÖ — formerly part of the FPÖ, which split 2005 into FPÖ and BZÖ. They are cleansing Graz of "corruption, asylum abuse, beggars, and criminality by foreigners").

Figure 2. "Bitte wählen Sie NICHT das BZÖ"
(Wojciech V., serial car thief, states: "Do not vote for the BZÖ because I would like to continue with my business dealings")

Figure 3. "Bitte wählen Sie NICHT das BZÖ"
(Amir Z, asylum seeker and drug dealer, states: "Please do not vote for the BZÖ so that I can continue with my business dealings").

4. Research method

According to Reisigl and Wodak (2001:1), racism/discrimination/exclusion manifests itself discursively: "racist opinions and beliefs are produced and reproduced by means of discourse… through discourse, discriminatory exclusionary practices are prepared, promulgated and legitimized." Hence, the strategic use of many linguistic indicators to construct in- and out-groups is fundamental to political (and discriminatory) discourses in all kinds of settings. It is important to focus on the latent meanings produced through pragmatic devices, such as implicatures, hidden causalities, presuppositions, insinuations and certain syntactic embeddings, as frequently manifest in the rhetoric of rightwing-populist European politicians, such as Jörg Haider, Jean Marie Le Pen or Silvio Berlusconi (see Wodak & Pelinka, 2002). To be able to analyze our examples, it is important to introduce some analytic concepts of the DHA:

Systematic qualitative analysis in the DHA takes four layers of context into account:

- the *intertextual and interdiscursive relationships* between utterances, texts, genres and discourses,
- the extra-linguistic social/sociological variables,
- the *history and archaeology of texts and organizations*, and
- institutional frames of the specific *context of a situation*.

In this way, we are able to explore how discourses, genres, and texts change due to socio-political contexts.

"Discourse" in the DHA is defined as being

- related to a macro-topic (and to the argumentation about validity claims such as truth and normative validity which involves social actors who have different points of view).
- a cluster of context-dependent semiotic practices that are situated within specific fields of social action;
- socially constituted as well as socially constitutive;

In sum, we regard (a) macro-topic-relatedness, (b) pluri-perspectivity, and (c) argumentativity as constitutive elements of a discourse (see Reisigl & Wodak, in press, for extensive discussions of particular aspects).

Furthermore, I distinguish between *discourse* and *text*: Discourse implies patterns and commonalities of knowledge and structures, whereas a text is a specific and unique realization of a discourse. Texts belong to *genres*. Thus a discourse on exclusion could manifest itself in a potentially huge range of genres and texts, for example in a TV debate on domestic politics, in a political manifesto on immigration restrictions, in a speech by an expert on migration matters, and so forth

(Wodak, 2008). A text only creates sense in connection with knowledge of the world and of the text.

Intertextuality refers to the linkage of all texts to other texts, both in the past and in the present. Such links can be established in different ways: through continued reference to a topic or to its main actors; through reference to the same events as the other texts; or through the reappearance of a text's main arguments in another text. The latter process is also labeled *recontextualization*. By taking an argument out of context and restating it in a new context, we first observe the process of de-contextualization, and then, when the respective element is implemented in a new context, of recontextualization. The element then acquires a new meaning, because, as Wittgenstein (1967) already demonstrated, meanings are formed in use. Hence, arguments from parliamentary debates on immigration or from political speeches are recontextualized in a genre-adequate way in the posters depicted above through the use of salient visual and verbal features and elements.

Interdiscursivity, on the other hand, indicates that topic-oriented discourses are linked to each other in various ways: for example, a discourse on exclusion often refers to topics or subtopics of other discourses, such as education or employment. Discourses are open and hybrid; new sub-topics can be created at any point in time, and intertextuality and interdiscursivity always allow for new fields of action.

A *genre* may be characterized as "a socially ratified way of using language in connection with a particular type of social activity" (Fairclough, 1995: 14). Thus, a proposal on "combating immigration" manifests certain rules and expectations according to social conventions, and has specific functions in a "discourse community" (Swales, 1990). The proposal itself follows certain textual devices, the contents follows an ideology or programme put forward by a specific political group (like trade unions).

The construction of in- and out-groups necessarily implies the use of *strategies of positive self-presentation and the negative presentation of others*. I am especially interested in five types of discursive strategies, which are all involved in positive self- and negative other-presentation. These discursive strategies underpin the justification/legitimization of inclusion/exclusion and of the constructions of identities. Strategy generally refers to a (more or less accurate and more or less intentional) plan of practices, including discursive practices, adopted to achieve a particular social, political, psychological or linguistic goal.[1]

First, there are *referential strategies* or *nomination strategies*, by which social actors are constructed and represented, for example, through the creation of in-groups

1. All these strategies are illustrated by numerous categories and examples in Reisigl and Wodak (2001: 31–90). It would be impossible to present all these linguistic devices in this chapter, due to space restrictions.

and out-groups. This is done through a number of categorization devices, including metaphors and metonymies, and synecdoches in the form of a part standing for the whole (*pars pro toto*) or a whole standing for the part (*totum pro parte*).

Second, social actors as individuals, group members or groups as a whole, are linguistically characterized through predications. *Predicational strategies* may, for example, be realized as evaluative attributions of negative and positive traits in the linguistic form of implicit or explicit predicates. These strategies aim at labeling social actors in a more or less positive or negative manner. They cannot be neatly separated from the nomination strategies.

Third, there are *argumentation strategies* and a fund of *topoi* through which positive and negative attributions are justified. For example, it can be suggested that the social and political inclusion or exclusion of persons or policies is legitimate.

Fourth, one may focus on the *perspectivation, framing* or *discourse representation* by means of which speakers express their involvement in discourse, and position their point of view in the reporting, description, narration or quotation of relevant events or utterances.

Fifth, there are *intensifying strategies* on the one hand and *mitigation strategies* on the other. Both of these help to qualify and modify the epistemic status of a proposition by intensifying or mitigating the illocutionary force of utterances. These strategies can be an important aspect of the presentation inasmuch as they operate upon it by either sharpening it or toning it down.

Positive self and negative other-presentation requires justification and legitimation strategies, as elements of "persuasive rhetoric." Reisigl and Wodak (2001) define "topoi" as parts of argumentation which belong to the obligatory, either explicit or inferable premises. Topoi are the content-related warrants or "conclusion rules" which connect the argument or arguments with the conclusion or the central claim. As such, they justify the transition from the argument or arguments to the conclusion. Topoi are central to the analysis of seemingly convincing *fallacious arguments*, which are widely adopted in prejudiced and discriminatory discourses (Kienpointner, 1996: 562).

In Table 1, I list the most common topoi which are used when writing or talking about "others," specifically about migrants. These topoi have been investigated in a number of studies on election campaigns (Pelinka & Wodak, 2002), on parliamentary debates (Wodak & Van Dijk, 2000), on policy papers (Reisigl & Wodak, 2001), on "voices of migrants" (Delanty, Wodak & Jones, 2008), and on media reporting (Baker et al., 2008; see below). Most of them are used to justify the exclusion of migrants through quasi rational arguments ("they are a burden for the society," "they are dangerous, a threat," "they cost too much," "their culture is different," and so forth). In this way, migrants are constructed as scapegoats; they are blamed for unemployment or for causing general discontent (with politics, with the European Union, etc.), for abusing social welfare systems or they are more generally perceived as a threat for "our"

Table 1. List of Prevailing Topoi in Immigration Discourse

1- Usefulness, advantage	6- Justice	11- Numbers
2- Uselessness, disadvantage	7- Responsibility	12- Law and right
3- Definition	8- Burdening	13- History
4- Danger and threat	9- Economy	14- Culture
5- Humanitarianism	10- Reality	15- Abuse

culture (see also the Introduction to Baker et. al., 2008). On the other hand, some topoi are used in anti-discriminatory discourses, such as appeals to human rights or to justice.

Similarly, there is a more or less fixed set of metaphors employed in exclusionary discourse (Reisigl & Wodak, 2001), such as the likening of migration to a natural disaster, of immigration/immigrants as avalanches or floods, and of illegal immigration as "dragging or hauling masses."

Furthermore, Reisigl and Wodak (2001) draw on Van Eemeren and Grootendorst (1994), when providing the list of general common fallacies. This list includes the following very frequently employed argumentative devices: *argumentum ad baculum*, i.e., "threatening with the stick," thus trying to intimidate instead of using plausible arguments; the *argumentum ad hominem*, which can be defined as a verbal attack on the antagonist's personality and character (of her or his credibility, integrity, honesty, expertise, competence, and so on) instead of discussing the content of an argument; and finally, the *argumentum ad populum* or *pathetic fallacy* which consists of appealing to prejudiced emotions, opinions and convictions of a specific social group or to the *vox populi* instead of employing rational arguments. These fallacies frequently prevail in rightwing populist rhetoric (see Rydgren, 2005).

Let us now return to the examples depicted above: The three posters which form the data of our brief pilot study condense many features of racist and discriminatory rhetoric; most importantly, the insinuation to Nazi rhetoric is apparent both in the choice of words, and in the use of visual metaphors and symbols (washing the streets with brooms). This also applies to the stereotypes of "drug dealing black asylum seekers," and "Polish thieves" (as nominations), which are common in Austria.

In this way, the BZÖ attempts to construct itself by applying several visual and verbal topoi to imply the "law and order" party, which could save Austrians and the citizens of Graz from "immediate and huge threats." The posters employ many nominative and predicative strategies whereby the "others" are named and certain characteristics are attributed to them. On the other hand, the BZÖ leaders are also labeled and characterized, albeit contrasted in positive ways.

Moreover, all posters utilize layout and fonts in black and white, and explicit paradoxical statements which serve as *presuppositions* to contrasting latent meanings:

the real and right norms and values are implied through the subtext — the opposite meanings. These persuasive strategies (*implicature by contrast*) all belong to the political sub-field of advertising.

If we continue briefly with a *multi-modal analysis*, we have to point to colors and contrast between dark and light which are salient features (see Kress & Van Leeuwen, 1996): dark for the "others," the bad people who steal and deal drugs; light, white and orange for the "good guys" who "will cleanse" the city of threatening inhabitants. In this way, the images combine *metaphorical, metonymic* and *pragmatic devices* in intricate ways. The latter devices are employed as *argumentation* and *intensification strategies*. The topoi range from "abuse, criminality" to "law and right" "threat for our culture" and "justice."

Due to the fact that we are discussing images where the depiction of the "others" employs biological characteristics, like skin color, certain hairstyles, dark eyes, etc., we necessarily conclude that racist meanings are intentionally (re)produced as persuasive devices. At this point, we should explore the context of the election campaign in much greater detail, the history of the two parties involved, as well as the broader historical context in Austria, where similar slogans and meanings were employed by Nazi rhetoric before and during WWII. The topos of "cleansing" streets/stores/towns of "others" (Jews, Slavs, Roma, etc.) stems from such fascist rhetoric and has now been redeployed and recontextualized to apply to Poles and migrants from Africa, among others, for this context.

Debates about immigration and nationhood are also crucially linked to *assumptions about place, thus to deixis*. "Our" culture belongs "here" within the bounded homeland, whilst the culture of "foreigners" belongs "elsewhere" (*topos of culture;* Billig, 2006). The theme of place is particularly threatening to groups who are seen to have no "natural" homeland, such as the Roma or other diasporic communities today, or the Jews in the first half of the twentieth century. Religion as a central condition for inclusion/exclusion, frequently triggered by indexical markers such as the "headscarf" worn by Muslim women, has recently become dominant in some EU countries.

5. Recent research

The DHA was first developed for a study that sought to trace in detail the constitution of anti-Semitic stereotyped images, as they emerged in public discourses in the 1986 Austrian presidential campaign of Kurt Waldheim, who, for a long time, had kept secret his National-Socialist past as a member of the German Wehrmacht (Wodak et al., 1990; Mitten, 1992; Heer et al., 2008). The interdisciplinary study combined several linguistic approaches with historical and sociological research while analyzing linguistic manifestations of anti-Semitic prejudices in their socio-political and historical contexts. The analyzed data comprised both oral and written texts: historical expert reports on Waldheim's past, three Austrian newspapers and the *New York Times*, statements by politicians, daily news broadcasts and TV news, interviews, TV discussions, hearings, news documentary series, discussions in various institutional settings, and the vigil commemorating Austrian resistance in the centre of Vienna were integrated into the analysis.

In the 1990s, the DHA was further elaborated in a number of studies, for example, on racist discrimination against migrants from Romania and on the discourses about nation and national identity in Austria (Matouschek, Wodak & Januschek, 1995; Wodak et al., 1999). The latter study analyzed the relationships between the discursive construction of national sameness and difference that lead to political and social exclusion of specific out-groups. The politics of inclusion and exclusion were further investigated in political debates on immigration in national parliaments of six EU member states, especially in debates on asylum and migration (Wodak & Van Dijk, 2000) and the discursive construction of European identities in speeches by German, British, and French politicians (e.g., Wodak & Weiss, 2007).

Most recently, the DHA was employed in a 5th EU framework project XENOPHOB, which investigated institutional and structural discrimination in eight EU countries. Again, multiple publics and genres were analyzed in interdisciplinary ways. It became obvious that historical socio-political traditions have had and continue to have a major impact on the politics of exclusion in each of the investigated countries (see Delanty, Wodak & Jones 2008). Nevertheless, some general patterns emerged which are characteristic for Western EU countries. First, exclusionary practices typically occur in situations of differential power. Second, the powerful actors need not possess a conscious goal or intention, indeed, they may deny that any discrimination/exclusion has occurred. Third, the powerful actors are likely to consider their own actions "reasonable" and "natural" and justify them, and fourth, the actions that lead to exclusion are typically conducted through "coded" language and very rarely use overt exclusionary language (see also Billig, 2006). Another project funded by the ESRC combined quantitative corpus linguistic methods with the DHA in a study of 10 years of news reporting by national and regional British newspapers on asylum seekers, migrants and refugees (see Baker et al., 2008). This project developed new methodologies for analyzing such huge corpora in systematic discourse-analytic ways; the results point to the development of a semantic merger: all three groups of foreigners are gathered into one group of "others" which are negatively connotated, regardless of their aims, histories, and plights.

6. Research proposal

In relationship to the pilot study summarized in this chapter, it would be of great interest to make a comparative study of election posters in two or more countries. The visual and verbal elements could be analyzed. One could also interview passersby and study the reception of such election materials. It would be necessary, however, to restrict the campaign materials to a specific theme within the election campaigns to make it comparable across countries and languages. It would also be of interest to investigate in more detail in which way such election materials on matters of immigration have changed over recent years. Possible macro-themes could be: campaigning for citizenship tests; campaigning for new/other/more restrictive/more general immigration laws; campaigning for more "law and order," and so forth.

A thorough DHA analysis would consist of an 8-stage program (see Reisigl & Wodak, in press):

1. **Activation and consultation of prior theoretical knowledge**
   (i.e., reading and discussing existing research)
2. **Triangulation: Systematic collection of data as well as contextual information from multiple genres**
   (news paper reporting, parliamentary debates, TV discussions; public spheres such as media, schools and semi-private conversations in focus groups)
3. **Selection/preparation of data for the specific analyses**
   (selection of relevant foci, downsizing huge corpora in relationship to important events, transcribing tape recordings, etc.)
4. **Specification of the research questions, formulation of assumptions and/or hypotheses**
   (on the basis of a literature review and first data analyses, initial assumptions can be formulated)
5. **Qualitative pilot analysis**
   (systematic pilot study of at least two and at most four posters allows testing categories and first assumptions)
6. **Detailed case studies**
   (after the pilot analysis has been conducted, the whole range of data can be systematically analyzed while applying the tools and categories tested in the pilot analysis)
7. **Formulation of critique**
   (the three levels of critique should be applied explicitly, interpreting the results, testing possible readings while including context information, etc.)
8. **Application of analytical results**
   (if possible, the results might be proposed for application; f.ex., the images of foreigners could be changed in school books, guidelines for non-discriminatory language use could be proposed, etc.)

Depending on the funding, time, and other constraints on the specific research, smaller studies are of course legitimate. This ideal-typical list relates to big interdisciplinary projects with enough time and money available. Nevertheless, I believe that it makes sense to be aware of such a thorough research design and to make explicit choices when devising one's own MA thesis or PhD dissertation, for example. In this case, one would certainly conduct only one or two case studies and would restrict the range of data collection (at most two genres, for example). One could also extend the pilot study and leave case studies for another follow-up project.

7. Practical relevance

Research based on the DHA has been applied in many ways. This has included devising guidelines for non-discriminatory language use, proposing changes in news production, in writing expert opinions for court cases against hate speech, by writing school books on "Language and Power," on "Multilingualism," on "Diversity," etc., proposing more comprehensible and less exclusionary communication patterns for police officers, doctors, teachers, and bureaucrats, among other practical applications (see Wodak, 1996, for some examples).

Results of detailed critical discourse analytic studies can be applied; however, application always implies a reduction in complexity. Moreover, other genres have to be selected, and non-academic writing in other genres needs to be trained and acquired. In my experience, the application of results of studies in the DHA tradition has been very successful and useful. Doctors, for example, have been oriented towards communicative patterns, which made it very difficult for patients to feel comfortable and to comply with recommendations. Many doctors were happy to change these subconscious patterns. This stage relates to the third level of critique formulated in Section 1, which suggests the application of results in ways which would transform and change hegemonic and/or discriminatory communicative patterns.

By critically monitoring election campaigns and detecting the reproduction and dissemination of prejudiced opinions and beliefs, researchers have been able to support NGOs concerned with and fighting for human rights.

Assignment

Analyze the following extract from G.W. Bush's speech (12/9/2001)

Extract

I just completed a meeting with **our** national security team, and **we**'ve received the latest intelligence updates. The **deliberate** and **deadly** attacks, which were carried out yesterday against **our** country, were more than **acts of terror**. **They** were **acts of war**. This will require **our** country to **unite in steadfast determination and resolve. Freedom and democracy** are under attack. The **American people** need to know **we**'re facing a **different enemy** than **we** have ever faced. This **enemy** hides in **shadows** and has **no regard for human life**. This is an **enemy who preys on innocent and unsuspecting people**, then **runs for cover**, but it **won't be able to run for cover forever**. This is an **enemy** that tries to hide, but **it won't be able to hide forever**. This is an **enemy** that thinks its harbors are safe, **but they won't be safe forever. This enemy** attacked not just **our** people but **all freedom-loving people everywhere in the world**.

The **United States of America** will use all **our** resources to conquer **this enemy. We** will rally the world. **We** will be **patient. We**'ll be **focused**, and **we** will be **steadfast** in **our** determination. This battle will take time and resolve, but make no mistake about it, **we** will win. The federal government and all our agencies are conducting business, but it is not business as usual. **We** are operating on heightened security alert. **America** is going forward, and as **we** do so, **we** must remain keenly aware of the threats to **our** country.

(George W. Bush, *The Deliberate and Deadly Attacks…Were Acts of War,* President's Address from Cabinet Room following Cabinet Meeting, 12 September 2001; highlighting by RW; http://www.americanrhetoric.com/speeches/gwbush911cabinetroomaddress.htm)

Key to the assignments

Chapter 1. Doing discourse analysis with possible worlds

Here we provide some pointers towards a productive strategy for the analysis of Obama's South Carolina Victory Speech.

With respect to the first step, the main world creating lexico-grammatical devices found in the final part of the speech are highlighted below in boldface, while a stylistic pattern which most obviously alludes to the final passage of Martin Luther King's "I have a dream" speech has been underlined.

> *The **choice** in this election **is not** between regions or religions or genders. It's **not** about rich versus poor; young versus old; and it **is not** about black versus white.*
>
> *It's about the past versus the future.*
>
> *It's about **whether** we settle for the same divisions and distractions and drama that passes for politics today, or **whether** we reach for a politics of common sense, and innovation — a shared sacrifice and shared prosperity.*
>
> *There are those who **will** continue to **tell** us we **cannot** do this. That we **cannot** have what we **long** for. That we are peddling false **hopes**.*
>
> *But here's what I **know**. I **know** that **when** people **say** we **can't** overcome all the big money and influence in Washington, I **think of** the elderly woman who sent me a contribution the other day — an envelope that had a money order for $3.01 along with a verse of scripture tucked inside. So **don't tell** us change **isn't possible**.*
>
> ***When I hear the cynical talk that** blacks and whites and Latinos **can't** join together and work together, I'm **reminded of** the Latino brothers and sisters I organized with, and stood with, and fought with side by side **for** jobs and justice on the streets of Chicago. So **don't tell** us change **can't** happen.*
>
> *When I **hear** that we'**ll never** overcome the racial divide in our politics, **I think about** that Republican woman who used to work for Strom Thurmond, who's now devoted to educating inner-city children and who went out onto the streets of South Carolina and knocked on doors for this campaign. **Don't tell** me we **can't** change.*
>
> *Yes we **can** change.*
>
> *Yes we **can** heal this nation.*
>
> *Yes we **can** seize our future.*
>
> *And as we leave this state with a new wind at our backs, and take this journey across the country we love with the **message** we've carried <u>from the plains of Iowa to the hills of New Hampshire; from the Nevada desert to the South Carolina coast</u>; the same **message** we had when we were up and when we were down — **that** out of many, we are*

> *one; that while we breathe, we hope; and where we are met with cynicism, and doubt, and those who* ***tell*** *us that we* ***can't,*** *we* ***will*** *respond with that* ***timeless creed*** *that sums up the spirit of a people in three simple words:*
>
> *Yes. We. Can.*

Some of the world-creating predicates highlighted above are rather simple to spot. They include speech and thought predicates such as *tell, say* and *think, know* respectively, as well as modal adjectives (*possible*) and modal verbs such as *will* and, obviously, *can* which is part of the three word campaign slogan *Yes We Can.*

Others are less obvious, such as the negations which appear in the first two lines (*The choice in this election* ***is not*** *between regions or religions…*). Even though negations can be assigned simple truth-functional semantics in logic without recourse to possible worlds, interpreting a negation from a discourse semantic viewpoint always requires the evocation of a dw where the negated proposition holds true. Negations are often interpreted polyphonically as referring polemically to the speech or thought of other people or to more abstract standpoints being refuted by the discourse. In our case the negated dw is clearly to identify with the discourse of the unnamed opponents, which is evoked more explicitly later on by constructions such as *I hear the cynical talk that.* The noun *choice* is another difficult case. We can see more clearly its role in introducing dws if we solve the anaphora in the fourth sentence: *It* [=the choice] *is about* ***whether*** p… *or* ***whether*** q. Here the propositions p and q hold true in different alternative possible futures corresponding to the outcomes of the choice. Finally, the conjunction *when* in the text is not purely temporal and functions as a world-creating predicate by setting up two dws linked by a conditional relation.

As regards the kinds of discourse worlds introduced, we can clearly see that three main broad types of dw dominate the speech: (1) reported speech worlds, (2) represented thought worlds, and (3) participant internal future-oriented dynamic modality (*can, possible, will*).

Reported speech worlds relate exclusively to the unnamed, faceless, voices of the opponents and skeptics. Represented thought worlds refer mostly to the speaker and include knowledge and the process of entertaining a mental image of people and situations (*think of…, think about…*). A special place is occupied by *creed* which introduces the belief and assent to a set of values. Given its collocation in the speech, this predicate is probably to interpret as closely related to King's *faith* in the "I have a dream" speech (cf. *This is our hope, and this is the faith that I go back to the South with*).

As for participant internal future-oriented dynamic possibility (*can*), its prominence is obviously intentional and plays a key role in the rhetoric of the campaign. This could not fail to be noticed by commentators in the media, who remarked: "His is the native tongue of possibility, which is the native tongue of the young." (*Time*, February 11th 2008, p. 36, cited in Capone, 2008).

Much less prominent is *deontic* modality, which is present in the imperative formula ***don't** tell us change can't happen.* In this case, the deontic modality refers first of all to the *dialectical obligation* to retract a standpoint in face of contrary evidence. At a certain level, then, the use of the imperative is just a way of introducing a refutation, but it does create a clearly perceivable moral overtone: advancing the refuted standpoint is seen not just as dialectically untenable but as flat out morally wrong.

Moving to the mapping of discourse worlds and their relations, we can see how the text is characterized by a deep embedding of dws. This is particularly apparent in the central rhetorical pattern of the passage, opposing for three times the anonymous voices of the opponents and skeptics to the vivid an personal images of people Obama affectionately *thinks of*, people who witness the possibility of "change," more with the example of their deeds than with words.[1] The figure below shows how these embeddings might be reconstructed:

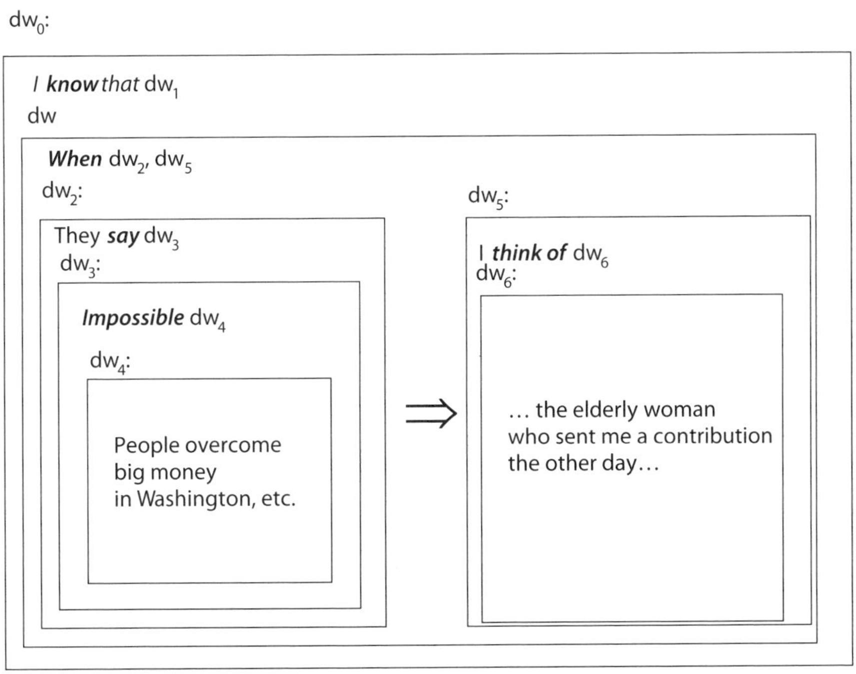

1. This rhetorical strategy can be further illuminated by looking at the findings of Capone (2008). In his study Capone focuses on how Obama's speech "is constituted by many voices" that is on its *polyphony*. Capone pursues the analysis of polyphony in two directions. On the one hand, by providing an accurate transcript of the pronounced speech, he looks at how the audience collaborates to the speech and how Obama's diction is designed to projecting audience response to his speech at strategic junctures — a feature which was prominent also in M.L.K.'s rhetoric. On the other hand, he looks at how Obama employs the strategy of personification, populating his speech with the "voices" of the people he seeks to represent as a candidate to the presidency.

Finally, a brief comment is in order on the comparison between this speech and King's *I have a dream* speech. Perhaps the most interesting way to approach the issue from our viewpoint is to compare the kind of discourse world introduced by King's *dream* with the one introduced by Obama's *can*. Both are future possible worlds, as suits political rhetoric, and both relate to a version of the American Dream (*that **timeless creed** that sums up the spirit of a people*), but they differ both at the level of their *modality* and at the level of their *propositional content*.

The modality of King's *dream* is complex and contains *bouletic*, *deontic* and *epistemic* overtones, as we have seen, while Obama's *can* is a more straightforward case of *dynamic* agent-oriented possibility. The content of King's dw — the future state of affairs *dreamed* of — is quite precise as it relates to one big issue: civil rights and the elimination of racial inequalities. In Obama's speech, the future change that *can* be operated has a much more diverse and also *vaguer* propositional content, which includes *overcome all the big money and influence in Washington.., change, …heal the nation, …seize our future*, etc. This befits the construction of a presidential campaign platform addressing a variety of issues and appealing to a variety of people. As observed also by Capone (in press), *vagueness* plays a strategic role in this kind of political communication.

Chapter 2. Discourses "off course"?

Task 1. This is a creative translation (I owe it to Agnieszka Szarkowska) of the Polish word *łże-elity*. The core word is *elity* (*elites*). The Polish *łże-elity* is a derogatory neologism used recently by members of the then ruling rightist party, *Law and Justice*, in their campaign against Polish intellectuals. Literally, the first part of the word, *łże* ("shamelessly lying"), can be rendered as *lie*, highlighted by the capitals. Yet, the meaning of the hybrid is more like "quasi-elites" or "pseudo-elites" (a competing translation was proposed by Jola Kozak — "*intellectualese*" — which however destroys the perceptual linking to "elite" in Polish and English alike, but finds a linguistic rationale, suggesting an intertextual linking to, say, *journalese*, or *legalese*).

Task 2. What may be perceptually established here is some similarity of *s**forward**ować* to the English word *forward* (the example from Dąbrowska, 2004: 266). The punctuation mark at the end is meaningful too in that it suggests that a question might be asked. The performative force of the sequence is still more transparent once we know that the sequence is a part of an e-mail message. Yet, the "full" meaning of this stretch requires some knowledge of Polish. This is then a "local" hybrid in that it is exploits first of all the resources of the Polish language (here the English form is inflected according to the Polish verb system). On the other hand, it is globally carrying as it invokes specialist knowledge of computer-based communication. That is, the text is meaningful first of all to those speakers of Polish who have some knowledge of or practical skill at using computers or mobile phones.

Task 3. This is an excerpt of a literary text that reads as: "Go to the backyard and dump the pot. Mop the floor and then wax it. Take the car insurance and go to Stanley at the corner, buy what I've told you. And watch while you drive, or you'll make an accident." (Edward Stachura, 1982, "Nocne popołudnie," Warszawa: Czytelnik, page 297, translated by J. Kozak)

The understanding of this text requires some knowledge of both languages, English and Polish. For a Pole, it demands a different type of socio-cultural knowledge than the previous text. Namely, the excerpt from Stachura parodies the talk of Polish emigrants in the States (usually of the older and poorly educated category). Some availability of this knowledge is necessary to appreciate the comic overtone of the writing (or speech).

Task 4. There are perceptual clues in how this image speaks to us. It bifurcates its intertextual potential along vision- and language-based search. On the verbal plane it is a hybrid too, directing towards two language domains: English and Polish. The picture shows a busy road (fast turning wheels dimly seen in the background). What stands to our attention is the zebra crossing with the white inscription "Look right," which contextualizes the picture in a particular physical place: road crossing for pedestrians. At the same time it localizes the scene in an English language country with driving on the left-hand side. For a Pole, a most likely addressee of this text, this information is an element of cultural knowledge. The function of the text may not be clear. It may be a part of an educational safe-roads campaign, targeted at foreign drivers in England. There is an intertextual dialogue between a Polish and an English text written on the crossing. In order to arrive the message it is necessary to be able to relate the two texts. We need to establish the relation between the two perceptually salient sequences: "*Wyglądaj dobrze?*" and "Look right." Once we start reading from the top, the question mark in the Polish text might suggest that what follows is an answer to a question. Yet the "right" order of reading is the opposite: you start with where you are located "in the material world" and what you can see right in front of your eyes. The inscription on the crossing says "Look right." It is not what may appear to you as the correct translation *Wyglądaj dobrze?* (in literal translation: *Look well?*). If you return to the bottom of the image, you find "the correct answer": *No, it means LOOK RIGHT. It is better to know some things.* The linguistic impact of the message capitalizes on an error in translating from English into Polish. This is part of a promotion campaign of a language school in Poland — *Archibald School of English.*

Chapter 3. Discourse across semiotic modes

In terms of the multimodal deployment of resources, the pages are very different. The left one is from 1994, the right from 1996 and so we cannot simply explain their differences according to different periods of production. The former is still largely a text-flow artefact, although the itemized list towards the bottom of the page struggles towards a table-like representation. The latter is far more of a page-flow artefact, with its information spread around the page in visually distinguished spatial regions. Moreover, within that page-flow we find textual, tabular, diagrammatic, photographic, iconic and image-flow contributions. Only some of these are to be found in the first page.

We can therefore ask very concretely what different rhetorical work is being done by the distribution of information around these distinct semiotic modes. What distinct discourse relations are signaled by these differences, and in what ways? Approaching concrete pages in this manner leads very quickly to subtleties of multimodal design while still maintaining an exact methodology for discussing the phenomena that are found.

Chapter 4. Schemes and tropes in visual communication: The case of object grouping in advertisements

WHAT?

1. What are the central claims expressed by these ads?

Guitar:	GUITAR IS (LIKE) ATOMIC BOMB (attributing notions like energy, strength)
Champagne	Getting better with time of champagne is like getting better with time of mushroom-shape (bomb into actual mushroom)
Beer	BEER IS (LIKE) ATOMIC BOMB (attributing notions like energy, strength)

Notice that only the first and third ad express a metaphorical analogy. Your answer should be explicit about the conceptual relation between the depicted objects (predicate in case of the first and third). Be aware of the fact that the message conveyed by the second ad is not metaphorical: the topic object (e.g., the champagne) is not part of the grouped objects (e.g., the atomic bomb and the mushroom). Conceptually speaking, there is no relation between the grouped objects. Mushrooms are not an attribute of atomic bombs, nor is the reverse true. Bombs are not conceptually associated to mushrooms, nor do they lead to mushrooms, etc.

How?

2. Which of these ads shows object grouping?

Guitar and Champagne.

3. What perceptual features are used?

Table a. Comparison of Guitar and Champagne ad

	Guitar	Champagne
objects have similar shape	no	yes
objects are made to have similar shape	yes	no
parts of objects have similar shape	not relevant	not relevant
objects have similar size	no	no
objects are made to have similar size	yes	no
objects are spatially aligned	yes	yes
objects are placed at equal distances from each other	not relevant	not relevant
objects have similar spatial orientation	yes	yes
more than one attribute depiction	not relevant	not relevant
image uses special pictorial techniques like enlarging objects or turning them	yes	no

Pleas note that the spatial orientation in the Guitar ad is achieved by depicting the topic in a non canonical way (e.g., "upside down").

Speculate why it is that the Champagne ad manages to achieve the same perceptual experience with much fewer grouping techniques. A hint: the mushroom has the prototypical shape of the atomic bomb and even has become polysemous in this respect.

Why?

4. Which of the ads uses the image of the bomb metaphorically?

The Guitar and the Beer ad.

5. Explain how the metaphorical relation between topic and attribute is expressed?

Guitar
The metaphorical relation is typically highlighted by the object grouping characteristics described above.

Beer
The Beer ad is a typical case of object fusion. One actually sees only one object instead of two, but this object is non-existent (e.g., homospatially).

The formal nature of object grouping can be used independently of the message the ads convey (Guitar versus Champagne). Note that the same metaphorical analogy can be expressed both with and without object grouping (Guitar versus Beer).

6. Explain the use of object grouping in the non-metaphorical ad(s).

One could say that the Champagne ad contains a visual scheme that is deprived of meaning. It only employs the shape of the two objects. If you think that the grouped objects are conceptually linked, try to be as explicit as you can about your reasons for claiming so.

7. Summarize the differences and commonalities of the three ads.

This should not pose much problems. However, we once again emphasize the fact that, unlike the other two the Champagne ad does not exploit either bombs or mushrooms to attain some attributes to the topic object. You are invited to find on the Internet more examples of ads (or editorial cartoons!), using the image of atomic bombs.

Chapter 5. Text types and dynamism of genres

In text (4), first three lines allude to the idea that the L'ESPACE 180 seat is comfortable. This is an echoic, interpretive utterance in the sense that the writer presupposes the thinking of most people (i.e., lying flat on one's back in the air is an illusion) and expresses his opposing view and attitude toward this general thought. In the following text, the writer uses interpretive utterances — quoting a hypnotist's speech to the person lying — *you* — in order to show the comfort of the L'ESPACE seat, rather than explicitly describing the comfort of the seat for the reader. The writer does not give any specific evidence about why L'ESPACE is comfortable. Readers may infer the comfort based on their background knowledge. Such an interpretation process may increase curiosity and interest in the good aspects of Air France and the text will bring about an evaluative effect.

In text (5), descriptive utterances are dominantly used where the writer moves from nonspecific to specific information (*a street — the street — Pincheon Street*) and consequently the interpretation of context is constrained by the text-internal information. Such an interpretation process may bring about an informing effect of the scene described in the text.

In this way, the interpretation of text (4) is less tightly constrained than text (5). These different degrees of interpretative constraint form different text types.

The coreference chains are for text (4):

your eyes
all you can hear
you – you – you – you – you – you (hypnotized *you*)
you (the reader *you*)
L'ESPACE 180 — it — its surface

For text (5):

a bystreet – the street – Pyncheon Street – Pyncheon Street
a rusty wooden house – the house – old Pyncheon house – antiquity – the weather beaten edifice
an elm tree – Pyncheon Elm – the great elm tree – antiquity – the great elm tree
one of New England towns – the town aforesaid

Chapter 6. Academic and professional written genres in disciplinary communication: Theoretical and empirical challenges

1: Important schools and approaches are — among others — the Sydney School (Halliday, Martin), the Rhetoric Approach (Freedman, Bazerman), the Language with Specific Purposes (Swales, Bhatia), the Semiolinguistic Approach (Charaudeau, Manguenau), and the Discourse Analysis (Van Dijk). The emphasis most detected in defining genres has been the social features, with minor or no interest in cognitive or linguistic features.
2: Discourse genres, through which students get access to disciplinary knowledge, not only play a key role in establishing membership and cultural identity, but also exclusion from the rest. These particular linguistic and symbolic forms of communication and meaning creation, constructed through genres, help transmit not only knowledge but also a sense of customs and practices typical to the disciplinary community. This is clear when texts embody a significant number of specialized terms and lexicogrammatical structures (such as in Chemistry and Construction Engineering) (see Parodi, 2005a, 2007b), or a particular symbolism of their own.

Highly relevant is to know the generic means students encounter in their university environments and also to detect similarities and points of differences. Important questions derive from these data, such as: Is the university system responsible for the academic literacy of university students of the genres they would face in the professional workplace?

Also, to have an in-depth description of academic and professional genres in a multidimensional perspective is highly valuable, because teaching implications could be established. Knowing the repertoire of genres employed in some disciplines would help organize the academic curriculum, and the way we want students to walk along the disciplinary domains. This means how to proceed from a more dissemination objective in order to open access to the core concepts (Textbooks and Didactic Guidelines), to more sophisticated and highly informative, abstract theoretical artefacts (Disciplinary Texts, Research Articles).

The relationship between the cognitive processing of information packed in some genres and the linguistic and rhetorical organizational patterns is a link not yet explored scientifically and with appropriate research tools. Only recently, some research studies have been addressing issues like this. This constitutes a challenging objective for the near future, if we believe that cognition and genres are highly related, as I proposed here.

3: The data collected reveals important differences between the academic and the professional corpus. The academic written communication in university settings show restricted forms of genre interactions, compared with the richer and more diversified repertoire of written genres employed in professional settings. Interesting cross-disciplinary similarities in genre occurrence in the academic corpus were detected, and also two extreme poles in a continuum of genre occurrence between Industrial Chemistry (only two genres) and Psychology (nine genre types). At the same time, intra-disciplinary variations in the academic and professional corpus are very revealing and show prototypical features of some genres.

Chapter 7. Why investigate textual information hierarchy?

Elements between square brackets are implied (usually from the cotext). The pair of elements chosen in one sentence when its coherence relation is established with another sentence might differ when the coherence relation is established with yet another sentence. For example, a3 ("these requirements") when the relation between S1 and S3 is investigated is not the same a3 ("science of discourse") when the relation between S3 and S4 is investigated. Unfortunately, no defined principles guide the choice of elements in sentences for the reconstruction of coherence. However, one should presume that most coherence relations rest on explicit elements so as not to render the reading comprehension, i.e., reconstruction of coherence by readers, too difficult. In practice, the choice is limited, and thus the analysis is not as arduous as it might look at first sight, especially with practice.

The explanation of how the relation of coherence was established on the basis of the pair of elements in each sentence is given in italics after the identification of the relation.

LK: linguistic knowledge
DK: domain knowledge
WK: world knowledge

1 p1= many formal methods (a1= generated automatically, inter-coder reliability)
2 [p2= many formal methods] (a2= analyst's unique insights)
→ relation 1: coordination (opposition)
p1 = p2 (LK) and a1 = non a2 (DK)

2 [p2= many formal methods] (a2= analyst's unique insights)
3 [p3= many formal methods] (a3= these requirements [=generated automatically, inter-coder reliability])
→ relation 1: coordination (opposition)
p2 = p3 (LK) and a2 = non a3 (LK, DK)

1 p1= many formal methods (a1= generated automatically, inter-coder reliability)
3 [p3= many formal methods] (a3= these requirements [=generated automatically, inter-coder reliability])
→ relation 1: coordination (elaboration)
p1 = p3 (LK) and a1 = a3 (LK)

3 p3= requirements (a3= science of discourse)
4 p4= constraints (a4= in no science [= in science, in general, there is no…]) [*if the text said, "in no other science," it would be parallelism, as "other science" is one of the sciences as the "science of discourse"*]
→ relation 9: superordination
p3 = p4 (LK) and a3 ⊂ a4 (LK, DK — "science of discourse" is part of "science [in general]")

4 p4= constraints (a4= theory)
5 p5= constraints (a5= its [=of the theory])
→ relation 1: coordination (elaboration)
p4 = p5 (LK) and a4 = a5 (LK)

5 p5= constraints (a5= its [= science, in general])
6 p6= unconstrained (a6= theories of a text)
→ relation 6: subordination (contrast)
p5 = non p6 (LK) and a6 ⊂ a5 (DK)

3 p3= requirements (a3= science of discourse)
6 p6= unconstrained (a6= theories of a text)
→ relation 1: coordination (opposition)

p3 = non p7 (LK) and a3 = a6 (DK — the "theories of a text" make up the "science of discourse")

6 p6= theories of a text (a6= constructing)
7 p7= theories (a7= validating, deciding among)
→ relation 2: coordination (parallelism)
p6 = p7 (LK) and a6 $\subset \Sigma$ and a7 $\subset \Sigma$, with Σ= set of preliminary stages before theory use (DK)

3 p3= science of discourse (a3= these requirements [= generated automatically, inter-coder reliability])
7 p7= theory of a text [i.e., when working in science of discourse] (a7= must encode the theories … and subject them…)
→ relation 2: coordination (parallelism)
p3 = p7 (LK) and a3 $\subset \Sigma$ and a7 $\subset \Sigma$, with Σ= set of conditions for theories (DK)

This paragraph is taken from an article published in an academic journal. It is therefore not surprising that domain knowledge (DK) is necessary for the reconstruction of its coherence. The article is supposed to be accessible to all experts in this field, whatever their culture. World knowledge (WK) was not used in this reconstruction of coherence.

Chapter 8. Implicit and explicit coherence relations

The next pages show the three different analyses from the RST-website. They can be found on the website under Analyses: Unpublished Analyses.

Alternative analyses for some of the segments can be found in Renkema (2006).

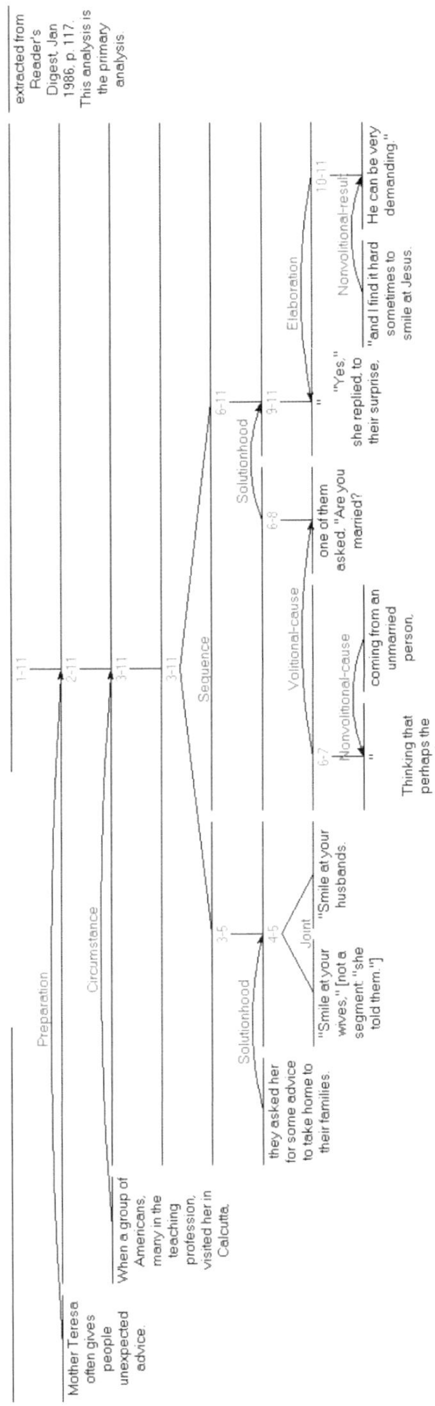

Figure a. Mother Teresa 1

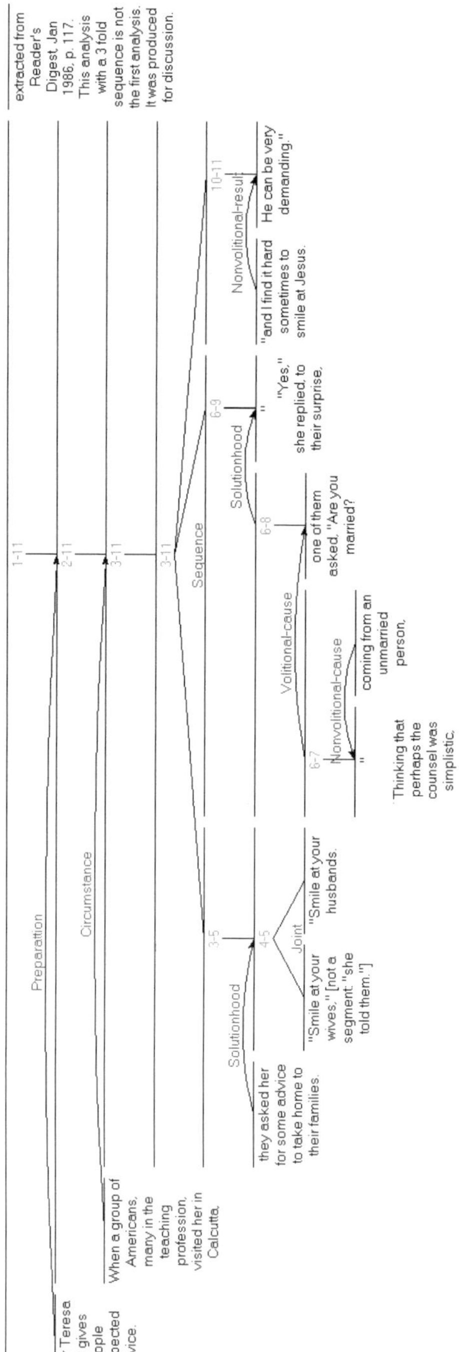

Figure b. Mother Teresa 2

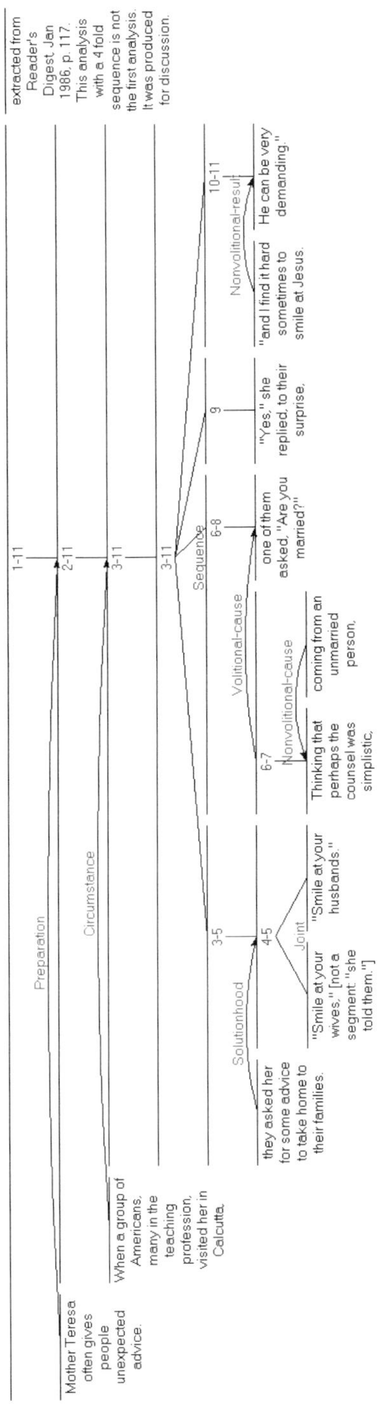

Figure c. Mother Teresa 3

Chapter 9. Style and culture in quantitative discourse analysis.

Based on the previous results, one can again predict that negative obligations (prohibitions) will be more frequent in American tourist websites, though generally not too many instances of prohibitions are to be expected in this genre and register. Indeed, the Austrian corpus contains only 19 instances of negative obligation in form of *may not*, *must not* and *not allowed*, while the American corpus contains 72.

Alternative ways of expressing prohibitions include phrases along the lines of *something is prohibited.* The Microsoft Office Word thesaurus lists the following adjectives as synonyms for prohibited: *forbidden, banned, barred, illegal, proscribed, taboo, outlawed, illicit.* Others that may come to mind include *not permitted, against the law* and *criminal.* Most of these words are indeed used in tourist websites, and their frequencies and usage reinforce our findings. Typical examples found on www.utah.com are:

- *Single-track riding is not allowed within the park*
- *Wood fires are prohibited, but charcoal fires are allowed at designated sites.*
- *Several rock and mineral specimens can be found here but rock collecting is prohibited inside the national park.*
- *Camping is prohibited one mile from road, or within 300 feet of a water source.*

In the corpus of tourist websites the above words are used 21 times in the Austrian files and 51 times in the American texts. There is a strong semantic association of these prohibitions with *camping* in both corpora. In addition to that, the American texts ban *pets* and *bikes* in certain *areas* and exclude *guests under a certain height* from participating in particular activities.

Chapter 10. Devices of probability and obligation in text types

In Text 1, the central modals verbs are *would, should* and *can. Would* and *can* appear twice each, and *should* occurs once. As a median value modal verb, *would* is used with the subject *I*, carrying the meaning of willingness. Should, as a median value modal verb, is used in the that-clause to express the modal meaning of obligation and probability. *Can* is used as a low value modal verb and thus carries the meaning of probability and permission. The use of median value and low value modal verbs shows that the author is trying to negotiate with the reader and to avoid giving the impression of imposition.

Text 2 is a legal text, in which obligations and responsibilities are prescribed. Here we find two instances of *must,* two instances of *may,* one instance of *would,* and one instance of *shall. Must,* as a high value modal verb, indicates the meaning of high probability, while *may* is used in the text to express permission and possibility and explain the rights authorized by the law. *Would* is a median value modal verb and carries the meaning of predication. *Shall*, used in this context, indicates the meaning of high probability and thus is a high value modal verb.

These instances of central modal verbs in the two text types show that their use is constrained by the communicative goal of the text, and is distributed differently across text types. The above analysis is done on small pieces of text. If we want to know the general picture of the pattern of use of central modal verbs in certain text types, the investigation should be conducted on a large scale.

In Systemic Linguistics, adjuncts of modality fall under the category of mood adjuncts. As mentioned in the previous sections, devices of probability and obligation include modal verbs, modal adjuncts, expansion of the Predicator and the metaphorical variant. Based on Halliday's (1994) categorization of mood adjuncts, adjuncts serving as devices of probability include *certainly*, *probably*, *possibly*, *perhaps*, and *maybe*. Adjuncts serving as devices of obligation include *definitely*, *absolutely*, *possibly*, *at all costs*, and *by all means*. As for the expansion of the Predicator, we have *required*, *supposed*, and *allowed*. We also have the metaphorical variants of *I think*, *I know*, and *I imagine*.

Four types of efforts are involved in examining the use of adjuncts in English legal documents and in the part of "general introduction to the University" in university websites. First, we should get a good understanding of the systemic theory about mood adjuncts. For this, we can refer to Halliday (1994) and Halliday and Matthiessen (2004). Second, we can search university websites and law websites for introductions and legal documents. Third, we can investigate the frequency of use of these adjuncts and find out their prominent use. Last, we can explain the functions of these prominent features in both registers, through the concept of context of situation.

Chapter 11. Analysis and evaluation of argumentative discourse

Initially, KLM seems to defend three separate standpoints, one of them remaining implicit:

Standpoints KLM

1 KLM has acted in a way that is formally justified.
(2 After the finishing off the squirrels KLM has acted in an appropriate way.)
3 The order from the government to destroy the animals was unethical.

Strategic maneuvering in confrontation stage

- The position of the accusers is portrayed as if they do not claim that KLM is to blame for the killing of 440 squirrels but have the less serious claim that KLM made an assessment mistake. KLM gives in right away to this last accusation. It is undeniable that the squirrels are finished off and an open denial of KLM responsibility would not be good for KLM's image.

- By stating that KLM has acted formally correct and implying that after the killing KLM did the right things, the blame is put on others: the governmental department.

Strategic maneuvering in opening stage

- Facts that are detrimental for KLM's position (the actual finishing off of the squirrels) are pushed to the background and wrapped in excuses.
- Facts that are positive for KLM are mentioned explicitly: KLM was given orders from higher up to finish off the animals. KLM sent the employee concerned home. This fact is not only relevant as a reason why KLM did the right thing after the incident, it also implies that there is something fishy going on with this employee: he is partly to blame. This interpretation is plausible if we take into consideration that KLM may accept part of the blame but in its least unacceptable form: blame for one of its employees. Apparently KLM is trying to defend another standpoint: the company as a whole is not to blame.

Strategic maneuvering in argumentation stage

- KLM uses the technique of dissociation to make sure that the company as a whole is not to be blamed but that only part of it is guilty: the employee. What is true for a part is certainly not true for the whole.
- To justify the claim that both KLM and the employee acted in a formally correct way, it is indicated that KLM and the employee did precisely what he was told to do from higher up. This argumentation is strong because this is exactly what acting formally right means. Again, this argumentation is meant to show that the real guilt lies not with KLM but with others: the government.

Revised analysis standpoints KLM

Based on these considerations, we achieve a different reconstruction of the standpoints involved: there are two main standpoints and both remain implicit:

(1) KLM is not to be blamed for the killing of 440 squirrels.
(2) The Department of Agriculture, Environmental Management and Fishing is to blame.

KLM uses a strategy of reducing its own responsibility and blaming others. In this endeavour, the associated claims are not explicitly stated, but only suggested.

Chapter 12. Embodied cognition, discourse, and dual coding theory: New directions

The "plain English" rewrites for the two examples are:

1. Children need good schools if they are to learn properly.
2. Thank you for your letter asking for permission to put up posters in the library. Before we can give you an answer we will need to see a copy of the posters to make sure they won't offend anyone.

Chapter 13. The cognition of discourse coherence

1: (1) is epistemic: from the argument in (b) the conclusion can be derived that Hamers must be the murderer;
(2) is content: in extra-textual reality there is a causal relationship between producing a surplus and exporting it;
(3) is a speech act relation because the situation in (a) legitimates uttering the judgment in (b).
2: Background: none of the above; Condition: if; Contrast: but, although; Restatement: in other words; Goal: in order to; Evidence: because, since; Cause-Consequence: as a result; Temporal Sequence: after; Elaboration: and.
3: If, either-or, because, in addition, and.

Chapter 14. A computational psycholinguistic algorithm to measure cohesion in discourse

(1) You probably have obtained pretty high similarity values for semantically related terms and synonyms, and values close to zero for unrelated terms. However, antonyms also tend to have high similarity values. The reason is that they are found in similar contexts. It is hard to find a pair of words with a strong negative similarity value (give it a try!) because it is rare to have words in strongly dissimilar contexts.

(2) The similarity results for sentences are a function of the meaning of their words. The more similar words they have in common, the more similar two sentences are.

(3) It can be argued that LSA is a useful computational tool, but not a model of human cognition, because it looks at semantic neighbors and not at the embodied aspects of meaning. For LSA a sentence like "John dried his feet with a towel/a shirt/glasses" does not differ much in meaning, but humans would find the second option acceptable and the third unacceptable (Glenberg & Robertson, 2000). However, see Louwerse (2007) and Louwerse and Jeuniaux (in press) for a discussion.

Chapter 15. Chinese questions and power relations in institutional dialogue

Some scholars hold that in casual conversation, all participants are peers or family members and have equal rights to speak and casual conversion is regarded as an equal power speech system. However, in the empirical study such a viewpoint cannot hold. In fact, the dichotomy between the symmetry and the equality of casual conversation and the asymmetry and inequality of institutional dialogue oversimplifies the nature of asymmetry and neglects the possible ways in which the participation in casual conversation may be asymmetrical. In casual conversation, asymmetry exists temporarily between the speaker and the hearer of a turn in a dialogue; between initiator and respondent in a sequence of interaction; between those who are active in shaping topics and those who are subordinate and inferior to produce topics.

Despite the seeming equality between participants in casual conversation, participants cannot be absolutely equal because some members in a family or in a circle of friends may have higher status than the others due to the privileged resources, involving age, wealth, sex, education, information and so on. As power is exercised on the basis of higher status, power in casual conversation is covert and not easy for people to scrutinize.

In fact, as power is covert in casual conversation, questions in casual conversation tend to be a latent means to exercise power. On the one hand, questions produce the immediate allocation of turn-taking. When a person asks a question, s/he obtains a turn and possesses a privilege to allocate the following turn to the next speaker. On the other hand, questions temporarily control topics because participants exchange the role of questioning alternatively. Therefore, in casual conversation, it is possible that a participant takes a lead in asking questions and has more opportunity to initiate a dialogue, to take turns and to control topics in a conversation.

Chapter 16. Towards a process view of preformulation in press releases

Here's an example of the kind of analysis that the reader should engage in.

On 12 June, 2008, worldwide media reported the news of a bid launched by Belgium-based InBev, one of the world's largest brewing companies, to take over American Anheuser-Busch. These are the first few lines of what the BBC news website has to say on the topic.

Takeover bid for Budweiser firm

US brewer Anheuser-Busch, the maker of Budweiser beer, has said it has received an unsolicited takeover bid from Belgian-Brazilian rival InBev.

The firm said the proposal was for $65 (£23.40) per share in cash — a deal that would be worth $46bn. Anheuser said that it would "review the merits" of a possible tie-up that would combine InBev's brands, including Stella Artois, with Anheuser's.

Brewers are looking to consolidate amid higher costs and a consumer downturn.

Anheuser said in a statement: "The board will review the merits of the proposal consistent with its fiduciary duties and in consultation with its financial and legal advisers. The board will pursue the course of action that is in the best interests of Anheuser-Busch's stockholders."

(…)

http://news.bbc.co.uk/go/pr/fr/-/2/hi/business/7449700.stm

It's interesting to note that the BBC seems to rely heavily on Anheuser-Busch as a source of information. In addition, the sourcing is acknowledged very explicitly. In fact, in only a couple of lines there are four expressions sourcing the information to an Anheuser-Busch "statement." If we compare the BBC's version of the story with the Anheuser-Busch press release issued the day before (and shown below), the only possible conclusion is that there is indeed massive, verbatim overlap, which implies that the press release was effectively preformulated.

Anheuser-Busch Acknowledges Receipt of Unsolicited Proposal from InBev

ST. LOUIS, June 11, 2008 — Anheuser-Busch Cos. Inc. (NYSE: BUD) announced today that it has received an unsolicited, non-binding proposal from InBev to acquire all of the outstanding shares of Anheuser-Busch for $65 per share in cash.

Anheuser-Busch said that its board of directors will evaluate the proposal carefully and in the context of all relevant factors, including Anheuser-Busch's long-term strategic plan. The board will review the merits of the proposal consistent with its fiduciary duties and in consultation with its financial and legal advisers. The board will pursue the course of action that is in the best interests of Anheuser-Busch's stockholders.

Anheuser-Busch's board expects to make its determination regarding InBev's proposal in due course.

Based in St. Louis, Anheuser-Busch is the leading American brewer, holding a 48.5 percent share of U.S. beer sales. The company brews the world's largest-selling beers, Budweiser and Bud Light. Anheuser-Busch also owns a 50 percent share in Grupo Modelo, Mexico's leading brewer, and a 27 percent share in China brewer Tsingtao, whose namesake beer brand is the country's best-selling premium beer. Anheuser-Busch ranked No. 1 among beverage companies in FORTUNE Magazine's Most Admired U.S. and Global Companies lists in 2008. Anheuser-Busch is one of the largest theme park operators in the United States, is a major manufacturer of aluminum cans and one of the world's largest recyclers of aluminum cans. For more information, visit www.anheuser-busch.com.

Chapter 17. Media discourse

1:

Text A
1: Headline, 2: Source of information, 3: Address, 4: TRANSACTION
5: Additional information, 6: Price, 7: Background, 8: Profit, 9: Commentary

Text B
1: Headline, 2: Source of information, 3: Address, 4: TRANSACTION, 5: Additional information, 6: Price, 7: Seller, 8: Buyer, 9: Background, 10: Profit, 11: Commentary

Chapter 18. Critical discourse analysis

Nomination

Only those speaking against immigration are nominated: Lord Turner, Shadow Home Secretary David Davis, and Sir Andrew Green. All other actors remain anonymous, including the Government. This biases the article against the Government's immigration policy and in favour of the anti-immigration point of view.

Lord Turner

Lord Turner is named and "titulated," and the article also functionalizes him, mentioning activities that underline his importance, his connection with issues that may concern readers, such as pensions and climate change, and his stance "above politics" (he is both a Labour adviser and strongly supported by the Shadow Home Secretary): "Senior Labour Adviser," "former CBI director," "headed Gordon Brown's Pension

Commission," "chairman of the Committee on Climate Change." All this is clearly aimed at lending credibility to his views. He is also called "an influential figure," which I would interpret as a "descriptivized" functionalization (he influences). Lord Turner is agentive throughout, though of speech acts rather than actual deeds: he "attacks," "accuses," "warns," "argues," and so on.

Immigrants

Immigrants are categorized in terms of provenance and recency of arrival ("foreign-born population," "newcomers"), functionalized in terms of low-ranking jobs ("workers," "office cleaners") and in terms of the act of immigrating itself ("arrivals from overseas"), in terms of numbers ("865") and objectivated ("migration" — instead of "immigrants" — is said to "affect communities," to "contribute to the economy," etc.). They are also always collectivized. As far as role allocation is concerned, immigrants are on the one hand agentive (though their actions are often nominalized: "influx," "arrival," "impact," etc) but they are also "patients" — of processes like "need" ["we do not 'need' immigrants"] and "control."

"Native" population

The "non-immigrant" population is referred to as a collective. The pronoun "we" constructs the paper and its readers as a "community" which clearly excludes immigrants. "Residents" is a categorization based on place of domicile. The "native" population is also referred to as "an already highly populated region," which is a "spatialization." And finally, they are agents of processes such as "need" (in "we do not 'need' immigrants") and "feel crowded," but "patient" (though only implicitly) of processes like "overcrowding," "impact," etc.

The Government

The Government is impersonalized in expressions like "the Government," "Labour" and "the Home Office." An (anonymous, collectivized) functionalization ("ministers") is the exception. This makes the Government's point of view less personalized and more remote from the readers. Although the Government is "patient" of Lord Turner's "attack," for the most part it plays an agentive role, as it actually implements and justifies the pro-immigration policy. However, its actions are often nominalized, so that agency is not explicitly signaled.

Nominalization

Nominalizations include the things immigrants do (such as "influx"), especially negative (or potentially negative) things like "overcrowding" and "impact." They also include the anti-immigration views of ordinary people, who are therefore not explicitly made responsible for such views: "racist backlash," "groundswell of opinion," and perhaps also "debate." The Government's arguments, too, are nominalized: "the *language* of a (...) shortage...." (instead of "The Government says..."), "the idea that we 'need' higher fertility..." (instead of "The Government believes"), and terms like "argument" and "contribution to the debate..." This allows the Government's views to be negatively evaluated, while at the same time not attributing them to anyone in particular, so that they can not be checked.

Legitimation

The article can be said to legitimate the anti-immigration point of view in a number of ways: (1) it creates an "us" and "them" relationship between the readers and "immigrants" (2) it lends credibility to the anti-immigration view and distances the reader from the Government's point of view (and from the immigrants as actual people seeking a better life) through a range of discursive strategies such as anonymization, de-personalization, collectivization and so on, and (3) it only *alludes* to the assumed anti-immigration feelings of "us," "residents," who, after all, are more easily branded as racist than those of the Conservative elite.

Chapter 19. Gendered discursive constructions of bank manager positions: Conflicting social identities.

1: The article starts with commenting on how women have gained access to the workforce and how they are now entering boardrooms and launching their own companies. The first paragraph thus refers to *gender in management*. The second paragraph introduces the idea of "male and female styles of leadership," which might indicate a gendered management perspective; however, as the text moves on to describe differences between male brains and female brains, the perspective is still a *gender in management perspective*. However, the third paragraph allows for a widening of perspective in that men and women are said to be "also molded by differing sets of social rules and expectations." This would indicate a combination of gender and gendered views as advocated by liberal feminists. In the rest of the article, though, the gender in management perspective prevails, which may be seen through the many stereotyped descriptions of men and women as leaders. However, in paragraph 10, there is again indication of a transient view in the claim that "women are lately demonstrating higher levels of traditional 'hard' or 'male' skills as well." The same view is carried over to paragraph 12, which suggests that "men are used to running the show and, for the most part, don't reward 'female' style management because they see it as weak." However, from this *gendered management perspective*, the writer reverts to a *gender in management perspective* by suggesting that "women have had to prove that their way of managing works, over and over again." The text thus discursively constructs men as "tough" managers and women as "soft" managers, while suggesting that tough managers should adopt soft management styles for the benefit of business. In other words, the text suggests that instead of focusing on *gender in management* there is a case for focusing on *gendered management*, however without really practicing what it preaches.

2: Female stereotypes: (1) Women managers tend to have more of a desire to build than a desire to win, (2) Women are more willing to explore compromise and to solicit other people's opinions, (3) Women are better than men at empowering teams and staff, (4) Women encourage openness and are more accessible, (5) Women leaders respond more quickly to calls for assistance, (6) Women are more tolerant of differences, so they're more skilled at managing diversity, (7) Women identify problems more quickly and more accurately, (8) Women are better at defining job expectations and providing valuable feedback, (9) Women delegate more readily and express their appreciation for hard work more often, (10) Women ask questions, (11) Women tend to be better at making staffers feel valued and rewarded, (12) Women have to prove themselves over and over again.

Male stereotypes: (1) Men often think if they ask other people for advice, they'll be perceived as unsure or as a leader, who doesn't have answers, (2) Men tend to be more speedy decision-makers, (3) Male managers are also more adept at forming what management psychologist Ken Siegel calls "navigational relationships," (4) Men tend to give answers, (5) Men are used to running the show, (6) Men see female style management as weak.

3: All the examples of stereotyping found in extracts 1 and 2, express attitudes towards people, which are in Appraisal categorized as Judgment. Evaluation is expressed in explicit terms and tends to be *positive* for women and *negative* for men. Women are generally appraised for being capable (they are more skilled at managing diversity; they identify problems more quickly and more accurately), dependable and courageous (they respond more quickly to calls for assistance; they are tolerant of differences), honest (they encourage openness) and beyond reproach (they prefer to build rather than to win; they are more willing to solicit other people's opinions), which earns them credit in the social sanction and social esteem categories. By emphasizing these qualities in women as positive, the writer at the same time implicitly evokes negative Judgment of male managers, who are then seen as lacking qualities when it comes to *capacity*, *tenacity*, *veracity* and *propriety*. It should be noted, however, that the analysis might produce different results in different cultures, depending on what the analyst accepts as good and true.

The linguistic features used to produce the stereotypes include comparison (better than, more than) (underlined in the text below), followed by a complement that identifies what women are better at. Unsurprisingly, the complements (highlighted in *italics*) share positive semantic traits, mostly conveyed by processes and goals for these processes: to build, to explore compromise, to solicit opinions, to empower teams, to be open and accessible, to respond quickly to calls, to be tolerant of differences, to be skilled at managing diversity, to provide valuable feedback. Many of the stereotypes resemble definitions in that a term is defined (women), followed by a differentiation (how they are different from men). This is also evident from the frequent use of the relational verb "to be."

Gender matters.
"Women managers tend to have more of a *desire to build* than a desire to win," says Debra Burrell, regional training director of the Mars-Venus Institute in New York. "Women are more willing to *explore compromise and to solicit other people's opinions.*" By contrast, she says, men often think if they ask other people for advice, they'll be perceived as unsure or as a leader who doesn't have answers.

- Women are better than men *at empowering teams and staff.*
- Women encourage openness and are more *accessible.*
- Women leaders *respond* more quickly *to calls for assistance.*
- Women are more *tolerant of differences*, so they're more *skilled at managing diversity.*
- Women *identify problems* more *quickly and more accurately.*
- Women are better at *defining job expectations and providing valuable feedback.*

Chapter 20. The semiotics of racism: A critical discourse-historical analysis

In a first brief analysis, we can clearly detect the relevant *social actors* "us" (we, I, freedom, democracy, America, freedom loving people, our country, United States of America) and "them" (enemy, hiding in the shadow, preys on innocents, runs for cover; note that the impersonal neutral pronoun "it" is being used, not "they" which would clearly indicate human beings). "We" are active and willing to confront the enemy (*material verbs*), whereas "the enemy" is described as being cowardly, hiding, immoral, a threat to all values of democracy and freedom. Once the opposing groups have been categorized, we can also observe several *rhetorical techniques* (repetitions of syntactic structures as well as lexical items), the use of *metaphors* to depict "the enemy" (hiding in the shadows), while "us" is attributed by very positive *flag-words* ('patient, steadfast, freedom-loving'). A *discursive contrast* between light and dark is constructed: the light relates to democracy, freedom, patience, and the whole freedom-loving world; the dark relates to a small group of enemies who are hiding and have "no regard for human life" and who commit "acts of terror" or even "acts of war." The construction of the contrast serves *argumentative-rhetorical means*: to *convince* the in-group (us, all Americans, the freedom-loving world) that acts of war (thus *redefining* "acts of terror") were committed against America (which is rhetorically *equated* with the "freedom loving world"), and therefore, a war seems a necessary measure against "the enemy." This speech marks the preparation for a "call-to-arms" (see also Young & Fitzgerald, 2006: 10–33).

About the authors

John Bateman (1957) is a full Professor of Applied Linguistics in the English and Linguistics Department of the University of Bremen. He studied Linguistics and Computer Studies at the University of Lancaster (UK) and received his PhD from the University of Edinburgh in 1986 with a dissertation entitled "Utterances in Context: Towards a Systemic Theory of the Inter-subjective Achievement of Discourse." He worked subsequently at research institutes and universities in Scotland, Japan, California and Germany. His areas of specialization include functional, computational and multimodal linguistics.

His current interests center on the application of functional linguistic and corpus methods to multimodal meaning-making, analyzing and critiquing multimodal documents of all kinds, the development of linguistically-motivated ontologies, and the construction of computational dialogue systems for human–robot communication. He has published widely in all these areas, as well as authoring several introductory and survey articles on natural language generation and Systemic Functional Linguistics. In 1991 he published *Text Generation and Systemic Functional Linguistics* (together with Christian Matthiessen) and in 2008 a new linguistically-inspired treatment of page-based documents in *Multimodality and Genre: A Foundation for the Systematic Analysis of Multimodal Documents.*

Currently he is a member of the editorial boards of the *Information Design Journal* and the journal of *Applied Ontology.*

John Bateman
Bremen University
FB10: Linguistics and Literary Sciences
Bibliothekstr. 1, Building GW2
28334 Bremen, Germany

bateman@uni-bremen.de

Anna Duszak (1950) is a Professor of Linguistics at the Institute of Applied Linguistics, Warsaw University, and Head of the Chair of Sociolinguistics and Pragmatics. Her research interests include Discourse Analysis, pragmatics, anthropological linguistics, cross-cultural communication, social semiotics and Critical Discourse Analysis.

She is the author of three monographs and some eighty papers in scholarly collections and journals. Her English-medium editorship includes: *Culture and Styles of Academic Discourse* (1997); *Us and Others. Social Identities across Languages, Discourses and Cultures* (2002); *Speaking from the Margin. Global English from a European Perspective* (with U. Okulska, 2004); *Identity, Community, Discourse: English in Intercultural Settings* (with G. Cortese, 2005); *Bridges and Barriers in Metalinguistic Discourse* (with U. Okulska, 2006).

Her recent research focuses on academic communication under globalization, education policies in academia (especially with reference to linguistics and specialist language studies) as well as social and communicative change in post-communist Poland (e.g., "Globalization as Interdiscursivity: On the Spread of Global Intertexts," in: *Speaking from the Margin: Global English in a European Perspective* (2004); "Between Styles and Values: An Academic Community in Transition," in: *Identity, Community, Discourse: English in Intercultural Settings* (2005); "Why 'New' *Newspeak*? Axiological Insights into Language Ideologies and Practices in Poland," in: *Language Ideologies, Policies and Practices: Language and the Future of Europe*, (2006); "Looking Globally, Seeing Locally: Exploring some Myths of Globalization in Academia," *Revista Canaria de Estudios Ingleses, 53* (2006); (with Jo Lewkowicz) "Publishing Academic Texts in English: a Polish perspective," *Journal of English for Academic Purposes, 7* (2008).

Anna Duszak
Warsaw University
Institute of Applied Linguistics
Browarna 8/10
00-311 Warsaw, Poland

a.duszak@uw.edu.pl

Bart Garssen (1964) is assistant professor in the Department of Speech Communication, Argumentation Theory and Rhetoric of the University of Amsterdam. His research interests are argument schemes, fallacies and empirical research of argumentation.

Together with Bert Meuffels and Frans van Eemeren he published several articles on laymen's judgments of argumentation. A joint monograph on this research project is in preparation. Together with Frans van Eemeren, he wrote a Dutch textbook on argumentative writing for a broader audience (2005).

Bart Garssen
University of Amsterdam
Department of Speech Communication, Argumentation Theory and Rhetoric
Spuistraat 210
1012 VB Amsterdam, The Netherlands

b.j.garssen@uva.nl

Geert Jacobs (1966) received a PhD in linguistics in 1997 from the University of Antwerp, where he wrote a dissertation on the metapragmatics of press releases. His research focuses on the study of professional and institutional discourse, with a special interest in news production processes and PR. He has recently founded the international NewsTalk&Text research group (NT&T) to promote and pool further efforts in this area. He has published research articles in a wide range of international, peer-reviewed journals including the *Journal of Pragmatics, Text, Public RelationsReview, Document Design, Pragmatics* and the *Journal of Sociolinguistics*. In addition, he has co-edited volumes on the *Pragmatics of Crisis* (2002), *Language, Communication and the Economy* (2005), *Discourse in Organizations* (2006) and *the Discourse of News Management* (2008).

He teaches business communication at the Department of Language and Communication at Ghent University (Belgium). He has recently co-authored a textbook for undergraduate students of Business English and he has supervised several on-line learning projects.

Geert Jacobs
Ghent University
Department of Language and Communication
Hoveniersberg 24
B-9000 Ghent, Belgium

geert.jacobs@ugent.be

Patrick Jeuniaux (1976) is a research assistant in the Department of Psychology and the Institute for Intelligent Systems at the University of Memphis. He studied psychology and statistics at Université catholique de Louvain, and artificial intelligence at Katholieke Universiteit Leuven, in Belgium. He has worked on a variety of topics including modeling coherence in texts, multimodal communication in humans and artificial agents, and word learning. He is currently pursuing a PhD in cognitive psychology and psycholinguistics at University of Memphis.

Patrick Jeuniaux
University of Memphis
Department of Psychology /
Institute for Intelligent Systems
400 Innovation Drive
Memphis, TN 38152, USA

pjeuniau@memphis.edu

Martin Kaltenbacher (1966) is a post-doc research fellow in English linguistics at the Department of English at the Paris-Lodron University of Salzburg, Austria. He studied English and Classics in Salzburg and Oxford and received his PhD in 2000 with a dissertation on "Universal Grammar and Parameter Resetting in Second Language Acquisition," which was published in 2001.

Currently, his research interests are in Systemic Functional Linguistics, Corpus Linguistics and multimodal Discourse Analysis. He has published a number of articles and co-edited the books *Perspectives on Multimodality* (2004) and *Empirical Approaches to Discourse Analysis* (2007).

Martin Kaltenbacher
University of Salzburg
Department of English
Akademiestr. 24
5020 Salzburg, Austria

martin.kaltenbacher@sbg.ac.at

Kenneth C. C. Kong (1969) is an Associate Professor of linguistics in the Department of English Language and Literature at Hong Kong Baptist University. His major academic interests are discourse analysis, intercultural pragmatics, multimodal analysis and English for specific purposes. He has published extensively in these areas in international journals such as *Text and Talk, Language in Society, Journal of Pragmatics* and *Discourse Studies.* His most recent publication is a research monograph (co-edited with Winnie Cheng) titled *Professional Communication: Collaboration between Academics and Practitioners.*

Currently he is involved in a number of research projects. They evolve around two areas: multimodality and professional discourse. His most current research project in multimodality is to develop a fully-annotated multimodal and bilingual corpus of news and advertisements, the first of its kind in the Asian-Pacific region. In the area of professional discourse, he is developing a detailed framework of intertextuality in studying the recontextualization of voices in different professional settings. He is also writing a research-oriented guidebook about professional discourse.

Kenneth Kong
Hong Kong Baptist University
Department of English Language and Literature
Waterloo Road
Kowloon, Hong Kong

kkong@hkbu.edu.hk

Inger Lassen (1948) is a Professor of Discourse in Professional Settings at Aalborg University. She obtained a Master's degree in translation and interpreting in 1990 from the Aarhus School of Business. In 1999 she received her PhD with the dissertation "Accessibility and Acceptability in Technical Manuals: A Survey of Style with the Emphasis on Grammatical Metaphor" from Aalborg University. She began her career at Aalborg University as a teaching assistant in 1990 to become a full professor in 2007. She has given open lectures at a number of universities including Ghent University in Belgium, Adelaide, Macquarie and Sydney University in Australia, University of Michigan, and Oulu University in Finland.

Her publications include a monograph on style, an edited anthology entitled *Mediating Ideology in Text and Image: Ten Critical Studies* and articles in international journals such as *Journal of Document Design*, *Journal of Discourse Studies* and *Journal of Critical Discourse Studies*. In addition she has written book chapters for international publications.

Inger Lassen is currently Head of the doctoral program Discourse and Contemporary Culture at Aalborg University, and she teaches and does research within the fields of genre and discourse studies, focusing on intercultural communication, discourses of science and technology and discourses of organization and management.

Inger Lassen
Aalborg University
Department of Language and Culture
Kroghstræde 3
DK-9220 Aalborg, Denmark

inglas@hum.aau.dk

Elisabeth Le (1959) is an Associate Professor of Applied Linguistics in the department of Modern Languages and Cultural Studies at the University of Alberta. She studied law (Paris II), political science (Paris II), Russian (INALCO-Paris III), and education (McGill University and OISE-Toronto), and received her PhD in Linguistics in 1996 at the Université de Montréal. In her dissertation, she elaborated a model of coherence analysis and compared the structures of articles published in French and English academic reviews of Public International Law.

Since then, most of her research has been done on newspapers' editorials. In a monograph, *The Spiral of Anti-Other Rhetoric* (2006), she compared how French and American editorialists in *Le Monde* and *The New York Times* wrote about Russia from 1999 to 2001, and examined how Russian journalists working for elite Russian dailies answered them in their writings. She is currently finishing a project on *Le Monde*'s role in society seen through its editorials.

Elisabeth Le
University of Alberta
Department of Modern Language and Cultural Studies
200, Arts Building
Edmonton, Alberta
T6G 2E6, Canada

elisabeth.le@ualberta.ca
www.ualberta.ca/~emle/

Max M. Louwerse (1970) is an Associate Professor in the Department of Psychology and the Institute for Intelligent Systems at the University of Memphis. He received his MA degrees in language and literature from the University of Utrecht and a PhD degree in Linguistics from the University of Edinburgh.

He has published over 80 articles in a variety of journals, books and conference proceedings, edited an interdisciplinary volume on thematics and received international awards for his teaching and research. He received funding from various organizations for research on intelligent tutoring systems, computational linguistics, and multimodal communication.

His interests cover a wide range of topics in interdisciplinary research related to cohesion and coherence, symbolic and embodied cognition, genre analysis, alignment of linguistic and non-linguistic communicative channels, and embodied conversational agents.

Max M. Louwerse
University of Memphis
Department of Psychology /
Institute for Intelligent Systems
400 Innovation Drive
Memphis, TN 38152, USA

mlouwerse@memphis.edu
http://www.psyc.memphis.edu/people/faculty/louwerse.shtml

Alfons Maes (1952) is a full Professor and Head of the Department of Communication and Information Sciences, Faculty of Humanities at Tilburg University (The Netherlands), and received his PhD in 1991. His work includes research on the way in which humans adapt their referential behavior to specific communicative conditions (like the type of task or addressee). Other areas of research are the design of multimodal documents in different communicative domains, including advertising, health communication, instructive communication and websites.

Alfons Maes
Tilburg University
Faculty of Humanities
Department of Communication and Information Science
PO Box 90153
5000 LE Tilburg, The Netherlands

maes@uvt.nl

Giovanni Parodi (1962) is currently Head of the Postgraduate School of Linguistics at Pontificia Universidad Católica de Valparaíso, Chile, and editor of *Revista Signos. Estudios de Lingüística*. He obtained an MA in Applied Linguistics and later received his PhD in Linguistics. His major fields of interest are Corpus Linguistics, genre theory, and discourse psycholinguistics (reading comprehension and written production processes). Currently he is conducting research in specialized academic/professional written genres, press media discourse analysis, and computational resources through three grants funded by major Chilean research foundations and international programs, such as *ECOS-CONICYT* and *UNESCO UNITWIN Chairs*. His publications include articles in Spanish and English journals and several books published by EUDEBA (2005), EUV (2002, 2003, 2005, 2007, 2008), and Arco/libros (2009). His most recent contribution is an edited book published in 2007: *Working with Spanish Corpora*. He has also edited four other interdisciplinary books.

Giovanni Parodi
Pontificia Universidad Católica de Valparaíso
Brasil 2830, 9th Floor
Valparaíso, Chile

gparodi@ucv.cl
www.postgradolinguistica.ucv.cl/gparodi

Joost Schilperoord (1957) is an Assistant Professor at the centre for information and communication, Humanities Faculty at Tilburg University. He studied communication studies at Utrecht University. He received his PhD in 1996 with a dissertation of cognitive processes in text production and has published several articles on this subject. Together with Ted Sanders (Utrecht University) and Wilbert Spooren (Free University Amsterdam) he edited a book on linguistic and psycholinguistic aspects of text representation.

His current interest concerns visual communication, and its communicative and persuasive aspects. His research focuses on possibilities of applying theories of verbal rhetoric and linguistic semantics on the analysis of visuals in advertisements and editorial cartoons: their structure (e.g., "grammar"), meaning and effects on audiences.

Joost Schilperoord
Tilburg University
Faculty of Humanities
Department of Communication and Information Science
PO Box 90153
5000 LE Tilburg, The Netherlands

j.schilperoord@uvt.nl

Jan Renkema (1948) is a Professor of Discourse Quality at Tilburg University. He studied General Linguistics at the VU University of Amsterdam and received his PhD in 1981 with a dissertation on "The Language of the Government." He was a professor of Cultural Studies at the Open University of The Netherlands. He has given guest lectures at various well-known universities, amongst which the universities of Berkeley, Kunming, Stellenbosch, Sydney and Valparaiso.

Among his writings for a broader audience are a Dutch style manual, of which over 400,000 copies have been sold. He also wrote an introduction to the field of text linguistics ("Introduction to Discourse Studies"), which was translated into English, Spanish, Korean and Japanese. A special Dutch edition of the book is expected to be available in China. He was author of the introduction to the Official Word List as stipulated by the Dutch Spelling Law in 1994 and one of the supervisors of the New Dutch Bible translation. He was also a general editor of the *Information Design Journal*.

Currently he is acting as a communications advisor for various government agencies; a member of the editorial boards of a number of journals and chairman of the International Association for Dutch studies.

Jan Renkema
Tilburg University
Faculty of Humanities
Department of Information and Communication Science
PO BOX 90153
5000 LE Tilburg, The Netherlands

j.renkema@uvt.nl
www.janrenkema.nl

Andrea Rocci (1970) is an Assistant Professor of Language Sciences at the Faculty of Communication Sciences of the USI (Lugano, Switzerland), where he teaches Discourse Analysis and Interpersonal Communication. His research interests lie at the intersection between semantics, discourse pragmatics, and the analysis of argumentation in professional and media genres, with a special focus on the discourse of finance. He wrote a book on the argumentative constraints encoded by the semantics of Italian modals (*La Modalità Epistemica tra Semantica e Argomentazione*, Milan, 2005) and several papers on the relationship between semantics, discourse structure and argumentation. He is currently directing a Swiss National Foundation research project on predictions and modality in the discourse of economic-financial newspapers.

He has been executive editor of the journal *Studies in Communication Sciences* (2003–2006) and currently serves as vice-president in the Swiss Association for Applied Linguistics (VALS-ASLA).

Andrea Rocci
Facoltà di Scienze della comunicazione
Università Della Svizzera Italiana (USI)
Via G. Buffi 13
CH 6900 Lugano

andrea.rocci@lu.unisi.ch

Mark Sadoski (1945) is a Professor and distinguished research fellow at Texas A&M University. He holds joint appointments in the Department of Teaching, Learning, and Culture and the Department of Educational Psychology in the College of Education and Human Development, and the Department of Humanities in Medicine and the Office of Educational Development in the College of Medicine. He received his PhD in 1981 from the University of Connecticut in Curriculum and Instruction with an emphasis on Reading and Language Arts.

He has published over 100 peer-reviewed articles and chapters on literacy research and theory in prominent journals and books including *Reading Research Quarterly, Journal of Literacy Research, Scientific Studies of Reading, Reading and Writing, Reading Psychology, Journal of Educational Psychology, Research in the Teaching of English, Review of Educational Research, American Educational Research Journal, Document Design, Medical Education*, and *Theoretical Models and Processes of Reading*. He has authored two books, including *Imagery and Text: A Dual Coding Theory of Reading and Writing* (2001, with Allan Paivio), and *Conceptual Foundations of Teaching Reading* (2004).

He has served on the editorial boards of *Reading Research Quarterly, Journal of Literacy Research, Reading and Writing, Reading Psychology, Document Design,* and *Information Design Journal.*

His current research interests are verbal and nonverbal cognition and curriculum and instruction across disciplines.

Mark Sadoski
Texas A&M University
Department of Teaching, Learning, and Culture,
4232 TAMU
College Station, TX 77843-4232, USA

msadoski@tamu.edu

Ted Sanders (1963) is a Professor of Dutch language use and discourse studies at Utrecht University, The Netherlands and received his PhD in 1992. His research concentrates on discourse structure and coherence. Central questions are: how can coherence be modeled? What are the linguistic signals of coherence (connectives, referential phenomena)? How do writers and readers use these signals in the cognitive processes of reading and writing? Striving for an interdisciplinary approach, he combines cognitive linguistics and text linguistics with the psycholinguistics of discourse processing, as well as an interest in text and document design: how can text quality be improved? Together with co-authors he published on these issues in several edited books and in international journals, such as *Cognitive Linguistics, Discourse Processes, Journal of Pragmatics, Reading and Writing, Text,* and *Written Communication.* He recently co-edited special issues of *Cognitive Linguistics* and *Discourse Processes* and with Joost Schilperoord and Wilbert Spooren he edited a book volume on *Text representation: Linguistic and psycholinguistic approaches* (2001).

Ted Sanders
University of Utrecht
Utrecht institute of Linguistics
Trans 4, kamer 0.59
3512 JK Utrecht, The Netherlands

ted.sanders@let.uu.nl

Wilbert Spooren (1956) is a Professor of Language and Communication at the Free University of Amsterdam, The Netherlands and received his PhD in 1989. His research focuses on issues of text structure and coherence. His research questions involve the use and processing of coherence relations and their linguistic signals, and how insights concerning such matters can be used to optimize text quality. He is interested in combining insights from fields like cognitive linguistics, text linguistics and psycholinguistics, and he applies various research methodologies (both qualitative and quantitative — the latter comprising corpus studies, experiments and survey studies). In order to stimulate interdisciplinary discussion of issues of text structure, he has been involved in the organization of a series of international biannual workshops called Multidisciplinary Approaches to Discourse (MAD) since 1995. He has published on discourse structure, genre, interestingness and persuasiveness, in edited volumes and in journals like *Cognitive Linguistics, Discourse Processes,* and *Journal of Research in Reading.* Together with Ted Sanders and Joost Schilperoord, he edited a book volume on *Text representation* (2001).

Wilbert Spooren
Free University of Amsterdam
Faculty of Arts
De Boelelaan 1105
1081 HV Amsterdam, The Netherlands

w.spooren@let.vu.nl

Maite Taboada (1970) holds a MA in English Philology from the Universidad Complutense de Madrid (Spain), an MSc in Computational Linguistics from Carnegie Mellon University (USA), and completed her PhD in English Linguistics at the Universidad Complutense in 2001. She is currently an Associate Professor of Linguistics at Simon Fraser University, in Vancouver, Canada.

She works in the areas of discourse analysis, Systemic Functional Linguistics and computational linguistics. Her book, *Building Coherence and Cohesion: Task-Oriented Dialogue in English and Spanish* (2004), is a cross-linguistic characterization of coherence and cohesion in spoken language, where she examines the strategies that speakers use to build a conversation. She has done research on coherence and cohesion, information structure and turn-taking. She has participated in research projects in natural language generation, machine translation and software agents. She was a post-doctoral research fellow at the University of Alberta (Edmonton, Canada), Visiting Chair in Cognitive Science at the University of Potsdam (Germany), and has also worked in industry, leading the development of a natural language processing system. Some of her current research projects are: cohesion and referring expressions in Spanish and English, combining cohesion and Centering Theory; Rhetorical Structure Theory; discourse parsing; evaluation and appraisal in text (and how to implement a system to perform automatic appraisal).

Maite Taboada
Simon Fraser University
Department of Linguistics
8888 University Dr.
Burnaby, B.C. V5A 1S6, Canada

mtaboada@sfu.ca
http://www.sfu.ca/~mtaboada

Frans H. van Eemeren (1940) is Professor of Speech Communication, Argumentation Theory and Rhetoric at the University of Amsterdam. Frans van Eemeren and Rob Grootendorst (1944–2000) are the founders of the influential Pragma-dialectical Argumentation Theory. This theory systematically combines normative insights from philosophical dialectics and dialogue logic with pragmatic insights from Speech Act Theory, Gricean theory and Discourse Analysis. The Pragma-dialectical Theory is applied in the analysis, evaluation and production of oral and written argumentative discourse.

Frans van Eemeren is (co-)author of some fifty book publications. Among them are *Speech Acts in Argumentative Discussions* (1984), *Argumentation, Communication, and Fallacies* (1992), *Reconstructing Argumentative Discourse* (1993), *Fundamentals of Argumentation Theory* (1996), A *Systematic Theory of Argumentation* (2004), and *Argumentative Indicators in Discourse* (2007). Currently he is completing a monograph based on his work with Peter Houtlosser (1956–2008), *Strategic Maneuvering in Argumentative Discourse*, which proposes an integration of rhetorical insights in the pragma-dialectical method for reconstructing and evaluating argumentative discourse.

Frans H. van Eemeren
University of Amsterdam
Department of Speech Communication, Argumentation Theory and Rhetoric
Spuistraat 210
1012 VB Amsterdam, The Netherlands

f.h.vaneemeren@uva.nl

Tom van Hout (1978) studied linguistics and journalism at the University of Antwerp and is currently employed as a research assistant at the Department of Language and Communication at Ghent University. He is finalizing his PhD — a linguistic ethnography of business reporters' writing practices, i.e., how business journalists write from news sources. He has taught Business English courses at the universities of Antwerp and Ghent and has guest-lectured at the universities of Utrecht, Leuven (Lessius) and Milan.

His research interests include organizational discourse, in particular journalism and new(s) media, ethnography, science popularization and applied linguistics. He is a published author and a founding member of two international research groups: *NewsTalk&Text* and *Discourse in Organizations.*

At Ghent University, he serves as an elected representative on the Arts Faculty Council for the research assistant body and he is involved in a number of science popularization initiatives. He also serves as an editor for *Tekstblad*, a popularizing Dutch language communication journal.

Tom van Hout
Ghent University
Dept. of Language & Communication
Sint-Pietersnieuwstraat 130/5
B-9000 Ghent, Belgium

tom.vanhout@ugent.be
http://www.ntt.ugent.be
http://www.dio.ugent.be

Theo van Leeuwen (1947) is a Professor of Media and Communication and Dean of the Faculty of Arts and Social Sciences at the University of Technology, Sydney. He has published widely in the areas of Critical Discourse Analysis, multimodality and visual semiotics. His books include *Reading Images — The Grammar of Visual Design* (with Gunther Kress); *Speech, Music, Sound*; *Multimodal Discourse — The Modes and Media of Contemporary Communication* (with Gunther Kress); *Introducing Social Semiotics* and *Global Media Discourse* (with David Machin). His latest book *Discourse and Practice — New Tools in Critical Discourse Analysis* was published in 2008. He is a founding editor of the journal *Visual Communication.*

Theo van Leeuwen
University of Technology, Sydney
Faculty of Arts and Social Sciences
PO Box 123
Broadway, NSW 2007, Australia

theo.vanleeuwen@uts.edu.au

Jinjun Wang (1968) is a Professor in the School of Foreign Languages at Yunnan University, China. She studied Functional Linguistics under the supervision of Prof. Xinzhang Yang at Xiamen University and obtained her PhD in 2004 with a dissertation entitled "A Critical Analysis of Questions in Dialogue." She has many academic interests, including Systemic Functional Linguistics, Discourse Analysis, sociolinguistics and pragmatics. Recently she has developed a special interest in Critical Discourse Analysis.

She has had many publications, including one book, nearly 20 articles in some key Chinese journals of foreign languages, and one article and some book reviews in international journals. Among them, "Questions and the Exercise of Power" made its appearance in *Discourse and Society, 17*(4), 2006. She has co-translated two English dictionaries (Macmillan English Dictionary and Oxford ESL English Dictionary) into their English-Chinese versions. Currently she has just edited a book and had it published.

Now she is a vice director of Foreign Languages and Literatures Research Institute of Yunnan University and is acting as a directing member of China Functional Linguistics Association.

Jinjun Wang
Yunnan Univeristy
School of Foreign Languages
Kunming 650091, China

jjwangkm@yahoo.com.cn

Sungsoon Wang (1960) is an Associate Professor of the General Education English Program at Sogang University in Seoul, Korea. She studied Text Linguistics at the Sogang University and received her PhD in 1998 with a dissertation on "Text Typology and Givenness Constraints on Interpretation." She also holds an MA in general Linguistics from Louisiana State University.

While teaching English as a Foreign Language, she wrote articles on genre based language teaching by applying text type and genre theories. Her research interest involves exploiting linguistic theories for the practitioners of language teaching and document design. She also taught "Discourse Studies" in the Sogang Graduate School of Education.

Sungsoon Wang
Sogang Universtiy
Room X506 GEEP
PO BOX 1142
Seoul, Korea

swang@sogang.ac.kr

Ruth Wodak (1950) PhD, Dr. Habil. is a Distinguished Professor of Discourse Studies at Lancaster University. Besides various other prizes, she was awarded the Wittgenstein Prize for Elite Researchers in 1996. Her research interests focus on discourse studies; gender studies; language and/in politics; prejudice and discrimination; and on ethnographic methods of linguistic field work.

She is member of the editorial board of a range of linguistic journals and co-editor of the journals *Discourse and Society, Critical Discourse Studies*, and *Language and Politics*, and co-editor of the book series *Discourse Approaches to Politics, Society and Culture* (DAPSAC). She has held visiting professorships in Uppsala, Stanford University, University Minnesota, University of East Anglia, and Georgetown University. In 2008, she was awarded the Kerstin Hesselgren Chair of the Swedish Parliament (at University Örebrö).

Recent book publications include *Ist Österreich ein 'deutsches' Land?* (with R. de Cillia, 2006); *Qualitative Discourse Analysis in the Social Sciences* (with M. Krzyzanowski, 2008); *Migration, Identity and Belonging* (with G. Delanty, P. Jones, 2008), and *The Discursive Construction of History. Remembering the Wehrmacht's War of Annihilation* (with H. Heer, W. Manoschek, and A. Pollak, 2008). The monograph *The discursive construction of politics in action: 'Politics as usual'?* (2009) is in press.

See http://www.ling.lancs.ac.uk/profiles/265 for more information on current research projects and recent publications.

Ruth Wodak
Distinguished Professor
Chair in Discourse Studies
Department of Linguistics and English Language
Bowland College
Lancaster University, LA1 4YT

r.wodak@lancaster.ac.uk
http://www.ling.lancs.ac.uk/profiles/Ruth-Wodak/
http://www.wittgenstein-club.at

Xinzhang Yang (1956) is a Professor of Linguistics at Xiamen University. He studied Linguistics at the University of Sydney and received his MA in 1990. He was a visiting scholar at Central Michigan University from 1998 to 1999. He has given guest lectures at various well-known universities, amongst which are the universities of Tsinghua, Sun Yat-sen, Wuhan, Jilin and Yunnan.

His main areas of study include functional linguistics and text analysis. So far, he has published 25 books and 60 papers. Among his writings is an introduction to the field of linguistics (*Introduction to Linguistics*), which has been used as a textbook in many universities. He has won one prize award for excellent teaching, and five prize awards for his research achievements in social sciences. Currently he is Dean of College of Foreign Languages and Cultures at Xiamen University, a member of the editorial boards of a number of journals, vice chairman of China Association of Functional Linguistics, and vice chairman of China Association of English-Chinese Discourse Analysis.

Xinzhang Yang
College of Foreign Languages and Cultures
Xiamen University
Xiamen, Fujian 361005, China

xzyang@xmu.edu.cn

References

Aakhus, M. (2003). Neither naïve nor critical reconstruction: dispute mediators, impasse, and the design of argumentation. *Argumentation, 17*, 265–290.

Ainsworth-Vaughn, N. (2001). The discourse of medical encounters. In D. Schiffrin, D. Tannen, & H.E. Hamilton (Eds.), *The handbook of discourse analysis* (pp. 453–469). London: Blackwell.

Alvesson, M., & Billing, Y.D. (1997). *Understanding gender and organizations*. London: Sage.

Alvesson, M., & Billing, Y.D. (2000). Questioning the notion of feminine leadership: a critical perspective on the gender labelling of leadership. *Gender, Work and Organization, 7*(3), 144–157.

Andrews, R. (2005). Models of argumentation in educational discourse. *Text, 25*(1), 107–127.

Armstrong, D.F., & Wilcox, S.E. (2007). *The gestural origin of language*. New York: Oxford University Press.

Askehave, I. (2009). What women want: A gendered, discourse analytical perspective on the job advertisement. Manuscript in preparation.

Askehave, I., & Swales, J. (2000). Genre identification and communicative purpose: A problem and a possible solution. *Applied Linguistics, 22*(2), 195–212.

Badger, R., & White, G. (2000). A process genre approach to teaching writing. *ELT journal, 54*, 153–160.

Baker, P. (2006). *Using corpora in discourse analysis*. London: Continuum.

Baker, P., Gabrielatos, C., KhosraviNik, M., Krzyżanowski, M., & Wodak, R. (2008). Qualitative and quantitative methodologies in analyzing racist utterances. *Discourse and Society, 18*, 273–306.

Bakhtin, M. (1981). *The dialogical imagination*. (C. Emerson & M. Holqusit, trans.) Austin, TX: University of Texas Press.

Bakhtin, M. (1986). *Speech genres and other late essays*. Austin, TX: University of Texas Press.

Barnhurst, K.G., Vari, M., & Rodríguez, Í. (2004). Mapping visual studies in communication. *Journal of Communication, 54*(4), 616–644.

Barthes, R. (1967). *Elements of semiology*. New York: Hill & Wang.

Barthes, R. (1970). *Mythologies*. London: Paladin.

Barthes, R. (1977). *Image-music-text*. London: Fontana.

Bateman, J.A. (2007). Towards a *grande paradigmatique* of film: Christian Metz reloaded. *Semiotica, 167*(1/4), 13–64.

Bateman, J.A. (2008). *Multimodality and genre: A foundation for the systematic analysis of multimodal documents*. London: Palgrave Macmillan.

Bateman, J.A., Delin, J.L., & Henschel, R. (2002). XML and multimodal corpus design: experiences with multi-layered stand-off annotations in the GeM corpus. In *Proceedings of the LREC'02 Workshop "Towards a Road-map for Multimodal Language Resources and Evaluation."* Las Palmas, Canary Islands, Spain.

Bateman, J.A., Kamps, T., Kleinz, J., & Reichenberger, K. (2001). Constructive text, diagram and layout generation for information presentation: the DArt$_{bio}$ system. *Computational Linguistics, 27*(3), 409–449.

Bauman, R., & Briggs, C. (1990). Poetics and performance as critical perspectives on language and social life. *Annual Review of Anthropology, 19*, 59–88.

Beck, I., McKeown, M., Sinatra, G., & Loxterman, J. (1991). Revising social studies text from text-processing perspective: Evidence of improved comprehensibility. *Reading Research Quarterly, 26*, 251–276.

Bell, A. (1985). One rule of English: geographical, social and historical spread. *Te Reo, 28*, 95–117.

Bell, A. (1991) *The language of news media*. Oxford, UK: Blackwell.

Bell, A. (1998). The discourse structure of news stories. In A. Bell & P. Garrett (Eds.), *Approaches to media discourse* (pp. 64–104). Oxford, UK: Blackwell.

Benwell, B., & Stokoe, E. (2006). *Discourse and identity*. Edinburgh, UK: Edinburgh University Press.

Berezowski, L. (1997). *Dialect in translation*. Wrocław, Poland: Wydawnictwo Uniwersytetu Wrocławskiego.

Berkenkotter, C., & Huckin, T.N. (1995). *Genre knowledge in disciplinary communication — cognition/culture/power*. Hillsdale, NJ: Lawrence Erlbaum.

Bestgen, Y., Degand, L., & Spooren, W. (2006). Towards automatic determination of the semantics of connectives in large newspaper corpora. *Discourse Processes, 41*(2), 175–194.

Bhatia, V.J. (2002). Applied genre analysis: Analytical advances and pedagogical procedures. In A.M. Johns (Ed.), *Genre in the Classroom* (pp. 279–283). London: Lawrence Erlbaum.

Bhatia, V.J. (2004). *Worlds of Written Discourse*. London: Continuum.

Bhatia, V.J. (2005). Generic Patterns in Promotional Discourse. In H. Halmari & T. Virtanen (Eds.), *Persuasion across genres: A linguistic approach*. Amsterdam: Benjamins.

Biber, D. (1988). *Variation across speech and writing*. Cambridge, MA: Cambridge University Press.

Biber, D. (1989). A typology of English texts. *Linguistics, 27*, 3–43.

Biber, D. (1994). Using register-diversified corpora for general language studies. In S. Armstrong (Ed.), *Using large corpora* (pp. 180–201). Cambridge, MA: The MIT Press.

Biber, D. (2006). *University language: A corpus-based study of spoken and written registers*. Amsterdam: Benjamins.

Biber, D., Connor, U., & Upton, T. (2007). *Discourse on the move*. Amsterdam: Benjamins.

Biber, D., Conrad, S., & Reppen, R. (1998). *Corpus linguistics: investigating language structure and use*. Cambridge, MA: Cambridge University Press.

Biber, D., Johansson, S., Leech, G., Conrad, S., & Finegan, E. (1999). *Longman grammar of spoken and written English*. London: Pearson.

Biber, D., & Tracy-Ventura, N. (2007). Dimension of register variation in Spanish. In G. Parodi (Ed.), *Working with Spanish corpora* (pp. 54–89). London: Continuum.

Billig, M. (2006). Discrimination in discourse. In *Elsevier Encyclopedia for Language and Linguistics*. Oxford, UK: Elsevier.

Block, C.C., Parris, S.R., & Whiteley, C.S. (2008). CPMs: A kinesthetic comprehension strategy. *Reading Teacher*, 61(6), 460–470.

Bloom, L. (1991). *Language development from two to three*. Cambridge, MA: Cambridge University Press.

Bloor, M., & Bloor, T. (1993). How economists modify propositions. In W. Henderson, T. Dudley-Evans, & R. Backhouse (Eds.), *Economics and language*. London: Routledge.

Boorstin, D.J. (1961). *The image or what happened to the American dream*. London: Weidenfeld.

Bordwell, D. (1989). *Making meaning. Inference and rhetoric in the interpretation of cinema*. Cambridge, MA: Harvard University Press.

Bourdieu, P. (1989). *The logic of practice*. Cambridge, UK: Polity Press.

Bowdle, B.F., & Gentner, D. (2005). The career of metaphor. *Psychological review, 112*(1), 193–215.

Brewis, J. & Linstead, S. (2004). Gender and management. In L. Fulop, S. Linstead, & S. Lilley (Eds.), *Management and organization. A critical text* (pp. 56–92). New York: Palgrave.

Buttler, D., Kurkowska, H., & Satkiewicz, H. (1971). *Kultura języka polskiego. Zagadnienia poprawności gramatycznej* [Culture of the Polish language. On grammatical correctness]. Warsaw, Poland: PWN.

Cabré, M.T. (1999). El discurs especialitzat o la variación funcional determinada per la temàtica: Noves perspectives. [Special discourse or the functional variation determined by theme: New perspectives] In T. Cabré (Ed.), *La terminología. Representación y comunicación. Una teoría de base comunicativa y otros artículos* (pp. 151–173). Barcelona: IULA.

Cabré, M.T. (2002). Textos especializados y unidades de conocimiento: Metodología y tipologización. [Specialized texts and units of knowledge: Methodology and typology]. In J. García & M. Fuentes (Eds.), *Texto, terminología y traducción* (pp. 122–187). Salamanca, Spain: Almar.

Cademártori, Y. (2003). La inscripción de las personas en textos de divulgación científica. *Revista latinoamericana de estudios del discurso, 3*(1), 9–28.

Caldas-Coulthard, C.R., & Counthard, M. (1996). *Texts and practices: Readings in Critical Discourse Analysis.* London: Routledge.

Caldas-Coulthard, C.R., & Van Leeuwen, T. (2002). Stunning, shimmering, iridescent: Toys as the representation of gendered social actors. In L. Litosseliti & J. Sunderland (Eds.), *Gender identity and discourse analysis* (pp. 91–108). Amsterdam: Benjamins.

Calsamiglia, H. (2000). Decir la ciencia: Las prácticas divulgativas en el punto de mira. [Say sience: The divulging practices in the front sight] *Discurso y Sociedad, 2*(2), 3–8.

Capone, A. (2008). Barack Obama's South Carolina speech. [Electronic version]. *RASK: International Journal of Language and Communication, 27*, 87–122. Retrieved from http://semantics-archive.net/Archive/DRmNWU2Z/

Carletta, J. (1996). Assessing agreement on classification tasks: The kappa statistic. *Computational Linguistics, 22*(2), 249–254.

Carlson, L., Marcu, D., & Okurowski, M.E. (2001). Building a Discourse-Tagged Corpus in the Framework of Rhetorical Structure Theory. In *Annual Meeting of the ACL.*

Carlson, L., Marcu, D., & Okurowski, M.E. (2002). RST Discourse Treebank, LDC2002T07 [Corpus]. Philadelphia, PA: Linguistic Data Consortium.

Cassell, J., Nakano, Y., Bickmore, W.T., Sidner, C.L., & Rich, C. (2001). Non-verbal cues for discourse structure. *Proceedings of the 41st Meeting of the Association for Computational Linguistics* (pp. 17–19). Toulouse, France.

Catalyst Report sponsored by General Motors Corporation (2005). Women take 'care', men take 'charge'. Stereotyping of US business leaders exposed. Retrieved from http://www.catalystwomen.org/files/full/Women%20Take%20Care%20Men%20Take%20Charge.pdf

Catalyst Report sponsored by IBM Corporation (2007). The double-bind dilemma for women in leadership: Damned if you do, doomed if you don't. Retrieved from http://catalyst.org/files/full/2007%20Double%20Bind.pdf

Charolles, M. (1997). L'encadrement du discours. Univers, champs, domaines et espaces. [The framing of discourse. Universe, fields, areas and spaces *Cahiers de recherche linguistique, 2*(6), 1–73. LANDISCO, URA-CNRS 1035, Université de Nancy.

Cheng, H.H. (2001). Consuming a dream: Homes in advertisements and imagination in contemporary Hong Kong. In G. Mathews & T.L. Lui. (Eds.), *Consuming Hong Kong* (pp. 205–236). Hong Kong: Hong Kong University Press.

Chouliaraki, L., & Fairclough, N. (1997). Discourse in late modernity: rethinking critical discourse analysis. Edinburgh, UK: University of Edinburgh Press.

Ciapuscio, G. (2003). *Textos especializados y terminología* [Specialized texts and terminologies]. Barcelona: IULA.

Cienki, A., & Müller, C. (Eds.). (2008). *Metaphor and gesture*. Amsterdam: Benjamins.

Clark, E.V. (2003). *First language acquisition*. Cambridge, UK: Cambridge University Press.

Clark, H.H. (1996). *Using Language*. Cambridge, UK: Cambridge University Press

Clayman, S., & Heritage, J. (2002). *The news interview: journalists and public figures on the air*. Cambridge, UK: Cambridge University Press.

Coates, J. (1987). Epistemic modality and spoken discourse. *Transactions of the Philological Society*, 110–131.

Coe, R. (2002). The new rhetoric of genre; Writing political brief. In A.M. Johns (Ed.), *Genre in the Classroom* (pp. 197–207). London: Lawrence Erlbaum.

Coffin, C., & O'Halloran, K. (2005). Finding the global groove: Theorising and analysing dynamic reader positioning using APPRAISAL, corpus, and a concordancer. *Critical Discourse Studies, 2*(2), 143–163.

Crompton, R. (1997). Women, employment and feminism in the Czech Republic. *Gender, Work and Organization, 4*(3), 137–148.

Crystal, D. (1979). Reading, grammar and the line. In D. Thackray, (Ed.). *Growth in reading*. London: Ward Lock.

Crystal, D. (2001). *Language and the Internet*. Cambridge, UK: Cambridge University Press.

Curthoys, A., & Docker, J. (1989). In praise of prisoner. In J. Tulloch & G. Turner (Eds.), *Australian television: Programs, pleasures and politics*. Sydney, Australia: Allen & Unwin.

Dąbrowska, M. (2004). English and its impact on electronic media communication. In A. Duszak & U. Okulska (Eds.), *Speaking from the margin. Global English from a European perspective* (pp. 261–274). Frankfurt/Main, Germany: Peter Lang.

Daneš, F. (1974). Functional sentence perspective and the organization of text. In F. Daneš (Ed.), *Papers on functional sentence perspective* (pp. 106–128). The Hague, The Netherlands: Mouton.

Daneš, F. (1989). Functional sentence perspective and text connectedness. In M.E.A. Conte (Ed.), *Text and discourse connectedness* (pp. 23–31). Amsterdam: Benjamins.

Danesi, M., & Rocci, A. (In press). *The Role of Language in Intercultural Communication. An introduction to global linguistics*. Berlin/New York: Mouton De Gruyter.

De Beaugrande, R. (1996). *New foundations for a science of text and discourse*. Norwood, NJ: Ablex.

De Beaugrande, R., & Dressler, W. (1981). *Introduction to text linguistics*. London: Longman.

Deerwester, S., Dumais, S.T., Furnas, G.W., Landauer, T.K., & Harshman, R. (1990). Indexing by latent semantic analysis. *Journal of the American Society for Information Science, 41*, 391–407.

Degand, L. & Sanders, T. (2002). The impact of relational markers on expository text comprehension in L1 and L2. *Reading and Writing, 15*(7–8), 739–758.

Delanty, G., Wodak, R., & Jones, P. (2008). *Identity, migration, and belonging*. Liverpool: University of Liverpool Press.

Delin, J.L., & Bateman, J.A. (2002). Describing and critiquing multi-modal documents. *Document Design, 3*(2), 140–155. Amsterdam: Benjamins.

Delin, J.L., Bateman, J.A., & Allen, P. (2002). A model of genre in document layout. *Information Design Journal, 11*(1), 54–66.

Den Ouden, H. (2004). *Prosodic Realizations of Text Structure*. Unpublished PhD dissertation, Tilburg University, Tilburg, The Netherlands.

Den Ouden, H., Van Wijk, C., Terken, J., & Noordman, L. (1998). *Reliability of discourse structure annotation* (No. 33, Annual Progress Report). Eindhoven: IPO Center for Research on User-System Interaction, Technical University of Eindhoven, The Netherlands.

Deutscher, G. (2005). *The unfolding of language. An evolutionary tour of mankind's greatest invention.* New York: Metropolitan Books.

Di Eugenio, B., & Glass, M. (2004). The kappa statistic: A second look. *Computational Linguistics, 30*(1), 95–101.

Do women make better managers? (2001). *FT Financial Times.* Wijeya Newspapers. Retrieved from http://lakdiva.org/suntimes/030914/ft/16%5D.htm

Dodd, R.J. (1990). Innovative techniques: Parlor tricks for the courtroom. *Trial, 26*(4), 38–43.

Drew, P., & Heritage, J. (Eds.). (1992). *Talk at work: Interaction in institutional setting.* Cambridge, UK: Cambridge University Press.

Du Bois, J.W., Chafe, W.L., Meyer, C., & Thompson, S.A. (2000). *Santa Barbara Corpus of Spoken American English* [CD-ROM]. Linguistic Data Consortium.

Duszak, A. (1998). *Tekst, dyskurs, komunikacja międzykulturowa.* [Text, discourse, cross-cultural communication]. Warsaw, Poland: PWN.

Duszak, A. (2004). Globalisation as interdiscursivity: on the spread of global intertexts. In A. Duszak & U. Okulska (Eds.), *Speaking from the margin. Global English from a European perspective* (pp. 117–132). Frankfurt/Main, Germany: Peter Lang.

Duszak, A. (2007). Discourse pragmatics and 'physicality' of texts. In P. Cap & J. Nijakowska (Eds.), *Current trends in pragmatics* (pp. 33–51). Newcastle, UK: Cambridge Scholars Publishing.

Eggins, S., & Slide, D. (1997). *Analyzing casual conversation.* London/Washington: Cassell.

Ehrlich, S. (1998). The discursive reconstruction of sexual consent. *Discourse and Society, 9*(2), 149–171.

Evers-Vermeul, J., & Sanders, T. (2009). The emergence of Dutch connectives; how cumulative cognitive complexity explains the order of acquisition. *Journal of Child Language.*

Fabricius-Hansen, C. (2005). Elusive connectives: A case study on the explicitness dimension of discourse coherence. *Linguistics, 43*(1), 17–48.

Facchinetti, R. (2003). Pragmatic and sociological constraints on the functions of *may* in contemporary British English. In R. Facchinetti, M. Krug, & F. Palmer (Eds.), *Modality in contemporary English* (pp. 301–330). Berlin/New York: Mouton de Gruyter.

Fairclough, N. (1989). *Language and power.* London: Longman.

Fairclough, N. (1992). *Discourse and social change.* Cambridge, UK: Polity Press.

Fairclough, N. (1995a). *Critical discourse analysis. The critical study of language.* London: Longman.

Fairclough, N. (1995b). *Media discourse.* London: Arnold.

Fairclough, N. (1996). A reply to Henry Widdowson. "Discourse analysis: a critical view." *Language and Literature, 5*(1), 49–5.

Fairclough, N. (2003). *Analysing discourse. Textual analysis for social research.* London/New York: Routledge.

Fauconnier, G. (1994). *Mental spaces. Aspects of meaning construction in natural languages.* Cambridge, UK: Cambridge University Press.

Fauconnier, G. (1998/2004). Mental spaces, language modalities, and conceptual integration. In M. Tomasello (Ed.), *The new psychology of language.* Mahwah, New Jersey: Erlbaum. (Reprinted in S. Davis & B.S. Gillon [Eds.], *Semantics: A reader* [pp. 346–365]. Oxford, UK: Oxford University Press).

Fauconnier, G., & Turner, M. (2002). *The way we think: Conceptual blending and the mind's hidden complexities.* New York: Basic Books.

Ferdinandusse, H. (2007). *Visuele schema's in advertenties. Een exploratief onderzoek naar de effecten van perceptuele groepering op de betekenis van geprinte advertenties.* [Visual schemes in advertisements. An exploratory research of the effects of perceptual grouping on the meaning of printed advertisements]. Unpublished Master's Thesis, Tilburg University, Tilburg, the Netherlands.

Fiig, C. (2009). *Money talks: Discourses on gender equality, leadership and recruitment in the Danish financial sector*. Manuscript in preparation.

Fishman, M. (1980). *Manufacturing the news*. Austin, TX: Texas University Press.

Forceville, C.J. (1996). *Pictorial metaphor in advertising*. London: Routledge.

Forceville, C.J. (2006). Non-verbal and multimodal metaphor in a cognitivist framework: Agendas for research. In G. Kristiansen, M. Achard, R. Dirven, & F. Ruiz de Mendoza (Eds.), *Cognitive linguistics: Current applications and future perspectives* (pp. 379–402). Berlin/New York: Mouton de Gruyter.

Forceville, C.J. (2007). [Review of the book *Multimodal Transcription and Text Analysis: A Multimedia Toolkit and Coursebook*]. *Journal of Pragmatics*, *39*, 1235–1238.

Forstorp, P.A. (1998). Reporting on the MS Estonia catastrophe: Media-on-media events and interpersonal boundary work. *Text*, *18*(2), 271–299.

Fowler, R., Hodge, R., Kress, G., & Trew, T. (1979). *Language and control*, London: Routledge & Kegan Paul.

Fowler, R., & Kress, G. (1979). Critical linguistics. In R. Fowler, B. Hodge, G. Kress, & T. Trew (Eds.), *Language and control* (pp. 185–213). London: Routledge & Kegan Paul.

Frenier, C. (1996). *Business and the feminine principle: The untapped resource*. Oxford, UK: Butterworth Heinemann.

Gaik, F. (1992). Radio talk-show therapy and the pragmatics of possible worlds. In A. Duranti & Ch. Goodwin (Eds.), *Rethinking context. Language as an interactive phenomenon*. Cambridge, UK: Cambridge University Press.

Galtung, J., & Ruge, M. (1973). Structuring and selecting news. In S. Cohen & J. Young (Eds.), *The manufacture of news* (pp. 62–72). London: Constable.

Garret, P., & Bell, A. (1998) Media and discourse: a critical overview. In A. Bell & P. Garret (Eds.), *Approaches to media discourse* (pp. 1–20). Oxford, UK: Oxford University Press.

Gavins, J. (2007). *Text world theory. An introduction*. Edinburgh, UK: Edinburgh University Press.

Gentner, D., Bowdle, B.F., Wolff, P., & Boronat, C. (2001). Metaphor is like analogy. In D. Gentner, K.J. Holyoak, & B.N. Kokinov (Eds.), *The analogical mind: Perspectives from cognitive science* (pp. 199–253). Cambridge, UK: MIT Press.

Geurts, B. (1999). *Presuppositions and pronouns*. Amsterdam: Elsevier

Gibbs, R.W. (2005). Embodiment in metaphorical imagination. In R.A. Zwaan & D. Pecher (Eds.), *Grounding cognition: The role of perception and action in memory, language and thinking* (pp. 65–92). Cambridge, UK: Cambridge University Press.

Gilabert, R., Martínez, G., & Vidal-Abarca, E. (2005). Some good texts are always better: text revision to foster inferences of readers with high and low prior background knowledge. *Learning and Instruction*, *15*, 45–68.

Givòn, T. (1995). Coherence in text vs. coherence in mind. In M.A.G. Gernsbacher & T. Givón (Eds.), *Coherence in spontaneous text*. Amsterdam: Benjamins.

Glenberg, A.M., & Robertson, D.A. (2000). Symbol grounding and meaning: A comparison of high-dimensional and embodied theories of meaning. *Journal of Memory and Language*, *43*, 379–401.

Godfrey, J.J., & Holliman, E. (1993). *Switchboard-1* [CD-ROM]. Linguistic Data Consortium.

Goetz, E.T., Sadoski, M., Stricker, A.G., White, T.S., & Wang, Z. (2007). The role of imagery in the production of written definitions. *Reading Psychology*, *28*, 241–256.

Goffman, E. (1981). *Forms of talk*. Philadelphia: University of Pennsylvania.

Goodman, S., & Graddol, D. (Eds.). (1996). *Redesigning English: new texts, new identities*. London/New York: Routledge and the Open University.

Gore, A. (2007). *The assault on reason*. New York: Penguin Press.

Gotti, M. (2003). *Shall* and *will* in contemporary English: A comparison with past uses. In R. Facchinetti, M. Krug, & F. Palmer (Eds.), *Modality in contemporary English* (pp. 267–300). Berlin/New York: Mouton de Gruyter.

Grabe, W. (2002). Narrative and expository macro-genres. In A.M. Johns (Ed.), *Genre in the classroom* (pp. 249–267). London: Lawrence Erlbaum.

Graesser, A.C., Gernsbacher, M.A., & Goldman, S. (Eds.), *Handbook of discourse processes*. Mahwah, NJ: Erlbaum.

Graesser, A.C., McNamara, D.S., Louwerse, M.M., & Cai, Z. (2004). Coh-Metrix: Analysis of text on cohesion and language. *Behavior Research Methods, Instruments, and Computers*, *36*, 193–202.

Graesser, A.C., Millis, K., & Zwaan, R.A. (1997). Discourse comprehension. *Annual Review of Psychology*, *48*, 163–89.

Graff, D. (1996). *North American News Text Corpus* [CD-ROM]. Linguistic Data Consortium.

Greco-Morasso, S. (2006). Towards a multidisciplinary context-dependent model of mediation practice. *Studies in Communication Sciences*, *6*(2), 281–292.

Greco-Morasso, S. (2008). *Argumentative and other communicative strategies of the mediation practice*. PhD Thesis. Faculty of Communication Sciences. University of Lugano.

Grimes, J.E. (1975). *The thread of discourse*. The Hague, The Netherlands: Mouton.

Hahn, U., & Mani, I. (2000). The challenges of automatic summarization. *IEEE Computer*, *33*(11), 29–36.

Halliday, M.A.K. (1978). *Language as a social semiotic: The social interpretation of language and meaning*. London: Arnold.

Halliday, M.A.K. (1989). *An introduction to functional grammar*. London: Arnold.

Halliday, M.A.K. (1994). *An introduction to functional grammar* (2nd edition). London: Arnold.

Halliday, M.A.K., & Hasan, R. (1976). *Cohesion in English*. London: Longman.

Halliday, M.A.K., & Hasan, R. (1985). *Language, context, and text: Aspects of language in a social-semiotic perspective*. Victoria, Canada: Deakin University Press.

Halliday, M.A.K., & Matthiessen, C.M.I.M. (2004). *An introduction to functional grammar* (3rd edition). London: Arnold.

Hamblin, Ch.L. (1970). *Fallacies*. London: Methuen.

Harris, S. (1995). Pragmatics and power. *Journal of Pragmatics*, *23*, 117–35.

Harvey, A. (2002). Representación e imagen del quehacer científico en los medios de comunicación. [Representation and image of the scientific task in mass media.] In G. Parodi (Ed.), *Lingüística e inter-disciplinariedad. Desafíos del nuevo milenio. Ensayos en honor a Marianne Peronard* (pp. 335–353). Valparaíso: EUV.

Hasan, R. (1985). Part B. In M.A.K. Halliday & R. Hasan (Eds.), *Language, context and text: aspects of language in a social-semiotic perspective* (pp. 63–64). Geelong, VI: Deakin University Press.

Hasan, R. (1996). *Ways of saying: ways of meaning: selected papers of Ruqaiya Hasan*. London: Cassell.

Hatim, B., & Mason, I. (1990). *Discourse and the translator*. London: Longman.

Hausenblas, K. (1966). On the characterization and classification of discourses. *Travaux Linguistiques de Prague*, *1*, 67–83.

Heer, H., Manoschek, W., Pollak, A., & Wodak, R. (Eds.). (2008). *The discursive construction of history*. Basingstoke: Palgrave/MacMillan.

Hejwowski, K. (2004). *Translation: a Cognitive-Communicative Approach.* Olecko, Poland: Wydawnictwo Wszechnicy Mazurskiej.

Helbig, J. (1996). *Intertextualität und Markierung* [Intertextuality and Marking]. Heidelberg: Universitäts-verlag C. Winter.

Hine, C. (2000). *Virtual ethnography.* London: Sage.

Hobbs, J.R. (1979). Coherence and coreference. *Cognitive Science, 3*, 67–90.

Hobbs, J.R. (1983). Overview of a formal theory of discourse interpretation. *Text, 3*(3), 241–246.

Hobbs, J.R. (1985). On the coherence and structure of discourse (No. CLSI-85-37): Leland Stanford Junior University — Center for the Study of Language and Information.

Hockett, Ch. (1966). The problem of universals in languages. In J. Greenberg (Ed.), *Universals of language* (pp. 1–29). Cambridge, MA: MIT Press.

Hodge, R., & Kress, G. (1993). *Language as ideology.* London: Routledge.

Hoey, M. (2005). *Lexical priming. A new theory of words and language.* London/New York: Routledge.

Hoey, M. (2006). Language as choice: what is chosen? In G. Thompson & S. Hunston (Eds.), *System and corpus. exploring connections* (pp. 37–54). London: Equinox.

Holmes, J., & Meyerhoff, M. (1999): The community of practice: theories and methodologies in language and gender research. *Language in Society, 28*, 173–183.

Holmgreen, L. (2009). Metaphorically speaking. Constructions of gender and career in the Danish financial sector. *Gender and Language.* Manuscript in preparation.

House, J. (1996). Contrastive discourse analysis and misunderstanding: The case of German and English. In M. Hellinger & U. Ammon (Eds.), *Contrastive sociolinguistics* (pp. 345–361). Berlin/New York: Mouton de Gruyter.

Hovy, E.H. (1988). Planning coherent multisentential text. *Proceedings of 26th Annual Meeting of the Association for Computational Linguistics* (ACL'88) (pp. 163–169). Buffalo, New York.

Hovy, E.H., & Maier, E. (1995). Parsimonious or profligate: How many and which discourse structure relations? Unpublished manuscript.

Hunston, S. (2002). *Corpora in applied linguistics.* Cambridge, UK: Cambridge University Press.

Hyland, K. (2000). *Disciplinary discourses: Social interactions in academic writing.* London: Longman.

Hyland, K. (2004). Disciplinary interactions: Metadiscourse in L2 postgraduate writing. *Journal of Second Language Writing, 13*, 133–151.

Hymes, D. (1972). Models of the interaction of language and social life. In J.J. Gumperz & D. Hymes (Eds.), *Directions in sociolinguistics: The ethnography of communication* (pp. 12–36). Amsterdam: Benjamins.

Ide, N., Romary, L., & De La Clergerie, E. (2003). International standard for a linguistic annotation framework. In *Proceedings of the HLT-NAACL'03 workshop on the software engineering and architecture of language technology.*

Illich, I. (1971). *Deschooling society.* Harmondsworth, UK: Penguin.

Jackendoff, R.S. (1987). On beyond zebra: The relation of linguistic and visual information. *Cognition, 26*, 89–114.

Jacobs, G. (1999). *Preformulating the news: An analysis of the metapragmatics of press releases.* Amsterdam: Benjamins.

Janssen, D., & Neutelings, R. (2001). *Reading and writing public documents.* Amsterdam: Benjamins.

Jenson, J.V. (1983). Metaphor in argumentation. *Rhetoric Society Quarterly, 13*, 201–208.

Johnson, M. (1987). *The body in the mind. The bodily basis of meaning, imagination and reason.* Chicago: University of Chicago Press.

Joy, L., Carter, N.M., Wagner, H.M., Narayanan, S. (2007). *The bottom line. Corporate performance and women's representation on boards.* Catalyst. Retrieved from http://www.catalystwomen.org/knowledge/files/Bottom%20Line%202.pdf

Kalantzis, M., & Cope, B. (Eds.). (2000). *Multiliteracies: Literacy learning and the design of social futures.* London: Routledge.

Kaltenbacher, M. (2004). Perspectives on multimodality: From the early beginnings to the state of the art. *Information Design Journal, 12*(3), 190–207.

Kaltenbacher, M. (2006). Culture related linguistic differences in tourist websites: the emotive and the factual. A corpus analysis within the framework of Appraisal. In G. Thompson & S. Hunston (Eds.), *System and corpus. Exploring connections* (pp. 269–292). London: Equinox.

Kaltenbacher, M. (2007). Systemic functional linguistics and corpus analysis: the language of exaggeration in web-sites of tourism. In H. Gruber, M. Kaltenbacher, & P. Muntigl (Eds.), *Empirical approaches to discourse analysis* (pp. 89–117). Frankfurt/Main, Germany: Peter Lang.

Kamalski, J. (2007). *Coherence marking, comprehension and persuasion: On the processing and representation of discourse.* Utrecht, The Netherlands: LOT.

Kamalski, J., Lentz, L., Sanders, T., & Zwaan, R. (in press). The fore-warning effect of coherence markers in persuasion: off-line and on-line evidence.

Kamp, H., & Reyle, U. (1993). *From discourse to logic.* Dordrecht, The Netherlands: Kluwer.

Karttunen, L. (1969). Discourse referents. Paper presented at *COLING 1969. International conference on computational linguistics,* Sånga Säby (Sweden). Preprint n. 70 available online at: http://portal.acm.org/citation.cfm?id=990490.

Kienpointner, M. (1996). *Vernünftig argumentieren. Regeln und Techniken der Diskussion* [Arguing reasonably. Rules and techniques of discussion]. Hamburg, Germany: Rowohlt.

King, M.L. (1998). The American dream. In C. Carson & P. Holloran (Eds.), *A knock at midnight: Inspiration from the great sermons of reverend Martin Luther King, Jr.* New York: Warner Books. Online version available at http://www.stanford.edu/group/King/mlkpapers/

King, M.L. (2001). "I have a dream." Address at March on Washington for jobs and freedom (28 August 1963). In C. Carson & K. Shepard (Eds), *A call to conscience: The landmark speeches of Martin Luther King, Jr.* New York: IPM/Warner Books. Online version available at http://www.stanford.edu/group/King/mlkpapers/

Kintsch, W. (1988). The role of knowledge in discourse comprehension: A construction-integration model. *Psychological Review, 95*(2), 163–182.

Kintsch, W. (1998). *Comprehension: A paradigm for cognition.* Cambridge, UK: Cambridge University Press.

Kintsch, W. (2002). On the notions of theme and topic in psychological process models of text comprehension. In M.M. Louwerse & W. van Peer (Eds.), *Thematics: Interdisciplinary studies* (pp.157–170). Amsterdam: Benjamins.

Kintsch, W., & Van Dijk, T. A. (1978). Toward a model of text comprehension and production. *Psychological Review, 85*(5), 363–394.

Klare, G.R. (1974–1975). Assessing readability. *Reading Research Quarterly, 10,* 62–102.

Kong, K.C.C. (2006). A taxonomy of the discourse relations between words and visuals. *Information Design Journal, 14*(3), 207–230.

Kong, K.C.C. (2006). Property transaction report: News advertisement or a new genre? *Discourse Studies, 8,* 771–796.

Kozak, J. (2004). Between catachresis and tautology. Multilingual discourses in translation. In A. Duszak & U. Okulska (Eds.), *Speaking from the margin. Global English from a European perspective* (pp. 145–158). Frankfurt/Main, Germany: Peter Lang.

Kranstedt, A., Kopp, S., & Wachsmuth, I. (2002). *MURML: A multi-modal utterance representation markup language for conversational agents.* (Technical Report 2002/05, SFB 360) Situated Artificial Communicators. Bielefield, Germany: Universität Bielefeld.

Kratzer, A. (1981). The notional category of modality. In H.J. Eikmeyer & H. Rieser (Eds), *Words, worlds and contexts.* Berlin: De Gruyter.

Kress, G. (2003). *Literacy in the new media age.* London: Routledge.

Kress, G., & Fowler, R. (1979). Interviews. In R. Fowler, R. Hodge, G. Kress, & T. Trew (Eds.), *Language and Control* (pp. 63–80). London: Routledge & Kegan Paul Ltd.

Kress, G., & Van Leeuwen, T. (1996). *Reading images: The grammar of visual design.* London: Routledge.

Kress, G., & Van Leeuwen, T. (2001). *Multimodal discourse: the modes and media of contemporary communication.* London: Arnold.

Kristeva, J. (1968). Problémes de la structuration du texte. [Problems with the structuring of text] *Linguistique et Littérature, 12*, 55–64.

Krzeszowski, T. (1997). *Angels and devils in hell.* Warsaw, Poland: Energeia.

Labov, W. (1972). The transformation of experience in narrative syntax. In W. Labov (Ed.), *Language in the inner city* (pp. 354–396). Philadelphia, PA: University of Pennsylvania Press.

Lakoff, G., & Johnson, M. (1999). *Philosophy in the flesh.* New York: Basic Books.

Landauer, T.K., & Dumais, S.T. (1997). A solution to Plato's problem: The latent semantic analysis theory of acquisition, induction and representation of knowledge. *Psychological Review, 104*, 211-240.

Landauer, T.K., Foltz, P.W., & Laham, D. (1998). Introduction to Latent Semantic Analysis. *Discourse Processes, 25*, 259–284.

Lassen, I. (2004). Ideological resources in biotechnology press releases: Patterns of theme/rheme and given/new. In L. Young & C. Harrison (Eds.), *Systemic functional linguistics and critical discourse analysis* (pp. 264–297). London: Continuum.

Lauerbach, G. (2004). Political interviews as hybrid genre. *Text, 24*(3), 353–397.

Lave, J., & Wenger, E. (1991). *Situated learning: Legitimate peripheral participation.* Cambridge, UK: Cambridge University Press.

Le, E. (1996). Structure discursive comparée d'écrits argumentatifs en français et en anglais — de leur linéarité. [Compared discursive structure of argumentation in English and French writings — of their linearity]. PhD thesis. Montréal, France: Université de Montréal.

Le, E. (1999). The use of paragraphs in French and English academic writing: Towards a grammar of paragraphs. *Text, 19*(3), 307–343.

Le, E. (2000). Pour une analyse critique du discours dans l'étude des relations internationales — exemple d'application à des éditoriaux américains sur la guerre en Tchétchénie. [For a critical analysis of discourse in the study of international relations — example of an application on American editorials about the war in Chetchnia]. *Études Internationales, 31*(3), 489–515.

Le, E. (2002a). The concept of Europe in Le Monde's editorials. *Journal of Language and Politics, 1*(2), 279–325.

Le, E. (2002b). Human rights discourse and international relations: Le Monde's editorials on Russia. *Discourse and Society, 13*(3), 373–408.

Le, E. (2002c). Themes and hierarchical structures of written texts. In M. Louwerse & W. van Peer (Eds.), *Thematics — interdisciplanary studies* (pp. 171–187). Amsterdam: Benjamins.

Le, E. (2003). Information sources as a persuasive strategy in editorials — Le Monde and The New York Times. *Written Communication, 20*(4), 478–510.

Le, E. (2004a). Active participation within written argumentation: Metadiscourse and editorialist's authority. *Journal of Pragmatics, 36*, 687–714.

Le, E. (2004b). The role of paragraphs in the construction of coherence — text linguistics and translation studies. *IRAL, 42*, 257–273.

Le, E. (2006a). Collective memories and representations of national identity in editorials: Obstacles to a renegotiation of intercultural relations. *Journalism Studies, 7*(5), 708–728.

Le, E. (2006b). *The spiral of 'anti-other rhetoric'. Discourses of identity and the international media echo.* Amsterdam: Benjamins.

Le, E. (2007). The power of the French 'ON' in editorials. *RAEL (Revista electrónica de lingüística aplicada)* [Special issue] *1*, 32–48.

Le, E. (in press). Editorials' genre and media roles: *Le Monde's* editorials from 1991 to 2001. *Journal of Pragmatics.*

Leech, G. (2003). Modality on the move: The English modal auxiliaries 1961–1992. In R. Facchinetti, M. Krug, & F. Palmer (Eds.), *Modality in contemporary English* (pp. 223–240). Berlin/New York: Mouton de Gruyter.

Leijten, M., & Van Waes, L. (2006). Inputlog: New perspectives on the logging of on-line writing processes in a windows environment. In K. Sullivan & E. Lindgren (Eds.), *Studies in writing: Vol. 18. Computer key-stroke logging and writing. Methods and applications* (pp. 73–94). Oxford: Elsevier.

Lemke, J. (2004). *Critical analysis across media: Games, franchises, and the new cultural order.* Paper delivered at the First International Conference on Critical Discourse Analysis, Valencia, May 2004.

Lenaerts, G. (2002). In pursuit of the functional quality of political press releases. *Document Design, 3*, 210–223.

Levy, M., & Ransdell, S. (Eds.). (1996). *The Science of Writing.* Hillsdale, NJ: Erlbaum.

Lewis, D.K. (1973). *Counterfactuals.* Oxford: Blackwell.

Lewis, R.L. (2003). Computational psycholinguistics. In *Encyclopedia of Cognitive Science.* London: Macmillon (Nature Publishing Group).

Li, C.N., & Thompson, S.A. (1981). *Mandarin Chinese: A functional reference grammar.* Berkeley/Los Angeles/London: University of California.

Linell, P. (1990). The power of dialogue dynamics. In I. Marková & K. Foppa, (Eds.), *The dynamics of dialogue* (pp. 147–177). London: Harvester Wheatsheaf.

Linstead, S., Fulop, L., & Lilley, S. (2004). *Management and organization. A critical text.* New York: Palgrave.

López, C. (2002). Aproximaciones al análisis de los discursos profesionales. [Approaches to the analysis of professional discourse]. *Revista Signos, 35*(51–52), 195–215.

Lorente, M. (2002). *Verbos y discurso especializado.* [Verbs and specialized speech]. Retrieved from http://elies.rediris.es/elies16/Lorente.html

Louwerse, M.M. (2004). Semantic variation in idiolect and sociolect: Corpus linguistic evidence from literary texts. *Computers and the Humanities, 38*, 207–221.

Louwerse, M.M. (2007). Symbolic or embodied representations: A case for symbol interdependency. In T. Landauer, D., McNamara, S. Dennis, & W. Kintsch (Eds.). *Handbook of latent semantic analysis* (pp. 107–120). Mahwah, NJ: Erlbaum.

Louwerse, M.M., Cai, Z., Hu, X., Ventura, M., & Jeuniaux, P. (2006). Cognitively inspired natural-language based knowledge representations: Further explorations of Latent Semantic Analysis. *International Journal of Artificial Intelligence Tools, 15*, 1021–1039.

Louwerse, M.M., & Graesser, A.C. (2005). Coherence in discourse. In P. Strazny (Ed.), *Encyclopedia of linguistics*. (pp. 216–218). Chicago: Fitzroy Dearborn.

Louwerse, M.M., & Jeuniaux, P. (in press). Language comprehension is both embodied *and* symbolic. In M. De Vega, A. Glenberg, & A.C. Graesser (Eds.), *Embodiment and meaning: A debate*. Oxford, UK: Oxford University Press.

Louwerse, M.M., Lewis, G., & Wu, J. (in press). Unigrams, bigrams and LSA. Corpus linguistic explorations of genres in Shakespeare's plays. In W. van Peer & J. Auracher (Eds). *New directions in literary studies*. Cambridge, UK: Cambridge Scholars Publishing.

Louwerse, M.M., & Van Peer, W. (2006). Waar het over gaat in cijfers. Kwantitatieve benaderingen in tekst- en literatuurwetenschap. [What it is about in numbers: quantitative approaches in text- and literary studies]. *Tijdschrift voor Nederlandse Taal- en Letterkunde, 122*, 21–35.

Louwerse, M.M. & Van Peer, W. (in press). How cognitive is cognitive poetics? The interaction between symbolic and embodied cognition. In G. Brone & J. Vandaele (Eds.), *Cognitive Poetics*. Berlin, Germany: De Gruyter.

Louwerse, M.M., & Zwaan, R.A. (in press). Language encodes geographical information. *Cognitive science*.

Lü, S. (1982). *A brief introduction to Chinese grammar*. (trans. from Chinese). Beijing: The Commercial Press.

Maes, A. (1997). Referent ontology and centering in discourse. *Journal of Semantics, 14*, 207–235.

Maes, A., & Schilperoord, J. (2008). Classifying visual rhetoric. Conceptual and structural heuristics in interpreting and classifying visual rhetoric. In B.J. Phillips & E.F. McQuarrie (Eds.), *Go figure: New directions in advertising rhetoric*. Armonk, NY: M.E.Sharpe.

Malmkjæker K., & Anderson, J. (1991). *The linguistic encyclopedia*. London: Routledge.

Mann, W.C., & Taboada, M. (2007). RST Website, from http://www.sfu.ca/rst.

Mann, W.C., & Thompson., S.A. (1988). Rhetorical Structure Theory: Toward a functional theory of text organization. *Text, 8*(3), 243–281.

Marcu, D., Romera, M., & Amorrortu, E. (1999). Experiments in constructing a corpus of discourse trees. *Proceedings of ACL Workshop on Standards and Tools for Discourse Tagging* (pp. 48–57). College Park, Maryland.

Marcus, M.P., Santorini, B., Marcinkiewicz, M.A., & Taylor, A. (1999). Treebank-3, LDC99T42 [Corpus]. Philadelphia, PA: Linguistic Data Consortium.

Marsh, E.E., & White, M.D. (2003). A taxonomy of relationships between images and text. *Journal of Documentation, 59*(6), 647–672.

Martin, J.R. (1992). *English text. System and structure*. Amsterdam: Benjamins.

Martin, J.R. (2000). Beyond exchange. In S. Hunston & G. Thompson (Eds.), *Evaluation in text* (pp. 142–175). Oxford: Oxford University Press.

Martin, J.R. (2001). Language, register and genre. In A. Burns & C. Coffin (Eds.), *Analysing English in a Global Context: a reader. Teaching English Language Worldwide* (pp. 149–166). Clevedon, UK: Routledge.

Martin, J.R. (2004). Mourning: how we get aligned. *Discourse and Society, 15*(2–3), 321–344.

Martin, J.R., & White, P.R.R. (2005). *The language of evaluation. Appraisal in English*. London: Palgrave.

Martinec, R., & Salway, A. (2005). A system for image-text relations in new (and old) media. *Visual Communication, 4*(3), 337–371.

Martín Zorraquino, M. & Portolés, J. (1999). Los marcadores del discurso. [The markers of speech]. In I. Bosque & V. Demonte (Eds.), *Gramática descriptiva de la lengua Española* (pp. 4051–213). Madrid, Spain: Espasa Calpe.

Matouschek, B., Wodak, R., & Januschek, F. (1995). *Notwendige Maßnahmen gegen Fremde? Genese und Formen von rassistischen Diskursen der Differenz.* [Necessary measures against foreigners? Birth and forming of racist discourses of difference]. Vienna: Passagen Verlag.

Matthiessen, C. (2004). *An introduction to functional grammar. Revised edition of Halliday's original grammar.* London: Arnold.

Mautner, G. (2005). Time to get wired: Using web-based corpora in critical discourse analysis. *Discourse and Society, 16*(6), 809–828.

McCawley, J.D. (1993). *Everything that linguists have always wanted to know about logic ... But were ashamed to ask* (2nd edition). Chicago: University of Chicago Press.

McCloud, S. (1994). *Understanding comics: the invisible art.* New York: Harper-Perennial.

McEnery, T., & Wilson, A. (2001). *Corpus Linguistics: An introduction* (2nd edition). Edinburgh, UK: Edinburgh University Press.

McNamara, D.S., Cai, Z., & Louwerse, M.M. (2007). Comparing latent and non-latent measures of cohesion. In T. Landauer, D.S. McNamara, S. Dennis, & W. Kintsch (Eds.), *Handbook of latent semantic analysis* (pp. 379–400). Mahwah, NJ: Erlbaum.

McNamara, D.S., & Kintsch, W. (1996). Learning from texts: effects of prior knowledge and text coherence. *Discourse processes, 22*, 247–288.

McQuarrie, E.F., & Mick, D.G. (1999). Visual rhetoric in advertising: Text-interpretive, experimental, and reader-response analyses. *Journal of Consumer Research, 26*, 37–54.

McQuarrie, E.F., & Phillips, B.J. (Eds.). (2008). *Go figure. New directions in advertising rhetoric.* Armonk, NY: M.E.Sharpe.

Miodek, J. (Ed.). (1996). *O zagrożeniach i bogactwie polszczyzny* [On the threats to and the richness of the Polish language]. Wrocław, Poland: Towarzystwo Przyjaciół Polonistyki Wrocławskiej.

Montolío, E. (2001). *Conectores de la lengua escrita.* [Connectors of written language]. Barcelona, Spain: Ariel Practicum.

Müller, M. G. (2007). What is visual communication? Past and future of an emerging field of communication research. *Studies in Communication Sciences, 7*(2), 7–34.

Mumby, D.K. (Ed.). (1993). *Narrative and social control: critical perspectives.* London: Sage.

Nebenzahl, D. (2007, October 20). Women at the top deliver at the bottom line. *The Gazette* (Montreal). Retrieved from http://working.canada.com/montreal/resources/story.html?id=ce0ec216-5ad5-466b-81a2-713807c7706c

Neumann, S. (2003). *Textsorten und Übersetzen: eine Korpusanalyse englischer und deutscher Reiseführer* [Text genres and translating: a corpus analysis of English and German travel guides]. Frankfurt/Main, Germany: Peter Lang.

Noordman, L. & De Blijzer, F. (2000). On the processing of causal relations. In E. Couper-Kuhlen & B. Kortmann (Eds.), *Cause, condition, concession and contrast: Cognitive and discourse perspectives,* 35–56. Berlin: Mouton de Gruyter.

Noordman, L. & Vonk, W. (1998). Memory-based processing in understanding causal information. *Discourse Processes, 26*, 191–212.

Norris, S. (2002). The implication of visual research for discourse analysis: transcription beyond language. *Visual Communication, 1*(1), 97–121.

Norris, S. (2004). Multimodal discourse analysis: a conceptual framework. In P. LeVine & R. Scollon (Eds.), *Discourse and technology: multi-modal discourse analysis* (pp. 101–115). Washington, DC: Georgetown University Press.

Obama, B.H. (2008). Remarks of senator Barack Obama: South Carolina victory speech, Columbia, SC. January 26, 2008. Retrieved from http://www.barackobama.com/2008/01/26/remarks_of_senator_barack_obam_42.php

O'Halloran K.L. (Ed.). (2004/2006). *Multimodal discourse analysis. A systemic-functional perspective.* London/New York: Continuum.

Östman, J.O. (2004). The postcard as media. *Text, 24*(3), 423–442.

Östman, J.O. (2005). Persuasion as implicit anchoring: The case of collocations. In H. Halmari & T. Virtanen (Eds.), *Persuasion Across Genres* (pp. 183–212). Amsterdam: Benjamins.

Paivio, A. (1971). *Imagery and verbal processes.* New York: Holt, Rinehart, and Winston. (Reprinted 1979, Lawrence Erlbaum Associates).

Paivio, A. (1986). *Mental representations: A dual coding approach.* New York: Oxford University Press.

Paivio, A. (2007). *Mind and its evolution: A dual coding theoretical approach.* Mahwah, NJ: Lawrence Erlbaum Associates.

Paltridge, M. (2002). Genre, text type and the English for Academic Purposes classroom. In A.M. Johns (Ed.), *Genre in the Classroom* (pp. 73–90). London: Lawrence Erlbaum.

Paltridge, M. (2006). *Discourse Analysis: An introduction.* London: Continuum.

Pander Maat, H. (2007). How promotional language in press releases is dealt with by journalists: genre-mixing or genre conflict? *Journal of Business Communication, 44,* 59–95.

Parodi, G. (Ed.). (2005a). *Discurso especializado e instituciones formadoras.* [Specialized speech and training institutions]. Valparaíso, Chile: EUV.

Parodi, G. (2005b). *Comprensión de textos escritos.* [Comprehension of written texts]. Buenos Aires, Argentina: Eudeba.

Parodi, G. (Ed.). (2007a). *Lingüística de corpus y discursos especializados: Puntos de mira.* [Linguistics of specialized corpora and speeches: Front sights]. Valparaíso, Chile: EUV.

Parodi, G. (Ed.). (2007b). *Working with Spanish corpora.* London: Continuum.

Parodi, G. (Ed.). (2008a). *Géneros académicos y géneros profesionales: Accesos discursivos para el saber y el hacer.* [Academic sorts and professional sorts: Discursive access of knowledge and doing]. Valparaíso, Chile: EUV.

Parodi, G. (2008). Lingüística de corpus. Una introducción al ámbito. [The linguistics of corpus. An introduction to the scope]. *Revista de Lingüística Teórica y Aplicada, 46*(1), 93–119.

Parodi, G. (in press-b). Pasos retóricos en el género *Manual*: exploración en cuatro disciplinas académicas. [Rhetorical steps in the genre Manual: exploration in four academic disciplines]. In G. Parodi (Ed.), *Géneros académicos y géneros profesionales: Accesos discursivos para el saber y el hacer.* Valparaíso, Chile: EUV

Parodi, G., & Gramajo, A. (2007). Technical-professional discourses: Specialized and dissemination text types. In G. Parodi (Ed.), *Working with spanish corpora* (pp. 145–172). London: Continuum.

Parodi, G., Venegas, R., Ibáñez, R., & Gutiérrez, R. (in press). Corpus académico y corpus profesional PUCV-2006: Construcción de definiciones multiniveles. [Academic corpus and professional corpus PUCV-2006: Construction of multilevel definitions]. In G. Parodi (Ed.), *Géneros académicos y géneros profesionales: Accesos discursivos para el daber y el hacer.* Valparaíso: EUV.

Passonneau, R. (2004). Computing reliability for co-reference annotation. *Proceedings of 4th International Conference on Language Resources and Evaluation, LREC.* Lisbon, Portugal.

Pelinka, A., & Wodak, R. (2002). *Dreck am Stecken. Politik der Ausgrenzung.* [Dirt on the stick. Politics of exclusion]. Vienna, Austria: Czernin Verlag.

Pelsmaekers, K., Braecke, C., & Geluykens, R. (1998). Rhetorical relations and subordination in L2 writing. In A. Sánchez-Macarro & R. Carter (Eds.), *Linguistic choice across genres: Variation in spoken and written English* (pp. 191–213). Amsterdam: Benjamins.

Peracchio, L.A., & Meyers-Levy, J. (2005). Using stylistic properties of ad pictures to communicate with consumers. *Journal of consumer research: an interdisciplinary quarterly, 32*(1), 29–40.

Perelman, Ch., & Olbrechts-Tyteca, L. (1969). *The new rhetoric. A treatise on argumentation* (J. Wilkinson & P. Weaver, trans.). Notre Dame: University of Notre Dame Press. (Original work published 1958).

Peterson, M.A. (2003). *Anthropology & mass communication. media and myth in the new millenium.* New York: Berghahn Books.

Phillips, B.J., & McQuarrie, E.F. (2004). Beyond visual metaphor: A new typology of visual rhetoric in advertising. *Marketing Theory, 4*(1/2), 113–136.

Pickering, M. (2001). *Stereotyping. The politics of representation.* New York: Palgrave.

Pilegaard, M., & Frandsen, F. (1995). Text type. In J. Verschueren, J.O. Ostman, & J. Blommaert (Eds.), *Handbook of Pragmatics, 1995 Instalment* (pp. 1–13). Amsterdam: Benjamins.

Pisarek, W. (Ed.). (1999). *Polszczyzna 2000* [The Polish language 2000]. Krakow, Poland: RJP PAN.

Pisarek, W., & Zgółkowa, H. (Eds.). (1995). *Kultura języka dziś* [Culture of language today]. Poznań, Poland: KURPISZ.

Plett, H. (1991). Intertextualities. In H. Plett (Ed.), *Intertextuality* (pp. 3–29). Berlin, Germany: Walter de Gruyter.

Polanyi, L. (1989). *Telling the American story.* Cambridge MA: MIT Press.

Polanyi, L. (1996). *The linguistic structure of discourse,* CSLI Technical Report, CSLI-96-200.

Polanyi, L. (2001). The linguistic structure of discourse. In D. Schiffrin, D. Tannen, & H.E. Hamilton (Eds.). *The handbook of discourse analysis.* Oxford: Blackwell.

Portolés, J. (1998). *Los Marcadores del discurso.* Barcelona, Spain: Ariel.

Quirk, R., Greenbaum, S., Leech, G., & Svartvik, J. (1972). *A grammar of contemporary English.* London: Longman.

Quirk, R., Greenbaum, S., Leech, G., & Svartvik, J. (1985). *A comprehensive grammar of the English language.* London/New York: Longman.

Rampton, B., Tusting, K., Maybin, J., Barwell, R., Creese, A., & Lytra, V. (2004). UK linguistic ethnography: A discussion paper, http://www.ling-ethnog.org.uk/

Redeker, G., & Egg, M. (2006). Says who? On the treatment of speech attributions in discourse structure. *Proceedings of the Workshop "Constraints in Discourse."* Maynooth University, Ireland.

Reisigl, M., & Wodak, R. (2001). *Discourse and discrimination.* London: Routledge.

Reisigl, M., & Wodak, R. (in press). The discourse-historical approach. In R. Wodak & M. Meyer (Eds.), *Methods of CDA.* London: Sage (2nd revised edition).

Renkema, J. (2004). *Introduction to discourse studies.* Amsterdam: Benjamins.

Renkema, J. (2006). How to proceed with ambiguity in discourse relations? A proposal based on connectivity variables. *Studies in Communication Sciences, 6*(1), 117–134.

Rigotti, E. (2005a). Towards a typology of manipulative processes. In L. Saussure & P. Schulz (Eds.). *Manipulation and ideologies in the twentieth century: Discourse, language, mind. Discourse approaches to politics, society and culture, 17.* Amsterdam: Benjamins.

Rigotti, E., & Rocci. A. (2006). Towards a definition of communication context. In M. Colombetti (Ed.), *The communication sciences as a multidisciplinary enterprise, studies in communication sciences,* 6(2) [Anniversary Issue], pp. 155–180.

Rocci, A. (2005a). *La modalità epistemica tra semantica e argomentazione.* [The epistemic modality between semantics and reasoning]. Milano, Italy: Pubblicazioni dell'ISU Università Cattolica.

Rocci, A. (2005b). Are manipulative texts coherent? Manipulation, presuppositions, and (in-)congruity. In L. Saussure & P. Schulz (Eds.), *Manipulation and ideologies in the twentieth century: Discourse, language, mind.* Amsterdam: Benjamins.

Rocci, A. (2008a). Analysing and evaluating persuasive media discourse in context. In M. Burger (Ed.), *L'analyse linguistique des discours médiatiques* (pp. 247–284). Québec, Canada: Nota Bene.

Rocci, A. (2008b). Modality and its conversational backgrounds in the reconstruction of argumentation. *Argumentation.* Pre-published online via SpringerLink: http://www.springerlink.com/content/5v56228pv5475846

Rocci, A. (2008c). If it's only worth a *might*, it probably isn't a story: possibility modals and argumentation in Italian financial news. Paper presented at the VALS-ASLA Colloquium *Changing societies. Methodological challenges for applied linguistics.* Lugano, February 7–9, 2008.

Rocci, A., & Palmieri, R. (2007). Economic-financial news stories between narrative and forecast. Paper presented at *IPRA 2007 10th International Pragmatics Conference — Göteborg, Sweden, 8–13 July 2007* as part of the panel *Les Narrativités médiatiques.*

Rosner, J.B. (1990). Ways women lead. *Harvard Business Review,* November-December (pp. 119–25).

Rutledge, L., Bailey, B., Van Ossenbruggen, J., Hardman, L., & Geurts, J. (2000). Generating presentation constraints from rhetorical structure. In *Proceedings of the 11th ACM conference on Hypertext and Hypermedia* (pp. 19–28).

Rydgren, J. (Ed.). (2005). *Movements of exclusion.* New York: Nova.

Sacks, H. (1995). *Lectures on conversation.* (Vols. I–II.) (Jefferson, G., Ed.) Oxford: Blackwell.

Sacks, H., Schegloff, E., & Jefferson, G. (1974). A simplest systematics for the organization of turn-taking for conversation. *Language, 50*(4), 696–735.

Sadoski, M. (1992). Imagination, cognition, and persona. *Rhetoric Review, 10,* 266–278.

Sadoski, M., Goetz, E.T., & Rodriguez, M. (2000). Engaging texts: Effects of concreteness on comprehensibility, interest, and recall in four text types. *Journal of Educational Psychology, 92,* 85–95.

Sadoski, M., Goetz, E.T., Stricker, A.G., & Burdenski, T.K. (2003). New findings for concreteness and imagery effects in written composition. *Reading and Writing: An Interdisciplinary Journal, 16,* 443–453.

Sadoski, M., Kealy, W.A., Goetz, E.T., & Paivio, A. (1997). Concreteness and imagery effects in the written composition of definitions. *Journal of Educational Psychology, 89,* 518–526.

Sadoski, M., & Paivio, A. (2001). *Imagery and text: A dual coding theory of reading and writing.* Mahwah, NJ: Lawrence Erlbaum Associates.

Sadoski, M., & Paivio, A. (2004). A dual coding theoretical model of reading. In R.B. Ruddell & N.J. Unrau (Eds.), *Theoretical models and processes of reading.* (5th edition). (pp. 1329–1362). Newark, DE: International Reading Association.

Sadoski, M., & Paivio, A. (2007). Toward a unified theory of reading. *Scientific Studies of Reading, 11,* 337–356.

Sanders, T., Land, J., & Mulder, G. (2007). Linguistic markers of coherence improve text comprehension in functional contexts. *Information Design Journal, 15*(3), 219–235.

Sanders, T., & Noordman, L. (2000). The role of coherence relations and their linguistic markers in text processing. *Discourse Processes, 29,* 37–60.

Sanders, T., Sanders, J. & Sweetser, E. (2008). *Causality, cognition and communication: a mental space analysis of subjectivity in causal connectives.* Manuscript submitted for publication.

Sanders, T. & Spooren, W. (2007). Discourse and Text structure. In Geeraerts, D. & Cuyckens, H. (Eds.), *Handbook of Cognitive Linguistics* (pp. 916–943). Oxford, UK: Oxford University Press.

Sanders, T., Spooren, W., & Noordman, L. (1992). Toward a taxonomy of coherence relations. *Discourse Processes, 15*, 1–35.

Sanders, T., Spooren, W., & Noordman, L. (1992). Toward a taxonomy of coherence relations. *Discourse Processes, 15*(1), 1–35.

Schilperoord, J. (2007). Oote. Retorische schema's (en tropen) in tekst en beeld. [Oote. Rhetorical schemes (and tropes) in text and image]. *Tijdschrift voor Taalbeheersing, 29*(1), 65–87.

Schilperoord, J., Ferdinandusse, H., & Maes, A. (2008). *Perceptual and conceptual rhetoric: The case of symmetric alignment.* Manuscript submitted for publication.

Schneider, D.J. (2004). *The psychology of stereotyping.* New York: Guilford Press.

Schriver, K.A. (1997). *Dynamics in document design: creating texts for readers.* New York: John Wiley and Sons.

Scollon R., & Scollon, S.W. (2004). Intertextuality across communities of practice: Academics, journalism and advertising. In C.L. Moder & A. Martinovic-Zic (Eds.) *Discourse across languages and culture* (pp. 149–176). Amsterdam: Benjamins.

Scollon, R., & Wong Scollon, S. (2003). *Discourses in place. Language in the material world.* London: Routledge.

Scott, L.M., & Batra, R. (2003). *Persuasive imagery: A consumer response perspective.* Mahwah, NJ: Lawrence Erlbaum Associates.

Semino, E., & Culpeper, J. (1995). Stylistics. In J. Verschueren, J.O. Ostman, & J. Blommaert (Eds.), *Handbook of Pragmatics Manual* (pp. 513–520). Amsterdam: Benjamins.

Seuren, P.A.M. (1985). *Discourse semantics.* Oxford, UK: Blackwell.

Shao, J. (1996). *On modern chinese questions.* (trans. from Chinese) Shanghai: East China Normal University Press.

Sinclair, J.M. (1991). *Corpus, concordance, collocation.* Oxford, UK: Oxford University Press.

Sinclair, W.A. (1944). *An introduction to philosophy.* London: Oxford University Press.

Sleurs, K., & Jacobs, G. (2005). Beyond preformulation: an ethnographic perspective on press releases. *Journal of Pragmatics, 37*, 1251–1273.

Sleurs, K., Jacobs, G., & Van Waes, L. (2003). Constructing press releases, constructing quotations: a case study. *Journal of Sociolinguistics, 7*, 192–212.

Smith, N. (2003). Changes in the modals and semi-modals of strong obligation and epistemic necessity in recent British English. In R. Facchinetti, M. Krug, & F. Palmer (Eds.), *Modality in contemporary English* (pp. 241–266). Berlin/New York: Mouton de Gruyter.

Sperber, D., & Wilson, D. (1995). *Relevance, communication and cognition* (2nd ed.). Oxford, UK: Blackwell.

Spooren, W. (1997). The processing of underspecified coherence relations. *Discourse Processes, 24*, 149–168.

Spooren, W., & Sanders, T. (2008). The acquisition order of coherence relations: on cognitive complexity in discourse. *Journal of Pragmatics, 40*(12), 2003–2026.

Stalnaker, R. (1973). Presuppositions. *Journal of Philosophical Logic, 2*, 447–457.

Star, S.L. (1989). The structure of ill-structured solutions: boundary objects and heterogeneous distributed problem solving. Working paper, Department of Information and Computer Science, University of California, Irvine.

Stede, M. (2004). The Potsdam commentary corpus. *Proceedings of the Workshop on Discourse Annotation, 42nd Meeting of the Association for Computational Linguistics.* Barcelona, Spain.

Stockl, H. (2004). *Die Sprache im Bild — Das Bild in der Sprache: Zur Verknüpfung von Sprache und Bild im massenmedialen Text. Konzepte -Theorien -Analysemethoden.* [The language in the picture — the picture in the language: To the linkage of language and picture in the mass-medial text. Concepts, theories, methods of analysis]. Berlin, Germany: Walter de Gruyter.

Stråth, B. (2006). The future of Europe. *Journal of Language and Politics, 5*(3), 427–448.

Strunck, J. (2008). *Gender and politeness in a Danish bank setting.* Manuscript in preparation.

Stubbs, M. (1996). *Text and corpus analysis.* Oxford, UK: Blackwell.

Stubbs, M. (1997). Whorf's children: critical comments on critical discourse analysis (CDA). In A. Ryan & A. Wray, (Eds.), *Evolving models of language.* Clevedon, UK: Multilingual Matters.

Stubbs, M. (2006). Corpus analysis: the state of the art and three types of unanswered questions. In G. Thompson & S. Hunston (Eds.), *System and corpus. exploring connections* (pp. 15–36). London: Equinox.

Swales, J. (1990). *Genre analysis: English in academic and research settings.* Cambridge, UK: Cambridge University Press.

Swales, J. (2002). On models of applied discourse analysis. In C.N. Candlin (Ed.), *Research and practice in professional discourse* (pp. 61–77). Hong Kong: City University of Hong Kong Press

Sweetser, E. (1990). *From etymology to pragmatics.* Cambridge, UK: Cambridge University Press.

Tabakowska, E. (2002). The regime of the other: 'us' and 'them' in translation. In A. Duszak (Ed.), *Us and others. Social identities across languages, discourses and cultures.* (pp. 449–461). Amsterdam: Benjamins.

Taboada, M. (2004). *Building coherence and cohesion: Task-oriented dialogue in English and Spanish.* Amsterdam: Benjamins.

Taboada, M. (2006). Discourse markers as signals (or not) of rhetorical relations. *Journal of Pragmatics, 38*(4), 567–592.

Taboada, M., Anthony, C., & Voll, K. (2006). Creating semantic orientation dictionaries. *Proceedings of 5th International Conference on Language Resources and Evaluation (LREC)* (pp. 427–432). Genoa, Italy.

Taboada, M., & Mann, W.C. (2006a). Rhetorical Structure Theory: Looking back and moving ahead. *Discourse Studies, 8*(3), 423–459.

Taboada, M., & Mann, W.C. (2006b). Applications of Rhetorical Structure Theory. *Discourse Studies, 8*(4), 567–588.

Tajfel, H. (1963). Stereotypes. *Race, 5*(2), 3–14.

Tajfel, H. (1981). *Human groups and social categories.* Cambridge, UK: Cambridge University Press.

Tannen, D. (1989). *Talking voices. Repetition, dialogue and imagery in conversational discourse.* Cambridge, UK: Cambridge University Press.

Tannen, D. (1994). *Gender and Discourse.* Oxford, UK: Oxford University Press.

Tanskanen, S.K. (2006). *Collaborating towards Coherence: Lexical Cohesion in English Discourse.* Amsterdam: Benjamins.

Teng, N.Y., & Sun, S. (2002). Grouping, simile, and oxymoron in pictures: A design-based cognitive approach. *Metaphor and Symbol, 17*, 295–316.

Teubert, W., & Cermakova, A. (2007). *Corpus Linguistics: A short introduction.* London: Continuum.

Thomas, M. (2007). Querying Multimodal Annotation: A concordancer for GeM. *Proceedings of the linguistic annotation workshop. Czech Republic*, 57–60.

Thompson, G., & Hunston, S. (2006). System and corpus: two traditions with a common ground. In G. Thompson & S. Hunston (Eds.), *System and corpus: Exploring connections* (pp. 1–14). London: Equinox.

Thompson, G., & Hunston, S. (Eds.). (2006). *System and corpus. exploring connections.* London: Equinox.

Thompson, J.B. (1995). *The media and modernity: a social theory of the media.* Cambridge, UK: Polity Press.

Thornborrow, J. (2002). *Power talk.* UK: Pearson Education Limited.

Thornborrow, J., & Fitzgerald, R. (2002). From problematic object to routine 'add-on': dealing with e-mails in radio phone-ins. *Discourse Studies, 4,* 201–223.

Titscher, S., Wodak, R., Meyer, M., & Vetter, E. (2000). *Methods of text and discourse analysis.* London: Sage.

Tognini-Bonelli, E. (2001). *Corpus linguistics at work.* Amsterdam: Benjamins.

Tolkien, J.R.R. (1937). *The Hobbit or there and back again.* London: George Allen & Unwin.

Toolan, M. (Ed.). (2002). *Critical discourse analysis: critical concepts in linguistics* (Vols. 1–4). London: Routledge

Traxler, M.J., Bybee, M.D., & Pickering, M.J. (1997). Influence of connectives on language comprehension: Eye tracking evidence for incremental interpretation. *The Quarterly Journal of Experimental Psychology, 50A,* 481–497.

Traxler, M.J., & Gernsbacher, M.A. (Eds.). (2007). *Handbook of psycholinguistics.* NewYork: Elsevier.

Trew, T. (1979). Theory and ideology at work. In R. Fowler, R. Hodge, G. Kress, & T. Trew (Eds.), *Language and control.* London: Routledge & Kegan Paul.

Tsur, R. (1992). *Toward a theory of cognitive poetics.* Amsterdam: Elsevier Science Publishers.

Tuchman, G. (1978). *Making news: a study in the construction of reality.* New York: The Free Press.

Tuchman, G., Kaplan Daniels, A., & Benet, J. (1978). *Hearth and home: Images of women in the mass media.* New York: Oxford University Press.

Twyman, M. (1979). A schema for the study of graphic language. In P.A Kolers, M.E. Wrolstad, & H. Bouma (Eds.), *Processing of Visible Language, 38,* pp. *117–150.* New York/London: New York Plenum.

Ungerer, F. (2000). News stories and news events: A changing relationship. In F. Ungerer (Ed.), *English media texts — past and present: Language and textual structure.* Amsterdam: Benjamins.

Ungerer, F. (2004). Ads as news stories, news stories as ads: The interaction of advertisements and editorial texts in newspapers. *Text, 24*(3), 307–328.

Unsworth, L. (2001). *Teaching multiliteracies across the curriculum: changing contexts of text and image in classroom practice.* Berkshire, UK: Open University Press.

Unsworth, L. (2007). Multiliteracies and multimodal text analysis in class-room work with children's literature. In T.D. Royce & W.L. Bowcher (Eds.), *New directions in the analysis of multimodal discourse* (pp. 331–360). Hillsdale, NJ: Lawrence Erlbaum.

Van Dijk, T.A. (1980). *Macrostructures.* Hillsdale, NJ: Lawrence Erlbaum.

Van Dijk, T.A. (1991). *Racism in the press.* London: Routledge.

Van Dijk, T.A. (1993). Principles of critical discourse analysis. *Discourse and Society, 4*(2), 249–283.

Van Dijk, T.A. (1998a). *Ideology: A multidisciplinary study.* London: Sage.

Van Dijk, T.A. (1998b). *News discourse.* Hillsdale, NJ: Lawrence Erlbaum.

Van Dijk, T.A., (2001). Critical discourse analysis. In S. Deborah, D. Tannen & H.E. Hamilton (Eds.), *The handbook of discourse analysis* (pp. 352–71). Oxford, UK: Blackwell.

Van Dijk, T., & Kintsch, W. (1983). *Strategies of discourse comprehension.* New York: Academic Press.

Van Eemeren, F.H. (1990). The study of argumentation as normative pragmatics. *Text; an interdisciplinary journal for the study of discourse, 10*(1/2), 37–44.

Van Eemeren, F.H. (Ed.). (2001). *Crucial concepts in argumentation theory*. Amsterdam: Amsterdam University Press.

Van Eemeren, F.H., & Grootendorst, R. (1984). *Speech acts in argumentative discussions. A theoretical model for the analysis of discussions directed towards solving conflicts of opinion*. Berlin/Dordrecht: de Gruyter/Foris.

Van Eemeren, F.H., & Grootendorst, R. (1992). *Argumentation, communication, and fallacies. A pragma-dialectical perspective*. Hillsdale NJ: Lawrence Erlbaum.

Van Eemeren, F.H., & Grootendorst, R. (Eds). (1994). Studies in pragma-dialectics. Amsterdam: International Centre for the Study of Argumentation, Sic Sat.

Van Eemeren, F.H., & Grootendorst, R. (2004). *A systematic theory of argumentation: The pragma-dialectical approach*. Cambridge, UK: Cambridge University Press.

Van Eemeren, F.H., Grootendorst, R., Jackson, S., & Jacobs, S. (1993). *Reconstructing argumentative discourse*. Tuscaloosa, AL: The University of Alabama Press.

Van Eemeren, F.H., Grootendorst, R., Jackson, S., & Jacobs, S. (1997). Argumentation. In T. van Dijk (Ed.), *Discourse studies. A multidisciplinary introduction, 1*, (pp. 208–229). London: Sage.

Van Eemeren, F.H., Grootendorst, R., & Snoeck Henkemans, A.F. (2002). *Argumentation: analysis, evaluation, presentation*. Mahwah, NJ: Erlbaum.

Van Eemeren, F.H., & Houtlosser, P. (2000). Rhetorical analysis within a pragma-dialectical framework. The case of R. J. Reynolds. *Argumentation, 14*(3), 293–305.

Van Eemeren, F.H., & Houtlosser, P. (2002). Strategic maneuvering in argumentative discourse: Maintaining a delicate balance. In F.H. van Eemeren & P. Houtlosser (Eds.), *Dialectic and rhetoric: The warp and woof of argumentation analysis* (pp. 131–159). Dordrecht, Holland: Kluwer Academic.

Van Eemeren, F.H., Houtlosser, P., & Snoeck Henkemans, A.F. (2008). Dialectical profiles and indicators of argumentative moves. *Journal of Pragmatics, 20*, 475–493.

Van Hout, T., & Jacobs, G. (2008). News production theory and practice: fieldwork notes on power, interaction and agency. *Pragmatics, 18*, 59–84.

Van Leeuwen, T. (1996). The representation of social actors. In C.R. Caldas-Coulthard & M. Coulthard (Eds.), *Texts and practices — Readings in Critical Discourse Analysis*. London: Routledge.

Van Leeuwen, T. (2000). Visual racism. In M. Reisigl & R. Wodak (Eds.), *The semiotics of racism*. Vienna, Austria: Passagen Verlag.

Van Leeuwen, T. (2005). *Introducing social semiotics*. London: Routledge.

Van Leeuwen, T. (2008). *Discourse and practice — New tools for Critical Discourse Analysis*. New York: Oxford University Press.

Van Mulken, M., Van Enschot-Van Dijk, R., & Hoeken, H. (2005). Puns, relevance and appreciation in advertisements. *Journal of Pragmatics, 37*, 707–721.

Venuti, L. (Ed.). (2000). *The translation studies reader*. London/New York: Routledge.

Verschueren, J. (1999). *Understanding pragmatics*. London: Arnold.

Vestergaard, T. (2000). That's not news: Persuasive and expository genres in the press. In A. Trosborg (Ed.), *Analyzing professional genres* (pp. 97–119). Amsterdam: Benjamins.

Vestergaard, T., & Schorder, K. (1985). *The language of advertising*. Oxford, UK: Blackwell.

Virtanen, T., & Halmarai, H. (2005). Persuasion across genres: Emerging perspectives. In H. Halmari & T. Virtanan (Eds.), *Persuasion across genres* (pp. 3–24). Amsterdam: Benjamins.

Waller, R. (1996). The origins of the information design association. In *The 1996 annual report of the IDA*. Information Design Association.
Waller, R., & Delin, J.L. (2003). Cooperative brands: the importance of customer information for service brands. *Design Management Journal, 14*(4), 63–69.
Wang, J. (2006). Questions and the exercise of power. *Discourse and Society, 17*(4), 529–548.
Wang, S. (2001). Text types and varying degrees of interpretative constraint. *Document Design, 2*(1), 34–57.
Wang, S. (2005a). The role of text type in genre based language learning. *Discourse and Cognition, 12*(2), 91–115.
Wang, S. (2005b). Persuasion for different communicative purposes in teaching writing. *Korean Journal of English language and Linguistics, 5*(3), 431–458.
Wenger, E. (1998). *Communities of practice: learning, meaning and identity.* Cambridge, UK: Cambridge University Press.
Wennerstrom, A. (2003). *Discourse Analysis in the language classroom*. Michigan: The University of Michigan Press.
Werth, P. (1999). *Text worlds. Representing conceptual space in discourse.* London: Longman.
West, C. (1984). *Routine complications: troubles with talk between doctors and patients.* Bloomington, IN: Indiana University Press.
White, P.R.R. (1998–2008). The language of attitude, arguability and interpersonal positioning. The Appraisal website: Homepage. Retrieved from http://www.grammatics.com/appraisal/
Whorf, B.L. (1956). *Language, thought and reality*. Cambridge, MA: MIT Press.
Widdowson, H.G. (1995). Discourse analysis: a critical view. *Language and Literature, 4*(3), 157–172.
Widdowson, H.G. (1996). Reply to Fairclough: Discourse and interpretation: conjectures and refutations. *Language and Literature, 5*(1), 57–69.
Widdowson, H.G. (1998). The theory and practice of critical discourse analysis. [Review]. *Applied Linguistics, 19*(1), 6–151.
Widdowson, H.G. (2000). On the limitations of linguistics applied. *Applied Linguistics, 21*(1): 3–25.
Widdowson, H.G. (2004). *Text, context, pretext. Critical issues in discourse analy*sis. Oxford, UK: Blackwell.
Williams, C.L. (1995). *Still a man's world: Men who do women's work.* Berkeley, CA: University of California Press.
Wilson, M. (2002). Six views of embodied cognition. *Psychonomic Bulletin and Review, 9*, 625–636.
Wittgenstein, L. (1967). *Philosophische Untersuchungen.* [Philosophical researches]. Frankfurt/Main, Germany: Suhrkamp.
Wodak, R. (1996). *Disorders in discourse*. London: Longman.
Wodak, R. (1997) Das Ausland and Anti-Semitic Discourse: The Discursive Construction of the Other. In S.H. Riggins (Ed.), *The language and politics of exclusion*. London: Sage.
Wodak, R. (2001). What CDA is about — a summary of its history, important concepts and its developments. In R. Wodak & M. Meyer (Eds.), *Methods of critical discourse analysis* (pp. 1–13). London: Sage.
Wodak, R. (2006). Review article: Dilemmas of discourse (analysis). *Language in Society, 35*, 595–611.
Wodak, R. (2007a). Discourses in European Union organizations: Aspects of access, participation, and exclusion. In C. Briggs (Ed.), Four decades of epistemological revolution: Work inspired by Aaron V. Cicourel. [Special Issue]. *TEXT and TALK, 27*(5/6), 655–680.

Wodak, R. (2007b). "Doing Europe": The discursive construction of European identities. In R.C.M. Mole (Ed.), *Discursive constructions of identity in European politics* (pp. 70–94). London: Palgrave/Macmillan.

Wodak, R. (2008). "Us" and "them": Inclusion/exclusion — Discrimination via Discourse. In G. Delanty, P. Jones, & R. Wodak (Eds.), *Migration, identity, and belonging* (pp. 54–78) Liverpool, UK: Liverpool University Press.

Wodak, R., De Cillia, R. Reisigl, M., & Liebhart, K. (1999). *The discursive construction of national identity*. Edinburgh, UK: University Press.

Wodak, R., & Matouschek, B. (1993). We are dealing with people whose origins one can clearly tell by just looking: Critical discourse analysis and the study of neo-racism in contemporary Austria. *Discourse and Society*, *4*(2), 225–248.

Wodak, R., & Meyer, M. (Eds.). (2001). *Methods of critical discourse analysis*. London: Sage. (2003. Metodos de analisis critico del discurso. Barcelona: Gedisa, Spanish translation)

Wodak, R., Pelikan, J., Nowak, P., Gruber, H., De Cillia, R., & Mitten, R. (1990). *Wir sind alle unschuldige Tater! Diskurshistorische Studien zum Nachkriegsantisemitismus*. [We are all innocent authors! Discursive-historical studies of "nightwar anti-Semitism."] Frankfurt/Main, Germany: Suhrkamp.

Wodak, R., & Pelinka, A. (2002). *The Haider phenomenon*. London/New Jersey: Transaction Press.

Wodak, R., & Van Dijk, T.A. (Eds.). (2000). *Racism at the top*. Klagenfurt, Austria: Drava.

Wodak, R., & Weiss, G. (2007). Researching European Identities. In R. Wodak & P. Chilton (Eds.), *A new agenda in (critical) discourse analysis*. Amsterdam: Benjamins (DAPSAC series).

Wolf, F., & Gibson, E. (2005). Representing discourse coherence: A corpus-based analysis. *Computational Linguistics*, *31*(2), 249–287.

Wolf, F., Gibson, E., Fisher, A., & Knight, M. (2005). Discourse GraphBank, LDC2005T08 [Corpus]. Philadelphia: Linguistic Data Consortium.

Woods, N. (2006). *Describing discourse: A practical guide to discourse analysis*. London: Arnold.

Wright, W. (1975). *Sixguns and society: A structural study of the Western*. Berkeley, CA: University of California Press.

Yang, X. (2006). English modals and text types. *Foreign languages and their teaching*, *202*, 1–4.

Young, L. & Fitzgerald, B. (2006). *The power of language. How discourse influences society*. London: Equinox.

Zbikowski, L.M. (2002). *Conceptualizing music: Cognitive structure, theory, and analysis*. Oxford, UK: Oxford University Press.

Zwaan, R.A., & Radvansky, G.A. (1998). Situation models in language comprehension and memory. *Psychological Bulletin*, *123*, 162–185.

Index